The *Lady's Magazine* (1770–1832) and the Making of Literary History

Edinburgh Critical Studies in Romanticism
Series Editors: Ian Duncan and Penny Fielding

Available Titles
A Feminine Enlightenment: British Women Writers and the Philosophy of Progress, 1759–1820
JoEllen DeLucia

Reinventing Liberty: Nation, Commerce and the Historical Novel from Walpole to Scott
Fiona Price

The Politics of Romanticism: The Social Contract and Literature
Zoe Beenstock

Radical Romantics: Prophets, Pirates, and the Space Beyond Nation
Talissa J. Ford

Literature and Medicine in the Nineteenth-Century Periodical Press: Blackwood's Edinburgh Magazine, 1817–1858
Megan Coyer

Discovering the Footsteps of Time: Geological Travel Writing in Scotland, 1700–1820
Tom Furniss

The Dissolution of Character in Late Romanticism
Jonas Cope

Commemorating Peterloo: Violence, Resilience, and Claim-making during the Romantic Era
Michael Demson and Regina Hewitt

Dialectics of Improvement: Scottish Romanticism, 1786–1831
Gerard Lee McKeever

Literary Manuscript Culture in Romantic Britain
Michelle Levy

Scottish Romanticism and Collective Memory in the British Atlantic
Kenneth McNeil

Romantic Periodicals in the Twenty-First Century: Eleven Case Studies from Blackwood's Edinburgh Magazine
Nicholas Mason and Tom Mole

Godwin and the Book: Imagining Media, 1783–1836
J. Louise McCray

Thomas De Quincey: Romanticism in Translation
Brecht de Groote

Romantic Environmental Sensibility: Nature, Class and Empire
Ve-Yin Tee

Romantic Pasts: History, Fiction and Feeling in Britain and Ireland, 1790–1850
Porscha Fermanis

British Romanticism and Denmark
Cian Duffy

The Lady's Magazine (1770–1832) and the Making of Literary History
Jennie Batchelor

Forthcoming Titles
Romantic Networks in Europe: Transnational Encounters, 1786–1850
Carmen Casaliggi

Romanticism and Consciousness
Richard Sha and Joel Faflak

Death, Blackwood's Edinburgh Magazine and Authoring Romantic Scotland
Sarah Sharp

Seeking Justice: Literature, Law and Equity during the Age of Revolutions
Michael Demson and Regina Hewitt

Remediating the 1820s
Jon Mee and Matthew Sangster

Mary Wollstonecraft: Cosmopolitan
Laura Kirkley

Visit our website at: www.edinburghuniversitypress.com/series/ECSR

The *Lady's Magazine* (1770–1832) and the Making of Literary History

Jennie Batchelor

EDINBURGH
University Press

Edinburgh University Press is one of the leading university presses in the UK. We publish academic books and journals in our selected subject areas across the humanities and social sciences, combining cutting-edge scholarship with high editorial and production values to produce academic works of lasting importance. For more information visit our website: edinburghuniversitypress.com

We are committed to making research available to a wide audience and are pleased to be publishing an Open Access ebook edition of this title.

© Jennie Batchelor 2022, 2024, under a Creative Commons Attribution-NonCommercial licence

Edinburgh University Press Ltd
The Tun – Holyrood Road
12(2f) Jackson's Entry
Edinburgh EH8 8PJ

First published in hardback by Edinburgh University Press 2022

Typeset in 10/13pt Sabon
by Cheshire Typesetting Ltd, Cuddington, Cheshire

A CIP record for this book is available from the British Library

ISBN 978 1 4744 8764 1 (hardback)
ISBN 978 1 4744 8765 8 (paperback)
ISBN 978 1 4744 8766 5 (webready PDF)
ISBN 978 1 4744 8767 2 (epub)

The right of Jennie Batchelor to be identified as the author of this work has been asserted in accordance with the Copyright, Designs and Patents Act 1988, and the Copyright and Related Rights Regulations 2003 (SI No. 2498).

Contents

List of Figures	vi
Acknowledgements	x
Introduction	1
1. Origins: The Birth of the Women's Magazine	12
2. Beginnings: The Making of the *Lady's Magazine* (1770–2)	42
3. Modes, Media and Miscellaneity: The Contents of the *Lady's Magazine*	80
4. Authors, Readers, Writing Cultures	124
5. Rivals: The Changing Face of the Women's Magazine	162
6. Achievements and Legacies: The *Lady's Magazine* in Literary History	210
Afterword	242
Notes	245
Select Bibliography	283
Index	297

Figures

1.1	Contents page for the *Lady's Magazine* for January 1803	17
1.2	Back wrapper from Wheble's *Lady's Magazine* for October 1771	19
1.3	Frontispiece to *The Female Spectator* (1744)	29
2.1	Frontispiece to the *Lady's Magazine* for 1776	55
2.2	'An Account of the Trial at Law', from Wheble's *Lady's Magazine* for July 1771	64
2.3	The two journeys of the sentimental traveller in Wheble's and Robinson's *Lady's Magazine* for August 1771	69
2.4	*A Lady with the Emblems of Spring in the Dress of April 1771* from Robinson's *Lady's Magazine* for April 1771	70
2.5	Illustration for the 'Lady's Biography' from Wheble's *Lady's Magazine* for June 1771	72
2.6	Table setting to accompany 'The Lady's Handmaid; or Housekeeper's Calendar' from Wheble's *Lady's Magazine* for April 1771	74
2.7	Frontispiece to Robinson and Roberts's *Lady's Magazine* for 1771	77
3.1	The *Lady's Magazine* for October 1798	82
3.2	'Home News' section from the *Lady's Magazine* for January 1775	89
3.3	Frontispiece to the *Lady's Magazine* for 1773	106
3.4	Frontispiece to the *Lady's Magazine* for 1780	107
3.5	*A Correct Map of England Adapted to the Use of the Ladies* from the *Lady's Magazine* for October 1776	121
4.1	James Hopwood after George Slater, *Mary Pilkington* (1812)	133
4.2	Engraving after Hubert-François Gravelot for R—'s 'Don Carlos' from the *Lady's Magazine* for June 1775	145

5.1	Frontispiece and title page from the first volume of Alexander Hogg's *New Lady's Magazine* (1786)	165
5.2	Layout changes in the *Lady's Magazine* for April 1778 and March 1812	168
5.3	*Rynwick Williams Commonly called The Monster!* from the *Lady's Magazine* for July 1790	170
5.4	*Falcon* from 'The Moral Zoologist' in the *Lady's Magazine* for June 1803	172
5.5	Joseph Collyer after Angelica Kauffman. Frontispiece to the *Lady's Magazine* for 1775	173
5.6	Thomas Stothard, *The Remonstrance*, from the *Lady's Magazine* for October 1780	176
5.7	James Heath after Henry Corbould, *The Abbot* from the *Lady's Magazine* for January 1821	177
5.8	Charles Heath after Robert Smirke, *The Light of the Haram*, from the *Lady's Magazine* for December 1822	178
5.9	*A Lady in Full Dress* from the *Lady's Magazine* for August 1770	180
5.10	*A New Pattern for a Winter Shawl* from the *Lady's Magazine* for December 1796	182
5.11	(Top) Embroidered shoes held by the Victoria and Albert Museum. (Bottom) Pattern (detail) for a pair of shoes from the *Lady's Magazine* for April 1775	183
5.12	*London Walking and Evening Dresses* from the *Lady's Magazine* for March 1812	186
5.13	*Two Ladies in the newest Dress From Drawings taken at Ranelagh* from the *Lady's Magazine* for May 1775	187
5.14	*Evening Dress* designed by Mrs Smith from the *Lady's Magazine* for April 1819	191
5.15	Back wrapper from the *Lady's Magazine* for September 1816	199
5.16	*Le Follet* insert in the *Lady's Magazine* for March 1832	207
6.1	*The Statue of Mrs. Macaulay* from the *Lady's Magazine* for October 1777	213
6.2	*Mrs Leigh Perrot* from the *Lady's Magazine* for April 1800	230

Acknowledgements

This is a book about a magazine and its place in literary history. It is also a book about community and about how reading and writing can facilitate friendships, inspire creative thought and initiate meaningful and lasting conversations and collaborations. In this context, it seems more than usually fitting to acknowledge the numerous debts I owe to organisations and individuals who have supported or otherwise sustained this book from the germ of an idea I had a decade ago to the reality it has become.

Without Adam Matthew Digital, who in 2011 gamely responded to my proposal that they undertake a digitisation of a complete run of the *Lady's Magazine* (published in 2013 as *Eighteenth-Century Journals V*), the research for this book would have been impossible.

Without the financial support of the Leverhulme Trust, who generously funded both a Research Project Grant on the *Lady's Magazine* (2014–16) and a Research Fellowship (2017), this book would never have been written. My fellow researchers on the *Lady's Magazine* project, Koenraad Claes and Jenny DiPlacidi, were the very best colleagues. Their tireless detective work and inventive research on the magazine's authors and contents were wonders to behold. My debts to them are enormous and I sorely miss our weekly chats over coffee and chocolate about the periodical. I am also grateful to Kim Simpson, who joined the project as a researcher at a late, yet crucial, stage, and who taught us that there was still so much to learn.

While conducting research for this book I have relied on the resources of many libraries and archives, as well as the expertise and generosity of their staff. I especially wish to thank staff at the Bayerische Staatsbibliothek, München, the Bodleian Library, the Borthwick Institute for Archives at the University of York, the British Library, Chawton House, Derbyshire Record Office, the Library of Birmingham, Manchester Central Library, the National Art Library, the National

Library of Scotland, Reading Central Library, Special Collections at the University of Kent, and the Women's Library at the London School of Economics. I extend particular thanks to Karen Brayshaw and Clair Waller at the Templeman Library, University of Kent, to Julian Pooley of the Surrey History Centre and to Alison Harvey, Archivist in Special Collections and Archives at the University of Cardiff, for her invaluable support of this project and digitisation of images from Cardiff's wonderful collection of the magazine.

Serendipity should be credited as the non-human co-author of this book. Without an unexpected invitation from Laura Stevens to revisit earlier work I had done on the *Lady's Magazine* for a special issue on women and periodicals for *Tulsa Studies in Women's Literature*, I probably would have devoted most of the last ten years to a project that did not matter to me nearly as much as this one has. Needless to say, I am very grateful to Laura for the invitation and her characteristically kind and wise feedback at the very earliest stages of this project. Since then, I have been fortunate to have benefited from the advice and critical questioning of many different audiences at conferences, public lectures and workshops. Tita Chico, Serena Dyer, Markman Ellis, Laura Engel, Michelle Levy and Betty Schellenberg (jointly), Tina Lupton and Anthony Mandal all extended generous invitations to present my work in progress at formative stages of its development.

In late 2014, Jackie Jones at Edinburgh University Press asked Nush Powell and me to co-edit *Women's Periodicals in Print Culture, 1690–1820s* (2018), the first in a multi-volume series. Working on that book undoubtedly delayed the writing of this one, but it has also made this much better than it would otherwise have been. I learned so much from our wonderful contributors to the collection and, most of all, from Nush, an extraordinary periodicals scholar, co-editor and all-round human.

A number of this book's arguments were teased out in conversations with friends and colleagues over email, in libraries and coffeeshops and at dinner tables. I particularly want to acknowledge the perspicuity and encouragement of Susan Carlile, Tita Chico, Sophie Coulombeau, JoEllen DeLucia, Hilary Davidson, Gillian Dow, Liz Edwards, Markman Ellis, Laura Engel, Elisabeth Gernerd, Declan Gilmore-Kavanagh, Michael Falk, Emily Friedman, Katie Halsey, Tina Lupton, Anthony Mandal, Elaine McGirr, Dave Mazella, Tina Morin, Melissa Mowry, Elizabeth Neiman, Megan Peiser, Nush Powell, Bethany Qualls, Yael Shapira, Kim Simpson, Chloe Wigston Smith and Angela Wright. Various individuals kindly sent me attribution leads, including Gillian Dow, Emily Friedman, Colin Shrimpton and Rosemary Wake. All of my colleagues (present and former) at Kent have been unfailingly supportive over the last few, difficult years. I would particularly like to thank Bashir Abu-Manneh, David Ayers, Megan Batterbee, Karen Brayshaw, Vybarr Cregan-Reid, Christine Davies, Jenny DiPlacidi, Naomi Donovan, Michael Falk, David Herd, Sarah James, Declan Gilmore-Kavanagh, Bernhard Klein, Donna Landry, Deborah Molloy, Will Norman, Catherine Richardson, Robbie Richardson, Kerry Stanley, Scarlett Thomas, Nuria Triana Toribio and Cathy Waters.

I am eternally grateful to those friends who commented on draft chapters of the book, namely: Susan Carlile, Tita Chico, Gillian Dow, Katie Halsey, Elaine McGirr, Melissa Mowry and Kate Ozment, and especially Chloe Wigston Smith who read a draft of the complete manuscript. I couldn't have asked for a group of kinder yet more incisive critics, and I hope I have done justice to their suggestions. Thank you, Melissa, for the online writing bootcamps, which helped me whip things into better shape while trying to complete the book during the first UK Covid lockdown. I owe deep personal debts to Susan Carlile, Tita Chico, Gillian Dow, Laura Engel, Hannah Greig, Elaine McGirr and Chloe Wigston Smith for being my cheerleaders and for helping me through various trials and tribulations. They will know what I am talking about.

One of the greatest pleasures of researching the *Lady's Magazine* has been the opportunity to recreate something of its sense of community online. Followers of the *Lady's Magazine* project on social media have been unfailingly generous in sharing their responses to the periodical and a range of its contents. I am delighted that a 250-year-old publication has brought us together in the twenty-first century and that I have even been able to meet some of you in real life.

From the start of writing this book, I hoped that Edinburgh University Press would publish it. Michelle Houston and Susannah Butler have been hugely supportive of this project from the beginning. I would also like to thank the series editors of Edinburgh Critical Studies in Romanticism, Ian Duncan and Penny Fielding, as well as the anonymous readers for the Press for their incredibly helpful comments.

Finally, David, Leah and Ben Motton have lived with this book for as long as I have, in Ben's case, for his whole life. I owe them the deepest thanks for their support of my work and their patience while listening to yet another of Mum's stories about the *Lady's Magazine* or while I told them to 'hang on' as I bit my nails waiting to see if my Ebay bid was enough to secure a coveted volume of the periodical for my personal collection. Thank you, Mottons.

Sections of Chapters 1 and 3 appeared in '"[T]o cherish Female Ingenuity and to conduce to Female Improvement: The Birth of the Woman's Magazine', in *Women's Periodicals and Print Culture in Britain, 1690–1820s: The Long Eighteenth Century*, eds Jennie Batchelor and Manushag N. Powell (Edinburgh: Edinburgh University Press, 2018), 377–92. It is reproduced with the permission of Edinburgh University Press. Part of Chapter 4 appeared first in 'Anon, Pseud and by a Lady: The spectre of anonymity and the future of literary history', in *Women's Writing, 1600–1830: Feminisms and Futures*, eds Jennie Batchelor and Gillian Dow (Palgrave Macmillan, 2016), 69–86. It is reproduced here with the permission of Palgrave Macmillan. Other parts of my discussion in Chapter 4 appeared in 'UnRomantic Authorship: The Minerva Press and the *Lady's Magazine* (1770–1820)', *Romantic Textualities*, eds Elizabeth Neiman and Christina Morin 3 (Summer 2020): 76–93 <https://doi.org/10.18573/romtext.73>, and is reproduced with permission.

Introduction

I am sorry Sir I did not exist forty or fifty years ago when the Lady's magazine was flourishing like a green bay tree – In that case I make no doubt my aspirations after literary fame would have met with due encouragement . . . and I would have contested the palm with the Authors of Derwent Priory – of the Abbey and of Ethelinda. – You see Sir I have read the *Lady's Magazine* and know something of its contents . . . I read them before I knew how to criticize or object – they were old books belonging to my mother or my Aunt; they had crossed the Sea, had suffered ship-wreck and were discoloured with brine – I read them as a treat on holiday afternoons or by stealth when I should have been minding my lessons – I shall never see anything which will interest me so much again – One black day my father burnt them because they contained foolish love-stories. With all my heart I wish I had been born in time to contribute to the *Lady's Magazine.*
Charlotte Brontë to Hartley Coleridge, 10 December 1840.[1]

By December 1840, Charlotte Brontë was already a prolific writer. Her manuscript juvenilia, much of which was co-written with her siblings, included histories, short fiction, reviews, imitation magazines and poetry.[2] In late 1836, while she was working as a teacher at Roe Head School, Brontë sent copies of some of her verse to Robert Southey, then Poet Laureate. His famous assessment of her work was grudgingly admiring, if ultimately disheartening: 'Literature cannot be the business of a woman's life: & it ought not to be'.[3] Yet Brontë's 'scribblemania', as her brother Branwell memorably described it, could not be cured.[4] By late 1840, she was in a position to send chapters of a novel – likely the unfinished 'Ashworth' – to poet and biographer Hartley Coleridge, under the cover of the pseudonym 'C T'.[5] Coleridge's appraisal of the manuscript-in-progress was less than positive. In a playful yet pointed epistolary response to this unwelcome feedback, Brontë defended her novel – 'the demi-semi novelette of an anonymous scribe' (241) – and her authorial ambition, by evoking two antecedents. Turning first to Coleridge's criticisms about her novel's putative scope and length, she exclaimed that her correspondent was so 'pitiless' that he would presumably have tried to 'cut short' Samuel Richardson's *Sir Charles Grandison* (1753) 'in its very commencement' (240). She then proceeded to offer a second and altogether different precedent for her fiction and literary aspirations: the *Lady's Magazine*.

The *Lady's Magazine; or Entertaining Companion for the Fair Sex*, to give the best known of its full titles, began life in August 1770, some seven years before the birth of Brontë's father, Patrick.[6] It was founded by John Coote, a copyright-owning bookseller and publisher who had a hand in at least twenty magazines between the 1750s and the 1770s, and was initially published by John Wheble.[7] The brine-soaked copies of the magazine that Charlotte Brontë refers to in her letter to Coleridge had been shipped from Penzance to Liverpool in 1812 by her mother, Maria, in preparation for her marriage. How many issues of the periodical Brontë's mother owned is unknown, but her collection must have included issues for 1797, when Maria was still in her teens. We know this because, despite Brontë's demurring that she was 'not quite certain of the correctness of the titles' of the tales she recalls in the letter, they coincide only in that year (240).[8]

By 1797, the *Lady's Magazine* had been in the hands of its longest-serving publishers, George Robinson senior and his associates, under the sign of Addison's Head, 25 Paternoster Row, London, for a quarter of a century.[9] With only brief interruptions, the periodical was published under one of a succession of Robinson family imprints for the best part of six decades.[10] In 1832, where this book ends and by which time the Robinsons' association with the publication had terminated, the *Lady's Magazine* entered into the first of two mergers with rival periodicals, which gave it an extended and altered afterlife until 1847, the year in which Charlotte Brontë's *Jane Eyre* was published.[11] By any measure, the *Lady's Magazine* was a huge success: it was one of the longest-lived periodicals of the eighteenth century, and the era's most successful women's magazine by a considerable margin.

Yet Brontë was conscious that she was writing in and for a different age, one in which Coleridge's 'candid' and unflattering appraisal of her novelistic efforts was supposed to be greeted with as much pleasure 'as if it had been one from Professor Wilson, containing a passport of admission to Blackwood' (241, 239). Hers was the age of the professional journalist and critic, of the male-dominated world of *Blackwood's Edinburgh Magazine* (founded April 1817), to which Coleridge was an occasional contributor, and of dominant literary personalities such as Christopher North (John Wilson). Brontë's nostalgic evocation of the *Lady's Magazine* in this context is knowingly double-edged. On the one hand, her letter acknowledges how old-fashioned this once popular title had come to seem in a professionalised Victorian periodical marketplace that had little regard for the kinds of 'foolish love-stories' and anonymous scribblers with which the *Lady's Magazine* was associated. On the other hand, she powerfully conjures the magazine as a once tangible, but now remote, link to two pasts of critical importance to her: the past of her deceased mother; and a literary past that was infinitely more congenial to the pleasures of female readers and the ambitions of women authors.

Brontë defiantly uses the *Lady's Magazine* to articulate her barely concealed anger at the literal and metaphorical violence directed at women's reading and writing, whether in the form of her father's pyromaniacal destruction of her own copies of a much-loved magazine that bound two generations of Brontë women, or in that of Southey's and Coleridge's verbal puncturing of her authorial aspirations. Moreover, she implies that the age of *Blackwood's* and the new formulations of the literary, the author and the reader that underpinned it, emerged at least in part out of concerted efforts to delegitimise models from the past. At the same time, she suggests that the recollection and reclamation of these discredited models could map alternative futures that might better serve women. Perhaps it was for these reasons that a woman writer who was not 'born in time to contribute to the Lady's magazine' herself continued to remind her readers of the periodical's existence throughout her career. Not only is the *Lady's Magazine* read by Caroline Helstone in Brontë's *Shirley* (1849), but plots from its fiction and the cultural debates about women's lives, education and work it intervened in resurface in various forms in all of her novels.

The central argument of this book is that the *Lady's Magazine* can, indeed, persuasively write back to a literary history that has traditionally marginalised it on the grounds of its unapologetic popularity and its association with women's reading pleasures. As the following chapters detail, there are many reasons why the *Lady's Magazine* should claim our attention beyond its broad contemporary appeal, although an estimated circulation figure of around 15,000 monthly copies at its height is arresting enough.[12] The *Lady's Magazine* was not the first periodical marketed directly at a female audience, of course, but it is arguably the first recognisably modern women's magazine. Between its launch in the year Lord North's ministry was founded to its last in the year the Reform Act was passed, the magazine ran to over 750 monthly issues.[13] The periodical survived publishers' bankruptcies and deaths, editorial misconduct, innumerable domestic and global crises, and saw off many rivals and imitators who attempted to poach its subscribers and contributors. It encouraged countless others in their 'aspirations after literary fame', helping to launch the careers of the likes of the poet George Crabbe and gothic novelist Catharine Day Haynes (later Golland), just as it galvanised those of the likes of Mary Russell Mitford, whose *Our Village* (1824–32) first appeared as sketches in the magazine in the early 1820s. The periodical's influence was felt widely within the literary world of its day, both in the form of reprintings of its original content in journals published in England, Scotland and America, and in the inspiration it gave to professional women writers in the making, including Jane Austen.[14] Equally importantly, the *Lady's Magazine* provided a publication opportunity for hundreds of amateur reader-contributors, for the most part unpaid, whose 'favours' it encouraged, and whose poems, puzzles, essays, translations and fiction sat alongside excerpts from the works of many of the best-known writers of the day.

Challenges

Edward Copeland, one of very few literary historians to pay attention to this resilient periodical, claims that '"Everybody" read the *Lady's Magazine*', or at least everybody who could 'afford a ticket to the local circulating library', where new and back issues of it could be obtained. Copeland exaggerates for effect, but the question that interests me more than 'How accurate is his claim?' is: 'Why are so few reading the *Lady's Magazine* now?'[15] Anyone game enough to try to do so, as I first attempted some sixteen years ago, certainly has several problems to overcome. The size of the magazine's print run – well over 40,000 pages – checks the enthusiasm of even the most determined. So too does its relative inaccessibility. No copyright library holds a 'complete' run of the periodical. Some public and research libraries have digitised individual volumes or shorter runs of the magazine from their holdings, but a 'complete' and fully searchable run was only recently made available in the form of Adam Matthew Digital's subscription database, *Eighteenth-Century Journals V* (2013). The impact of *ECJ V* is already being felt in scholarship and in the classroom. Without it, neither the University of Kent's Leverhulme Trust-funded 'The *Lady's Magazine* (1770–1818): Understanding the Emergence of a Genre' (2014–16), nor this book would have been possible.[16]

Yet as my scare quotes caution, completeness is always an illusion in periodical studies. Indispensable though it is, the *ECJ V* digitisation reproduces only the Wheble issues of the magazines for 1771 and 1772, not the concurrent Robinson issues that I discuss in Chapter 2.

Moreover, digitised volumes are only as complete as the unique copies that have been scanned. I have never seen what might be considered a complete bound volume of the *Lady's Magazine*, nor have I even seen two identical bound volumes for the same year. It is not unusual to find text-based material, including editorial addresses to readers, indexes and sometimes individual items of content missing from such volumes, often because they appear to have been cut out and scrapbooked or commonplaced by their owners. Wrappers (covers) and advertisements are almost always absent, and non-text-based materials such as the engravings, fashion plates, embroidery patterns and song sheets that I discuss in Chapter 5 have been frequently excised pre- or post-binding.

Such issues will be familiar to anyone who works on periodicals from any century. Other of the challenges I faced when researching this book are specific to the *Lady's Magazine*. A particularly intransigent problem has been that the *Lady's*, unlike the *Gentleman's Magazine* (founded 1731), has no editorial or publisher archive of which to speak.[17] In trying to reconstruct as much as I could about the day-to-day running of the magazine and its connections to the rest of the Robinson catalogue, I have scoured thousands of letters, receipts, bankruptcy files, parish records and wills connected with George Robinson senior, his business associates, friends and family, as well as those connected with the magazine's various printers, engravers and identifiable contributors. I have spent months in records offices and on genealogy websites, following up on even the slightest lead a contributor's dateline might give to their identity. Many leads resulted in dead ends. Others, happily, did not. Much of what I have been able to piece together can be found in the following pages, but there is still more to find out and much that may never be established with certainty.

These methodological and logistical difficulties are more than matched by the disciplinary challenges presented by the miscellaneity of the magazine format. The *Lady's Magazine* includes: fiction; poetry; essays on subjects such as science, history and education (sometimes in and translated from foreign languages); life-writing; reviews; advice; and news. It is also multi-media. For much of its run, it contains monthly song sheets, embroidery patterns and later fashion plates, and its entire run is ornamented with 'embellishments' (copper-plate and, later, steel engravings). Frequently, the tone, import and argument of this eclectic and wide-ranging content blend and clash in ways that initially make little sense. And despite what we know about the Robinson family's radical leanings, the magazine's politics can seem bewilderingly incoherent. Yet even these questions are less baffling than trying to fathom who provided the periodical's fifty-six pages of monthly letter-press.

The *Lady's Magazine* was an enthusiastic participant in the culture of reprinting endemic in the periodical trade, and thus a good proportion of its content was repurposed from already published, but not always acknowledged, sources.[18] However, a significant percentage of the publication was original, the work of a large community of obscure volunteer reader-contributors: of Constantia Marias and Y. Z.s; of Lucindas who may have been Lucases; and of Strephons who might have been Daphnes. Even when payment for copy was introduced in the 1810s and finally embedded in the 1820s, the *Lady's Magazine* continued to support the culture of pseudonymous and anonymous authorship. The magazine, in short, resists many of the analytical categories – of genre, discipline, author, politics, period and gender – on which literary-historical scholarship relies. One of the key contentions of this book is that this resistance to the conventional categories or crutches of literary analysis is precisely what makes this periodical so vital. Reading the *Lady's Magazine* forces us not only to re-read the period of literary history in which it flourished, but also to reassess a number of the assumptions that underpin Romantic scholarship.

Overview

The 'rise of periodical studies', to borrow Sean Latham and Robert Scholes's phrase, has left its mark on eighteenth-century and Romantic studies in a wealth of recent monographs, journal articles, online databases and bibliographies.[19] The women's magazines that came to prominence in the last third of the eighteenth century have largely fallen beneath the scholarly radar, however. To date, no major study of the period's most famous and long-lived example of the genre exists, although the *Lady's Magazine* has garnered some attention from literary scholars (Robert D. Mayo, Ros Ballaster et al., Copeland, Jacqueline Pearson, Richard de Ritter), book historians (Jan Fergus) and historians of gender (Cynthia White, Alison Adburgham), as part of wider surveys of periodical print culture or histories of reading and the book trade.[20] The *Gentleman's Magazine* has been helpfully illuminated by a number of journal articles, PhD theses and digital projects, and by Gillian Williamson's recent and important book.[21] Yet it remains something of an exception in eighteenth-century periodicals scholarship, which tends to focus most intently on essay-periodicals, especially those published in the first half of the century. Scholarship on the Romantic-era periodical, for its part, has been largely dominated by 'literary' magazines and Reviews, in which otherwise well-established (and often male) writers, such as William Hazlitt, Leigh Hunt and Charles Lamb, were involved or in which some of the central categories of Romanticism were formulated.[22] In such studies, magazines oriented explicitly at women readers are generally presented as the foils to these more serious journals. David Stewart's important *Romantic Magazines and Metropolitan Literary Culture* (2011) is typical in the short shrift it gives to the *Lady's Magazine* in the one sentence of dedicated commentary devoted to this 'prominent' periodical: 'The *Lady's Magazine* balanced the claims of fashion and learning, neither as instructive as the *British Lady's Magazine* nor as stylish as *La Belle Assemblée*'.[23]

Most literary historians have, in fact, written off the *Lady's Magazine*. Where it has been registered, its unwieldy periodisation – which straddles the long eighteenth century and a generously defined Romantic period – means that it features most commonly either as a postscript to accounts of essay-periodicals such as the *Tatler* (1709–11) and *Spectator* (1711–12, 1714), or as a preface to studies of the Victorian women's magazine. Epitomising this first approach, Kathryn Shevelow argued that the launch of the *Lady's Magazine* in 1770 marked a regression in the periodical form that had lasting, and damaging, implications for women. The 'new configuration of feminine "learning"' as imagined by the *Lady's Magazine*, Shevelow contends, signalled an abandonment of the educational ambition of earlier periodicals such as Charlotte Lennox's *Lady's Museum* (1760–1) in favour of 'instruction' in 'the arts of femininity' – 'manners and morals', 'cookery, needlework, and fashion' – as a means of regulating women's behaviour.[24] Shevelow's decline-into-domesticity thesis, as I elaborate in subsequent chapters, has indelibly shaped subsequent studies of eighteenth-century periodicals, which are almost universally end-bracketed by the emergence of the women's magazine in the 1770s.[25] Margaret Beetham, by contrast, presents the *Lady's Magazine* as the naïve, and by the nineteenth century already outmoded, origins of a genre yet to fulfil its potential in its old-fashioned styling and policy of 'inviting [women] readers to write' at a time when 'the growing professionalization of journalism ... meant [this occupation] was increasingly a male preserve' (21).[26] The common denominator that justifies the neglect of the *Lady's Magazine* in the divergent critical positions occupied by Shevelow, Beetham and others is the periodical's association with amateurism, the ephemeral, the feminine and the non-intellectual and diverse offerings of its non- and/or unprofessional contributors.[27]

This book challenges these and associated arguments by offering the first sustained account of the *Lady's Magazine*. Its aims are: to document the periodical's achievements and influence, and to elucidate how these achievements and legacies contributed foundationally to the making of literary history. I begin these stories by taking a long view of the plurality of established periodical formats and cultures upon which the *Lady's Magazine* drew and from which it departed. Chapter 1 offers a wide-ranging account of the magazine's precedents – including question-and-answer sheets, essay-periodicals and miscellanies from the 1690s to the 1760s – to test scholarly assumptions about the emergence of the so-called 'women's magazine'. Locating the *Lady's Magazine* within this broader context undermines claims that its launch marked a decisive and retrograde moment in the history of women's relationship with periodical print culture, and starts to bring into focus many of the publication's most important and distinctive innovations.

The extraordinary first two years of the magazine's run – during which rival versions of the periodical were produced by neighbouring Paternoster Row publishers – are the subject of Chapter 2. This fraught period, I show, was formative in establishing the periodical's aspirations, its content range and the relationships between editorial staff, contributors and readers that were integral to its longevity. The chapter begins by considering the important roles played by the men behind the *Lady's Magazine* and examines the fallout of its founder-proprietor, John Coote's, decision to sell the periodical to booksellers George Robinson and John Roberts in early 1771, thus denying John Wheble the right to produce future issues. Wheble's determination to continue publishing the magazine despite the sale, and even after Robinson and Roberts's serial was legally declared the legitimate continuation of Coote's original, raises a number of important questions about what he saw in this new periodical venture. The terms in which Wheble attempted to defend his investment in the magazine in the courtroom illuminate his hopes for the publication and offer valuable insights into how it was run. The final sections of the chapter examine the rich and evolving contents of the two rival *Lady's Magazine*s issued between April 1771 and December 1772, when Wheble's version finally ceased publication. Wheble and Robinson and Roberts's efforts to push each other out of business through a combination of what we would now refer to as brand consolidation and innovation were essential, I demonstrate, in cementing the magazine's reputation and success over the following decades.

Throughout this book, I am committed to uncovering the reading practices that the magazine – as opposed to, say, the novel or essay-periodical – fostered and these practices' connection to the magazine format's pedagogical claims. Chapter 3 develops the arguments about the agile, discontinuous reading practices that I begin to map out in the closing sections of Chapter 2 through close attention to the *Lady's*

Magazine's diverse, multimodal and multi-media contents. My discussion captures many of the periodical's most prominent content types – including essays, fiction, translation, poetry, travel writing and news – but is organised around subject matter rather than genre or media. Such an approach is vital, I argue, because the magazine is not a static repository of different types of content, but a dynamic, multi- and intermedial network in which meaning is generated by interaction, remediation and juxtaposition. I pursue these meanings in relation to two key areas: news and politics, and advice and education. The intensity of the *Lady's Magazine*'s preoccupation with, and treatment of, these topics undermines conventional characterisations of the periodical as a training guide in passive femininity. More importantly, their distinctive mode of expression sheds important light on the habits of reading and thinking that Robinson's magazine demanded of its readers in order to navigate its coverage of these issues.

Chapter 4 turns from reading to readers of the *Lady's Magazine*. Establishing the periodical's readership is far from straightforward. Diaries and correspondence identify some individual and indeed notable subscribers, while regional bookseller ledgers and publisher archives offer some insight into subscription patterns and demographics at certain moments in time. For the most part, however, the question of who read the *Lady's Magazine* has to be divined from internal evidence. Its monthly 'Correspondents' columns, in which editors entered into dialogue with readers, is one such source. More valuable still are the magazine's contents. As I have already noted, until the 1820s when the likes of Mitford, Amelia Opie and Barbara Hofland were writing for payment for the magazine, most of its original content was penned by volunteer reader-contributors. If the magazine's editors are to be believed, these contributors favoured the periodical with thousands of poems, essays, works of fiction and translations every month, with only the very best finding their way into print. The magazine's reliance on reader-contributors, I argue, was a significant source of its commercial appeal and integral to the sense of community it created among generations of readers. It was the aspect of the magazine that Brontë celebrated most loudly, yet it is the feature of the magazine that has proved the most damaging to its reputation. This chapter offers a comprehensive reappraisal of the magazine's contributors and documents how their widely read and often determinedly professional work for the magazine figured in their lives and wider careers. Based on extensive attribution and archival work, the chapter offers career biographies for a host of writers – from Radagunda Roberts, John Legg and George Crabbe, to Ann Kendall, George Moore, Mary Pilkington, Sophia Troughton,

Charlotte Caroline Richardson and Mitford. Collectively, I contend, these writers and their careers represent a largely hidden culture of 'unRomantic authorship': ordinary, often precarious and unacknowledged writing lives that fail to align with, or that actively flouted, soon-to-be-normative assumptions about professional authorship.

The final two chapters of the book focus on different aspects of the magazine's evolutions over time. Chapter 5 tracks how it responded to the incursions made by the many periodical rivals that emerged in its wake from the 1780s to the 1820s. Despite repeated editorial claims that it never lost sight of its founding plan to 'cherish Female Ingenuity and to conduce to female Improvement', the form and content of the *Lady's Magazine* went through numerous refreshes designed to maintain subscription levels in the face of shifting tastes and ever more varied and sophisticated periodical competition (12 (January 1781): iv). While each of the changes I track in this chapter – changes to the magazine's format and production values, the introduction of new content and the jettisoning of old – was incrementally introduced, their cumulative effect by the late 1820s and early 1830s was to divorce the publication from its founding principles. As the final section of the chapter demonstrates, by 1831, when the magazine finally fell out of the hands of the Robinson publishing house, the publication was almost unrecognisable to readers and even to its editorial staff. Yet the magazine's achievements do not stand or fall on these last troubled years. In Chapter 6, I return to the questions foregrounded in this Introduction to identify the *Lady's Magazine*'s legacies, especially: its self-appointed role as an agent in women's literary history and curator of women's reputations and works for posterity; its championing of women's reading, writing and education; and its influence on individual writers, particularly Austen. Underpinning each of these achievements, as I argue throughout the book, was the magazine's commitment to fostering community among women in and across time and within and across nations and spheres of activity.

Attentiveness to the history, contents and multiple legacies of the *Lady's Magazine* offers an alternative literary history of what we commonly refer to as the Romantic period. The excerpted content that the periodical determined worthy of preservation, the reader-penned works it published and the genres it encouraged do not always map neatly onto the stories we have told ourselves about the late eighteenth- and early nineteenth-century literary marketplace. Conventional narratives about the rise and fall of particular genres and shifting literary tastes that structure standard literary histories are revised by close study of the *Lady's Magazine*, which reveals, for instance, the precocity of the sonnet before Charlotte Smith's supposed revival of it, and of the Gothic before the hey-day of Ann Radcliffe and Matthew Lewis. Volume after volume attest to the resilience of epistolary fiction, decades after Frances Burney and Austen abandoned the form, and to the tenacity of the oriental tale, the dominance of which waxed and waned but was never totally eclipsed during the magazine's run. And it is not only stories about what was being read in the Romantic period that the *Lady's Magazine* undermines, but the related questions of who was being read and considered worth reading. The enduring appeal of earlier and presumed-to-be-forgotten women writers such as Eliza Haywood and Delarivier Manley is confirmed by its contents pages, but it is the magazine's hundreds of pseudonymous translators, poets, essayists, memoirists and fiction writers who most powerfully disrupt our sense of literary history. The work of these now largely forgotten writers sat in columns alongside excerpts from the most famed poets, novelists and essayists of their generation and reached readerships of which many of these famous writers could only dream to find through volume publication alone.

In all of these ways, and in many others documented in the following chapters, the *Lady's Magazine* puts conventional narratives about Romantic literary history under irrevocable strain. Historically, the periodical's deviations from normative definitions of genre, reader, and author have been interpreted as signs that the magazine was out of step with the world beyond its pages. Such perceptions, this book shows, arise from a very selective vision of what constitutes Literature – for which *Blackwood's* is shorthand in Brontë's letter – and, we should note, a vision of Literature that the *Lady's Magazine* challenged in its emergence. For all Patrick Brontë's fears that the periodical was full of 'foolish love-stories', this book concludes, the periodical was resolutely unRomantic.

Chapter 1

Origins: The Birth of the Women's Magazine

WHEN you consider the eagerness with which mankind make their addresses to the shrine of beauty, you may not be a little surprized, that you should be totally neglected by the learned. The press groans with monthly collections calculated for the peculiar entertainment or improvement of men; and variety of articles are strewed, with no sparing hand, by those who would steal into the notice of the public, by catching the favourite inclinations of the times. Yet, as your sex is in this age more employed in reading, than it was in the last, it is something surprising that no periodical production should at present exist calculated for your particular amusement, and designed to improve as well as to delight.

'Address to the Fair Sex', *Lady's Magazine* 1 (August 1770)

So opens the inaugural issue of the *Lady's Magazine; or Entertaining Companion for the Fair Sex*. For his opening gambit, the magazine's unidentified editor blends the familiar and the fresh, asserting, on the one hand, the popularity and ubiquity of various periodical formats and, on the other, an inexplicable gap in the market that his publication will fill.[1] By the time the *Lady's Magazine* launched in August 1770, declarations that women were a 'totally neglected' periodical readership were proverbial. They were also groundless. As Manushag N. Powell reminds us, although 'there was no strong presence of what we would think of as women's magazines' until 'the last third of the eighteenth century', periodicals whose titles declared or implied a primarily male readership had always courted and found women readers.[2] Moreover, following the publication of the short-lived *Ladies Mercury* in 1693, these male-oriented publications jostled for sales with dozens of journals that presented themselves as designed specifically for the 'particular amusement' of women readers. For all the innovations it introduced, the *Lady's Magazine* had more in common with these predecessors than its editorial claims to novelty imply.

'[E]ntertainment' and 'improvement' are unsurprising watchwords for a periodical or indeed any novel, romance, poetry volume or essay collection from the eighteenth century. Yet the *Lady's Magazine* adopted what it cast as a distinctly woman-centred approach to realising these objectives in its avowed commitment to rendering female readers' 'minds' and 'persons' equally 'amiable' ('Address', 1 (January 1770): n.p.). Alongside contributions representing '[e]very branch of literature', the magazine promised 'engravings' designed to 'inform distant readers with every innovation that is made in the female dress'. It vowed also to capitalise on the 'progressive improvement made in the art of *pattern-drawing*' by publishing 'elegant patterns for the Tambour, Embroidery, or every kind of Needlework' ('Address').[3] Boasts that the publication was value for money were legitimate. One of the magazine's needlework patterns alone would have cost double the periodical's sixpence cover price from a haberdasher, in addition to which *Lady's Magazine* subscribers were provided with dozens of pages of double-columned text content and between two and four copper-plates every month. This was an impressive bill of fare by any standard, a veritable feast of a miscellany in the spirit of Edward Cave's *Gentleman's Magazine* (launched 1731). Yet the *Lady's Magazine* was no slavish imitator. Promising 'Interesting Stories, Novels, Tales, Romances', travel writing and fashion intelligence, it promised to be a distinctive and forward-looking publication: a magazine for all women, from the 'house-wife' to the 'peeress' ('Address').

Exaggerated though its claims to novelty are, scholars have tended to agree that the launch of the *Lady's Magazine* marks an important moment in the history of print media: the birth of the recognisably modern women's magazine. This is despite the fact that the term 'women's magazine', as Shawn Lisa Maurer notes, is a 'problematic appellation' in an eighteenth-century context.[4] Periodicals had always been 'very interested in women as both subjects and readers', and despite the fact that the trade was male-dominated, women were active as distributors, publishers, editors of, as well as subscribers and contributors to, periodicals and magazines from the late seventeenth century onwards.[5] Abigail Baldwin, for instance, published the *Female Tatler* (1709–10) after its unknown author left its original publisher, Benjamin Bragge.[6] Delarivier Manley edited several issues of the Tory *Examiner* (1710–14), after taking over from Jonathan Swift. Lady Mary Wortley Montagu authored an essay (no. 573) for the *Spectator* in July 1714, some twenty years before she launched her political periodical, the *Nonsense of Common-Sense* (1737–8).[7] At mid-century, the number of female-conducted and female-oriented periodicals rose substantially with the publication of titles including Eliza Haywood's *Female Spectator* (1744–6), Frances Brooke's *Old Maid* (1755–6) and Charlotte Lennox's *Lady's Museum*

(1760–1).[8] The *Lady's Magazine* was thus far from the first periodical that directly addressed female readers, nor, as we will see, was it even the first journal to possess this particular title. On what grounds, then, could the editors claim innovation and, more to the point, why has periodicals scholarship been so quick to judge the magazine's launch in 1770 as marking a decisive step-change in eighteenth-century periodical culture and its relationship to women?

This book does not dispute that the *Lady's Magazine* shaped the development of the women's periodical in decisive ways. It does, however, challenge the basis for, and nature of, these assertions, particularly the decline-into-domesticity thesis I outlined in the Introduction. In so doing, it offers a very different account of the magazine's objectives and successes.[9] This chapter lays the foundations for these claims: first, by surveying the *Lady's Magazine*'s antecedents as well as the periodical formats and cultures from it emerged and deviated; and second, by reassessing the scholarly assumptions about different periodical types and cultures that have shaped the critical reception of Robinson's magazine.[10] The overwhelming number of periodicals published during the first two-thirds of the century means that the following discussion is not exhaustive. Nor is my presentation of the material in the sections that follow entirely chronological, a decision that reflects: first, that the periodical was always a plural print form, or multiform as I explain in Chapter 3; and second, that women's relationship to this plural form was a mixed bag of gains and losses over time. Magazines, the most magpie-like and, superficially at least, the most undisciplined type of serial publication, drew freely on diverse and co-existing periodical traditions while making innovations of their own. The *Lady's Magazine* was no exception to this general rule of thumb. Understanding Robinson's publication in relation to those periodicals that came before it allows us more accurately to assess its role in the development of the 'women's magazine', a form whose scope and limits were still very much to be determined in 1770. Only by integrating it into a longer and broader history of eighteenth-century periodical culture can the *Lady's Magazine*'s contribution to media and literary history come into focus.

When Is a Periodical Not a Periodical? When It's a Magazine . . .

When it comes to periodical studies, terminology matters. An array of words has been and is still used to describe serial publications from this period. In the eighteenth century itself, many periodicals – such as the

Spectator (1711–12; 1714), *Parrot* (1745), *Female Spectator* or *Old Maid* – avoid specific allusion to their format in their titles, which are drawn instead from the publications' mediating eidolons or guiding textual persona.[11] Other serial publications explicitly styled themselves as journals, repositories, museums, miscellanies and magazines. Today the catch-all 'periodical' encompasses all these and other forms, including newssheets, annuals, pocket-books, advice columns, Reviews, essay-periodicals and even certain kinds of essay collections.[12] There is often considerable slippage between these periodical types, but there are also important differences and, as we will see, scholarly perceptions of these differences have had significant implications for the reception of individual titles and for the women's magazine more widely.

The most important of these differences – especially when considering women's relationship to periodical print culture – is that between the 'periodical' and the 'magazine'. The difference between a 'periodical' and 'magazine' is essentially a technical one, but it is one that is frequently overlaid with implied qualitative judgements. Almost all magazines – one-shops and bookazines aside – are periodicals. Not all periodicals are magazines, however, and not all periodicals are created equal. Periodicals are defined temporally, by frequency and regularity of publication. Magazines, by contrast, are defined formally. They might be published weekly, fortnightly, monthly or even annually, but what unites magazines is their miscellaneity and the absence of the kind of unifying perspective provided by essay-periodical eidolons such as Mr Spectator or the Old Maid.

Many of the differences between the periodical and the magazine can seem arbitrary from a reader's point of view, but they have far-reaching consequences for the formats' perceived respectability. It is common in eighteenth-century studies to pit the polite, original and improving essay-periodical against the commercially driven, derivative and ephemeral magazine. Iona Italia puts the contrast most starkly. While the essay-periodical – epitomised by the *Tatler* (1709–11) and the *Spectator* – evidenced clear 'aspirations to literary gentility' and widely influenced literary culture, the eighteenth-century magazine was a 'second-rate', 'unscrupulous' genre that, in its reliance on repurposed content to pad out original contributions, reveals a 'growing disparity between literary values and journalistic practice'.[13] The differences between periodicals and magazines became still more marked after 1770, Italia continues, in no small part due to the launch of the *Lady's Magazine*. Although acknowledging that magazines of the 'late eighteenth century form a vital link in the history of journalism', Italia concludes that they necessitate 'a very different approach' from 'their predecessors up to 1770', because they are fundamentally different kinds of publication in terms of tone, form and quality.[14] Unlike the posterity-oriented essay-periodical's, the magazine's ambition is cast as a short-term and cynical print form.

That such judgements have their origins in the eighteenth century itself can be inferred from the titles of miscellanies whose editors and publishers adopted other nomenclature. Susan Carlile is surely right that Charlotte Lennox's decision to call her periodical miscellany a 'Museum' was a pointed move to dissociate it from the magazines that preceded it. Lennox's title, according to Carlile, communicated her ambition to provide learned content that was envisaged to be a 'long-lasting . . . and durable part of the reader's library'.[15] Yet if Lennox did reject the term 'magazine' in order to distance her miscellany from associations with the trashy and the perishable, then her decision was at odds with the spirit of the term as it had been adopted by Cave when he launched the *Gentleman's Magazine* three decades earlier. Samuel Johnson may have defined the magazine at mid-century as a 'miscellaneous pamphlet', but he defined it also as 'a storehouse . . . or repository of provisions'.[16] This latter descriptor more nearly captures the aims of Cave and later adopters such as the *Lady's Magazine*'s publishers and editors, who used the term to signify the medium's provision of an armoury of knowledge, information and entertainment – both original and tried and tested – that could be ransacked for edification and amusement for decades or even centuries to come.

That magazine editors and publishers forecast their publications' durability is clear from the physical formats of their works. It is rare today to read magazines from this period as the individual stitched issues that readers first encountered. Library collections primarily hold bound, annual or semi-annual volumes. Often the only signs of these volumes' single-issue origins are the tell-tale needle marks revealed by weakened bindings (Figure 1.1) and the absence of the handsome engravings, song sheets, embroidery patterns and fashion plates that were filleted from individual issues for scrapbooking or extra-illustration prior to binding. Yet even in magazines' more transient original formats, there are clear signs that their publishers envisaged their longevity and preservation by readers. Contents lists and indexes direct readers to items of particular interest long after an initial reading (Figure 1.1). Readers routinely relied upon these orientational tools, as is clear from the many moments in the *Lady's Magazine*'s history when contributors acknowledge using them to locate articles published months or even decades earlier. Catharine Bremen Yeames, a regular contributor to Robinson's periodical, did just this in May 1803 when she responded to a reader request for a cure for hair loss with a recipe by the one of the magazine's medical

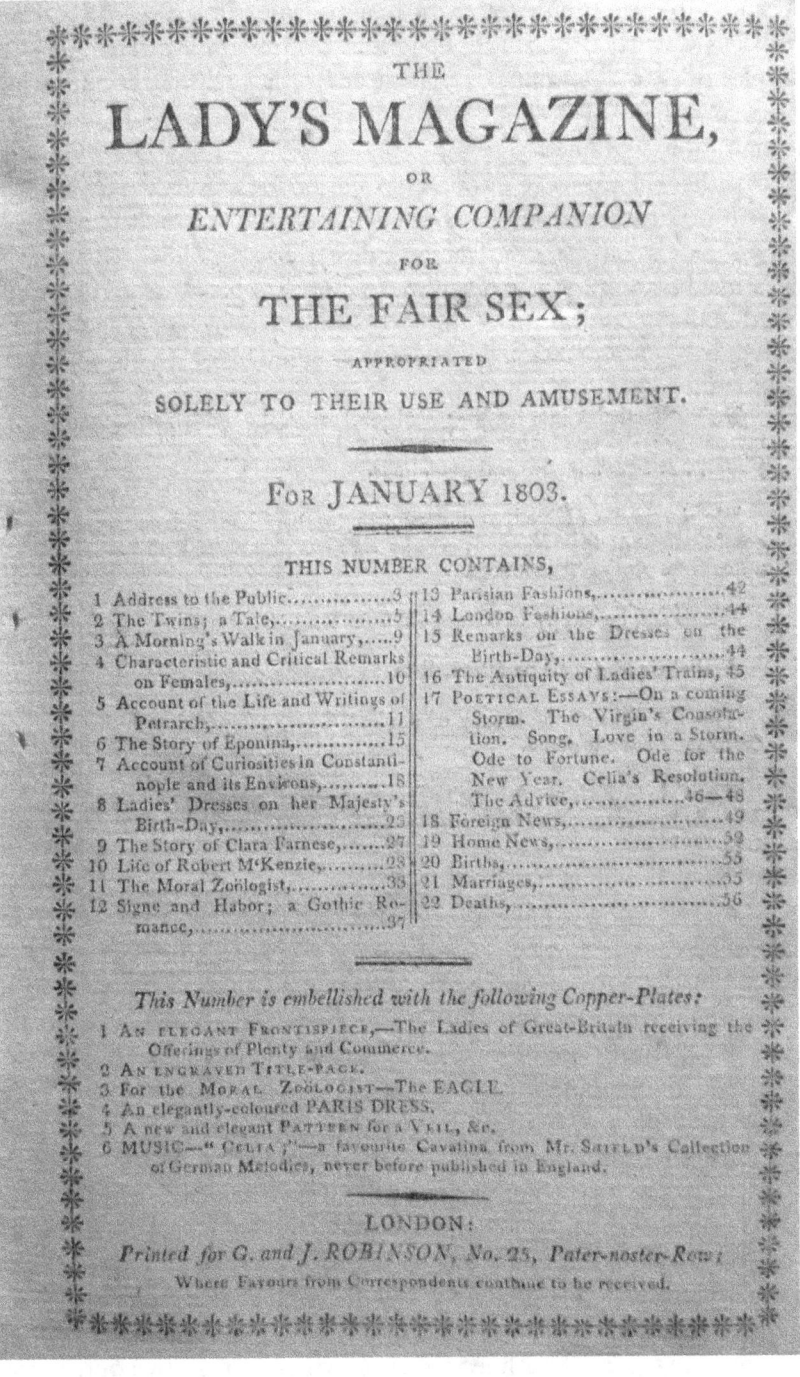

Figure 1.1 Contents page for the *Lady's Magazine* for January 1803. Private collection.

columnists that had appeared in the magazine in 1784, a year before her birth (34 (May 1803): 252). Ephemeral was probably the last adjective to come to Yeames's mind, or that of any of her fellow readers, when considering the *Lady's Magazine* and the rich archive of retrievable information it contained.

Yet neither the presence of these navigation aids, nor the fact that the eighteenth-century magazine survived to be read by multiple generations of readers, has been sufficient to dispel scholarly allegations of the form's insubstantiality. This insubstantiality has been most commonly located in the notorious mixed messages churned out by the magazine's 'open-ended, heterogeneous, fragmented' contents, which marketed a series of ideals and commodities.[17] The magazine – especially the women's magazine – is often assumed to be a more aggressively commercial medium than its essay-periodical counterparts – a myth that persists partly because it is extremely unusual today to be able to read essay-periodicals in the single-issue printings that contained their advertisements. The vast majority of notices for forthcoming books, cosmetic and medicinal preparations or insurance that appeared on the wrappers of the *Lady's Magazine* have not survived in bound volumes (Figure 1.2). Yet its fashion plates, patterns and essays on dress in the main body of the publication have seemed to offer proof enough of the magazine's investment in the selling of things, from frocks to the very idea of femininity itself. Such associations have cast a long shadow over our understanding of the relationship between historic women's magazines, including the *Lady's Magazine*, and their readers. Tellingly, eighteenth-century women who subscribed to periodicals are neutrally categorised as *readers*; readers of eighteenth-century women's magazines, however, are frequently described as '*consumers*', 'educated', in the words of Maurer, 'in the consuming practices that would increasingly come to validate their worth and desirability as women'.[18] Magazines, so the argument goes, turn their readers into passive figures who are enjoined to buy into the feminine ideals that these publications tout under the spurious guise of improvement. If the periodical sharpens the mind, then the women's magazine blunts it through contradictory messaging and its privileging of the realm of goods over the world of ideas.

These criticisms have a long history. Number 60 of Henry Mackenzie's Edinburgh weekly, the *Lounger*, for example, took satiric aim at early women's magazines for their spurious promise that they provided an 'excellent education' for subscribers.[19] Taking the form of a letter to the editor, *Lounger* 60 outlines an 'entirely new' 'plan' by contributor, Projector Literarius, for a miscellany intended solely for women and comprising: news; anecdotes; fashion; essays by women writers; reviews;

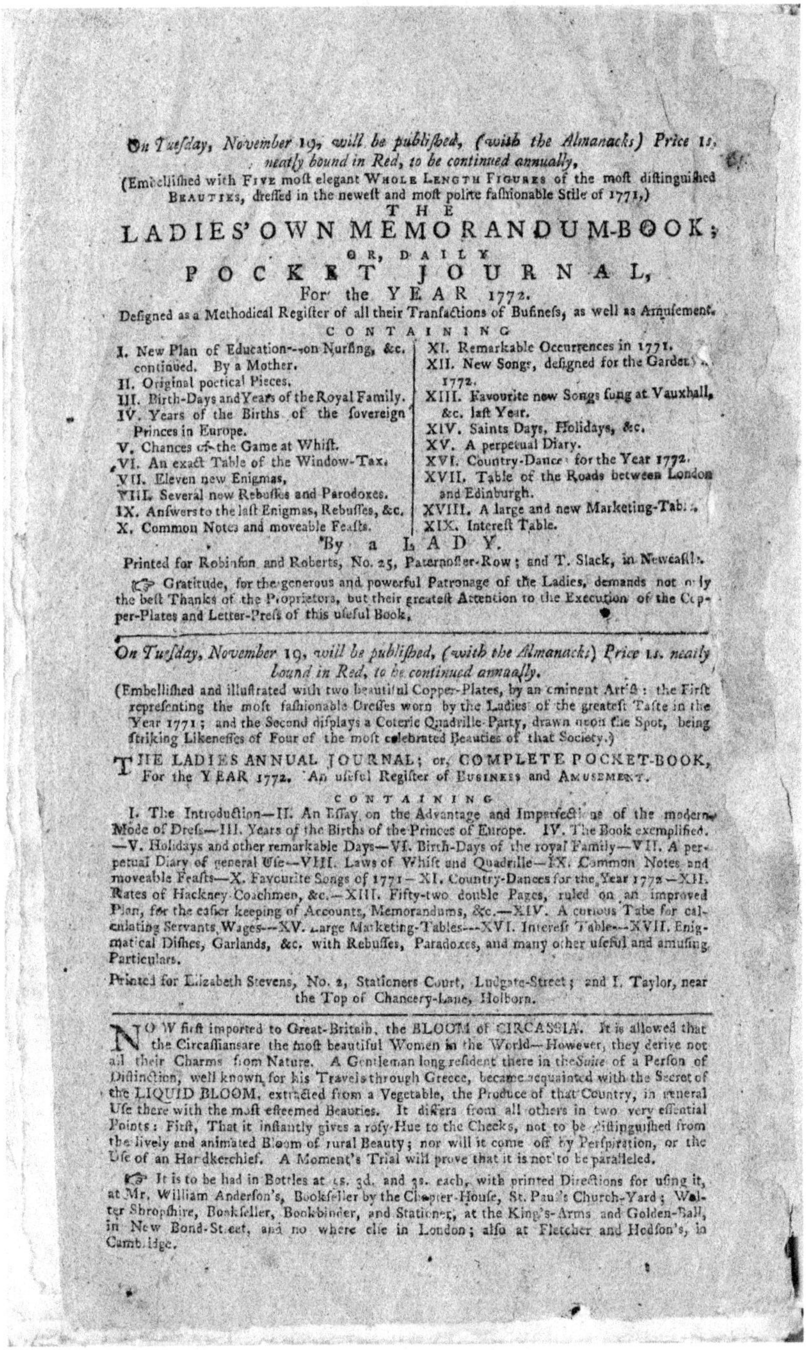

On Tuesday, November 19, will be published, (with the Almanacks) Price 1s. neatly bound in Red, to be continued annually,
(Embellished with FIVE most elegant WHOLE LENGTH FIGURES of the most distinguished BEAUTIES, dressed in the newest and most polite fashionable Stile of 1771,)

THE
LADIES' OWN MEMORANDUM-BOOK;
OR, DAILY
POCKET JOURNAL,
For the YEAR 1772.

Designed as a Methodical Register of all their Transactions of Business, as well as Amusement.

CONTAINING

I. New Plan of Education—on Nursing, &c. continued. By a Mother.
II. Original poetical Pieces.
III. Birth-Days and Years of the Royal Family.
IV. Years of the Births of the sovereign Princes in Europe.
V. Chances of the Game at Whist.
VI. An exact Table of the Window-Tax.
VII. Eleven new Enigmas,
VIII. Several new Rebusses and Parodoxes.
IX. Answers to the last Enigmas, Rebusses, &c.
X. Common Notes and moveable Feasts.
XI. Remarkable Occurrences in 1771.
XII. New Songs, designed for the Garden, 1772.
XIII. Favourite new Songs sung at Vauxhall, &c. last Year.
XIV. Saints Days, Holidays, &c.
XV. A perpetual Diary.
XVI. Country-Dance for the Year 1772.
XVII. Table of the Roads between London and Edinburgh.
XVIII. A large and new Marketing-Table.
XIX. Interest Table.

By a LADY.

Printed for Robinson and Roberts, No. 25, Paternoster-Row; and T. Slack, in Newcastle.

☞ Gratitude, for the generous and powerful Patronage of the Ladies, demands not only the best Thanks of the Proprietors, but their greatest Attention to the Execution of the Copper-Plates and Letter-Press of this useful Book.

On Tuesday, November 19, will be published, (with the Almanacks) Price 1s. neatly bound in Red, to be continued annually.
(Embellished and illustrated with two beautiful Copper-Plates, by an eminent Artist: the First representing the most fashionable Dresses worn by the Ladies of the greatest Taste in the Year 1771; and the Second displays a Coterie Quadrille-Party, drawn upon the Spot, being striking Likenesses of Four of the most celebrated Beauties of that Society.)

THE LADIES ANNUAL JOURNAL; or, COMPLETE POCKET-BOOK,
For the YEAR 1772. An useful Register of BUSINESS and AMUSEMENT.

CONTAINING

I. The Introduction—II. An Essay on the Advantage and Imperfections of the modern Mode of Dress—III. Years of the Births of the Princes of Europe. IV. The Book exemplified.—V. Holidays and other remarkable Days—VI. Birth-Days of the royal Family—VII. A perpetual Diary of general Use—VIII. Laws of Whist and Quadrille—IX. Common Notes and moveable Feasts—X. Favourite Songs of 1771—XI. Country-Dances for the Year 1772—XII. Rates of Hackney-Coachmen, &c.—XIII. Fifty-two double Pages, ruled on an improved Plan, for the easier keeping of Accounts, Memorandums, &c.—XIV. A curious Table for calculating Servants Wages—XV. Large Marketing-Tables—XVI. Interest Table—XVII. Enigmatical Dishes, Garlands, &c. with Rebusses, Paradoxes, and many other useful and amusing Particulars.

Printed for Elizabeth Stevens, No. 2, Stationers Court, Ludgate-Street; and I. Taylor, near the Top of Chancery-Lane, Holborn.

NOW first imported to Great-Britain, the BLOOM of CIRCASSIA. It is allowed that the Circassians are the most beautiful Women in the World—However, they derive not all their Charms from Nature. A Gentleman long resident there in the Suite of a Person of Distinction, well known for his Travels through Greece, became acquainted with the Secret of the LIQUID BLOOM, extracted from a Vegetable, the Produce of that Country, in general Use there with the most esteemed Beauties. It differs from all others in two very essential Points: First, That it instantly gives a rosy Hue to the Cheeks, not to be distinguished from the lively and animated Bloom of rural Beauty; nor will it come off by Perspiration, or the Use of an Handkerchief. A Moment's Trial will prove that it is not to be paralleled.

☞ It is to be had in Bottles at 1s. 3d. and 3s. each, with printed Directions for using it, at Mr. William Anderson's, Bookseller by the Chapter-House, St. Paul's Church-Yard; Walter Shropshire, Bookseller, Bookbinder, and Stationer, at the King's-Arms and Golden-Ball, in New Bond-Street, and no where else in London; also at Fletcher and Hodson's, in Cambridge.

Figure 1.2 Back wrapper from a rare surviving single issue of Wheble's *Lady's Magazine* for October 1771 containing adverts for publications and a cosmetic preparation. Templeman Library, University of Kent.

and, more ominously, works of 'Freethinking' (240). The naïve Projector undermines this fictional plan with every word. Drawn to fashion, scandal in high life and a lubricious interest in the '*marriage* ceremonies of distant countries' (238), the education that his periodical promises is evidently nothing of the kind. Barbara Benedict has read *Lounger* 60's articulation of 'the infamous triad of the feminine, the sentimental, and the modern' as indicative of the eighteenth-century tendency to view miscellany publications as 'reflect[ing] the sins of a decadent culture'.[20] Yet the criticism runs more locally and deeper. Specifically targeting 'monthly Miscellanies' for and by a sex 'hitherto ... excluded' from the 'republic of letters' (237), *Lounger* 60 borrows directly from the rhetoric of the annual 'Addresses' that prefaced publications such as the *Lady's Magazine*. The letter's satire may be many-pronged, but its argument is unambiguous: women's magazines, unlike essay-periodicals such as the *Lounger*, could never meet their promise to 'enlarge the sphere of female knowledge' (237). The heterogenous here-today-gone-tomorrow magazine format, which offered readers the 'liberty of dipping' into, without fully engaging with, its multifarious content, guaranteed its pedagogical failure (239).

Lounger 60 and more recent scholarly accounts arrive at the same conclusion from different starting points: eighteenth-century women's magazines are all show and no substance. According to Mackenzie's periodical, the heterogeneous form and enervating content of women's magazines engendered shallow and promiscuous reading habits. For scholars such as Shevelow and Maurer, female-oriented magazines encouraged reader passivity and appeals to women's bodies rather than minds in the service of a particular model of domestic femininity. The following sections of this chapter challenge these triangulated claims about the relationship between form, content and gender by revisiting women's engagement with a broad range of periodical forms from the 1690s to the 1760s. As we will see, neither the essay-periodical nor the magazine had a monopoly on female improvement and individual titles varied greatly in their treatment of, and ambitions for, women readers. The *Lady's Magazine*'s adoption of the miscellany format was no doubt in part a commercial decision – an attempt to capitalise on the success of Cave's long-running journal and the more modest triumphs of earlier magazines marketed at women readers. Yet as we will see, it was also a declaration of faith in the efficacy of miscellaneity as a mode particularly well 'calculated ... to improve as well as to delight' through its conversational form, its showcasing of different viewpoints and its promotion of active reading habits.

Fair-sexing It?: The 1690s to the 1710s

The first periodical specifically to target women subscribers was the weekly question-and-answer sheet, the *Ladies Mercury* (1693). The editorial that opened the first of the four issues comprising the complete run of this lively journal was very different from the one that opened the *Lady's Magazine* eight decades later.[21] Taking the form of a letter addressed to the 'Gentleman' behind John Dunton's *Athenian Mercury* (1690–7), to which the *Ladies Mercury* served as supplement and counter, it begins with an expression of 'Esteem' for its predecessor and a promise not to 'encroach' upon the earlier title's expansive 'Province': 'Learning, Nature, Arts, Sciences, and indeed the whole World' (28 February 1693).[22] The *Ladies Mercury*, by contrast, vowed to restrict its 'narrow Speculation' to 'that little Sublunary, Woman' and the dishing up of 'a small Treat of Love' in each of its weekly papers (1.1). As such, the editor reassured, the *Ladies Mercury* posed no competition to its namesake. Catering to these less lofty topics would, moreover, benefit the Athenians by saving them from the embarrassment of having to condescend to the 'wast [sic] Paper-lumber' of 'Foolish Tatlers and Gossips' – that is, the queries on such matters submitted by women correspondents to the *Athenian* (1.1).[23] Only after identifying itself as a repository for the Athenians' hand-me-downs does the *Ladies Mercury* finally address women readers directly. The address concludes with a dedication to the 'fair Sex', in whose collective service the editor promises to answer 'all Questions' female correspondents might 'vouchsafe to send', and in such a manner as 'not [to] force a Blush into a Virgin-Cheek' (1.1)

In this last sentence, the rhetoric of the *Ladies Mercury* begins to approximate that of the later *Lady's Magazine*, which similarly emphasised that its content was designed to 'confirm chastity and recommend virtue' ('Address', 1 (August 1770): n.p.). The tone of the two publications is otherwise poles apart. If the *Lady's Magazine*'s manner of address is polite and companionable, then that of the *Ladies Mercury* is playful, sometimes prurient, yet pre-eminently savvy in its meditations on subjects ranging from private marriages to male impotence, sex before marriage and adultery. The first of the sixteen questions the *Mercury* published very much sets this tone. Its inaugural female querist introduces herself as 'a very young Woman ... of some little Quality' and endowed with more beauty than fortune. Enjoying a better fate than many of the women who would later write to the *Lady's Magazine*'s agony aunt, the Matron, the correspondent writes that she is married to a wealthy, kind and handsome man upon she whom she dotes (1.1). Yet despite having 'every thing that's happy', she declares herself the 'miserablest of Women' because she lives with the 'Pangs and Torments' of guilt over a secret premarital affair. Fearful of disclosure, and emaciated by distress at the thought that her spouse might discover her former liaison and reject her, the querist begs the Mercurians to advise on how to 'support her self in this deplorable Calamity' (1.1). In response, the Mercurians acknowledge the correspondent's 'sin', but deny her 'Infamy' and absolve her of 'Guilt' (1.1). Evoking the precedent of Jacob's deception of Isaac, they declare 'Hypocrisie' no crime and simply urge the 'lovely penitent' to turn her eyes to the 'bright Heaven before thee' rather than 'the sullen shade behind thee' (1.1).

Had the querist failed to perform penitential self-flagellation in her query, the Mercurians might have been unforgiving. Elsewhere, the paper exhibits less tolerance of women's sexual behaviour. This is especially true when that behaviour is abstinence. The last question the *Ladies Mercury* printed in the final 17 March 1693 issue, for instance, articulates the concerns of a wife whose previous, difficult pregnancy prompted warnings from 'Physicians' that future attempts to bear children would 'hazard [her] life'. Content that she can 'easily persuade' her 'Husband' against 'that part of the Matrimonial Ingagement' that endangers her, she is nonetheless concerned about whether she can 'lawfully' abstain from sex (1.4). The Mercurians respond, first, by casting doubt that any woman could accomplish such a feat of self-denial as chastity even to preserve her life, and second, by questioning whether any wife could have such 'entire Ascendance' over their husband as to ask the same of him. They conclude by urging the querist to 'perform [her] Conjugal Duty, and trust to Providence to a Good Cause' (1.4). In its attempts to reconcile the checks of law and cultural norms against the balance of individual desires and women's right (or not) to exert control over their own bodies, the *Ladies Mercury* is nothing if not pragmatic.

An early attempt to capitalise on the rise of the periodical format through specialisation, the *Ladies Mercury* attempted to carve out a specialist corner of the market by devoting itself to the subject of love and to the social, economic, legal and cultural contexts that legitimise or prohibit love's pursuit. Like later periodicals specifically marketed at female subscribers, the *Mercury* also marked out women's experience as a neglected realm that merited attention and textual space for the articulation. Matters of 'Love', of course, are not solely women's concern and, as if to prove the point, exactly half of the queries that the *Ladies Mercury* published were submitted by self-identified male querists. Yet even though male correspondents feature prominently, the

Mercury is titularly, thematically and structurally 'woman championing', an phrase that Eve Tavor Bannet uses to describe serial publications that: occupied 'a middle ground between mainstream and woman authored periodicals'; encouraged women's participation in periodical print culture; and presented this participation as a way for women to renegotiate their position in society.[24] In its epistolary dialogue with the Athenian Society and its often startlingly frank responses to its querists, the *Ladies Mercury* boldly put the question of women's relationship to an expanding and increasingly competitive periodical print culture on the table.

This was a conversation extended by the *Mercury*'s contemporary, Peter (Pierre) Anthony Motteux's *Gentleman's Journal: or, the Monthly Miscellany* (1692–4).[25] Inspired, in part, by the French *Mercure Galant* (1627–1724), Motteux's monthly contained a diverse range of material including news, poetry, enigmas, translations, theatre criticism, scientific information, amatory fiction and song sheets. Although the periodical's title seems to anticipate an exclusively male readership, the *Gentleman's Journal* made clear from the outset that the 'fair Sex' were part of its intended audience and that its contents were designed so as not to provoke them to 'Blush'. Indeed, Motteux had good reason to declare his publication 'no less the *Ladies Journal* than the *Gentlemens'* (1 (January 1692): 1).[26] His miscellany was not only partly written for women, but it also contained many contributions by 'a Lady' or published under female signatures and pseudonyms. Identified women writers whose work appeared in the *Gentleman's Journal* include Aphra Behn, Anne Finch and Anne Wharton.[27]

As Margaret J. M. Ezell documents, Motteux's miscellany overturns the 'common assumption that the literary world of seventeenth-century England was, in general, aristocratic and male, an exclusive men's club, in effect'.[28] Indeed, the October 1693 issue of the *Gentleman's Journal* contained so many items authored by women that Motteux dubbed this issue 'the *Lady's Journal*' and prefaced its contents with a four-page address 'To the Fair Sex', in which the editor declared his 'Constancy' to female readers and his desire to 'vindicate' them through his periodical (2 (October 1693): 324). Such rhetorical flourishes were more than gallantry. In devoting so much of his publication to the work of women writers, Motteux claimed that he was not condescending to female subscribers, but simply paying them their due for their 'productions and those of others which you have occasion'd' (324). By enthusiastically including women writers within its mixed-sex periodical community, the *Gentleman's Journal* accommodated early modern scribal and coterie practices to the 'commercial medium' of print.[29] It was a move that would have long-lasting implications for the miscellany format, as I discuss in more detail in Chapter 6. If the *Ladies Mercury* is a landmark publication for its opening up of the periodical form to include women's voices and experiences, then the entertaining and literary *Gentleman's Journal* is significant in the history of women's relationship to periodical print culture as the first publication of its kind to give women's writing and the woman writer their due within that culture.

Despite their significance to the development of the form, however, both the *Ladies Mercury* and the *Gentleman's Journal* quickly receded from collective memory. When mid- to late-century journals reflected on women's prior engagement with the periodical format, they looked not to these titles but to the *Tatler* and *Spectator*. Women, of course, occupy a central place in the worlds of Addison and Steele's periodicals. These pathbreaking journals, which famously sought to model and promote new forms of politeness, sociability and virtue in public and private life, remain the century's best-known serial publications. Since women's projected role in these periodicals' efforts to reform the nation's morals and manners has been so thoroughly examined, there is no need to re-tread much ground in order to understand why they have been accorded the status they have in the history of women's relationship to periodical print culture.[30] My interest here, therefore, is less in how the *Tatler* and *Spectator* projected and responded to their female readers than in how our understanding of these projections and responses has conditioned, and sometimes distorted, our reading of their periodical successors.

From the outset, the thrice-weekly *Tatler* and the daily *Spectator* identified women as an important constituency of their readerships. The confirmed yet amorous bachelor Isaac Bickerstaff opens the first issue of the *Tatler* by announcing the paper's ambition to 'offer something' to public-spirited 'Gentlemen . . . of strong Zeal', but affirms also a resolve 'to have something which may be of Entertainment to the Fair Sex, in Honour of whom I have invented the Title of this Paper' (1: 15).[31] As Shevelow observes, even though the *Tatler*'s titular nod to the female sex is a rather 'back-handed compliment', women were central to the periodical's programme.[32] The behaviour and virtues of the female sex were closely surveyed throughout the *Tatler*'s run; letters from female correspondents were actively solicited; and various numbers feature paraphrased or purportedly verbatim letters from female correspondents. The *Tatler* even had its own occasional female eidolon in the form of Jenny Distaff, Bickerstaff's younger half-sister, who takes up the 'Cause of [her] Sex' in six *Tatler* papers (no. 247, vol. 3, p. 261). True to the promise of its inaugural number, the *Tatler* covered news and politics – although its coverage of these topics dwindled over time – and devoted considerable attention to domestic life, manners and the civilising effects of female conversation and sociability. The periodical's public scrutiny of private life produced 'a definitive and normative image of feminine duties', a construction founded upon the presumption of biologically determined sexual difference, or what Steele notoriously referred to in *Tatler* no. 172 as 'a Sort of Sex in Souls' (vol. 2, p. 144).[33]

The *Spectator* extended the *Tatler*'s project by placing women at its rhetorical and ideological heart. There was 'none', Mr Spectator claimed, 'to whom this Paper will be more useful, than to the female World'.[34] The periodical's aim was to bring 'Philosophy out of Closets and Libraries, Schools and Colleges, to dwell in Clubs and Assemblies, at Tea-Tables, and in Coffee-Houses' (no. 10, vol. 1, p. 44). Addison's famous and idealised formulation seems to imagine the male preserve of the coffee-house and the feminised tea-table as parallel sites, linked by the conversable sociability facilitated by his periodical and its circulation within these spaces. This vision of the periodical left an important legacy. It was one that the *Lady's Magazine* willingly inherited even if, as I return to in Chapter 3, Robinson's periodical strenuously challenged the gendered assumptions that underpinned its forerunner's conversational mode. For, as the *Lady's Magazine* acknowledged, the rational, masculine realm of the coffee-house and the 'female', domestic 'world' of the tea-table were not understood by Addison and Steele's periodical as precisely the equivalents that Mr Spectator's rhetoric implies. When Mr Spectator declares his paper's ambition to 'furnish *Tea-Table Talk*' 'among reasonable Women' he has no intention of bringing the idealised world of rational-critical coffee-house debate to the drawing room (no. 4, vol. 1, p. 21). He aims instead merely to 'divert the Minds of my female Readers' from the trifles that are the 'Business' of their leisure hours and to lead them through all the becoming duties of Virginity, Marriage, and Widowhood' (no. 4, vol. 1, pp. 21–2). The *Spectator*'s imagined female reader is no everywoman: she moves in a more 'exalted Sphere of Knowledge and Virtue' than 'Ordinary Women' and unites the 'Ornaments' of physical and mental accomplishment so as to inspire 'Awe and Respect, as well as Love, into their Male Beholders' (no. 4, vol. 1, p. 21). The *Spectator*, like the *Tatler*, characterises women's virtues and spheres of intellectual and material life as different from, and valuable only in relation to, those of men.

The *Tatler* and *Spectator*'s commitment to what Jonathan Swift pejoratively termed 'fair-sexing it' has been well-documented.[35] As Shevelow observes, the *Tatler* and *Spectator* turn on an insidious paradox: their attentiveness to women ultimately serves 'an emerging ideology that . . . constructed women as essentially – that is, both biologically and socially

– "other" than men'.³⁶ These essentialist views, which as Erin Mackie points out were linked to an emerging consensus about sexual difference in the early eighteenth century, are understood to have had lasting implications for women's relationship to periodical print culture.³⁷ Although Italia detects a 'proto-feminist agenda' in the *Tatler* and *Spectator*'s championing of 'women's intellectual capabilities', the dominant scholarly view is that these early attempts to 'fair-sex' the periodical led inexorably to an increasingly normative vision of womanhood that magazines from the second half of the eighteenth century unquestioningly exploited for commercial and ideological gains.³⁸ Subsequent chapters of this book reassess these assertions in relation to the *Lady's Magazine*, which harboured much greater ambitions for itself and its women readers than these accounts suggest. These were ambitions that were, in part at least, fuelled by the emergence at mid-century of a number of 'woman championing' and woman-led periodical initiatives that are commonly read as instituting vital – if temporary – interruptions in the decline-into-domesticity narrative.

The Mid-century: Eliza Haywood, Frances Brooke and Charlotte Lennox

The mid-century set a highwater mark for women's involvement in the periodical marketplace. Eighteenth-century literacy rates are difficult to calculate with precision, but the evidence points to a significant – around 50 per cent – growth in the number of literate adults between 1700 and 1750. From 1760, when Lennox's *Lady's Museum* launched, rising literary rates – especially among women – coupled with an expanding population, grew readerships significantly. By 1830 – when the *Lady's Magazine* entered its seventh decade – the adult reading public in England had grown by more than three million (or by 238.4 per cent, according Michael Suarez's estimate) since 1700.³⁹ Periodicalists took advantage of these developing readerships and demographics. Leading the way was a group of women whom Kathryn R. King has dubbed the 'new (if unheralded) female triumvirate of wit': Brooke, Haywood and Lennox.⁴⁰ All three writers enjoyed impressive literary careers and worked across various genres. While they are still known best as novelists, all also wrote for the stage and were skilled translators. Lennox was additionally an accomplished poet and literary critic, and Haywood wrote advice literature and many other texts that cross genres or resist our efforts to categorise them. Periodicals by all three women were actively remembered by the *Lady's Magazine*, which liberally reprinted material from them and other of their editors' works over the course of many years.

Haywood was the most prolific periodicalist of the triumvirate. She was editor of the *Female Spectator*, which is my focus here; the more sustainedly political *Parrot* (1746); a sequel to the *Female Spectator* entitled *Epistles to the Ladies* (1748); and the *Young Lady* (1756), which was purportedly led by one of the women from the Spectator Club described in Haywood's first periodical venture.[41] The *Female Spectator*, *Old Maid* and *Lady's Museum* have much in common. First, all three periodicals are mediated by female eidolons. The Female Spectator presents herself as a former 'Coquet', although reports of her reform are somewhat exaggerated.[42] Brooke's Old Maid is a woman 'on the verge of fifty' (15 November 1755: 2). And Lennox's Trifler, the columnist whose essays open all eleven issues of the *Lady's Museum*, describes herself a young 'coquet' of eighteen in possession of 'a strong passion for intellectual pleasures' as well as 'fashionable amusements' (1.1: 3–4).[43] Despite their age differences, all three personae are united by their status as singletons, to borrow Brooke's term, and all find authority in their spinsterhood. Second, while all three periodicals cover considerable thematic and topical ground, each places the question of women's education at its heart, and each promotes female intellectual ambition, albeit in differently calibrated terms. Third, like the *Tatler* and *Spectator* before them, each publication adopts a range of strategies to build rhetorical consensus around its dominant preoccupations. Finally, all three periodicals present themselves, and are still widely understood today, as 'by-women-for-women' publications, although as we will see, such claims are at least as fictional as the personae Haywood, Brooke and Lennox adopted. These formally innovative, wide-ranging, witty and ambitious publications more than earn the scholarly regard in which they are held. Nonetheless, conventional accounts that identify these periodicals' achievements partly at the expense of late-century magazines' perceived shortcomings are misleading, not least because they fail to identify the many through-lines between these earlier titles and those that followed. The *Female Spectator*'s, *Old Maid*'s and *Lady's Museum*'s collective questioning of what could and should constitute the business of a periodical for the fair sex, as well as their extended meditations on how the periodical form might uniquely serve women readers' interests and aspirations, were instrumental in creating the conditions, and setting the agenda for, the *Lady's Magazine*.

The first 'Book' of the monthly *Female Spectator*, published in April 1744, is a rhetorical tour de force in which Haywood establishes her eidolon's authority and positions her publication confidently within the by-now decades-long tradition of periodical writing. The 'Female Spectator' herself appears before readers in a guise that is both recognisable and distinctive. Although her declared aim to be 'both useful and entertaining to the Publick' is conventional, her claims to personal authority and her work's utility are not (18). Neither moral nor socioeconomic credentials authorise the Female Spectator's pronouncements; rather it is her past indiscretions, combined with 'a Genius tolerably extensive, and an Education more liberal than is ordinarily allowed to Persons of my Sex', that fuel her insights and 'Ambition' (18). Her periodical is pitched as reformist in the manner of Addison and Steele's journals, but from the outset, its methods and perspective are marked out as different. Instead of being 'a spectator of mankind rather than ... one of the species', the Female Spectator insists that she is very much of the world. She has 'Spies' in the city and fashionable resorts, and this intelligence, combined with her own 'Experience' and hard-won recognition of its self-defeating pleasures, offers a more inclusive and perspicacious perspective on the topics she addresses than her namesake does (19, 18). This perspectival shift, as Bannet argues, allows Haywood's periodical to offer a 'woman-centred' vision of society that 'vigorously contest[s] *The Spectator*'s attempts to exclude women from the public sphere'.[44]

The sense of inclusivity and worldliness so attentively cultivated by the *Female Spectator* in its first 'Book' is reinforced by the multiplicity of voices it contains. These voices include the periodical's correspondents, whose real or editorially manufactured letters about a range of ethical, social and political matters are printed in its pages, as well as those of Female Spectator club members (Figure 1.3): Euphrosine, a young merchant's daughter, the 'excellent ... Wife' Mira, and an unnamed 'Widow of Quality' (19). Collectively, the club members represent the three stages of a woman's life – 'Virginity, Marriage and Widowhood' – through which the *Spectator* promised to guide its female readers, with the Female Spectator herself embodying a fourth possibility not countenanced by her namesake: that of the well-educated, unmarried and childless woman. Crucially, it is her perspective that overrides and models into consensus all others that find their way into the periodical. The form of the *Female Spectator* mimics this controlled diversity of voice and viewpoint. The periodical includes anecdotes, fiction, correspondence and polemical essays, the meaning of which varied content is contained and remediated by the essay-periodical form in ways that are fundamentally different than if the same content were presented as a succession of discrete items jostling for page space in a miscellany. The result is a periodical that provides a nuanced and incisive account of the force of 'Custom' in dictating the scope of women's lives (book 10:

Figure 1.3 Frontispiece to *The Female Spectator* (1744). Courtesy of the General Collection, Beinecke Rare Book and Manuscript Library, Yale University.

358). Haywood's eidolon advocates forcibly that women should act in the world according to reason, not custom. She argues passionately that they should acquire the 'knowledge' requisite to form those principles and be allowed access to forums – 'public Places', including the medium of print – in which to act upon those principles (book 10: 358).

The *Female Spectator* enjoys a privileged place in Haywood scholarship, where it has traditionally, if rather inaccurately, been viewed as proof of the author's capitulation to changing literary sensibilities mid-century.[45] It has also been cast as marking an important development in women's relationship to the periodical through its feminisation of the form itself. According to Ros Ballaster, the *Female Spectator* signals a move away from earlier eighteenth-century periodicals – like the Tory *Female Tatler* – that attracted women and were associated with party politics or gossip and towards the late-century, 'popular women's magazines' that defined readers 'in terms of domestic enclosure and their absence from or lack of interest in state, as opposed to sexual, politics'.[46] Italia similarly concludes that the *Female Spectator* refashioned 'journalism' – formerly seen as 'louche and disreputable' – as 'decorous and socially exclusive' because of its 'persistent focus on gentility', distancing from 'political debate', and insistence upon 'the necessity of maintaining female decorum'.[47]

Such accounts uphold the *Female Spectator*'s status as a by-women-for-women periodical: a label that warrants at least partial qualification. For Ballaster, Haywood's periodical provided 'a conduit for dialogue and exchange between women produced collectively by women' and created a 'community in which its readers could participate from the isolation of their homes'.[48] Yet the *Female Spectator* club is an elaborate conceit, of course, and at least some of the so-called reader letters that provide internal evidence of the strength of its print community are likely editorial fabrications. A more substantive fiction is the notion that Haywood's periodical creates a community populated exclusively by women whose concerns are rooted in matters of personal rather than national or political interest. There is some evidence to suggest that Haywood might have co-authored the journal with male writers, but regardless, men nevertheless inhabit the world of the *Female Spectator* as correspondents. As King documents, the exchange between one of these letter writers, Curioso Politico, and the *Female Spectator* is particularly instructive in exposing as 'inadequate the by-to-and-about-women characterisation' of Haywood's journal.[49] This is not simply because of the male Curioso's presence within a so-called 'women's periodical', but because the nature of his exchange turns on, and complicates, the question: What is a 'women's periodical' anyway?

Curioso Politico's letter upbraids the journal's editor for failing to document 'turns and counter-turns in politics' and events in the ongoing War of Austrian Succession (1740–8). The Female Spectator retorts that such accusations are unjust and uses her correspondent's perverse criticisms of a women's periodical's seeming lack of interest in current affairs as an occasion to reflect on the nature of her journalistic enterprise. Enumerating 'Armies marching,—Battles fought,—Towns destroyed,—Rivers cross'd, and the like' is beyond the 'Province of a *Female Spectator*', she contends, but not because hers is a periodical by, for, or about women (book 8: 295). Indeed, as Catherine Ingrassia has documented, politics and martial culture, and their relationship to the domestic sphere, are central concerns of the *Female Spectator*, in which women readers are presented with a sophisticated take on the 'effects of global conflicts on domestic life'.[50] Curioso Politico's inability to see politics in the periodical, Haywood implies, derives rather from his narrow understanding of the term. The *Female Spectator* was no newspaper and asserted freely that it had no business and little interest in duplicating political information already in the public domain or catering to the 'coffee-house tastes' satisfied by Addison and Steele's earlier ventures.[51] Neither did it see politics in the round as outside its remit. Its business was instead to cultivate readers' habits of private reflection upon matters of public concern in order that they could inhabit the world more contentedly and usefully.

If living usefully entailed the cultivation of political literacy for women and men, then the *Female Spectator* was clear that it also required level of knowledge and education, to which end the periodical recommended to its women readers the study of history, mathematics, geography, science and philosophy. The periodical's advocacy of women's intellectual pursuits is circumscribed, however. Despite asserting, contra the *Tatler*, that there 'is undoubtedly, no Sexes in Souls', the *Female Spectator* ostensibly concedes that women's 'Duties' are largely 'confined to the Management of her Family' (book 10: 355–6). This, though, is no argument for perpetuating female 'Ignorance' (358). Knowledge, Haywood writes acerbically, 'is a light Burthen' for those who possess it, yet have fewer opportunities than men to exercise it. Furthermore, she preaches to the unconverted, the acquisition of 'learning' via the kinds of reflective and varied reading promoted by the *Female Spectator* would allow women better to fulfil their culturally mandated roles as 'good *Mothers*' and 'good *Wives*' (358, 357) by ensuring they perform 'those Duties more through Principle than Custom' (356). The vision of domesticity conjured by Haywood's periodical is every bit as strategically judged to appeal to readerly sensibilities as the *Female Spectator* persona. Haywood's 'most ambitious and successful journalistic undertaking', the *Female Spectator* was a landmark periodical in ways that its somewhat misleading by-and-for-women label only partly captures.[52] Its legacies, particularly its modelling of consensus and community and framing of debates about politics, learning and the women's periodical, shaped the form for decades to come.

Something of the *Female Spectator*'s immediate influence can be traced in Brooke's brilliant and still understudied weekly, the *Old Maid by 'Mary Singleton'*. Like Haywood's periodical, the *Old Maid* presents itself as female led and female oriented, a work written 'chiefly' for the amusement' of its editor's 'own sex' (no. 2 (22 November 1755): 12). In fact, we know that some contributions to the periodical, even some to which Singleton's signature was attached, were written by men and, like most periodicals of the time, the *Old Maid* appealed to readers of 'both sexes' (no. 1 (15 November 1755): 8).[53] Styled in its inaugural number as 'an odd attempt', Brooke's journal is strikingly original (15 November 1755: 1). Singleton eschews a heavy-handedly reformist agenda in favour of a light-touch, alternative take on the Horatian *dulce et utile* imperative. The opening sentences of the first issue suggest that little more than whim motivated Singleton to establish the journal and 'buz [sic] amongst' the many other periodicals that like 'summer insects just make their appearance, and are gone' (1). Quickly, however, her ruse is exposed. Singleton's eccentricity – an eccentricity she is aware readers will take as synonymous with her spinsterhood – only lightly masks her searing intellect. In Brooke's deft hands, the 'useless and insignificant' spinster is transformed into a cultural authority, who asserts her 'natural right' to communicate her 'prodigious wisdom' in the 'service' of her 'community' (4). Singleton claimed to have 'no regular plan' for her 'work, being too much a free-Born Briton to submit to any thing like rule' (no 2: 12). Yet there is little capricious about the *Old Maid*, a meticulously conducted periodical for which Brooke acted in triple capacity of author, editor and manager. Although its form more nearly approximates Haywood's essay-periodical than Lennox's later miscellany or the still later *Lady's Magazine,* the *Old Maid* foreshadows these subsequent publications in its wide-ranging contents, which included essays and letters on coffee-house culture, the stage, courtship and marriage, literary criticism, women's education, female Amazonianism, discussions of topical concerns such as the prospect of French invasion, as well as poetry.

Arguably the most important contribution the *Old Woman* made to the development of the women's periodical was its reanimation of the debate about the cultural and literary authority of 'odd' women sparked by Haywood's *Female Spectator*. In a brilliant, but all too rare, appraisal of the *Old Maid*, Powell observes that Brooke's journal, through the Singleton persona, 'flirts with but also rejects popular gender stereotypes' and 'capitalises on the affiliation between femininity and periodical culture without absolutely deferring to the loss of gravitas that a feminised periodical rhetoric implies'.[54] Eighteenth-century scholarship, as Harriet Guest reminds us, has historically been too quick to accept the pervasiveness of the ideal domestic woman in conduct books from the period as evidence that women were bound by increasingly restrictive and normative ideals of propriety. Yet domesticity was always, in Guest's words, 'a contested proposition', and the periodical was one of the principal sites of its contestation.[55] Wise and learned old maids in the Singleton mould continued to enrich and bedevil later women's magazines by refusing to abide by the conventional femininity with which the form would, ironically, become so closely associated.

Lennox's *Lady's Museum* was 'designed' more specifically for its editor's own 'sex' than either the *Old Woman* or the *Female Spectator*. It shares Haywood's and Brooke's conviction in women's rational capacity and fitness for intellectual pursuits, but advances these claims differently.[56] Its first departure from periodical tradition is in its construction of the 'Trifler', whose column reads like a series of compressed instalments of issues of the *Female Spectator* and the *Old Maid*. Yet unlike the Female Spectator or the Old Maid, whose authority rests on the unique perspective permitted by their social marginality, the Trifler unequivocally characterises herself as a model domestic woman. Declaring herself motivated by a benignly feminine 'desire to please', and slightly more suspect 'desire of fame' (1.1: 2), she is quick to point out that she does not deserve the 'odious appellation of coquet' that the Female Spectator willingly co-opts (3). And for all the vigour with which the Trifler unapologetically pursues 'intellectual pleasures' (4), she is not 'odd' like Singleton, and takes 'pleasure' in using her education to be 'a useful as well as agreeable companion' to her brother of whose 'well-ordered' family home she is 'mistress' (9).

Yet if the Trifler appears more outwardly conventional than Haywood's and Brooke's periodical personae, the form of the *Lady's Museum* as a whole breaks with periodical tradition in order to make good on its promise to provide 'Information and Amusement' through a 'Course of Female Education . . . for the Ladies'.[57] A miscellany in spirit if not in title, the *Lady's Museum* boasts an impressive range of content across diverse genres including: the Trifler column, which included interpolated reader letters; translations from the French (including an important translation of François Fénelon's 1687 *Traité de l'éducation des filles*); essays on botany, history, geography, astronomy and natural philosophy; biographies of notable women such as Joan of Arc and Boudica; a serial fiction in the form of 'Harriot and Sophia' (published subsequently, in 1762, as the novel *Sophia*); as well as non-textual material such as engravings, song sheets and maps. Diverse and expansive though these contents are, the *Lady's Museum* is, in the words of Carlile, 'a cohesive and interrelated enterprise'.[58] Unlike Haywood's and Brooke's periodicals, this cohesion is thematically achieved rather than manufactured by a mediating editorial persona. All of the material that the *Lady's Museum* published speaks to its pedagogical agenda, and its catalogue of contents offers an ambitious 'curriculum' for women's edification.[59] Every item in the *Museum* either reflects on the personal and cultural value of women's learning or identifies reading material to furnish that education in the privacy of its readers' homes.

The *Lady's Museum* is near-unanimously celebrated by scholars today for its opening up of 'diverse possibilities for women's intellectual and internal lives'.[60] For these same scholars, the periodical's 'pedagogical work' is all the more important because of what followed in its wake: the founding of publications, such as the *Lady's Magazine*, that lacked Lennox's vision for the women's periodical as a 'serious educational vehicle'.[61] That the *Lady's Museum* is forward-thinking and intellectually rich is irrefutable, but the presumed discontinuity between it and magazines like Robinson's *Lady's Magazine*, which in many ways followed its example, is exaggerated. So too are some of the claims made about the progressiveness of the *Lady's Museum*'s views on female education. The diverse and intellectually ambitious contents of the *Museum* implicitly endorse the *Female Spectator*'s surface claim that women should be allowed to enlarge their understanding in order to be 'more happy' in, and more 'worthy' of, their domestic roles. To quote the author of the *Museum*'s serial 'Philosophy for the Ladies' – possibly Lennox herself – it is precisely because 'the fair' are '[u]ndisturbed by the more intricate affairs of business', 'political entanglements' or the 'pursuit of fame or fortune', that their minds are 'vacant to receive and to retain the regular connection of a train of events' and to 'form deductions' that in turn 'render their lives more agreeable to themselves, and the more serviceable to everyone around them' (1.2: 129–30). To put it another way, women's minds are educable because their leisure gives them the freedom to cultivate their ductile minds and, in the cultivation, to become better women. Whether such circular arguments are genuine or performative – another knowing example of the periodical's desire to please by seeming to say what readers wanted to hear – is a moot point.

Lennox's vision for the periodical form is more ambitious than the *Museum*'s stated views on women's education. And her periodical's key innovation was its conviction in miscellaneity as method: a mode of organising and delivering content that was germane to its ambitions. 'Variety', in the words of the author of 'Philosophy for the Ladies', 'is the soul of study'. Learning that is 'bound up in the cluster' is 'almost impossible to overcome', but knowledge that is broken down into 'pieces' can more easily be 'mastered' (1.2: 132). The miscellany materialises this pedagogical principle of variety in its formal atomisation of knowledge and places the onus of knowledge mastery onto readers. Without a mediating eidolon to act as mediator or gatekeeper of this knowledge, the pedagogical work necessary to master, navigate and interpret falls to readers whose minds are left 'to range and form' what they read 'into systems according to his pleasure' (1.2: 132). In articulating as much, the *Lady's Museum* asked future editors, publishers and readers to accept the miscellany format's potential to cultivate knowledge through active, discontinuous reading practices. The gauntlet thrown down was enthusiastically picked up by many women's periodicals in the decades to come and most successfully by the *Lady's Magazine*.

Ladies' (and Gentlemen's) Magazines before the *Lady's Magazine*

Lennox was not the first editor to offer extended reflections on the periodical miscellany's unique affordances. Although she rejected the term magazine as a descriptor for her *Museum*, editors had been insistently making the case for the miscellany's utility since the founding of the *Gentleman's* three decades earlier. Cave's market-changing and indomitable publication played a formative role both in theorising the magazine and in establishing this new print medium's success. As we have seen, virtually all eighteenth-century periodicals presented themselves as original enterprises when they first launched. Yet Cave had more reason than most to cast his publication in such terms, even while openly acknowledging that a good percentage of its contents was repurposed from pre-existing sources. Indeed, the *Gentleman's Magazine* presented its reliance upon previously published content as one of the sources of its novelty and indispensability. The inaugural 'Advertisement' for the magazine positioned the publication as a direct response to a dizzying proliferation of print media. The number of 'News-Papers', in particular, had 'so multiply'd' in the decades prior to the magazine's founding that the editor opined that it was 'impossible' for any reader to digest their contents or to benefit from the information they contained.[62] The *Gentleman's Magazine* was accordingly launched in the spirit of preserving what otherwise would be lost or go unnoticed in the print deluge by 'treasur[ing] up, as in a Magazine, the most remarkable Pieces' of 'Amusement and Intelligence' ('Advertisement' (January 1731): n.p.). This was a project characterised by 'Reasonableness', in the double sense of being both a rational enterprise and one that represented good value for the periodical's subscribers. For just sixpence a close-printed, twin-columned forty-eight-page octavo issue, the *Gentleman's Magazine* offered a 'View of all the Pieces of Wit, Humour, or Intelligence daily offer'd to the Publick' in the form of essays on various subjects, poetry, domestic and foreign news, lists of births, marriages, deaths, bankruptcies and books published, and a calendar of events ('Advertisement' (January 1731): n.p.). By mid-century, the number of original items that sat alongside this content had significantly increased and eventually came to dominate the first half of the magazine, but the periodical's principal function as an accessible repository of published material of public interest remained intact.[63]

The legacies of the *Gentleman's Magazine* for the dozens of subsequent titles it inspired and with whom it competed were multiple. Two are of particular significance in the context of this chapter. First is the culture of reprinting that the *Gentleman's Magazine* endorsed and that came, as noted earlier, eventually to cement the eighteenth-century magazine's reputation as a second-hand or plagiarised print medium 'lacking in [the] fundamental originality' of alternative serial formats such as essay-periodical.[64] Of all the accusations levelled, plagiarism is perhaps the least warranted or even useful in describing the excerpting and copying practices that were widespread in newspapers and magazines throughout the eighteenth century. The Statute of Anne (1710), which defined the legislative context for periodical publications for much of the century, specifically addressed the copyright of 'books'. As Will Slauter elucidates, however, the absence of references to periodicals in the legislation did not mean 'that writers, publishers, and readers at the time did not view them as literary property in the same way' as 'books'.[65] Some periodicals were, in fact, registered with the Stationer's Company, and a number of booksellers attempted to sue periodical proprietors who excerpted works to which they owned the copyright. Cave was himself taken to legal task for reprinting extracts of published works by Joseph Trapp (in 1739) and Haywood (in 1743) in the *Gentleman's Magazine*.[66] Nonetheless, the legal situation with regard to reprinting in and among serial publications was 'ambiguous' to say the least.[67] Tacit acceptance of the reprinting of previously published excerpts in magazines quickly became widespread, not least, as Cave pointed out to readers of the *Gentleman's*, because the practice could benefit copyright owners and authors by increasing the circulation and visibility of books covered by the Statute. These benefits also extended to the reading public, for whom the magazine acted as a compendium of material 'deserving Attention' and of 'universal Benefit' to which they might not otherwise have ready access ('Advertisement' (January 1731): n.p.).

A second, formative legacy of Cave's magazine was its emphatic demonstration of the commercial viability of gender specialisation. In the words of Gillian Williamson, the appeal of the *Gentleman's Magazine* was inextricably bound up with its representation and reinforcement of 'normative, institutional masculinity', even though many women read and wrote for the publication.[68] The success of Cave's periodical, even its very title, emboldened several rival publishers to launch magazines marketed explicitly at women readers, although few before the 1750s enjoyed impressive runs. What seems to have been the first *Lady's Magazine* – the *Lady's Magazine; or Universal Repository*, published by John Roberts of Warwick Lane – was published just two years after the *Gentleman's* launched. No copies of this periodical seem to have survived, nor do we know how many issues were published. Evidence of at least a first issue for March 1733 exists in an advertisement in the *Universal Spectator and Weekly Journal* dated 7 April of that year, which indicates that the periodical carried very similar contents to the *Gentleman's Magazine*: 'Political, Moral, Theological, Controversial, and Humorous Essays' from 'the News-Papers'; poetry; 'foreign Affair[s]'; 'Domestick Intelligence', including birth marriages and deaths; and lists of new publications.[69] Nothing in the advertisement suggests that the periodical made any particular accommodations to the gender of its addressed readership. Indeed, as implied by the *Universal Spectator* advertisement, the most obvious difference between the contents of this *Lady's Magazine* and the *Gentleman's* was the former's cover price of a shilling as opposed to the sixpence levied by Cave's. What led to the demise of Roberts's obscure magazine is unknown, although the subscription fee seems recklessly optimistic. Little more is known about a second and much cheaper *Lady's Magazine* – the *Lady's Magazine; or, the Compleat Library* – which launched in late 1736 (1738–9?). All that survives of this tuppence weekly is a contents page for its eighteenth number (dated 3 February 1739) and a handful of surviving newspaper advertisements, which suggest that it was solely comprised of excerpted contents from already published works that included earlier periodicals such as the *Tatler* and *Athenian Mercury*.[70]

A later namesake, the *Lady's Weekly Magazine,* also survives only in an inaugural copy dated 19 February 1747.[71] Published 'under the Direction of Mrs. Penelope Pry', this periodical claimed to be more explicitly tailored to its intended demographic than its predecessors. An address by its 'proprietors' asserted that while 'the Knowledge of *Mankind in general*' would be its focus, the *Lady's Weekly* would nonetheless ensure that its content – all of which was 'original' – would be 'properly adapted' to female readers and intended to serve 'Principles of Virtue and Morality' ([1]). In addition to 'Essays' and news, the magazine promised female intelligence from Pry and her 'Emissaries' on 'Masquerades', 'Balls' and other fashionable entertainments, although it eschewed the 'mischievous Custom of publishing scandalous Advertisements' ([1]). No such content is present in the only extant issue of the magazine, around three out of four pages of which are devoted to news and current affairs, specifically to a long discussion about the War of Austrian Succession, about which Curioso Politico was so exercised when writing to Haywood's *Female Spectator*. Part of a projected serial, 'The Present History of the Transactions of the World' takes the form of a 'Dialogue' between a Lady Manley, a Miss Bloom and Pry herself, an 'easy, familiar' discursive format that is presented as more congenial to women readers and more 'likely to make the strongest Impressions upon the Memory' than that of wearisome 'Political Dissertations' ([1]). The *Lady's Weekly Magazine* was here one moment and gone the next, but the dialogic, conversational mode it adopted for 'The Present History' became a central feature of later magazines, especially Robinson's *Lady's Magazine*.

More successful and enduring than any of these early efforts to rival the *Gentleman's* was the fortnightly *Ladies Magazine: or, the Universal Entertainer* (1749–53), edited by the likely pseudonymous 'Jasper Goodwill, of Oxford, Esq'. Goodwill asserted the magazine's cultural legitimacy with a confidence that eluded even the most brazen of his predecessors. The address 'To the Publick', printed on the contents page of each issue of his periodical, takes for granted that the 'general Advantage and Utility' of the magazine format was 'so well known' that it required no reiteration, and its editor confidently entrusts his publication's fate to the 'impartial Judgment' of readers. Those readers belonged to a much wider demographic than the magazine's social- and gender-inclusive title implies. In Goodwill's magazine, 'ladies' is a group encompassing women of all ranks who were literate and could access the journal through loan, occasional purchase or regular subscription. Its modest cover price made this aspiration feasible. Haywood's *Female Spectator* – which cost one shilling per monthly stitched issue or one pound and four shillings for a complete unbound run of twenty-four numbers – had emphatically proved that by mid-century, journals marketed at women could command substantial subscriptions.[72] Yet just three years after it ceased publication, Goodwill's *Ladies Magazine* sold for a mere two pence a number or four shillings and sixpence for a year's worth of twenty-four issues plus an annual Supplement. Claiming to be 'the cheapest Thing of the Kind and Price ever yet published', his *Ladies Magazine* appealed to readers of all ages, including 'young Masters and Misses' who had the leisure to spend their day in the 'parlour', as well as those who spent their days in the 'Shop' or 'Compting-house' (title page). For their modest subscription, Goodwill's readers enjoyed a vibrant and entertaining array of contents that would become the standard fare of the eighteenth-century women's magazine: fiction, anecdotes, question-and-answer dialogues, trial reports, reviews, abridgements of novels, songs, enigmas and news.

The immediate influence of Goodwill's magazine is registered in the second best known *Lady's Magazine* of the eighteenth century: the *Lady's Magazine; or, Polite Companion for the Fair Sex* (1759–63), which is often, if somewhat misleadingly, referred to as Goldsmith's *Lady's Magazine*.[73] Goldsmith certainly wrote essays for this *Lady's Magazine* in its first months and seems at some point to have become its editor, but the periodical's official figurehead was the fictional Honourable Mrs Caroline Amelia Stanhope. The production values of Stanhope's *Lady's Magazine* spoke to the polite ambitions advertised in its subtitle. Unlike Goodwill's *Ladies* or Cave's *Gentleman's Magazine*, the journal was single-columned, which gave the publication an uncluttered and sophisticated look that was enhanced by multi-media embellishments including song sheets and engravings. These higher production values were accompanied by important shifts of emphasis and viewpoint. Whereas Goodwill's magazine provided a 'View of the Polite and busy World' to those on its fringes (title page), Stanhope's *Lady's Magazine* expected its readers to be of that world even if they required help navigating its imperatives. As the advertisement for its first issue declares, Stanhope's periodical was designed to be 'highly useful for every one, who is desirous to acquire and support the Character of the Polite, Well-bred, and accomplished Woman'.[74] And while the editor admitted the possibility of male subscribers, she presented her *Lady's Magazine*, contra Goodwill's, as a magazine by and for women: 'Men write for Men', Stanhope asserted, and 'Women should write for Women, or at least on such Topics as more immediately relate to them'.[75] Between its covers, readers were presented with an eclectic mix of 'original Pieces, viz. History, Novels, Essay[s], Poems, and such other pieces of

LITERATURE' as were designed with the 'Delicacy of our Sex' in mind. Over time, additions were made to these staple genres. Some of these improvements came at the behest of readers, such as the inclusion in the issue for December 1759 of a reproduction of a fashion plate displaying the 'Habit of a Lady'.[76]

Scholarly accounts of Stanhope's *Lady's Magazine* emphasise its inclusion of 'light essays' on stereotypically female matters such as fashion and conduct.[77] Yet the editor vehemently denied that hers was a frivolous publication. Inspired by the 'WRITINGS' of her spiritual 'Sisters' – Charlotte 'LENOX' [sic] and translator Elizabeth 'CARTER' – and the rise of 'Female Genius' on the continent, Stanhope envisaged her periodical as promoting the 'Talents' of her 'Sex' and offering incontrovertible proof 'that Women are not inferior to Men in Point of Genius'.[78] Instruction lies at the heart of Stanhope's *Lady's Magazine*, which imagined its subscribers less as readers than as 'students' (1 (September 1759): 9). While these 'students' are not imagined as scholars in the tradition of Carter, the magazine persistently makes the case for women's fitness for learning and provides them with access to a range of instructional content that covers impressive topical and disciplinary terrain. The first issue alone includes poetry and readers' letters on moral questions, as well as essays on geography, recent military conquests, 'the Present War in Germany', 'the beauties of the vegetable world', the mysteries of longitude and electricity. Later issues included numerous articles and serials promoting women's education, including 'Defence of Women', a serial translation of Spanish Benedictine monk Benito Jerónimo Feijoo's vindication of women's intellectual and cultural achievements, *Defensa de las Mujeres* (1726), which would later be translated for Robinson's *Lady's Magazine*. As correspondent C— L— of Chelsea noted in a letter to the editor printed in the magazine's second issue, Stanhope's mission to 'enlarge the knowledge, correct the judgment [sic], and polish the manners of the fair sex' was an 'important' one that would inspire future periodical publishers and editors (1 (October 1759): 64). One of these imitators was the author of the letter to Stanhope, one Charlotte Lennox, who just a few months later would launch the *Lady's Museum* in her rival bid to 'demand the attention and merit the encouragement of . . . inquisitive' women.[79]

Yet for all the similarity of their intellectual investments, Lennox's miscellany is quite different from Stanhope's magazine, and in ways that have cemented the critical reception of both titles. Chief among these differences is the former's apparently greater reliance on copy provided by subscribers. Purported reader contributions in Stanhope's *Lady's Magazine* took various forms. Some are commonplaced items: that is, extracts of published or manuscript works offered up by readers for the notice and edification of other subscribers. Others are original pieces, the variable quality of which was sometimes lamented by its editor.[80] The majority of this latter type of contribution are letters to the editor, some of which directly engaged with correspondence submitted by other contributors and purportedly designed to facilitate contributors' mutual instruction. Scholarship on periodicals has taken a less positive view of such strategies, identifying in Stanhope's magazine's heterogeneity and thematic and formal emphasis on conversation early warning signs of the periodical's waning authority and a declining ambition for women journal readers that Robinson's later *Lady's Magazine* has come to epitomise.[81]

Yet as we have seen throughout this chapter, periodicals had always demonstrated considerable variety in their aspirations for female subscribers, just as they had always believed that there was more than one way to skin the cat of readerly improvement. Setting aside the thorny question of how successfully – or not – individual titles achieved their declared objectives in these areas, many editors argued forcefully that the miscellaneous, conversational mode was as germane to the magazine's ambitions for its readers as the essay format was to that of the *Tatler*, or the *Female Spectator*. If this holds true for Stanhope's *Lady's Magazine*, then it is truer still for Robinson's later *Lady's Magazine*, which explicitly linked its objectives to promote women's reading, women's writing and women's literary history to the generative dynamism of its heterogenous, dialogic format and the distinctive reading practices it facilitated. In making such connections between its form and ambition, Robinson's magazine was not an entirely novel enterprise. Indeed, as subsequent chapters illuminate, its innovations were partly the product of sustained and critical reflection on the rich and varied periodical traditions and modes documented above. The question of how these reflections informed the *Lady's Magazine*'s emerging brand in its first two, troubled years of publication is the focus of the next chapter.

Chapter 2

Beginnings: The Making of the Lady's Magazine (1770–2)

> Inspired by gratitude for the favourable reception which this new production has met with from the Ladies, the Proprietors would be inexcusable if they were not to seize the very earliest opportunity of returning thanks to their Fair Supporters. Ambitious of pleasing them alone, no labour, no expense, will be spared to render our Magazine equally instructive and amusing . . . The vast sale of this performance sufficiently shews the encouragement it meets with from that sex to whose use it is particularly adapted, it is upon them our fate depends . . .
> Advertisement for the *Lady's Magazine* in the *Middlesex Journal* (29 September–2 October 1770)

As we saw in the previous chapter, women were well established readers of periodicals by the time the *Lady's Magazine; or Entertaining Companion for the Fair Sex* launched in the late summer of 1770. The seven decades' worth of periodicals, miscellanies and magazines marketed specifically at women readers that preceded its publication offered the men behind the *Lady's Magazine* grounds for caution as well as optimism. Those men were the journal's founder-proprietor John Coote and its first publisher John Wheble, both of whom were swiftly replaced by business partners George Robinson and John Roberts when they bought the magazine from Coote in the spring of 1771. All four had prior experience of the ruthlessly competitive periodical marketplace and embarked upon their project with their eyes open to the possibility of its failure. Yet their publication evidences little sense of self-doubt and its confident rhetoric was well placed. The popularity of the *Lady's Magazine* showed immediately. Although the precise size of the inaugural issue's print run is unknown, it sold out so quickly that it had to be reprinted before the next month's was published.[1]

This was an encouraging start, but there was no room for complacency. As acknowledged in the *Middlesex Journal* advertisement from which this chapter's epigraph is drawn, the periodical's 'fate' was dependent upon the loyalty of subscribers. Like its predecessors, the *Lady's Magazine* presented itself as a periodical designed to serve readers through a specially selected range of edifying as well as entertaining content and media. Yet the reality was that it needed readers more than readers needed the magazine. Its longevity was absolutely dependent upon its purchasers' 'protection' and continued 'favour', the latter a term used to describe both readers' patronage of the periodical and the written contributions they were encouraged to submit for publication. The relationship between the magazine, its editorial staff and its readers was sorely tested in the periodical's early years. Wheble's anger at Coote's sale of the journal to Robinson and Roberts, and his insistence that he still be allowed to publish it, culminated in a trial before Lord Chief Justice Mansfield that was documented in painstaking detail within the pages of the magazine itself. Wheble, as we will see, lost the argument, but the verdict failed to resolve the ongoing dispute. The debates about the nature of periodical property staged during the trial proceedings spilled out of the courtroom into a bitter war of words played out in the newspapers and on the pavements of Paternoster Row as the doggedly determined Wheble continued to issue his own version of the *Lady's Magazine* for a further eighteen months.

This chapter documents the turbulent, but formative, early years of *Lady's Magazine*'s history. I begin with biographical accounts of the men who laid the foundations for the periodical's success, before honing in on the first issues of Wheble's magazine and their defining emphases on both literal and imaginative journeying and on conversation as a navigational tool. I then turn to Coote's sale of the magazine within a few months of its founding and the trial transcript that reveals Wheble's stake in the periodical and offers rare insights into the publication's day-to-day running. The final sections of the chapter look closely at the two rival *Lady's Magazine*s published between April 1771 and December 1772 as Wheble and Robinson and Roberts aggressively competed for readers and their respective publications' futures. Reading the earliest contents of *Lady's Magazine* in the context of this dispute over the periodical's ownership sheds important light on: what and who made the *Lady's Magazine*; how its earliest editors and readers understood the publication; and how it became the enduring and influential print phenomenon it was.

The Men behind the *Lady's Magazine*: Coote, Wheble, Robinson and Roberts

For all but the last few months of its run, Paternoster Row appeared on every *Lady's Magazine* wrapper and contents page.[2] Flanked by St Paul's Churchyard to the south, Warwick and Ave Maria Lanes and Ludgate Street to the west, Newgate Street to the north and Cheapside to the east, the Row, as it was commonly known, was a long, narrow and densely populated street right in the heart of the City of London. The area's association with the book trade was of longstanding, but the first decades of the eighteenth century saw a pronounced rise in the number of men and women stationers, bookbinders, printers and publishers working out of Row premises. The address quickly became synonymous with 'the bookselling business'.[3] Indeed, for the next two hundred years, until the aerial bombing in 1940 that would lead to its destruction, Paternoster Row was one of the most important publishing centres in Europe.[4] All manner of books and pamphlets were printed, published, sold and distributed to provincial towns and British colonies from the Row, but, as James Raven notes, it was as a 'centre of magazine and periodical publishing' that the area gained particular renown in the second half of the eighteenth century.[5] An extraordinary number of serial publications from this period owed their existence to collaborations between Row tenants who regularly did business with one another. Other periodical titles, including some direct competitors of the *Lady's Magazine*, owed their demise to the fierce rivalries that erupted between these neighbours at almost equal intervals.[6]

In the eighteenth century as now, a magazine was the work of many hands. Periodicals were run by proprietors, publishers and printers, often with one or two people assuming a combination of these responsibilities. They also employed editors and/or compilers who worked with the staff writers, engravers and music publishers responsible for the magazine's multi-media contents. While these latter three roles were well defined, there is a lack of clarity about the others. In part, this is because some of these job titles – printer and publisher, editor and compiler, proprietor and publisher or even proprietor and editor – were often used interchangeably in the trade, and also because there was considerable variation in how these roles were executed. Reconstructing the network of individuals involved in the *Lady's Magazine*'s publication is difficult and the identity of, and division of labour between, staff is as obscure now as it would have been to the periodical's first readers.[7]

All the information I have been able to piece together is presented in the main text and footnotes of this book.

Before the production of the *Lady's Magazine* moved, in the spring of 1771, to Robinson and Roberts's establishment at 25 Paternoster Row, it was linked to at least three other addresses just yards away. The periodical's founder, John Coote (1733–1808), had moved from the Strand to 16 Paternoster Row in 1758, having entered the book trade earlier in the decade. According to John Nichols, Coote had long harboured ambitions of a career in the theatre, although the opera and five farces he penned early in his career were never staged. Coote more than compensated for his lack of success in his chosen career with bookselling entrepreneurialism. As Nichols grudgingly conceded, Coote 'evinced fertility in the invention of schemes'.[8] Those schemes included successful collaborations with George Kearsley, with whom Coote published Tobias Smollett's *The Adventures of Sir Launcelot Greaves* (1762), and with John Newbery, with whom he published Charlotte Lennox's *Lady's Museum* (1760–1).[9] Aside from his well-documented associations, Coote is a rather shadowy figure and the few surviving biographical accounts we have are scarcely complimentary. It is nonetheless clear that he was a shrewd businessman, and one who was unfailingly industrious in his efforts to protect his financial stake in the many serial publications and bookselling ventures in which he was involved. As Barbara Laning Fitzpatrick documents, Coote's career was animated by a will to exert 'direct control of his property', an ambition achieved by a heavy reliance on compilers who would solicit and arrange content for him while his own work on, and property in, a periodical would remain partly or wholly concealed from the publication's readers.[10] These questions of control and property proved central to the trial that followed Coote's termination of his business arrangement with the first publisher of the *Lady's Magazine* less than a year after its launch.

When Coote was asked during that trial how far he lived from its original publisher, John Wheble (1746–1820), he replied 'four or five doors, I cannot tell exactly'. In fact, when the *Lady's Magazine* was founded, Wheble lived and worked exactly four doors away from Coote at 20 Paternoster Row.[11] Wheble had moved to London in 1758 – the same year that Coote moved to the Row – when he took up an apprenticeship with John Wilkie, publisher of *The Bee* (1759) and Stanhope's *Lady's Magazine* (1759–63).[12] A decade later, Wheble became the first publisher of the *Middlesex Journal, or Chronicle of Liberty*. The histories of the *Lady's Magazine* and the *Middlesex Journal* are importantly intertwined, although the connection is rarely acknowledged. Coote resolved to sell his interest in the magazine in February 1771, the same month that Wheble was called before the Commons for breaching the privilege of the House by reporting parliamentary debates in his *Journal*. When Wheble refused to obey the summons, a reward was offered for his arrest. The charges were dropped only after the intervention of his friend John Wilkes.[13] Wheble's defiance of the oft-flouted prohibition on reporting parliamentary debates has earned him a celebrated place in the history of the freedom of the press, but it sounded the death knell for his association with the *Lady's Magazine*.[14] It is unclear whether the controversy was the only reason why Coote broke with Wheble, but the events and attendant publicity undoubtedly compromised the men's working relationship. As the March 1771 issue was being printed, Coote made the decision to sell his share in the periodical for 500l to Robinson and Roberts who took the magazine's publication in house.

George Robinson senior (1736–1801) is a much better-known figure than either Coote or Wheble and by far the most important man in the story of the *Lady's Magazine*. Described by his associate William West as 'the pride of Paternoster Row' and 'king of Booksellers', Robinson was a tour de force in the eighteenth-century publishing world.[15] He enjoyed enduring friendships with many of the leading writers of the day and was known for his financial generosity in his dealings with authors. Many of Robinson's earliest biographers laud his liberality of spirit and note his unstinting, if occasionally riotous, hospitality at his gatherings in the Row and at his family villa in Streatham. Like Coote and Wheble, the Cumbrian-born Robinson moved to London in the 1750s, around the age of eighteen. As Wheble underlined in his annotations on the printed trial transcript, however, Robinson was not formally apprenticed to the book trade (Wheble 1 (July 1771): 41). He instead gained informal experience by working for John Rivington and William Johnston before entering into a partnership with Roberts. Robinson met Roberts (1733–72) in 1763 when the latter was working out of 25 Paternoster Row with a 'Mrs Richardson, whose business he conducted'. Shortly after their meeting, the men made an offer to buy out Richardson, who had taken over her husband's bookselling business after his sudden death that same year.[16] A 'new firm' was 'established in the names of Robinson and Roberts', facilitated by the financial support of bookseller Thomas Longman and loans and credit from printer and publisher Archibald Hamilton senior (1719–93).[17] The partnership between Robinson and Roberts was a happy one for nearly a decade when it was abruptly terminated by Roberts's premature death in January 1772.[18]

Robinson and Roberts were associated with many different kinds of publication during their partnership. These included: instructional works; poetry volumes; collected works of the likes of Henry Fielding and John Locke; and reprinted editions of canonical texts such as *Paradise Lost*, Alexander Pope's translations of the *Iliad* and *Odyssey* and Samuel Johnson's *Rambler* (originally published 1750–2). Prior to their purchase of the *Lady's Magazine*, Robinson and Roberts's main involvement in the periodical line was as booksellers of the *Town and Country Magazine* (1769–96). Often referred to as the sister publication of the *Lady's Magazine*, the *Town and Country* was published by Archibald Hamilton junior (d. 1792) and printed by Archibald Hamilton senior. Robinson's partnership with the Hamiltons consolidated after Roberts's death. In 1774, Robinson purchased a stake in the *Critical Review* (founded 1756), which Archibald senior published. In the same year, Archibald senior and junior each bought a one-sixth share in the *Lady's Magazine*.[19] As I document in Chapter 5, the Hamilton family would continue to play a vital role in the day-to-day running of the *Lady's Magazine* for the next five decades.[20]

From the mid-1770s onwards, the Robinson list grew to be every bit as eclectic as the contents of the *Lady's Magazine*. It included poetry, drama, travel writing, translations, historical, medical, mathematical and scientific works, as well as books on gardening and agriculture, law, ethics and politics including, notably, William Godwin's *An Enquiry Concerning Political Justice* (1793). Godwin was just one of several radical men and women writers whose works Robinson published or distributed.[21] Other of the writers with whom he was closely associated include: Thomas Holcroft; Elizabeth Inchbald; Charlotte Smith; and Ann Radcliffe, whom Robinson famously paid a generous five hundred guineas for the *Mysteries of Udolpho* (1794). Under successive Robinson family imprints, and bolstered by the establishment of strong national and international distribution networks and informal partnerships, the Robinson firm built up one of the most impressive publishing catalogues of the period, earning '25 in the Row' a well-earned reputation as 'the most extensive publishing and wholesale book establishment in Europe'.[22] The *Lady's Magazine*, was a pillar of the firm's success. Its impressive sales figures of 15,000 monthly copies at its height are cited in all of the nineteenth-century accounts of Robinson's career upon which I have drawn above as irrefutable evidence of the unrivalled achievements of the King of the Row.

Wheble's *Lady's Magazine*: Imaginative Travelling

The first issues of the *Lady's Magazine* were crucial in establishing the periodical's place and readership in an overpopulated market in which many titles disappeared before they were even noticed. Eighteenth-century readers were catholic and fickle in their consumption of serial publications. Jan Fergus's analysis of the surviving archives of Midlands booksellers, the Clays, suggests that more than a third of magazine subscribers in the 1770s took in multiple periodicals, and dropped and restarted subscriptions frequently.[23] The *Lady's Magazine*'s impressive run, the longevity of its relationships with many of its contributors, and the limited available subscription evidence we have, all point to the fact that this was a periodical that was peculiarly adept at what Jon P. Klancher describes as 'audience-building': that is, at attracting and maintaining a core readership.[24] Not only do its subscribers seem to have been uncharacteristically loyal, but Fergus's analysis also credits the *Lady's Magazine* with significantly growing periodical subscriptions in the provinces.[25]

Various factors likely contributed to the *Lady's Magazine*'s expansion of the periodical reading audience and increase of its market share. The rise in women's literacy from the 1760s onwards doubtless played a part, as did the periodical's self-styling as a women's magazine, although as the previous chapter demonstrated, targeting a female readership was no guarantee of commercial viability. The key to the *Lady's Magazine*'s appeal was perhaps more prosaic. In the words of Ros Ballaster, it seems simply 'to have struck the right chord with an eager reading public'.[26] Hitting the right notes was not the work of instant, however, and the periodical's tune changed many times during its run. The first eight issues that Coote oversaw and Wheble published established the blueprint for the *Lady's Magazine*, a blueprint that was refined over the course of the following eighteen months in which Wheble's and Robinson's concurrent versions of the magazine went head-to-head. My account of the magazine's early history in this and subsequent sections of this chapter seeks to capture those features that did most to establish the periodical's distinctiveness and what we now call its brand. For Wheble's magazine, the most important of these features were the publication's preoccupation with travel and with generating conversation around the imaginative journeying in which readers engaged as they navigated the periodical's contents. These preoccupations ran across various genres and media – travel accounts, fictions, translations and essays – all of which moved readers to engage critically in a range of questions about women's lives that remained central to the magazine for the rest of its run.

As if to announce the centrality of literal and metaphorical journeying to the periodical, the opening feature in the inaugural August 1770 *Lady's Magazine* is 'A Sentimental Journey. By a Lady', a fictional domestic travel narrative authored by an anonymous writer elliptically referred to as being of some 'eminence in the literary world' ('Address', 1 (August 1770): n.p.). To underline the serial's headline status, an impressive engraving illustrating the dramatic overturning of the stagecoach that galvanises the initial action was commissioned. Further engravings did not follow, but 'A Sentimental Journey' remained the periodical's lead item for most of the more than seven years over which it ran. Part-homage to, and part-parody of, its Sternean namesake, this picaresque serial begins by announcing that it will follow an unnamed, independent female protagonist 'during her progress through this kingdom' and, subsequently, on 'the continent' (n.p.). The European ambition remained unrealised when the serial was unceremoniously terminated in 1777 'on account of the desire of many Correspondents' (13 (October 1782)). Robert D. Mayo, in his study of eighteenth-century magazine serials dismisses 'A Sentimental Journey' as 'the most tedious, the most affected, and (in its entirety) the most unreadable of all contemporary works of magazine fiction – except perhaps for other works in the same class'.[27] Tedium and unreadability are terms that are perhaps too subjective to dispute, although it is worth noting that eighteenth-century readers tired of the series far less quickly than Mayo. Charges of affectation are harder to contest, although as Paul Goring elucidates, this is largely because 'A Sentimental Journey' wears its efforts at literary impersonation so self-consciously.[28]

'A Sentimental Journey' was one of the principal innovations of Wheble's magazine. His periodical was not the first to publish serial fiction, of course. Earlier examples such as 'The Fortune-Hunter' (*Royal Female Magazine*, 1760), Tobias Smollett's 'The Life and Adventures of Sir Launcelot Greaves' (*British Magazine*, 1760–1), the extravagantly titled 'The Disasters of Tantarobobus' (*Universal Museum*, 1762), and Charlotte Lennox's 'Harriot and Sophia' had been key features of the mid-century periodicals in which they appeared. Coote had a stake in all but one of these four periodicals and therefore had first-hand knowledge of the commercial appeal of magazine serials when he launched the *Lady's Magazine* with Wheble.[29] 'A Sentimental Journey' capitalises on the popularity of such serials while also departing from the emerging tradition of magazine fiction. Although it leans heavily on familiar sentimental tropes, tableaux and character types, it is not recognisable as a novel, even as a novel in parts. Readers of the periodical were well aware that the travelogue was a work of fiction, not least because they were occasionally compelled to correct misinformation about the locations visited (4 (November 1773): 568).[30] Yet by the standards of the novel – even by the standards of the Sternean novel – its plotting is tenuous, as the editor himself admitted when describing the series as 'a meer vehicle to covey unconnected reveries' (Robinson 3 (January 1772): 1). Instalments of the serial read less as internally coherent individual parts than as a patchwork of textual fragments. The nine-page part for September 1770, for instance, is broken up by a typical ten sub-headings – 'The Post-Chaise', 'The Dream', 'The Highwayman', 'The Narrative', and so forth – which are loosely tacked together by the thread of the heroine's movement. The serial broke also with the emerging conventions of serial fiction by parodying the use of cliff-hangers with which Smollett, in particular, had experimented. The same heavily punctuated September 1770 instalment sees the heroine dramatically held up at gunpoint in the middle of the instalment only for the text to conclude bathetically with her vacillating about what to have for dinner at Red Lion inn: 'Among all these niceties, what shall I chuse, said I. – [*To be continued*]' (1 (September 1770): 58].

Metafictional moments in this vein delighted readers for many years. Yet for all its parodic elements and self-evident fictionality, the magazine asked readers to take 'A Sentimental Journey' as seriously as they would any other piece of travel writing designed to expand their imaginative horizons via its accounts of 'visit[s] to other towns, cities, or countries' than those in which subscribers were 'born and educated' (1 (August 1770): 5). It is this sentiment, more than any of those extravagantly demonstrated by characters in the serial itself, that makes 'A Sentimental Journey' such a fitting opener for the *Lady's Magazine*, a periodical in which travel writing quickly became a mainstay and in which the act of reading, as we will see, was frequently conceptualised as imaginative travel. In the magazine's first two years, extracts from and serialisations of already-published travel writing occupy a relatively small amount (under 10 per cent) of its overall page count, a percentage that would rise significantly in the 1780s. Yet travel thematically dominates the magazine from the start, especially in the form of the many oriental tales and translations it published. Like the more conventional magazine travel narratives that JoEllen DeLucia has recently examined, such content served to make 'the world a smaller and more delicate place', and, in expanding readers' knowledge of the customs, governance, economics and politics of other places, nations and cultures, extended 'the parameters of the feminine sphere'.[31] More explicitly than 'A Sentimental

Journey', the imaginative moves prompted by readers' vicarious travels to other lands and times via the *Lady's Magazine*'s contents allowed subscribers to reorient their perspective on the here and now of their own lives.

In the first issues of Wheble's *Lady's Magazine*, both non-fictional and imaginative travel narratives highlight the cultural status of women via unflinching depictions of courtship, marriage and sexual threat. The tone and nature of the conversations that these narratives generate are established in the August 1770 issue, which features two extracts from Giuseppe Marco Antonio Baretti's *Journey from London to Genoa, through England, Portugal, Spain and France* (1770). The most disquieting of these is the gruesome 'History of the Origin of the Convent of Monserate in Spain', which relates the seduction of a Catalonian princess by Guarino, an agent of the devil, who cuts the princess's throat and buries her body under a pile of stones after impregnating her (25). Guarino seeks and fails to obtain absolution for his crimes from the Pope, and is forced to walk back to his homeland naked and on all fours like a beast. Taken for a wild animal, he is beaten and imprisoned before eventually learning that the princess survived his attack. She forgives her seducer and would-be murderer and the excerpt concludes with her founding the convent on the site where 'Guarino had treated her so barbarously' and where she lives out the rest of her days (26). Like all appropriated content in the periodical, the excerpt from *A Journey to Genoa* is thoroughly remediated by the magazine format in which it is reprinted. Decontextualised from its original surrounding text – much of which is concerned with descriptions of Catalonian agriculture and industry – the anecdote reads less straightforwardly as piece of factual travel writing than as a stopping place in a diverse and richly textured landscape of a magazine in which generic and geographic boundaries are fluid and unstable.

Despite its European setting, 'the Convent of Monserate' formally, stylistically and thematically echoes the oriental tales that flank it within this particular issue and that featured prominently in the magazine for the first half of its run. Wildly popular for decades before the *Lady's Magazine* launched, oriental tales emotionally and imaginatively transported Western readers to textual worlds in ways that generated feelings of identification, desire or revulsion.[32] Wheble's *Lady's Magazine* capitalised on these possibilities, bringing tales of female lives in the Orient and in Europe into the homes of British periodical readers as part of a wider and ongoing dialogue that the publication staged about the cultural status and treatment of women. Many of these early oriental tales follow the pattern in the anecdote from Barretti's *Journey* in tracking the fate of women who defy and transcend male abuse. 'The Vizier's Daughter' (October 1770), for instance, tells of the eponymous Ghulnaz, whose rivalry in beauty to Prince Aladdin's daughter occasions such profound jealousy in the latter that she becomes dangerously ill, causing Aladdin to instruct the vizier to sell his daughter into slavery. Ghulnaz is purchased by a water-carrier, who falls in love with his slave only to be duped by a rival into believing that she is having an affair. In a passionate rage, he stabs the innocent Ghulnaz, who escapes only to find herself prey to the stratagems of a succession of men before eventually returning to her homeland in male garb. Assumed by all to be the man her costume makes her appear, the vizier's daughter ascends the throne and becomes a respected ruler. Years into her reign, and in a bid to find her beloved water-carrier, she commissions a portrait of herself to be painted 'in the character of a *Queen*' (108), and gives 'orders' to her spies that they should 'bring every one to her, who should fetch a sigh, or give the least signs of grief, on beholding the picture' (108). Over the following days all the men who have wronged Ghulnaz view the painting and are forced to repent of their crimes. Ghulnaz then reveals her true identity and marries the water-carrier.

Extraordinary though its plot is, 'The Vizier's Daughter' is otherwise characteristic of oriental magazine fiction of this period, which, as Mark L. Kamrath observes, encodes '"non-traditional" elements of female subjectivity, desire, pleasure, and sexual empowerment' while also reinforcing 'sexual stereotypes of submission and virtue'.[33] True to form, Ghulnaz's journey from dutiful daughter to autonomous ruler is both striking and non-threatening. She rebels against tyrants and usurps their rule, but only when compelled to by the relentless objectification and threats of men. Moreover, in the tale's conclusion, she relinquishes her well-earned authority by conceding 'her throne' to her future husband in a manner similar to that in which the princess in the 'Convent of Monserate' miraculously returns from death to the world, only to retire from it forever in a nunnery. Like so much of the fiction in the early *Lady's Magazine*, 'The Vizier's Daughter' offers a fantasy of female empowerment that is partially defused both by narrative closure and by the spatial and temporal remoteness of the text's setting from British female subscribers' lives. Yet at the same time, as countless other contributions in the magazine attest, the central themes of 'The Vizier's Daughter' – the commodification of women and their vulnerability to male predation and fitness for public life – were concerns that were close to home for many of the periodical's readers, and for whom Ghulnaz's triumph over extraordinary adversity might not only have provided poetic justice, but a form of wish-fulfilment.

That the magazine encouraged readers seriously to contemplate the seductive alternative realities opened up by such narratives is evidenced by the prevalence of oriental tales and anecdotes in the monthly translation competitions introduced in the magazine's second issue, which remained a regular feature until the early 1780s. The first piece the editor selected for reader translation was 'Générosité d'un Egyptien', another tale of violence, retribution and serendipitous resolution taken from Denis Dominique Cardonne's *Mélanges de Littérature Orientale*' (1 (September 1770): 57). *Mélanges de Littérature Orientale* – which is also the source text for the 'Vizier's Daughter' – contains close to a hundred tales and anecdotes from Arabic, Turkish and Persian sources and was mined promiscuously by Wheble's *Lady's Magazine*.[34] Foreign-language works and translations were ubiquitous in eighteenth-century magazines and provided a crucial, though commonly overlooked, conduit for the intellectual back-and-forth travel over what Margaret Cohen and Carolyn Dever term the 'Literary Channel'.[35] The *Lady's Magazine* was no exception: extracts from, and full translations of, foreign language works (especially from the French, but also from the German, Italian, Spanish, Latin, Greek, Chinese and Russian) are common. Most foreign language works in the magazine were offered to readers as competitive translation exercises, the first prize for which was publication in the following issue of the magazine.

The exercises served multiple functions. Along with poetry prizes and enigmas, they promoted reader engagement with, and loyalty to, the magazine, connecting men, women and children who lived in the metropolitan centres and provincial towns through which 'A Sentimental Journey' travelled to the distant and exotic locations described in their source texts. The exercises also underscored the magazine's pedagogical aspirations and championing of the active critical reading habits that I discuss further in Chapter 3. Indeed, many of the entrants to the competitions were schoolchildren. 'Générosité d'un Egyptien', for example, prompted several '*very good translations*' from young ladies at the likes of Mrs *Lintot's* boarding school in Worcester and Mrs Wilder*'s at Cheshunt* (1 (September 1770): 108). For schoolchildren, as for aspiring magazine contributors of all ages, translation was a safe way to test the authorial waters. As Gillian Dow observes of the practice in general in this period, translation 'offered ... a "safe" way to enter the literary marketplace ... removing the stigma of "original" publication'.[36] The translation exercises in the *Lady's Magazine* offered precisely such a low-risk apprenticeship in publication. To advertise this point to readers, the magazine followed its first exercises with an extract of a work from a figure offered up to readers as a kind of role model: 'Miss Roberts', the 'translatress of Marmontel's Tales' (October 1770: 111). The still little-known Radagunda Roberts, whose *Select Moral Tales from Marmontel* had been published in 1763, was a respected and important translator in her lifetime. As I document in Chapter 4, she was also an important figure in the *Lady's Magazine*'s early history.

But perhaps most importantly, the foreign language oriental tales offered by Wheble's magazine for reader translation opened up imaginative and creative possibilities that aligned with the magazine's self-declared mission to act as a kind of travelling companion or guide for readers as they navigated their daily lives. Ballaster figures the reading of eighteenth-century oriental fictions 'as a kind of transmigration: the projection of ... "spirit" into the place/space/time of an "other" or many "others", which requires a constant shifting of consciousness and perspective that transforms the reading self'.[37] Translating oriental fictions of female triumph over subjugation similarly urges movements of consciousness and perspective that have the power to transform the *writing* self, a notion that chimes with the *Lady's Magazine*'s promise to '*enlarge* the mind' of readers who journeyed through its contents ('Sentimental Journey', 1 (August 1770): 5).[38] Offering such opportunities for vicarious travel was vital for women readers, the periodical claimed, because they were routinely denied the uninhibited freedom of movement enjoyed by the strikingly unencumbered protagonist of 'A Sentimental Journey'. In the words of Wheble's regular columnist, 'The Female Rambler', 'Men [can] roam abroad, and get practical information, by conversing with mankind', but women were denied the intellectual mobility afforded by literal travel on the grounds that the 'world' was too dangerous and 'miscellaneous a work for their chaste perusal' (Wheble 2 (May 1771): 468). The vicarious journeying afforded by the magazine's travel writing, oriental tales and translation exercises circumvented this stricture, allowing them to experience other worlds and ideas that could be useful to the traveller without endangering her.

The Female Rambler was one of dozens of contributors to the *Lady's Magazine* to liken the world to a 'work' and to imagine the heterogenous form of the magazine as a textual proxy for the miscellaneity of life beyond its pages. The metaphor can be traced back to only the second article published in the magazine – the short essay 'Friendship: An Allegory' – in which the world is similarly likened by its author to 'a large volume, that will instruct those who know how to read in it' (1 (August 1770): 19). Teaching women how to travel through the world was the tantalising promise of Wheble's *Lady's Magazine*. Its annual frontispiece engravings pictorially realised this ambition in illustrations picturing a young reader or group of readers being assisted on a

Figure 2.1 Frontispiece to the *Lady's Magazine* for 1776. Private collection.

journey to wisdom by a Minerva figure holding a copy of the magazine in her hand (Figure 2.1). But as the following section elaborates, readers were expected to be no more passive in these travels than the heroine of 'A Sentimental Journey' or the respondents to the magazine's translation exercises. Subscribers instead imagined themselves to be active participants in the magazine's print community, which gave them an opportunity to participate in an ongoing and widespread conversation about the world and women's place within it. The terms of that conversation would not be settled during Wheble's tenure, but his periodical's initiation of this conversation was crucial in setting the course of the *Lady's Magazine* for the next few decades.

Starting the Conversation: or, whose magazine is it anyway?

As we saw in Chapter 1, the periodical had styled itself as a conversational print medium from its inception in the seventeenth century. The *Lady's Magazine* made this feature its key selling point by explicitly yoking the dialogic, miscellany format to its aspirations for its female readership. The 'Female Rambler', who lamented the restrictions imposed on women's movement, was one of many contributors who placed conversation at the centre of her arguments for women's education. In her first column in May 1771, she argues that since 'conversation' is the bedrock of sociability and the female sex is 'by nature and habit adapted' for polite discourse, women should be the 'life of a polished society' (467). And yet 'custom' has trumped prerogative. Debarred from formal education for the 'gratification and convenience of men', women have been denied access to the very ideas that should be the subject of the polite discourse for which they are suited (468–9). The Female Rambler offers up her column and the magazine that gave it a home as a salve for this problem. Over the coming decades, the periodical's editors and countless other contributors built on such claims to argue for the cultural, intellectual and pedagogical benefits of the magazine's discursive format to readers of both sexes, and most especially to women. Yet at the same time, there was vigorous disagreement among the periodical's readers about how or whether gender should dictate the scope and limits of the periodical's conversations. If, as Edward Copeland argues, much of the significance and appeal of the *Lady's Magazine* rested in its provision of 'a genuine forum for women's issues' in which readers were key participants, then the first numbers of Wheble's periodical are all the more interesting because the questions of what these issues were and who was best placed to arbitrate upon them were not yet settled.³⁹

An early and recurrent flashpoint in these debates was who had the right to participate in the conversations the magazine staged. The explicit calls to 'bar the male creatures' from the *Lady's Magazine* that would feature in the 1780s were some way off at this point in the periodical's history (11 (March 1780): 125). Yet even as early as the magazine's third issue, female correspondents were pointing out that male readers were taking up more than their fair share of page space. The first reader to make such a claim was Clarinda, a 'young Lady, not yet fourteen'. Clarinda's name first appears in the 'Correspondents' column for September 1770, which notes that the packet of manuscript material she had submitted for editorial consideration would be 'attended to in our next' (84). The October issue made good on that promise when it published her acrostic poem, 'Verses to a Young Gentleman' (135). Clarinda's verse is accompanied by a letter to the editor in which the poet avers that since she 'imagine[s the] new Magazine is open for the reception of favours from the Ladies as well as the Gentlemen' whose 'favours' crowd its columns, she feels justified in troubling them with her own poetic trifle (135). The self-deprecatory tone is hard to decipher. Clarinda's demure attitude may not be entirely performative and is certainly in keeping with the deferential tone of her poem, which begins with expressions of fear that as an '[u]nskill'd' and 'untutored' girl she is ill-equipped to do justice to her subject: 'A Milton's fire! Should sing the best of men'. Yet for all her avowed fears, this Milton's daughter did pick up the poetic mantle, sent her work to the magazine and, in doing so, took the opportunity to assert politely that women deserved more than a mere 'corner' in publication that was supposed to have been designed for their amusement and edification (135).

Clarinda's criticisms, first, that 'Gentlemen' were more visible in the magazine than its title implied they should be and, second, that male writers' visibility might discourage women writers, were on point (135). In a statistical analysis of the periodical's 'Correspondents' pages, Jean E. Hunter estimated that never less than a third and sometimes a much higher percentage of the *Lady's Magazine*'s content was produced by contributors publishing under male signatures. Hunter's conclusions are hard to corroborate, not least because they fail to account for male contributors who adopted female pseudonyms, for contributors who left their work unsigned and for those who used gender-neutral pseudonyms.⁴⁰ Nor does the analysis account for the fact that a good deal of material mentioned in the 'Correspondents' pages never actually appeared in the magazine, and that much that was published is not acknowledged in the 'Correspondents' columns at all. Attempting to put a percentage on the number of contributions and extracts by women and men in a single issue of the magazine is therefore impossible. Nevertheless, a significant number of the writers whose work was published in the poetry sections of the first issues of the magazine identify as men either by signature or write from explicitly male subject positions (in love poetry to an anonymous female beloved, for instance).[41] It is easy to see why Clarinda was concerned that a disproportionate number of men were finding their way into the *Lady's Magazine*, though the publication of her acrostic evidently put some of her fears to rest. Further poems and responses to monthly enigmas by Clarinda appeared until Wheble's magazine ceased publication at the end of 1772. While she does not seem to have followed other readers and contributors to Robinson's *Lady's Magazine* when Wheble's terminated, her legacy lives on in the complaints of later female contributors who also questioned the space the magazine gave to male writers and demanded that women were given a right of reply to these unwelcome interlocutors.

Dozens of early female contributors to the magazine argued that if the periodical continued to publish essays, letters and poems by men, then it was vital that women were given at least equal representation in the conversations that their works generated. This was particularly the case when male correspondents used the magazine to pronounce upon female conduct before or after marriage. If education is the magazine's dominant preoccupation, as I argue in Chapter 3, then marriage is one of many close seconds. Marital advice, from variably qualified sources, is in plentiful supply throughout the periodical's history. Yet the conservative, conduct-book-style prescriptions with which the magazine has become associated rarely go unquestioned when articulated. As much as the periodical recognised marriage as the likely destiny of most of its readers' lives, the cumulative picture of wedlock it generates through intertextual dialogue and contributor debate is resolutely pragmatic and often cynical.[42]

To illuminate how this conversation about marriage unfolds in the periodical, we need look no further than the November 1770 issue, which opens with the month's instalment of 'A Sentimental Journey' before forcing readers onto less comfortable terrain by asking them to navigate a series of texts about marital discord. 'The Cruel Father', an oriental tale from the French about domestic tyranny, adultery and infanticide, immediately follows the travel serial. This is succeeded by 'The History of Isabella', a cautionary tale about a fatally indulged woman who ill-advisedly marries a young officer who despises his wife for having no fortune and who drives his spouse into 'a habit of drinking' which 'terminate[s] her life' (159). As if to temper these unflinchingly bleak depictions of marriage, 'The Cruel Father' and 'History of Isabella' are followed by what initially seems a more idealistic portrayal of 'happy marriage'. 'Letter to a Lady on the Point of Marriage' is an extended extract submitted, along with a prefatory letter, by Amelia. Amelia does not name the source text for her excerpt beyond acknowledging that it was 'published not many years since', although it had 'not met with the attention it deserves' (159). Some of the magazine's readers would likely have recognised its origins in Frances Brooke's *History of Emily Montague* (1769), a novel that as Katherine Sobba Green describes, transplants 'the British novel of courtship to the New World' to offer 'a new multicultural perspective from which to view the institution of marriage and the role of women in British society'.[43]

Amelia's 'Letter' is an important contribution to the magazine's emerging conversation about marriage and an object lesson in the multiple effects of excerpting and miscellaneity. As I elaborate in Chapter 3, periodical remediation – the transplantation of extracted and reprinted texts into the dynamic media ecology of the miscellany format – agitates meanings dormant in the original source. In Brooke's work, the excerpted text appears in the context of a letter on the subject of companionate marriage by the novel's bachelor hero, Ed Rivers, to his newly married sister, Lucy. Rivers cautions his sibling that 'PRUDENCE and virtue' are insufficient to 'secure esteem' from a partner, before proceeding to quote liberally from Madame de Maintenon's letters: '"do not hope that your union will procure you perfect peace"'; '"do not hope to bring back a husband by complaints, ill humour, and reproaches"'; '"Men are naturally tyrannical, they will have pleasure and liberty, yet insist that women renounce both"; and women must '"know only to suffer and to obey, with a good grace"'. Rivers then attempts to reassure his surely perturbed sister that she should not be 'alarmed' by Maintenon's cynical views of wedlock before concluding with his own idealised view of marital partnership.

Amelia's excerpt from Rivers's letter is extensive, but it is not entirely faithful. Significantly, she omits from Brooke's original the hero's subsequent arguments that marriage should be based on 'Equality' and that 'the word OBEY' should be 'expunged from the marriage ceremony', skipping instead to Rivers's concluding advice that a contented wife is one who does not affect 'knowledge' and is ever so careless as to 'lose the mistress in the wife' (161). Amelia's redaction – assuming it is hers and not that of an editorial hand – opens the original text to new meanings and divergent interpretations that are contingent upon the excerpt's relationship both to its source text and to the contents with which it is surrounded in the *Lady's Magazine*. The editing out of some of the more controversial assertions in Brooke's original might lead readers to conclude that Amelia – or the magazine – endorses spousal passivity: in order to be happy in marriage, subordinate your happiness to that of your husband. But such a reading requires at least a partial act of will to overlook the stark criticisms of matrimonial tyranny the extract retains, criticisms amplified by the accounts of marital cruelty and dysfunction in the 'Cruel Father' and 'History of Isabella'. Read in dialogue with these intertexts, the prospect of conjugal felicity gestured at in Amelia's 'Letter' seems remote at best.

Arguably, however, it is not what the 'Letter' says about marriage but to whom its insights are addressed that most forcefully animates Amelia's criticism. Her reframing of the Brooke extract complicates the already dizzying gender dynamics of its source text: a female-authored novel in which marital advice is given to a sister by a male character who builds his case for companionate marriage on the foundation of the wisdom of an influential French woman writer and educationalist. Amelia's re-presentation of the extract adds additional layers of mediation, and brings to the foreground a question with which the magazine remained deeply preoccupied: who had the right to pronounce upon women's lives and happiness? Remediated both by Amelia and by the relational, miscellany context in which the extract appears, Rivers' words signify and orient differently. His pronouncements are less authoritative in Amelia's text than in *Emily Montague*, and women's voices – Amelia's, Maintenon's and, more obliquely, Brooke's – come to the fore. In this way, Amelia's extract implicitly pursues the complaints of fellow contributors, like Clarinda, who had objected that men were taking up too much space in what was, after all, a 'lady's magazine'. Indeed, as she explains in an accompanying letter, Amelia had felt compelled to write to the periodical because she found sufficient evidence in its pages to prove Maintenon's point that '[m]en are naturally tyrannical' in the unsolicited advice they dished out to women. Amelia enjoins the magazine's female readers not to accept such prescriptions and to interject via the medium of the periodical itself. But ultimately, she reveals, it is 'the Editor' and 'his sex in general' who, she hopes, will most heed her contribution. If the publication of her letter and excerpt alerts these gentlemen to what female readers already know – that male tyranny has no place in marriage or magazines – her efforts will have hit their mark (160).

Amelia's arguments are underlined a few pages later in a plea from Caroline, a contributor who writes to the magazine's editor to solicit advice on how to repair her unhappy marriage. Her letter opens by echoing Amelia's and Clarinda's unease that the *Lady's Magazine* was in danger of becoming a forum for men's writing and opinions. Fearing that she may have 'mistake[n] the intention' of a publication she thought was 'designed as a kind of Spectator for the fair sex', Caroline expresses amazement that the magazine's first three issues had not been more attentive to the plight of 'distressed damsel[s]' (171). Offering herself as the first, she proceeds to document her husband's misplaced jealousy of other men and the time she spends nursing their infant son. Having 'no friend to complain to', Caroline claims the magazine as her only avenue for possible redress. She 'beg[s]' the editor to publish her letter, in the hopes that it will 'have some effect' by staging a conversation about her spouse's behaviour in print that it was impossible to have with him in person (172–3).

Caroline may not be a genuine correspondent, of course, and if she is, we cannot know whether her letter had the desired effect. No direct reply to her correspondence was published in the magazine, although the editor mentions that one contributor saw fit to translate her original plea into French for their own amusement ('Correspondents' (December 1770: n.p.). An oblique response to Caroline did, however, follow a few months later in the form of a 'Short Essay upon Marriage' contributed by I. Aldrich of Pall Mall. Aldrich's 'Essay' cautions idealists among the magazine's readership to set the bar of marital expectation low and issues a series of rational checks on premarital enthusiasm. Contra Amelia and Caroline, Aldrich is determined to lay the responsibility for a happy marriage (or its inverse) at the feet of women, whose conduct is subject to ever more pompous pronouncements as the 'Essay' unfolds. A husband's burden, Aldrich concludes, is that he is 'blameable for [his wife's] conduct'. Reasonable women who expect fair treatment and fidelity from their husbands should understand this, recognise that their husband is their 'master', and regulate their behaviour accordingly (March 1771: 364). The message for the Isabellas, Amelias and Carolines of the magazine's readership could not be clearer: their plight is their responsibility and theirs alone.

Aldrich's 'Essay' endorses the overall picture of marital discord the magazine sketched over the course of previous issues, only this time this picture is achieved by discrediting the voices and experiences of previous correspondents. The move provoked outrage and was challenged directly by regular correspondent Theodosia one month later in a riposte entitled 'Advice to Married People'. 'Advice' opens by conceding that Aldrich's essay contained some guidance 'acceptable to every woman of sense', before launching into a masterclass in undermining antifeminists. Theodosia essay systematically discredits each and every one of the arguments of Aldrich's 'Essay' in the service of her counterclaim that '[m]arriage ought to be a state of mutual obligation' in which wives should be recognised as their husbands' equals and 'partners' (394). If, she asserted, men conceded that women were 'reasonable beings', then they must also accept that wives could not rationally be 'bound to obedience' to a spouse who indulged in 'tyrannical behaviour'. Such behaviour invalidated the terms of the marriage contract and rendered husbands solely accountable for the 'anarchy and perpetual discord' that followed (394–5). Theodosia's bold and brilliant intervention into the magazine's ongoing conversation about marital disharmony may be specifically addressed to Aldrich's 'Essay', but it also speaks back to, and vindicates, the views and arguments advanced by the 'History of Isabella', Amelia's excerpt and Caroline's and Clarinda's letters.

The debate occasioned by Aldrich's opinion piece is echoed in the hundreds of heated conversations the magazine published on subjects as diverse as women's education, domestic and international politics and fashion. To what extent these conversations were editorially stage-managed or grew organically is impossible to determine. The *Lady's Magazine* likely employed staff writers to produce copy, and editorial decisions about the selection and placement of content undoubtedly mediated how that content was experienced by readers. Yet contributors to the magazine undoubtedly guided these conversations also. Traditionally, periodicals scholarship has been suspicious about the authenticity of historic correspondents, often assuming that some, most or all such correspondents were fabrications. This may have been the case for some of the *Lady's Magazine*'s contributors, especially in the early days of Wheble's magazine when it was still growing its subscription list. In an important sense, though, whether or not any or all of these early correspondents were real or manufactured is beside the point. Far more important was the impression the magazine created of being an open forum in which all readers and potential contributors could participate freely. Controversial material like Aldrich's 'Essay' might not have been popular with readers such as Theodosia, but its publication underlined the periodical's openness as well as emphasising the magazine's contention that the world was riven with tensions that it would help women readers navigate. As I elaborate in Chapter 3, the *Lady's Magazine* did not claim, nor did it seek, to solve these tensions on behalf of its readers. The periodical's default position was, instead, to encourage subscribers to negotiate these challenges through their imaginative navigation of the diverse terrain of the magazine's contents. The first issues of Wheble's *Lady's Magazine* worked hard both to promote reader involvement in its conversations about these dilemmas and to cultivate the sense of belonging that played such an important part of the periodical's appeal and longevity. Indeed, it was so successful in this regard that it was easy from Robinson and Roberts to wrest it from the man whose name originally appeared on its imprint. As would be proved in court in the summer of 1771, the *Lady's Magazine* brand was bigger than, and thus separable from, any of the individuals with which it was first associated.

'[N]ot a colour for property in the title': The *Lady's Magazine* in the Courtroom

Wheble's refusal to give up on the *Lady's Magazine* after Coote's sale to Robinson and Roberts set in motion a series of events that had a decisive impact on the periodical. The most significant of these events in the short term was the court case that Robinson and Roberts brought against Wheble for continuing to issue his own version of the magazine under the same title and out of the same street as its new publishers. The ensuing trial by special jury was held on 8 July 1771 at the King's Bench, Guildhall, London, and was presided over by Lord Chief Justice Mansfield. Wheble had the trial proceedings taken down in shorthand and reprinted them in full along with copious, wounded annotations in the July 1771 issue of his *Lady's Magazine* (Figure 2.2). Questions of property and profit loom large in the transcript. The counsel for the defence alleged that Wheble's attempt to pass off his *Lady's Magazine* as a 'continuation of the same work' founded by Coote after the sale to Robinson and Roberts was tantamount to fraud and demonstrated an intention 'to injure and deprive' the periodical's new owners of 'the benefit and property of it' (Wheble 2 (July 1771): 41). Coote agreed, explaining to the court that Wheble was motivated by spite after Robinson and Roberts refused to take him on as publisher. Wheble disputed this narrative, claiming that any *Lady's Magazine* in which he was not involved was specious because the magazine's success was inextricably tied to the tireless 'industry' he had put into establishing it over the previous eight months. In arbitrating between Robinson and Roberts's and Wheble's competing arguments, the court was asked to consider a range of factors. The extent and nature of Coote's work for the periodical's first issues was heavily scrutinised, but ultimately did little to clarify the legal questions at stake. The world of periodical publication was evidently obscure in the eyes of the law and, in order to form a judgement, Mansfield had first to understand how the trade operated. A range of witnesses from the *Lady's Magazine*'s staff and the trade in general were called upon during the trial to shed light on the

(41)

An Account of the Trial at Law, respecting the Right of Property in the Publication of the LADY's MAGAZINE. *With Observations on the same.*

Proceedings on the Trial at Guildhall, London, before Lord Chief Justice MANSFIELD, Monday July 8, 1771;

ROBINSON and ROBERTS, Plaintiffs.———J. WHEBLE, Defendant.

This Cause was tried by a Special Jury*.

Counsel for the Plaintiffs,	Counsel for the Defendant,
Mr. Dunning,	Mr. Wallace,
Mr. Walker,	Mr. Davenport.
Mr. Mansfield.	

MR. Mansfield opened the cause, stating, That ——— Robinson and ———Roberts were the Plaintiffs, and John Wheble the Defendant. That this is an action upon the case :—That Plaintiffs were proprietors of a pamphlet called the Lady's Magazine, published monthly, and had been published for seven months;—a great number had been published for the eighth month, which was in April last, Defendant knowing this, and intending to injure and deprive them of the benefit and property of it, did himself publish another under the same name of the Lady's Magazine, as a continuation of the same work, to the great damage of the Plaintiffs ;—which Defendant denies.—We shall call our witnesses, and prove our case, and then you will, I make no doubt, give them a verdict, with such damages as you shall think proper.

Mr. *Dunning.* May it please your lordship, and you gentlemen of the jury, I am likewise of counsel for the Plaintiffs Robert Robinson and ———Roberts, who are eminent booksellers, and are the proprietors of a work called the Lady's Magazine.—They bring this action against the Defendant John Wheble, who is of the same trade †, for the injury which he had done their property by the invasion of it, complained of in the declaration. Gentlemen, this was a periodical publication, which began in the month of August, 70, under the direction of Mr. Coote, a bookseller ‡. Mr. Coote intending to commence a new Magazine to be published monthly, did for the purpose engage the sort of assistance which the conduct of such a work required. He engaged proper persons to write in this pamphlet, himself was to receive, and to judge of such compositions as should be sent to him ‖ in consequence of his engaging himself to the public for a performance of the work he had begun §, and he was to form such a work as would answer his views; the public were to receive information and entertainment upon the one hand, and he was to receive profit upon the other. He engaged likewise proper engravers to embellish this work, proper printers to print it, and amongst others a publisher. That publisher was the Defendant Wheble. For the purpose of carry-

---

* On this circumstance it is to be remarked, that all the special jury not attending, as indeed they seldom do, an advantage was some how taken in the choice of talesmen, to fix on one of the very booksellers who had signed the combination against Wheble : and who to be sure could not have been planted there for the purpose, as he was so very expeditious to get himself sworn in, before the counsel on the part of the Defendant observed it. But as the action itself was too notoriously litigious and oppressive, this officious juryman had the modesty, on a reprimand from the bench, to retire.

† That the Plaintiffs are eminent booksellers is indisputable ; but, like the faithful Irishman, they are too eminent to have been brought up to a *trade!* The Defendant Wheble indeed served a regular apprenticeship to a bookseller, and is accordingly a free member of the Stationers company. How the Plaintiffs became masters of the *same trade* is best known to themselves.

‡ Not so. The *publication* was under the direction of the Defendant Wheble.

‖ Not so. Mr. Wheble was to receive them.

§ Not so. Mr. Coote's name was not mentioned to the public. He never engaged for the performance of the work at all. It must be on the credit of Wheble's name the public relied, if they relied on the name of any body.

G   ing critical matters of how and by whom a periodical was made in a bid to clarify the question of wherein periodical property lay.

The first witness sworn in was the *Lady's Magazine*'s printer, John Johnson, who was called upon to explain how the periodical was compiled.[44] He explained that while the title page of the magazine asked readers to address correspondence to Wheble's establishment in Paternoster Row, it was Coote who decided what was 'fit to be published'. Accordingly, it was from the magazine's proprietor, not its publisher, that Johnson collected the paper, engravings and manuscript copy for each issue of the magazine before delivering them to 'Mr. Anderson [a bookbinder] to be folded and stitched up' (46). Johnson stops short of calling Coote the magazine's editor in his testimony, but the printer is clear that the magazine's founder had a much more hands-on role in its day-to-day running than we might assume from the title 'proprietor'.[45] Robinson and Roberts's counsel leant on Johnson's claims, arguing that Wheble had grossly misrepresented his labour for the periodical, which they contended consisted largely of administering reader correspondence and submissions, and selling the stock once Johnson delivered it. Wheble's representative counterclaimed that it was in fact Coote who overstated his involvement in the magazine and questioned why, if he was so intimately involved in its daily workings, he had not identified himself on its title page or elsewhere in its contents. Coote's response was illuminating: he had not declared his editorial role in the magazine, he asserted, because he was already 'publisher and proprietor' of another journal. In truth, he was involved in several. His fear was that if readers of the *Lady's Magazine* knew as much then they might suspect him of recycling material between these different titles and the recognition might dent sales: 'it is a conceived notion amongst people', Coote observed, 'that if they do publish three or four, they are made up of one another' (47). The court was convinced by Coote's account and persuaded that he had every right to sell his property in the magazine to Robinson and Roberts.

A host of thornier issues remained, however, especially in relation to the central question of whether Robinson and Roberts's *Lady's Magazine* could be legitimately described as a continuation of Coote's original. Particular sticking points were serials whose instalments crossed Wheble's and Robinson and Roberts's issues. Two such works featured prominently in the ensuing debate: 'The Pyrenean Hermits' (March–April 1771); and 'A Sentimental Journey' (August 1770–April 1777). Serials connect individual issues of a periodical and conjure a sense of coherent print identity. But, as the court was asked to consider, could serials meaningfully connect issues published or authored by different people?

Both sides agreed that the integrity of serials was vital in determining who had the right to call their *Lady's Magazine* a 'genuine' continuation of the original venture. Robinson and Roberts's counsel asserted that their clients had taken appropriate steps to ensure that the serials continued over from Wheble's magazine were legitimate sequels of prior instalments because the original authors had been commissioned to pen subsequent parts for them. Wheble undermined these claims in accusatory footnotes to the printed trial transcript. The 'Pyrenean Hermits', he pointed out, was a translation from the French and, as such, could not be owned by the writer in the way that originally authored work could be: 'any body had an undoubted right to translate' it, and therefore anyone, and indeed several people, could translate future instalments without impugning the text's or magazine's integrity.[46]

As an original work, 'A Sentimental Journey' was a different matter, as Wheble understood, and proving continuity of its authorship was a pressing and potentially decisive matter. Wheble claimed that the anonymous 'Lady' who originally produced the serial still worked for him and that the writer who produced Robinson and Roberts's version of the serial was an imposter and not even a woman, 'unless a short Parson's long petticoats entitle him to that appellation' (44). Robinson and Roberts claimed that this allegation was false, and that the serial's original author was now working solely for them. Johnson, who was kept on as printer of the magazine by its new owners, corroborated the assertion. He testified that the manuscripts for the parts of 'A Sentimental Journey' that he originally printed for Wheble and those that he now printed for Robinson and Roberts 'were in the same handwriting' (46).

Further testimonies and lengthy cross-examinations followed. But the eventual verdict proved something of a damp squib. In his closing remarks, Mansfield identified the question of property that had been so hotly debated by all parties during the trial was a red herring, after all. Following lengthy testimonies about how the periodical trade operated, he was forced to conclude there was simply 'not a colour for property' in serial publications (50). Periodicals changed hands and publishers regularly and, as had been pointed out during the trial, many different *Lady's/Ladies' Magazine*s had surfaced over the previous decades without troubling the court about whether any 'invasion of the name occurred' (50). Mansfield nonetheless upheld Robinson and Roberts's claim for damages on the grounds that Wheble had disingenuously attempted to pass off his magazine as a genuine continuation of the original founded by Coote, for whom Wheble had acted principally as 'servant or agent' (51). Nominal damages of a shilling were awarded, but ultimately, Mansfield conceded that the fate of Wheble's magazine could not be settled in the courtroom. Its future was in the hands of its readers, who were left to judge whether they would buy his periodical or transfer their loyalty to Robinson and Roberts (52). Over the next year and half, both *Lady's Magazine*s worked strenuously to win over subscribers by consolidating the most successful elements of Wheble's first issues and innovating new content. This competition and its implications for the magazine's future are the subject of the following section.

Two *Lady's Magazines*: Robinson vs Wheble

The first editorial 'Address' to readers that appeared in Robinson's *Lady's Magazine* was published in the August 1771 issue, the fifth published out of 25 Paternoster Row.[47] As the inaugural notice in Wheble's magazine had previously done, this 'Address' pays '[t]ribute' to the magazine's patronesses and contributors, and confirms the editor's commitment to 'Novelty', 'Utility' and to the 'improve[ment of] . . . the Female Mind' (3). Yet Robinson's *Lady's Magazine* was clearly not about to rest on its laurels. The editor acknowledges the magazine's 'amazing success' since its launch a year earlier, but refuses to give any credit for this success to Wheble, who is dismissed – along with the rival publication he was still unapologetically issuing – as a 'FRAUD' (3–4). Robinson's periodical, the editor continues, is the only title that has the right to call itself the *Lady's Magazine*, and he appeals to the sense of 'Justice . . . so conspicuous in the Breasts of our fair Countrywomen' to leave off Wheble's magazine once and for all (4). In return for their loyalty, the editor promises that he and his staff will use their 'utmost Endeavours' to deserve the 'Approbation' the magazine had earned since its founding, while continually 'opening new Stores for their [readers'] Amusement' and 'Education' (3–4).

As the carefully calibrated rhetoric of the 1771 'Address' reveals, Robinson's periodical had to toe a fine line. On the one hand, stiff competition from Wheble's magazine meant that his periodical needed to differentiate itself in order to survive. On the other hand, his journal needed to maintain continuity with past issues if it wanted to trade on the *Lady's Magazine*'s established popularity and to avoid giving further ammunition to Wheble, who was still arguing loudly that the periodical's new publishers were ill placed to ensure continuity with its original design and plan. Robinson's efforts to negotiate these competing imperatives were a resounding success, and in less than two years Wheble's magazine folded. It did no go down without a fight, however. Over the coming months, Wheble's periodical introduced a host of improvements to which Robinson's publication was forced to respond. The energetic battle for readers' hearts, minds and subscriptions fees described below continued to shape the *Lady's Magazine* long after the eventual demise of Wheble's publication in December 1772.

Accounts of the early history of the *Lady's Magazine* usually conflate the two versions of the periodical that ran concurrently from April 1771 to the end of 1772 and indeed most fail to acknowledge even that there was any other version of the magazine at the time than Wheble's. This anomaly can partly be explained by the fact that the majority of the surviving bound volumes from 1771 to 1772 in library collections are Wheble's rather than Robinson's.[48] Whether the greater survival rate of Wheble's magazine is accidental or it is simply the case that more of Wheble's magazine were printed is unclear.[49] Whatever the facts, and we will likely never know for sure, reading 1773 issues of the *Lady's Magazine* can be a very odd experience given that much of their content comprises continuations of serials from earlier Robinson's volumes that have largely fallen out of the literary-historical record.[50] In the following discussion, I pay close attention to these earliest issues of Robinson's magazine, identifying its debts to Wheble's periodical as well as to innovations it introduced to ward off its former publisher's aggressive efforts to maintain his readership.

In some ways, the April 1771 issue of Robinson's magazine proceeds seamlessly from Wheble's March issue. It picks up the female traveller of 'A Sentimental Journey' where readers left her at the Bear Inn, Oxford (Figure 2.3), although her subsequent journeying plots an amusingly different course from that followed in Wheble's magazine. The same issue also contains the concluding part of the 'Pyrenean Hermits' and a solution to the French translation exercise set in Wheble's issue for March. Coote appears to have passed on these materials to help smooth the transition from Wheble's to Robinson's ownership.[51] These are not the only lines of continuity. The sheet music for Robinson's magazine was set by the same 'master' – Mr Hudson – who had provided scores for Wheble, a fact offered up as 'incontrovertible proof' of the magazine's continuity with the periodical Coote had launched (3 (January 1772): 2).[52] Robinson's magazine also continued the tradition, established in Wheble's magazine, of duplicating material that had appeared in other of Coote's journals. For instance, a number of the theatrical reviews printed in early issues of Wheble's magazine – such as those for *Almida* (January 1771) and Richard Cumberland's *The West Indian* (February 1771) – are identical to those in Coote's *Oxford Magazine*. Robinson

Figure 2.3 The two different journeys of the sentimental traveller in Wheble's (left) and Robinson's (right) *Lady's Magazine* for August 1771. Private collection.

carried on this practice, issuing reviews such as that for Samuel Foote's *Maid of Bath* that appeared simultaneously in their *Lady's Magazine* and the *Oxford Magazine* for June 1771.[53]

The first issue of Robinson's magazine exhibits notable points of departure as well as lines of continuity, however. One of the most striking new directions is the magazine's publication of 'An Essay upon the present Fashionable Dress of the Ladies' (April 1771), an article that was accompanied by a 'fine Copper-plate, beautifully coloured' illustrating the latest metropolitan style (Figure 2.4). That illustration – 'A Lady with the Emblems of Spring' – is likely the first mass-produced, hand-coloured British fashion plate. A costly inclusion, its commission was a flamboyant gesture on the part of the magazine's new owners to poach *Lady's Magazine*'s readers who had publicly registered their disappointment that Wheble had 'promised to give ... the most early intelligence of every transition in female dress', but had only provided 'two plates upon that subject' in his issues of the magazine (Robinson 3 (October 1772): 459). As a declaration of intent, however, the publication of the plate proved hollow. Fashion reports and illustrations, as I return to in

Figure 2.4   Hand-coloured fashion plate displaying *A Lady with the Emblems of Spring in the Dress of April 1771* from Robinson's *Lady's Magazine* for April 1771. Bayerische Staatsbibliothek München, Bibl. Mont. 861–1. Urn:nbn:de:bvb:12-bsb10713981-3.

Chapter 5, remained only sporadic inclusions in the *Lady's Magazine* until 1800 because of the expense and complex logistics of sourcing month-by-month fashion coverage. The 'Court Mirror' column, which also launched in the April 1771 Robinson issue, was a lower-effort and certainly lower-cost attempt to entice the more fashion-preoccupied of Wheble's readers by bringing the lives and scandals of the St James's *bon ton* into the homes of the magazine's readers. Much more in keeping with the spirit of the gossip-saturated *Town and Country Magazine* than the *Lady's Magazine*, the 'Court Mirror' is one of very few editorial missteps made by Robinson's periodical. The column abruptly terminated after just two numbers.

Wheble responded to the new content in Robinson's *Lady's Magazine* by introducing three new initiatives to his own. The first of these was the ancient-and-modern memoir series, the 'Lady's Biography' (April 1771– March 1772) (Figure 2.5), which featured 'lives' of notable women from the worlds of politics, court, learning and letters including: the Queen of Sheba, Hyaptia, Catherine Parr, Lady Jane Grey, Elizabeth Thomas, Ninon de l'Enclos and Madame de Maintenon, who featured in Amelia's extract from Brooke's *Emily Montague*. The text for the series originates in various previously published sources, most prominently the *Biographium Faemineum* (1766), but it makes an original and important contribution to the magazine for which it is repurposed. Earlier periodicals, such as Lennox's *Lady's Museum,* had included accounts of the likes of Joan of Arc and Bianca Cappello. Yet as Hannah Doherty Hudson has explained, the eighteenth-century magazine biography was not exactly 'an equal-opportunity genre', and men remained the most memorialised subjects in periodicals.[54] The *Lady's Magazine*, as I return to in Chapter 6, helped to change this by putting female lives centre stage. Long after Wheble's connection with the periodical ceased, the 'Lady's Biography' continued to spawn popular sequels, such as 'Sketches of Female Biography' (July 1776–January 1777) – largely extracted from George Ballard's *Memoirs of Several Ladies of Great Britain* (1752) – and a sequel based on Ann Thicknesse's *Sketches of the Lives and Writings of the Ladies of France,* which appeared near-simultaneously with their volume publication between 1778 and 1781.[55] These multi-part serials were accompanied by hundreds of standalone biographies of notable women and men. By the time the *Lady's Monthly Museum*, the *Lady's Magazine*'s rival and later partner, launched in 1798, regular biographies, including and especially 'illustrious examples' of eighteenth-century British female worthies, were not merely standard magazine fare, but headline items designed to promote 'female ambition' among subscribers.[56]

Figure 2.5 Illustration for the 'Lady's Biography' from Wheble's *Lady's Magazine* for June 1771. Private collection.

The second of Wheble's initiatives was the launch of dedicated opinion and advice columns led by a range of female and male authorities. The first of these was the aforementioned 'Female Rambler', which began in May 1771. Bearing little resemblance to its Johnsonian namesake, the 'Female Rambler' is reminiscent of the *Lady's Museum*'s 'Trifler' column in dedicating itself to the cause of advancing women's education, and like Lennox's series, generated a postbag of correspondence from readers that the columnist answered within the magazine. Robinson's periodical responded swiftly by launching a regular advice column of its own, 'The Lady's Counsellor . . . by a young Philanthropist of Finchley' (July 1771–December 1771). Devoted to moral conundrums and life predicaments, the first instalments of the column are almost exclusively essay based and univocal. Like Wheble's 'Female Rambler', however, 'The Lady's Counsellor' quickly developed a life of its own and gradually evolved into the magazine's first agony aunt – or technically agony uncle – column. The December 1771 instalment published the first letter directly addressed to the Lady's Counsellor: a plea for advice from Maria, who is torn between her parents' desire for her to make a match against her will and following her heart and marrying the man she loves.

Advice of a rather different kind was issued in the third of Wheble's content additions. 'The Lady's Handmaid, or Housekeeper's Calendar' (Wheble July 1771–July 1772) is a recipe series complete with diagrammatic table plans illustrating how to set and dress the table once the elaborate meals described have been prepared (Figure 2.6). Magazine readers were not expected to cook these dishes themselves, but to familiarise themselves with menus, recipes and preparation methods in order to manage their servants more effectively. The 'Lady's Handmaid' was supplemented by other series in a similar vein such as 'The oeconomy of Female Life' (Wheble July 1771–January 1772), which consisted of numerous – and unacknowledged and edited – extracts from the popular conduct book *The Whole Duty of Woman* (1753).[57] Like the introduction of the 'Female Rambler', Wheble's inclusion of content devoted to practical household management was watched attentively by Robinson. A few months after these series launched, their magazine introduced 'The Modern Cook' (Supp 1771–December 1772), a column that was purportedly authored 'by a person eminent in his profession' and boasted a greater number and more seasonal recipes than Wheble's 'Lady's Handmaid' ('Preface' 3 (January 1772): 2).

Every time Wheble's magazine attempted something new, Robinson's followed and strove to do better. Equally, every time Robinson's magazine innovated, Wheble sought out new content to encourage readers back to his periodical. There was, however, one critical area over which

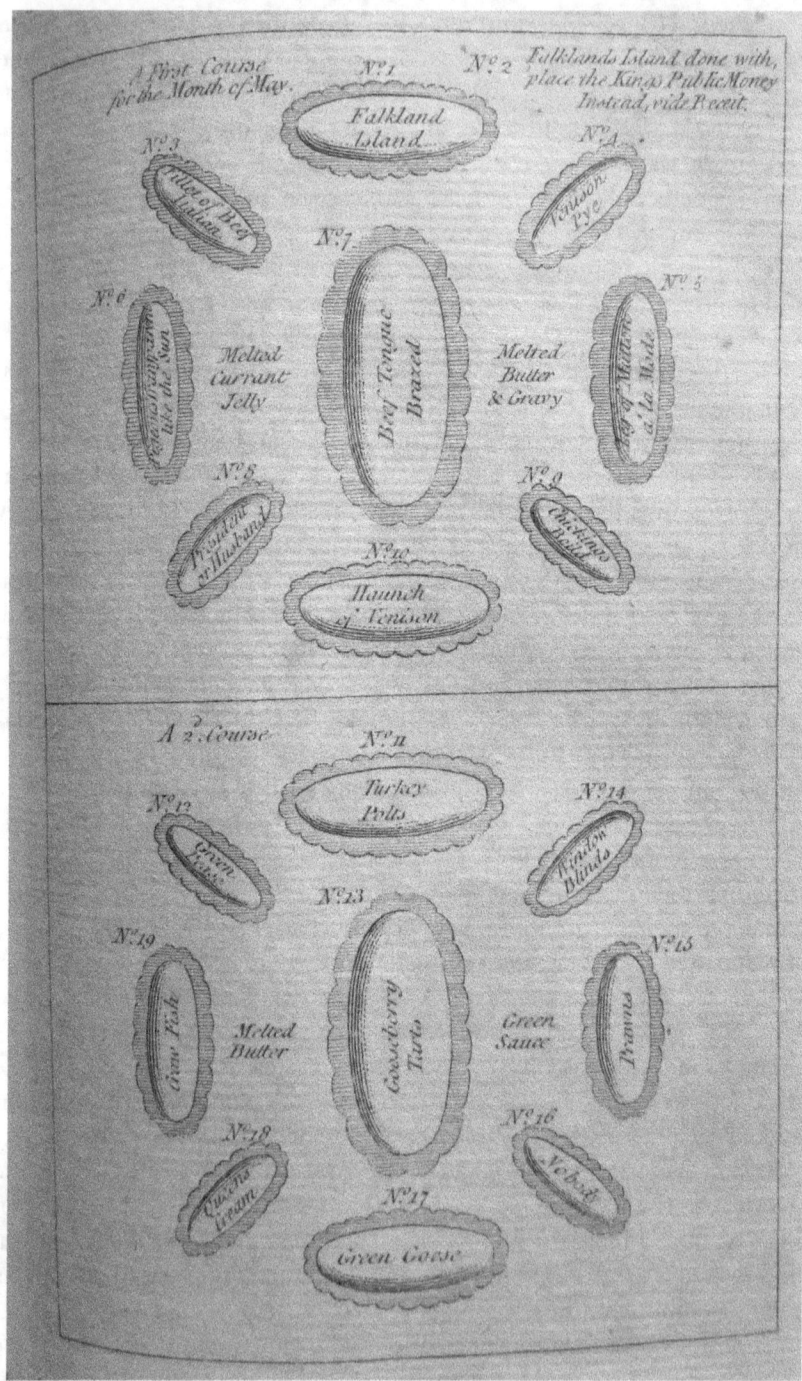

Figure 2.6 Table setting to accompany 'The Lady's Handmaid; or Housekeeper's Calendar' from Wheble's *Lady's Magazine* for April 1771. Private collection.

Robinson's and Wheble's journals decisively parted company: serial fiction. Robinson's *Lady's Magazine* included serialised novels from their very first issue. 'Memoirs of a Young Lady of Family: Written by herself and Addressed to a Female Friend' launched in Robinson's magazine in April 1771. It ran throughout the entire duration of Robinson's rivalry with Wheble, concluding in December 1772, the same month that saw the publication of the last issue of Wheble's magazine. Eighteenth-century magazine fiction, with only notable exceptions such as 'The Life and Adventures of Sir Launcelot Greaves' and 'Harriot and Sophia', has generally been given short shrift by its critics.[58] Mayo's *The English Novel in the Magazines* (1962) – the only book-length study of eighteenth-century periodical fiction to date – is indispensable, but strangely marginalises the very material it brings to light. The author's conclusion that most magazine fiction from this period is 'trashy, affected, ... egregiously sentimental' and 'lacking in vigour and permanent value' because written by hacks and amateurs, has been widely endorsed by subsequent scholars.[59] In Chapter 4, I offer a more comprehensive account of the merits and influence of the writers of, and fiction in, the *Lady's Magazine*, yet even a brief survey of 'Memoirs of a Young Lady' gives sufficient grounds to counter such characteristic dismissals.

'Memoirs of a Young Lady' may well have been written by an amateur – the author was almost certainly unpaid for her work – but 'trashy, affected and egregiously sentimental' it is not. An epistolary novel, albeit one in which the correspondence is entirely one-sided, 'Memoirs' revolves around two plots: the first follows the heroine, Charlotte's, tortuous road to marital harmony; the second charts her long process of reconciliation with her widowed father, which is finally achieved in the serial's last instalment. The serial closely foreshadows Frances Burney's *Evelina* (1778), although in this case, the heroine's struggle to navigate her entrance into the world is not caused by rural naivety, but by the inadequate education she receives at the fashionable boarding school to which she is sent by her aunt after her mother dies. While at the boarding school, Charlotte becomes involved in private theatricals of the kind that turn the Bertram household upside down in Jane Austen's *Mansfield Park* (1814). Against her father's will, Charlotte marries the young actor who plays Lothario in a performance of *The Fair Penitent* (perf. 1702) in which they are both involved, a role that her spouse continues to play in the couple's unhappy and abusive marriage. Charlotte's husband eventually dies, but only after plunging his wife and their child into a life of misery. The narrative concludes shortly after Charlotte's second, happy marriage to Mr Falkland, and a reconciliation with her father who accepts his own complicity in the numerous distresses endured by his daughter since her mother's death.

Unromantic, yet pacey and affecting, 'Memoirs of a Young Lady' struck a chord with readers, and like many of the magazine's most successful items and serials, generated a rich and extended conversation among them that was played out in the magazine's pages. At least one reader wrote to the magazine to request that the publishers consider issuing the seventy-thousand-word serial as 'a separate Volume', a request that the editor claimed was being seriously considered. No such volume appears to have seen the light of day, but fans of the serial were eventually rewarded with a sequel devoted to the life of Charlotte's close friend, entitled the 'The History of Lady Bradley' (Supp 1776–August 1778). 'Lady Bradley' opened with a brief introduction that assumed readers' acquaintance with the original despite the four-year time lag between the two works. Like its predecessor, 'The History of Lady Bradley' is an unsentimental tale of women's experiences of courtship and marriage that, as Jenny DiPlacidi notes, highlights the prevalence of spousal abuse and women's difficulty in establishing property in their inheritances, their children or even their own bodies.[60] Serial novels on these and related themes would play an ever more significant role in the overall make-up of the *Lady's Magazine* in the years to come. An early indication of how central such fiction was to the identity of Robinson's magazine (Figure 2.7) can be found in its 1771 frontispiece, which features a cherub guiding the periodical's reader towards the path of wisdom emblematised by a scroll carrying just two legible entries: the first is for a 'Sentimental Journey'; the second reads simply 'Novels'. Where Robinson's readers followed, Wheble did not. Although his magazine continued to run its fictional travelogue 'A Sentimental Journey', as well as further examples of the kinds of short oriental and moral tales discussed above, it did not respond by launching original serial novels of its own. With hindsight, this was a serious mistake.

The introduction of serial novels was likely not the only reason why readers and contributors started to abandon Wheble's magazine in favour of Robinson's, but abandon it many certainly did. Evidence that allegiances were shifting soon became visible in the pages of the two publications. In the weeks following Coote's sale of the periodical, poet James Thistlewaite started to hedge his authorial bets by submitting poems for the editorial consideration of both *Lady's Magazine*s.[61] He was not a unique case. George Crabbe began his poetic career as a contributor to Wheble's magazine while working as a doctor's apprentice. His winning entry for the periodical's monthly poetry competition was published in the September 1772 issue and was soon followed by a

Figure 2.7 Frontispiece to Robinson and Roberts's *Lady's Magazine* for 1771. Bayerische Staatsbibliothek München, Bibl. Mont. 861–1. Urn:nbn:de:bvb:12-bsb10713982-8.

further three poems that appeared in Wheble's magazine for December. Simultaneously, Crabbe was sending verse to the rival *Lady's Magazine*. Two further poems – 'Solitude' and a 'Song' – appeared in Robinson's periodical for September 1772; 'Emma' appeared in the October issue; and a further three verses appeared in November.[62] Enthusiastic enigmatist and sometime poet, G. Lacey of Bridport, made a more decisive break. His signature can be found just once in Wheble's magazine, in March 1771, before he became a regular contributor to Robinson's magazine from April 1771. A similar pattern can be found in the case of long-term contributor R./R—, to whom I return in the following chapter. R./R— made her first appearance in the inaugural issue of the *Lady's Magazine* and continued to feature in Wheble's periodical until July 1771 when she made the move to Robinson magazine, for which she served as a regular contributor for more than a decade.

Precisely why Wheble's periodical folded when it did is unknown. By December 1772, readers were responding enthusiastically to the new content in Robinson's magazine and several of Wheble's contributors were migrating to it. Additional, undocumented factors may also have come into play. Wheble could certainly be excused of tiring of his involvement in a publication that had led him to the court room and had pitted him against not only his neighbour, but also against many other booksellers in the Row and beyond. The list of thirty-nine booksellers whose names appeared in a widely circulated advert condemning Wheble's decision to continue publishing the *Lady's Magazine* after Coote's sale is a veritable who's who of the eighteenth-century publishing world. Faced with formidable, publicly documented opposition not only from Robinson and Roberts, but also from the likes of Thomas Cadell, Joseph Johnson, Edward and Charles Dilly, Kearsley, Longman, Newbery, John Rivington and Wilkie, it seems surprising that Wheble sustained his determination to publish the magazine for as long as he did.[63] The last issue of Wheble's magazine for December 1772 leaves only a partial and tantalising clue to the publisher's thoughts at the time. Buried in the middle of the magazine, and sandwiched between a half-column essay, 'On the Improvement of the Mind', and the recently begun but soon-to-end 'Theatrical Intelligencer' column, is a one-page letter addressed to the 'fair and candid readers' of the *Lady's Magazine* dated 29 December 1772, bidding them to follow its 'female editor' as she prepares to work for a different publisher, 'J. Bell, near Exeter Exchange'. The editor explains that the 'property' of the magazine had 'lately changed hands' and was to be published, under the same title, by Wheble's associate John Bell from January 1773 (541).[64] Bell became one of the most important publishers of the later eighteenth century and went on to publish the *Lady's Magazine*'s elegant rival and eventual partner, *La Belle Assemblée* (1806–32). No record of a Bell's *Lady's Magazine* survives beyond this letter. It marks an inauspicious end to Wheble's involvement in the *Lady's Magazine*, a periodical whose identity, readership and conversations were indelibly shaped under the watch of this remarkably tenacious publisher.

Chapter 3

Modes, Media and Miscellaneity: The Contents of the *Lady's Magazine*

> Among the many advantages derived to society from the invention of the Art of Printing, perhaps the Publication of Periodical Repositories for Fugitive Pieces, and the first efforts of the dawning genius, is not to be esteemed one of the least. The variety of literary amusements . . . they contain, cannot fail to furnish something agreeable to every taste, which may convey instruction without the trouble of laborious study. Whatever exercises the mind, tends to expand and invigorate its faculties, and that mental exercise which is required for the perusal of a Monthly Miscellany, will neither cause any great consumption of the time of the busy, nor exhaust the patience of the idle. The utility of Miscellanies of this kind, for the promotion of knowledge and the liberal arts, need not be insisted on.
>
>   'Address to the Public', *Lady's Magazine* 26 (1795)

Few people today would have trouble defining the 'women's magazine', even people who claim rarely or never to read it. Over the course of the nineteenth and twentieth centuries, the form came to epitomise an ever-expanding media industry devoted to fuelling, and promising to satisfy, the personal and (latterly) professional desires of women. At the same time, it became synonymous with the impossible set of contradictions that define femininity. Yet the women's magazine is not now, nor ever was, a monolithic entity. At any given time in its history, it has taken many different material forms issued at different price points and frequencies, and it has always oriented itself towards different readerships for diverse commercial and ideological reasons. The magazine's traditional bill of fare has changed relatively little over the centuries. A mix of editorial, features, fiction, reader letters, advice columns, celebrity lives, visual content and advertisements were as common in eighteenth-century magazines as they are in those published today. Yet the weighting and flavour of these different ingredients has varied markedly between titles issued at any given moment in time. The women's magazine has always been unapologetically heterogeneous.

This heterogeneity – the latest celebrity-endorsed diet trend appearing next to indulgent recipes for home baking, for instance – often feels indicative of the form's crushingly impossible demands upon women. Yet as we have seen, early magazines – and not just those marketed specifically at women – presented their topical as well as generic and even political diversity as hallmarks of their utility. The *Lady's Magazine* was no different. Its annual reader addresses repeatedly argued that the miscellany format was better able to achieve the Horatian imperative to entertain and educate than any other print medium. To quote from this chapter's epigraph, the 'utility of Miscellanies', lay in their ability to corral both already published ('Fugitive') pieces and original items written specifically for the magazine ('the first efforts of the dawning genius') from a 'variety' of genres and media into a format readily accessible to the time- or cash-poor.

This chapter continues the story I began in my last about the active, critical reading habits that the *Lady's Magazine* sought to cultivate. It explores also how these habits were inseparably linked to: the periodical's dialogic, multimodal and multi-media form; its presentation of the world as an unstable environment that required careful navigation; and its educational agenda for women. The principal focus of the following discussion is the staggering 'variety of literary amusements' that the magazine provided readers across its run. Attempting to survey these contents is daunting, not least because of the sheer volume of material that appeared in the periodical's tens of thousands of pages. It is a task made all more challenging by the fact that the most intuitive method of providing an overview of these contents – one organised around the many genres that populate the magazine's columns – is antagonistic to the miscellany format in which they were presented to readers. As Margaret Beetham notes, historic magazines are 'difficult to accommodate within the traditional taxonomy of literary forms'.[1] The binding of single issues into the book-like, bound volumes preserved in library collections creates an illusion of coherence that the magazine's generically diverse and multimedia contents quickly dispel (Figure 3.1).

The magazine undoubtedly has form, but in the plural. It is multiform. We often refer to 'the magazine' as a genre in its own right (like 'the novel'), but the designation is complicated by the miscellaneity that is its most important formal characteristic. According to David Mazella, the magazine is 'not simply a *container* of smaller sub- or micro genres', but a 'complex genre' that 'helps to mediate and transform the smaller genres found within its frame'.[2] While I largely agree with Mazella's claim, the process of writing this book has led me to view genre – whether understood complexly or simplistically – as a red herring when

Figure 3.1 An instalment of a gothic novel, a serialised travel writing and an embroidery pattern from the *Lady's Magazine* for October 1798. Private collection.

it comes to eighteenth-century magazines.³ Although genre can provide a useful taxonomy for charting changes in a magazine's composition over time, as I do in Chapter 5, genre is only one, and arguably the least important, mediator of the experience of reading the periodical. Indeed, the most notable generic feature of 'the magazine' is its *unfixing* of genre, and with genre often voice, perspective, authorship and import.

Magazine contents present interpretative questions and challenges that are unique to the format in which they published, a format in which the meaning of texts and media emerges relationally through their interaction on the page and in the reader's mind. We saw in Chapter 2 how Frances Brooke's epistolary novel, *The History of Emily Montague* (1769), is transformed by its repackaging in the *Lady's Magazine*. These kinds of generic remediation – of novels being reformulated as letters to the editor and essays, for instance – are frequently overlaid in the *Lady's Magazine* with a temporal remediation that passes off old wisdom as new. In Chapter 6, I turn to one especially striking example of this kind of double remediation in the magazine's surprising repackaging of Delarivier Manley's *The New Atalantis* (1709) as a series of pithy maxims for conduct in modern life. In this particular example, readers are alerted in the article's title to its origins, but in countless similar cases they were not. We cannot know how many readers of the November 1789 issue would have recognised Christopher Curious's 'Thoughts on Modern Gardening' as an edited extract of Alexander Pope's 'On Gardens', which had appeared in the *Guardian* no. 173 (29 September 1713). More to the point, would it have mattered if they did? And what about excerpts where not only the textual and generic origins, but also the national contexts in which works were originally produced are obscured? How would a reader have encountered a seemingly quintessentially British anecdote on the 'Surprising and Pleasant Effects of the Cold' (Supp 1785) that was in fact a reader-submitted, annotated extract from Thomas Holcroft's English translation of Stéphanie Félicité de Genlis's *Les Veillées du Chateau, ou, Cours de morale à l'usage des enfants* (1784)?

In worrying away at these questions in the following discussion, I am indebted to the insights of recent scholarship on re/mediation. In its broadest sense, mediation refers to the materiality of the medium, to those features that, in the words of Christina Lupton, 'invite readers to think about the long journey that brings a published text to hand' while also self-consciously projecting the medium's circulation and reception.[4] For magazines, mediators include a publication's material qualities, such as wrappers, advertisements, binding protocols and the font and page layouts, paper and print quality, to which I return in Chapter 5. They also include the dialogue between the magazine's editors, contributors and readers, editorial notes and corrections, monthly 'Correspondents' columns and annual 'Addresses' to the 'Public'. Further mediating features can be found in the many moments when editors and contributors imagine the magazine's past or future circulation. Such moments, like the epigraph with which this chapter opens, invariably reveal the magazine's self-styling as a new and distinctive medium for the production, communication and circulation of information, entertainment and knowledge. In so doing, the periodical anticipates Clifford Siskin and William Warner's recognition of the birth of the magazine as a 'cardinal' point in the history of mediation, marking as it does the emergence of one of many 'new channels and stopping places for new genres and formats to circulate' and, moreover, one that opened up 'new possibilities and expectations for what mediation could accomplish'.[5]

The newness of the channel should not obscure the indebtedness of the medium, however. The magazine is simultaneously derivative and innovative; it is both old and new; familiar and pathbreaking. For this reason, principally, I find *re*mediation a more helpful term for thinking about the magazine's form and contents, and about the distinctive reading experiences that emerge from the friction between form and content. Jay David Boulter and Richard Grusin are primarily concerned with late twentieth-century visual and digital media when they theorise remediation as a 'complex kind of borrowing in which one medium is itself incorporated in another medium', but it is hard to imagine a more apposite description of how eighteenth-century magazines operate, particularly in light of the endemic culture of reprinting in which they participated.[6] And it is not only a magazine's excerpted material that falls into the category of remediated content. Everything in the *Lady's Magazine* – even an original contribution – is remediated because once part of the dynamic and interactive multi-media ecology of the magazine, an essay, a short story, a translation or a poem becomes something more and other than merely itself. Periodical remediation re-situates one medium in relation to another in ways that reconstitute the meaning and identity of both. If this is true at the macro level of the medium itself then it is also true on the micro level of the medium's many messages. In the case of the contents of the *Lady's Magazine*, these messages appear in the often unpredictable ways in which themes, arguments, perspectives and meanings emerge, not from individual articles so much as by the intertextual conversation produced by their juxtaposition.

Periodicals studies draws on a number of linguistic and formal theories and vocabularies to describe these interactions, from Bakhtin's heteroglossia and dialogism, to theories of intertextuality and intermediality. My approach is more directly influenced by theories of emergence, which have come to prominence in nineteenth-century and Modernist periodicals scholarship, partly in response to the challenges posed by digitisation. Digital platforms make periodicals more accessible than ever before, not least because of keyword searching, which allows us to trawl huge quantities of textual material in a matter of seconds. Mining periodicals for content in this way promotes idiosyncratic reading practices that, superficially, might seem entirely consonant with a miscellany format that was tailor-made to be read non-sequentially and selectively. But it would be a mistake to confuse digital discontinuity – produced by disciplined keyword searching and datamining – with the more unruly and generative forms of reading facilitated by print discontinuity.[7] The instrumentality of professional digital 'reading' risks evacuating articles not only of their context, but, in Mark Parker's words, 'a mode of emergence which radically affects [their] meaning'.[8] Magazine contents need to be read both synchronically – as items in explicit or implicit conversation with others in the same issue – and diachronically – as items in dialogue with other pieces of content published in multiple issues over time. The distortions produced by failing to take this into account can be briefly illustrated by the *Lady's Magazine*'s attitude to one of its favourite and most contested subjects: fashion.

In the April 1783 issue, contributor W— G— wrote to the periodical's agony aunt, the Matron, to condemn the fashion for riding habits, which he laments give women a 'masculine appearance'. The Matron indicates that her 'sentiments agree entirely' with W— G—'s, but says no more for 'want of room' (14: 206). Reading this exchange in isolation – as a keyword search for 'advice' or 'fashion' invites – would lead anyone to conclude that the *Lady's Magazine* was anti-fashion and gender conservative. Reading discontinuously and associatively, however, undermines the supposition. In the next month's issue, the Matron retroactively modifies her initial response in a second in which she reflects that riding habits are 'more compact and convenient' than alternatives, and that *'single ladies'* surely have the right to wear them 'uncensured' even if married women ought to be wise enough only to wear what is 'becoming in the eyes of their husbands' (May 1783: 267). After a brief digression expressing concern about the recent fashion for extravagant feathered garments, the Matron signs off by noting that '[m]oderation . . . in dress' is 'most becoming' (268).

With this, the Matron steers a carefully plotted course: she checks a contributor's misogyny while simultaneously seeming to circle back to the sartorial and gender conservatism of her first reply. Reading her second within its immediate publication context alters the picture again, however. The Matron's response in the May 1783 issue is immediately followed by a fashion report describing the latest styles popularised by poet, actress and celebrity Mary (Perdita) Robinson. There is no matronly moderation in the ensuing and indulgent descriptions of the Rutland gown with its petticoats 'tied back at the sides in the form of a Sultana's robe', the '*Robinson hat*' trimmed with a 'panache of [the] white feathers' that the Matron rejects, or in the closing reference to 'Riding habits', which readers are now told, are 'much worn in the morning; the most fashionable are the Perdita's pearl colour' (14 (May 1783): 268). In the disjunction created by the placement of the report next to the advice column – a disjunction repeated many times in a single issue of the *Lady's Magazine* and thousands of times across its run – the periodical evidences its textual, formal and ideological complexity.

Examples such as this underline the aptness of Jeffrey Drouin's characterisation of historic magazines as networks in which the signification of 'individual pieces and their larger relations' – conceptual, political, personal and formal – emerge through editorial juxtaposition as 'a mutually constitutive whole'.[9] These juxtapositions need not be intentional to affect meaning. We will never know – and it arguably matters little – whether or not the editor of the *Lady's Magazine* instructed the fashion report to appear next to the Matron's belated response to W— G—. Nor, as that jarring example clarifies, is the effect of such juxtapositions necessarily the 'thematic coherence' that Drouin identifies.[10] The intermedial interactions I discuss throughout this chapter reveal numerous instances of thematic fluidity and instability, although meanings and patterns nonetheless emerge from superficial incoherence. In order to dive deeply into these juxtapositions, the following discussion is organised in two parts around four interrelated topics: news and politics; and advice and education. These are useful focal points not only because they are among most prevalent, contentious and ideologically fraught of the magazine's preoccupations, but also because sustained consideration of them undermines the conventional characterisations of the *Lady's Magazine* as a training guide in femininity. In pursuing these topics, the chapter is attentive to many of the magazine's array of genres and media, locating their significance in their re/mediated interactions, rather than in their intrinsic characteristics.[11] Although it acknowledges the impossibility of capturing exactly how individual readers encountered this material, the chapter also seeks to account for the specific kind of 'mental exercise' that the periodical claimed was required to navigate 'variety of literary amusements' and to elucidate how this 'exercise' was inextricably linked to the magazine's aspirations for its female readers.

Part 1: News and Politics – An Introduction

News and politics might seem unconventional axes for this chapter. Most of the few studies of the *Lady's Magazine* to date fail to mention these topics at all, and those that do tend to assert the periodical's uninterest in current affairs. Mary Poovey, for instance, identifies the principal difference between the *Gentleman's* (1731–1922) and the *Lady's Magazines* as the latter's only rare references to 'political events'. The *Lady's*, she contends, was invested in creating 'a reassuring picture of stability and continuity' that it disrupted only rarely and when it considered news items suitable for the 'polite conversations' of female readers.[12] Margaret Beetham detects even less interest in news and politics in the periodical, going so far as to claim that it 'was precisely the absence of "news" which came to distinguish the magazine from that other kind of periodical, the newspaper'.[13]

The pages of the *Lady's Magazine* give some ammunition for these charges. Numerous contributor letters and essays decry the 'female politician' as a grotesque contradiction in terms or inveigh against politics as destructive to women's manners, happiness or even their complexions.[14] Successive editors repeatedly assured readers that matters of government and party politics were beyond the publication's remit, and marvelled in self-congratulatory tones that the magazine was so successful when it refused to join its brethren in 'incit[ing] the Rage of the Populace' and 'expos[ing] the Frivolity of domestic Failings' ('Address', 14 (January 1783): n.p.). The periodical's most bold assertions along these lines came at the most politically fraught times, as when the editor declared in April 1789 that 'Politics can have no place in our Magazine' ('Correspondents', 20: n.p.). Like many such declamatory statements, this claim is misleading and was undercut even at the moment of its utterance. In this instance, the editor's comments were prompted by the submission of an article called 'The Triumph of Virtue' for editorial consideration. Nothing more is said about the piece – its genre, author or subject – other than that it had 'a political Tendency' and could not, therefore, be published. The pronouncement seems decisive, except that in denying the place of politics in the magazine, the editor unwittingly betrays his interest in current affairs. Although the reader is left in the dark as to what political 'Sentiments' the 'Triumph of Virtue' espouses, the editor's, we are told, 'agree with those of the Writer' (n.p.). The *Lady's Magazine* was political after all.

The periodical was no newspaper, however, and its coverage of news and politics departs from practices espoused by contemporary magazines such as the *Gentleman's*. Nevertheless, current affairs are much more than occasional concerns of the *Lady's Magazine* and, as Koenraad Claes demonstrates, its readers were much 'better informed about ongoing political debates than we have long presumed'.[15] It would be odd if this were not the case. George Robinson senior was well known for what JoEllen DeLucia has described as his 'dangerous and unwavering commitment to radical politics'.[16] As the publisher of *The Critical Review* (1756–1817) and *New Annual Register* (1780–1817), he and his firm were publicly criticised by conservative journals including the *Anti-Jacobin Review* (1798–1810) as 'disaffected to government' and 'enemies to the establishment'.[17] The *Lady's Magazine* is conspicuously absent from the *Anti-Jacobin*'s list of anti-establishment periodicals published by the Robinsons, but the publishing house's support of Jacobin writers, including William Godwin, Thomas Holcroft, Elizabeth Inchbald, Charlotte Smith, Thomas Paine and Helen Maria Williams – all of whom were published in the *Lady's Magazine* – was widely known. Admittedly, the *Lady's Magazine*'s politics are murkier than the works produced by any of these authors, and much less clear than Robinson senior's. Indeed, on many issues, the magazine's politics are wilfully ambiguous. Nevertheless, news, political events and controversies are much more prominent in the periodical and much more central to its editors' understanding of its female readers' lives and interests than has been commonly acknowledged.

Once you start looking for news and politics in the magazine you find them everywhere: in its births, marriages and deaths columns; in the chronicles of 'remarkable events' it published for many years in Supplement issues; in its detailed, often illustrated and multi-part accounts of state events, such as the funerals of William Pitt, Princess Charlotte and Lord Nelson, for instance; and in the transcripts of the trials of Warren Hastings, John Horne Tooke and Thomas Paine. The magazine also contains hundreds of pieces about most of the major political events and controversies of the period, including: the unfolding American Revolution; the Gordon Riots; the horrors of the French Revolution; the passing of the Acts of Union; the rise and fall of Napoleon; and parliamentary and electoral reform, which culminated in the magazine's celebration, in the June 1832 issue, of the passing of the Reform Bill.

The magazine's current affairs coverage is consistently visible in its 'foreign' and 'home news' sections – later dubbed 'foreign affairs' and 'domestic occurrences' and subsequently collapsed into a single news item called the 'Chronicle' that occupied the magazine's back pages until its new series launched in 1820.[18] The news sections in the earliest volumes of the magazine published by Robinson closely resemble those printed in the *Lady's Magazine*'s sibling publication, the *Town and Country* (1769–96). In fact, for the best part of twenty-five years, these periodicals' news sections are practically indistinguishable. Although separately typeset, they frequently begin and end with the same news items. The swollen domestic news section of the January 1775 *Lady's* and *Town and Country Magazine*s, for example, is identical, with both periodicals giving over five pages to the 'alarming situation of American affairs' (Figure 3.2). Such extensive coverage of 'American news' – which migrated between the home and foreign sections of the magazine amid the political confusion of the coming months and years – means that both the *Lady's* and *Town and Country Magazine* were forced to suspend the publication of birth, marriage and death listings for the month. (These lists were almost always identical also.)

Sometimes either the *Lady's* or the *Town or Country* interpolates a short editorial or news item or two into its columns that is not carried in

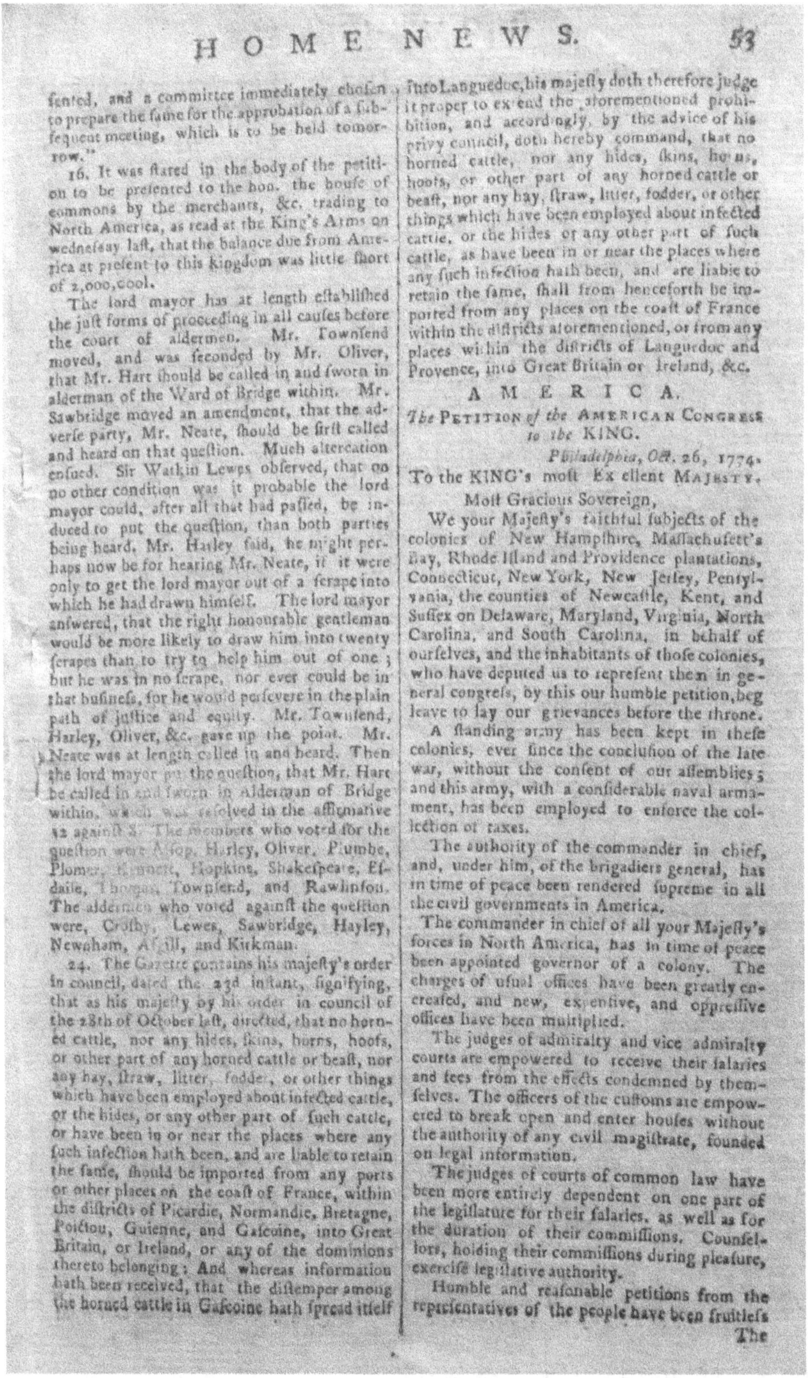

HOME NEWS. 53

ſented, and a committee immediately choſen to prepare the ſame for the approbation of a ſubſequent meeting, which is to be held tomorrow."

16. It was ſtated in the body of the petition to be preſented to the hon. the houſe of commons by the merchants, &c. trading to North America, as read at the King's Arms on wedneſday laſt, that the balance due from America at preſent to this kingdom was little ſhort of 2,000,000l.

The lord mayor has at length eſtabliſhed the juſt forms of proceeding in all cauſes before the court of aldermen. Mr. Townſend moved, and was ſeconded by Mr. Oliver, that Mr. Hart ſhould be called in and ſworn in alderman of the Ward of Bridge within. Mr. Sawbridge moved an amendment, that the adverſe party, Mr. Neate, ſhould be firſt called and heard on that queſtion. Much altercation enſued. Sir Watkin Lewes obſerved, that on no other condition was it probable the lord mayor could, after all that had paſſed, be induced to put the queſtion, than both parties being heard. Mr. Harley ſaid, he might perhaps now be for hearing Mr. Neate, if it were only to get the lord mayor out of a ſcrape into which he had drawn himſelf. The lord mayor anſwered, that the right honourable gentleman would be more likely to draw him into twenty ſcrapes than to try to help him out of one; but he was in no ſcrape, nor ever could be in that buſineſs, for he would perſevere in the plain path of juſtice and equity. Mr. Townſend, Harley, Oliver, &c. gave up the point. Mr. Neate was at length called in and heard. Then the lord mayor put the queſtion, that Mr. Hart be called in and ſworn in Alderman of Bridge within, which was reſolved in the affirmative 12 againſt 8. The members who voted for the queſtion were Alſop, Harley, Oliver, Plumbe, Plomer, Kennett, Hopkins, Shakeſpeare, Eſdaile, Thomas, Townſend, and Rawlinſon. The aldermen who voted againſt the queſtion were, Croſby, Lewes, Sawbridge, Hayley, Newnham, Aſgill, and Kirkman.

24. The Gazette contains his majeſty's order in council, dated the 23d inſtant, ſignifying, that as his majeſty by his order in council of the 28th of October laſt, directed, that no horned cattle, nor any hides, ſkins, horns, hoofs, or other part of any horned cattle or beaſt, nor any hay, ſtraw, litter, fodder, or other things which have been employed about infected cattle, or the hides, or any other part of ſuch cattle, or have been in or near the places where any ſuch infection hath been, and are liable to retain the ſame, ſhould be imported from any ports or other places on the coaſt of France, within the diſtricts of Picardie, Normandie, Bretagne, Poictou, Guienne, and Gaſcoine, into Great Britain, or Ireland, or any of the dominions thereto belonging: And whereas information hath been received, that the diſtemper among the horned cattle in Gaſcoine hath ſpread itſelf into Languedoc, his majeſty doth therefore judge it proper to extend the aforementioned prohibition, and accordingly, by the advice of his privy council, doth hereby command, that no horned cattle, nor any hides, ſkins, horns, hoofs, or other part of any horned cattle or beaſt, nor any hay, ſtraw, litter, fodder, or other things which have been employed about infected cattle, or the hides or any other part of ſuch cattle, as have been in or near the places where any ſuch infection hath been, and are liable to retain the ſame, ſhall from henceforth be imported from any places on the coaſt of France within the diſtricts aforementioned, or from any places within the diſtricts of Languedoc and Provence, into Great Britain or Ireland, &c.

A M E R I C A.

The PETITION *of the* AMERICAN CONGRESS *to the* KING.

Philadelphia, Oct. 26, 1774.

To the KING's moſt Excellent MAJESTY.

Moſt Gracious Sovereign,

We your Majeſty's faithful ſubjects of the colonies of New Hampſhire, Maſſachuſett's Bay, Rhode Iſland and Providence plantations, Connecticut, New York, New Jerſey, Penſylvania, the counties of Newcaſtle, Kent, and Suſſex on Delaware, Maryland, Virginia, North Carolina, and South Carolina, in behalf of ourſelves, and the inhabitants of thoſe colonies, who have deputed us to repreſent them in general congreſs, by this our humble petition, beg leave to lay our grievances before the throne.

A ſtanding army has been kept in theſe colonies, ever ſince the concluſion of the late war, without the conſent of our aſſemblies; and this army, with a conſiderable naval armament, has been employed to enforce the collection of taxes.

The authority of the commander in chief, and, under him, of the brigadiers general, has in time of peace been rendered ſupreme in all the civil governments in America.

The commander in chief of all your Majeſty's forces in North America, has in time of peace been appointed governor of a colony. The charges of uſual offices have been greatly encreaſed, and new, expenſive, and oppreſſive offices have been multiplied.

The judges of admiralty and vice admiralty courts are empowered to receive their ſalaries and fees from the effects condemned by themſelves. The officers of the cuſtoms are empowered to break open and enter houſes without the authority of any civil magiſtrate, founded on legal information.

The judges of courts of common law have been more entirely dependent on one part of the legiſlature for their ſalaries, as well as for the duration of their commiſſions. Counſellors, holding their commiſſions during pleaſure, exerciſe legiſlative authority.

Humble and reaſonable petitions from the repreſentatives of the people have been fruitleſs

The

Figure 3.2 The 'Home News' section section reporting on latest events in America in the *Lady's Magazine* for January 1775. Private collection.

the other. The differences are usually arbitrary rather than instructive, though. It would be misleading to accord significance to the fact that the January 1792 *Lady's Magazine*'s foreign news column gave space to a notice from Rome that on 9 December 1791 'His holiness . . . was attacked by an apoplectic fit', while the *Town and Country* did not (22: 50). Nor does it illuminate the politics of either magazine to note that the *Town and Country*'s February 1792 domestic news column is identical to that in the *Lady's Magazine,* except for the latter's inclusion of additional items on an audacious attempted robbery from the Prince of Wales's drawing room; a meeting about the 'proprietary settlement of the island of Bulam' [sic]; the settlement of Sierra Leone by Nova Scotians; and the number of families participating in the abolitionist sugar boycott in Birmingham (107–8). The *Lady's Magazine* was no more interested in Catholicism than the *Town and Country,* and the *Town and Country* was just as interested in the royal family, the abolitionist cause or the economics and logistics of freed slave colonies as the *Lady's Magazine*. A more arresting conclusion – since it runs counter to prevailing assumptions – is that the *Lady's Magazine* is clearly interested in all of these political issues. In fact, often it is more determinedly interested in such matters than the *Town and Country*.

The sources of news content for the *Lady's Magazine* are hard to pin down, but its columns often duplicate material from newspapers. The periodical kept a keen eye on the press, and a significant percentage of its news items – like its essays, theatrical reviews, poems and opinion pieces – were reprinted from national and provincial titles of both Tory and Whig affiliation: the *Cheltenham Chronicle, Daily Advertiser, Gazetteer, London Gazette, Lloyd's Evening Post, Morning Chronicle, Observer, Oracle, St James's Chronicle* and *Salisbury and Winchester Journal,* to name just a few. This truncated list does not include the scores of items that the magazine reprinted from European newspapers and those published in India or the Americas. Various items from the *Lady's Magazine* were, in turn, reprinted in newspapers. For all their differences, magazines and newspapers from this period have much in common. As Jeremy Black reminds us, the difference between the two types of serial publication is 'more of size and frequency' rather than of 'content'.[19] The most obvious aspect of the shared currency of these print forms was the news paragraph. As Will Slauter documents, news paragraphs, which were imported from various print and manuscript sources, were portable forms of current affairs coverage that could 'easily be detached from one source and inserted into another'. Although occasionally editors and publishers of the source text complained about material from their publications being reprinted elsewhere without consent, the culture of copying such material was widespread, not least because newspaper and magazine editors relied on the circulation of these paragraphs to fill their own columns. Reprinting was a widely accepted mechanism to ensure the circulation of news throughout the nation and empire.[20] The widespread recirculation of material in provincial, metropolitan and colonial publications meant that news was 'the property of the public'. As a consequence, it became 'increasingly difficult to argue that accounts of current events could be owned'.[21]

The promiscuous circulation of news paragraphs means that it is frequently impossible to align news coverage in periodicals with a particular political or ideological position. The difficulty is compounded by the remediation of these items in news listings, sometimes compiled from multiple unidentifiable sources. In the *Lady's Magazine*, as in most contemporary magazines, news paragraphs were conventionally placed in date order, so their position within the news section offers no sense of perceived priority. A further problem in determining the significance of a news item in the *Lady's Magazine* is the brevity of the coverage. News paragraphs are usually written in stripped back prose, and sometimes ran to half a column or more, but they commonly consisted of one or two sentences. The paragraph on the aforementioned Birmingham sugar boycott is representative: '*Birmingham, Jan. 26*. We are informed that upwards of a thousand families in this town have left off the sugar, as slow but certain steps towards the emancipation of the negro-slave' (23 (February 1792): 102). The description is informative in one sense, but its succinctness poses deeper questions raised by thousands of other similar news items in the periodical: What is the publication's stance here? Does the magazine support abolition or is it documenting the boycott merely for the sake of public interest? Might the neutrality of the prose even mask antagonism to the abolitionist cause? The answer to such questions is far from straightforward and becomes clearer only when we read such reports alongside the wide range of other material the magazine published that spoke directly or indirectly to abolition and the slave trade over many decades.

Slavery and Abolition

The *Lady's Magazine* tracked developments in the abolitionist campaign from Lord Mansfield's judgement in the Somerset case – reported in the July 1772 issues of both Wheble's and Robinson's magazines – through the failures to secure parliamentary support for bills to abolish the slave trade, to the passing of the British Abolition Act in 1807. Its news columns reported on slave rebellions and insurrections, including the Revolution in Saint Domingue, and uprisings on West Indian plantations were even sometimes used as pre-Austenian plot devices to move characters to the periphery of some of the periodical's short fiction.[22] The magazine also documented continued opposition to slavery in America and British colonies post-1807. As with political matters generally, the editors regularly asserted that abolition had no place in the periodical outside the monthly news columns. In much the same manner as the 'Triumph of Virtue' was condemned, a contribution on 'THE *question* on the *Slave-Trade*' was rejected for being 'of too political a nature to accord with our plan' ('Correspondents', 23 (April 1792): n.p.). Yet the reality was that before and long after this rejection, the periodical published numerous contributions that addressed the very issues its editors claimed to keep at arm's length. Whether in the form of fictionalised fantasies of oriental slavery, contributions in which white authors co-opted metaphors of slavery to discuss women's rights, or in explicit discussions about the abolitionist cause, 'the question on the *Slave-Trade*' was a longstanding and vital concern of the *Lady's Magazine*.

The first time the word 'slave' appears in the periodical was in its inaugural issue. 'Happiness the Effect of Misfortune' (August 1770) is a moral tale about a man of feeling, who like the hero of Henry Mackenzie's later novel of the same name, is too good for the world. As melancholy as he is generous, Lord D—'s efforts to better the lives of others are met with so much ingratitude that he craves the 'asylum' of death. As he contemplates suicide, Lord D— 'compare[s] the condition of his soul to that of a slave, who is impatient of his chain, and composes himself at the dawn of day, which he hopes will finish his pains by shipwreck' (1: 13). This use of slavery as a metaphor for other forms of oppression and exploitation is pervasive in the magazine, and indicative of what Srividhya Swaminathan and Adam R. Beach describe as the 'multipl[icity]' that characterises 'invocations of slavery in eighteenth-century print culture'.[23] Such invocations sit alongside the many exotic and often eroticised accounts of slavery in the oriental tales that, as we saw in Chapter 2, were prevalent throughout the magazine's run. Some of their characters are figuratively or literally enslaved men, such as the unnamed, illegitimate son of the malicious merchant, Kebal, in the 'Cruel Father' (November 1770), a translation from Denis Dominique Cardonne's *Mélanges de Littérature Orientale* (1769). More frequently, however, enslaved characters in the magazine's oriental tales are young and exceptionally beautiful women, who triumph over their oppression and in so doing become focal points for the hopes and disappointments of the magazine's white women readers.

The 'young Circassian', Zeineb, in 'The Generous Prince', is paradigmatic (1 (September 1770): 58).[24] A model and vision of 'perfection' (58), Zeineb is raised in the harem and purchased as a bride for a man she loves, only to be abducted before her wedding by an agent of the Calif. After being captured and imprisoned in a second harem, Zeineb's intended attempts to rescue her and is himself captured in the process. The doomed lovers are freed eventually by the power of narrative. The Calif's sister is won over by Zeineb's beauty and the enslaved woman's self-evident moral and intellectual superiority. She listens to Zeineb's story and repeats it to the Calif. Affected by her plight and love for her intended, the Calif repents of his tyranny, frees the couple and 'impos[es] no other conditions ... but that of loving each other as long as they lived' (65). Zeineb's story is retold with only minor variations in the dozens of other oriental captivity narratives the *Lady's Magazine* published over the next few decades. While these tales have different plots, the depictions of physically and morally exemplary enslaved women at their centre are almost indistinguishable. The women's interchangeability and their common trajectory of rising above oppression were part of the pleasure that these fictions provided readers: the pleasure of reassuring conformity to a popular narrative formula that, like the less exotic sentimental novel, rewards the virtue of the distressed heroine. This interchangeability worked also to connect orientalised enslaved women with their subjugated female readers in the West, whose own endings, the magazine frequently reminded readers, were invariably much less romantic than those projected in the tales.

The force of the comparison builds through accretion (the cumulative depiction of female oppression built up over time) and juxtaposition (the tales are frequently placed alongside sanguine essays and articles on the condition of women). A reader momentarily seduced by Zeineb's rise from slavery to marriage and wealth quickly comes back down to earth as her eyes scan the essay that follows the tale. 'Miscellaneous Thoughts on Women: From the French' is a thoroughly depressing list of aphorisms that grimly reveals that the beauty and virtue Zeineb possesses offer no immunisation against marital unhappiness in the real world. The first nugget of advice proffered speaks volumes: 'IF you marry ... you will do *well*; if you do not marry, you will do *better*' (65). The remaining 'Thoughts' are even less encouraging. Women, like Zeineb, who possess no fortune stand little chance of marital harmony in eighteenth-century England, it turns out: 'Though some women without fortunes have made the marriage state happy', readers learn, it was only because 'their husband had fortune enough for both'. And if such women managed to secure such a match, any subsequent attempt to exert mastery over themselves or their husbands would prove illusory. 'Woman' is like 'a little animal', 'timorous, and dangerous'. She 'fights only to be conquered, and conquers when it ceases to defend itself'. In the battle of the sexes, women lose most at the moment of seeming victory: the point of marriage (65).

Although 'Miscellaneous Thoughts' stops short of directly comparing the situation of European women to those of Asian or African slaves implied by the juxtaposition with 'The Generous Prince', other articles made the connection without compunction. One of the most striking of these articles, 'On Matrimonial Obedience', appeared in the magazine for May 1789, the same year that saw the publication of Olaudah Equiano's *Interesting Narrative*. The essay is framed by a letter signed Collector, who claims that the piece s/he has submitted was previously published in an unspecified outlet but demands a wider readership than the 'confined circle' it initially reached. The essay proper, signed 'A Matrimonial Republican', is an extended reflection on the injustice of matrimonial power relations. The marital vow, the author claims, infantilises women. It is open to abuse and contrary to moral and natural law. To take such a vow, 'Matrimonial Republican' continues, is to become 'a slave to all intents and purposes' (237). Marriage, she laments, is 'a contract between a superior and an inferior' rather than a reciprocal 'union of interests'; it turns a woman into 'a slave', though none is born as such (238). In developing these arguments, 'Matrimonial Republican' joins many of the magazine's contributors in mobilising what Moira Ferguson dubs the 'problematic of slavery' to open up 'a much wider cultural dialogue' about women's and slave rights' that assume a 'white patriarchal class system as its enemy'.[25]

The analogy drawn between Western women's subjugation and colonial or harem-based slavery was a potent rhetorical weapon in both the feminist and abolitionist causes. It was also riven with complications, not least the grotesquely self-evident disparity between the situation of enslaved and white European women obscured by the comparison. The *Lady's Magazine* was not averse to underlining the privilege of its white women readers, however, especially when these women were complicit with the institution of slavery. This potentially uncomfortable subject was addressed in an exchange between J. B. – a 'West-India merchant' recently returned to England with his daughter, Caroline – and the Matron (March 1788). J. B. explains that he has allowed his daughter to travel to England with her black servant, Nelly, but is unable to tolerate the physical and verbal cruelty to which Caroline subjects her. He tells the Matron that he has advised his daughter 'that there will soon be an act passed to liberate the slaves' and that his daughter 'will undoubtedly suffer both here and hereafter for the barbarous treatment' of Nelly before soliciting advice from Mrs Grey on further action he might take (133). As per her custom, the Matron's reply is held over to the following month's issue, thus allowing readers to arbitrate on the matter before getting the benefit the of columnist's wisdom. When it does appear, she begins by gently berating the father for Caroline's upbringing in a county in which the 'spirit of tyrannising has prevailed too much'. Mercifully, she continues, the tide of critical opinion has turned and there is reason 'to hope ... that if our slave-trade is not totally abolished' it might be made 'less productive of scenes shocking to the pitying eye of the philanthropist, and not to be described by the man of feeling without the most painful sensations' (193). The Matron's position is clearly ameliorist rather than abolitionist, but her words mark an important moment in the *Lady's Magazine* in which one of its key authorities speaks out against the slave trade.[26]

As in her response to W— G—, however, the Matron concludes her letter by tempering her views and stepping back from her arguments against the institution of slavery to focus on the local problem of a white mistress and her black servant. The retrenchment is an uncomfortable move, albeit one familiar from much contemporary literature on the slave trade. She advises J. B. to remove Nelly, but seems primarily motivated by a desire to teach Caroline a lesson by forcing her to lose a good domestic, rather than by a particular wish to keep Nelly from harm. By appealing to the passion of 'self-love', the Matron hopes that Caroline will no longer 'trample' over her servant and see how she might benefit from Nelly's gratitude. The experience of the Matron's acquaintances, 'who have lived both in the eastern and western parts of the globe', is that when 'Negroes and Indians ... are treated like friends', they are 'most faithfully attached to those whom they serve' (193). The Matron's reliance, here, on the figure of 'the grateful slave' – a figure exploited by both abolitionists and those seeking to naturalise racial difference and oppression in the period – does not wholly blunt her argument against the slave trade, but qualifies it substantially.[27]

Other magazine contributions on the institution and practice of slavery were less equivocally outspoken. Abolitionist verse – and political verse in general – is understood to be largely absent from eighteenth-century periodicals, because, in the words of Jennifer Batt, it 'had the potential to alienate readers of opposing perspectives' and to 'bore those who were not interested in politics'.[28] For the first three decades of its run, the *Lady's Magazine* largely bears out Batt's assertion, although the periodical's reprinting of verse by abolitionists such as Hannah More, Amelia Opie, Helen Maria Williams and later Susanna Moodie (née

Strickland), partly bucks the trend. From 1800, as the abolition of the slave trade became a dawning reality, the picture changed dramatically. In 1800, the magazine printed 'The Slave', a 'Plaintive Ballad' by Henry Frances and dedicated to William Wilberforce in which the eponymous slave – a 'sad son of Africa, worn out with grief' – condemns the hypocrisy by which the British espouse 'liberty's cause' while 'bereav[ing] the POOR BLACK of its joys'. A bleak and despairing work that rehearses tropes familiar from the poetry of William Cowper, More and Ann Yearsley, the poem concludes with the slave's death.[29] Original contributor poems on the slave trade such as Frances's were increasingly accompanied in the magazine by reprintings from prominent abolitionist collections like James Montgomery's *The West Indies, and other poems, on the abolition of the slave trade* (1810), poems from which appeared in 1811.[30] Extracts from collections of Montgomery's verse continued to appear in the magazine until the 1830s, and in November 1827 the magazine published a laudatory biography of the poet, with accompanying portrait, which praised his 'attach[ment] to the glorious cause of freedom'.[31]

This was an attachment that united a small group of other mostly unidentified and pseudonymous contributors to the magazine, whose explicitly abolitionist prose found a home within its pages. Letters and essays on slavery in the periodical take many forms, but the vast majority are linked by their conviction in the inevitability of the demise of the slave trade. For instance, 'On Improvements', an essay by A. B. in the Supplement for 1789, proposes the 'use of electrical apparatus in the West Indies' as an extension of the Christian mission to send 'our fellow-sufferers a share of the good things conferred on us by Providence' (20: 683). A. B. is unidentified, although his approving reference to 'Dr. [Thomas] Coke' – an important figure in transatlantic Methodism – gives clues as to his religious affiliations. Like many opponents of the slave trade, A. B. is both an apologist for colonialism and an abolitionist and sees no contradiction between these positions. The missionary impulse behind his projected improvements is writ large: should they be introduced, he continues, 'we may view the revival of the Gospel in those islands . . . the grand object of forming colonies in foreign parts'. Simultaneously, he retains faith that the will of God will be enacted upon earth and that the 'African trade' stopped 'before long' (683–4).

In the coming years, a series of articles centred around the lives of freed slaves underscore A. B.'s position. In 1793, Eliza M. of Stafford submitted an excerpt from the proceedings of a *'Meeting of the Pennsylvanian Society for promoting the abolition of slavery, and the relief of free Negroes, unlawfully held in bondage'* to 'convince those who still wish to oppress and torture ... that, if [slaves] are not such rational and excellent creatures as themselves, they at least possess something that strongly resembles reason (24 (October 1793): 530). Eliza's seeming condescension turns quickly into pointed criticism through her excerpt's demonstration of the intellectual equality or, in many cases, superiority of the men whose cases were discussed at the meeting. The first example is that of twenty-six-year-old Christian doctor James Denham, who was born into slavery in New Orleans. The education of the bi-lingual Denham at the hands of a succession of white medical men is detailed at length in the article, as is his professional skill. Denham's example is followed by that of seventy-year-old Virginian Thomas Fuller, an illiterate mathematical 'genius'. The last words of Eliza's excerpt are those of Fuller himself, who responds to suggestions that it was 'a pity he had not an education equal to his genius', with the resignation that it was for the '"best"'. After all, '"many learned men be great fools"' (532).

In uncomfortably resting its case for abolition on the grounds of the exemplarity of individuals, Eliza's article rehearsed a strategy common in abolitionist fiction outside the magazine and sometimes within it, as in 'Lanzou and Yuna', a tale in the style of *Oroonoko* (1688), in which a 'noble' warrior and his beautiful and dignified lover are enslaved by a tyrannical conqueror who vows to send Lanzou away when he learns of his love for a woman whom he wants exclusively for himself. In an affray as he is forced onto a slave ship, Yuna accidentally kills Lanzou, who in death 'recovered his liberty' (28 (September 1797): 410). The unsigned narrative is powerfully told and could only make its case that there is no more obviously improper 'practice among enlightened and civilised nations ... than the buying and selling of rational creatures' (417) more effective if it did not insist so determinedly on the exceptionality of the 'noble savage[s]' at its centre (418).

Much more self-consciously affecting than any of these essays, anecdotes or short stories is the magazine's printing of a widely reprinted extract from the English translation of August von Kotzebue's brutal play *The Negro Slaves* in which an enslaved woman is found with her murdered child (Supp 1796).[32] In a dialogue between the benevolent William, the white brother of a plantation owner, and his black servant and friend, Truro, the woman explains how she was kidnapped as a child before being forced to work on a sugar plantation. The three miscarriages brought on by the overwork that she endured in the coming years were a relief to her, she continues, because it meant that her children were not born into slavery. But her fourth pregnancy resulted in a live birth. Just three days after her child came into the world, the exhausted mother was viciously beaten for being too weak from the delivery to '"press some sugar beneath some heavy metal cylinders"' (27 (Supp 1796): 585). After the assault, she could only produce only blood, rather than breastmilk, to succour her infant, and driven by 'maternal duty' and 'love' for her innocent child, she drove a nail through the infant's heart. Distraught over reliving through her conversation with William, she runs away and disappears from the narrative (585). Her harrowing story lingers, however, and grimly cheers Truro, who hopes that the revulsion sparked in William will motivate him to reverse the chain of horrible events set in motion by his tyrannical brother on the plantation. Kotzebue's original play was less unambiguously optimistic. Instead of one ending, the dramatist provided two. One fulfils Truro's hopes and sees William's emancipation of the slaves on his brother's plantation. In the other, the black woman commits suicide.

Circumventing Kotzebue's destabilising double-ending through the editing of the excerpt, the *Lady's Magazine* extract is single-mindedly effective: it presents its horrific subject matter viscerally and powerfully stages the affective response required from readers in the form of William's reactions. But the extract's wider significance in the periodical emerges only when considered as part of the broader and sustained dialogue that the *Lady's Magazine* staged around slavery over many decades. The various ways in which the language and subject of slavery appear in the magazine give further weight to Swaminathan and Beach's claim that in the eighteenth century and Romantic periods slavery is 'a trope that crosses genre' in the period, to invoke 'multiple conditions of exploitation', from the atrocities of the slave trade and plantation system to the subordination of women.[33] The news paragraphs, letters, short tales, essays, extracts and poems discussed in this section do not amount to a campaign against slavery. They are fewer in number than in some other magazines and many newspapers, and their politics are invariably complex and sometimes unpalatable. But there is certainly no dead silence about the slave trade in the *Lady's Magazine*, despite what its editors intimated. Indeed, contrary to editorial pronouncements, the magazine's contents suggest that its staff writers and contributors understood the publication to be an active part of what John R. Oldfield has described as the transatlantic 'information highway' of books, pamphlets and newspapers that made 'abolitionism work and gave it its purchase'.[34]

The Under-plots of the Grand Story: Inter/national Conflict on the Home Front

Alongside slavery and abolition, the *Lady's Magazine* devoted considerable coverage to major political controversies and international conflicts, such as the American, French Revolutionary and Napoleonic Wars, and it dwelt on moments of national crisis. Whether in descriptions of these events' month-by-month unfolding in the periodical's news columns, in its topical poems and fiction, or in its anecdotes and biographies of public figures, current affairs and their effects on readers' lives were recurrent matters of concern. Attempting to establish an editorial position on the more politically divisive of these news items is nonetheless challenging. In its coverage of the 1790s revolution debates, for example, the periodical affords space to commentators across political divides – including Edmund Burke, Thomas Paine and Mary Wollstonecraft – without giving obvious precedence to any one of these writers or to any one of their arguments.[35] My interest in the magazine's presentation of current affairs, here, is not in trying to resolve these multiple perspectives; rather, it lies in uncovering the periodical's more coherent and sustained political commitment to legitimising 'the under-plot of the grand story': that is, in how the events and controversies described in its news sections came into contact with the lives of civilians who witnessed or were otherwise affected by them (57 (August 1826): 443).[36] The magazine provided an outlet for many of the most famous of these witnesses, such as Helen Maria Williams, whose letters from France the magazine generously excerpted between 1792 and 1796, and Amelia Opie, whose original serial, 'Recollections of a Visit to Paris in 1802', appeared between July 1831 and February 1832.[37] It allocated considerably more space to the views and experiences of subscribers. The periodical printed hundreds of contributions in which readers reflected on matters including how the death of public figures was felt in the homes of private families and the effects of war on those left on the home front. These contributors' stories, essays and poems reveal the diverse and profound ways in which events on the world stage had an impact on the lives of domestic subjects who, in turn, critically remediated the magazine's official news coverage.

The fact that the magazine expected readers to register political events in their contributions, despite ceaseless editorial protestations of political uninterest, is multiply reinforced throughout the periodical's history. Sometimes editors were direct about the matter, such as when one issued a metaphorical wrist-slap to an oblivious Bessy Bluitt, who repeatedly requested a recipe for successfully melting butter without flour as the

Gordon Riots were causing chaos in the capital ('Correspondents', June 1780). The magazine devoted considerable column inches over several months to the Riots, just as it did to other moments of national emergency. Its coverage of the deaths of Nelson (1805) and of Princess Charlotte and her baby in childbirth (1817) was particularly extensive. Official accounts of these events, in the form of the news reports, anecdotes, memoirs, obituaries and engravings that circulated widely across periodicals and newspapers, were reprinted over many successive issues of the *Lady's Magazine*. It also commissioned exclusive items to mark these sombre moments of national mourning. The magazine's 1806 frontispiece figured Britannia weeping over Nelson's ashes, while the affecting 1818 frontispiece imagined 'The Apotheosis of Princess Charlotte & her Infant' as witnessed by her devastated husband, Prince Leopold. These emotionally charged engravings represent stark departures from the usual allegorical themes and iconography of the periodical's annual engravings. Ultimately, though, it was the public's, rather than the official, national response to these crises, that was privileged by the *Lady's Magazine*.

Readers' share in Britannia's and Leopold's grief is expressed in their contributions across multiple genres. 'Noontide Walks', a series of reflective excursions authored by long-term *Lady's Magazine* contributor James Murray Lacey meditates upon Nelson in more than one instalment.[38] The 'Walk', published in the 1805 Supplement issue – and immediately following an extract from Nelson's will – opens with extended 'thanksgiving' for the 'victory of Trafalgar' and its 'immortal hero' (36: 696). The next month's instalment gives a first-hand account of Nelson's funeral as observed by Lacey, in which he focuses not on the procession itself, but on the actions and words of the crowd who gathered with him to watch it (37 (January 1806): 26). Lacey was one of dozens of the magazine's contributors who submitted a personal commemoration of Nelson's death. Many of these fellow mourners were women, such as Lydia – whose own account of the funeral procession appeared alongside Lacey's – and Horatia Marina of Coleshill (Mary Dodwell).[39] The poem of regular contributor Dodwell on Nelson's heroism acknowledges the nation's gratitude and sadness for his sacrifice, but asks it to 'restrain' its 'grief' to support his successor Cuthbert Collingwood (36 (November 1805): 606). Collingwood would have neither the opportunity nor the charisma to rival Nelson in the public imagination, and the magazine continued to indulge readers' appetite for Nelsoniana in the form of prayers, anecdotes, descriptions of his public and private lives and other tributes for many years. By far the strangest of these is Eusebia's 'A Fragment of a Letter to an Inhabitant of the Planet Remote from the Earth, of a Superior Race of Beings', which describes Nelson's funeral procession as if through the eyes of an enlightened alien visitor who is baffled by the emotional restraint exhibited by mourners (40 (April 1809): 167).

No such detachment is present in subscribers' responses to Princess Charlotte's death. The poetry section of the November 1817 *Lady's Magazine* – Charlotte had died on the sixth – was almost entirely given over to expressions of national mourning. Some of these poems, like 'November' by C., attempted to raise a 'paralyz'd' nation's spirits (48: 517), while Henry Neele's 'Consolation' sought to allay the concerns of pregnant women who feared they might share the fate of the young royal (519). Other poems dwelt unapologetically on the tragic theme. They register the grief of the Prince Regent – 'thou hast much to bear' – and Leopold, to whom 'not the sweetest sounds / Of soft condolence ... can aught avail' (520) – as well as to every Briton to whom Charlotte is imagined to belong: the royal is described as 'our Princess' (520), 'Britain's Princess' (520), and 'darling of the nation!' (521). The sentiment is not entirely self-indulgent. Underlying each of these poems is an acute consciousness of the political ramifications of a domestic tragedy. Charlotte's death is the death of 'hope', the loss not only of a princess and a future heir to the throne, but of a 'nation' and an 'empire', the future of which suddenly seemed less certain (520).

The tragic deaths of Charlotte and her son were felt so keenly partly because of the stability they offered both to a monarchy beleaguered by ill health and marital scandal and to a nation that had been involved in international conflict or trying to quell domestic unrest since the *Lady's Magazine* began publication in the 1770s. The periodical registers this instability at every turn. The world it conjures is as fragmented, contingent and unstable as the miscellany form it adopted. As moral tale after moral tale, poem after poem and advice column after advice column writ large, the world of the *Lady's Magazine* is one in which fortunes, reputations and even lives are made or lost in a heartbeat.[40] The most decisive and tragic of these make-or-break scenes of life is the battlefield, which is as ominous a presence in the magazine's short fiction and poetry as it is in the records of losses that were printed in its news columns. Patriotic accounts, anecdotes and memoirs of British military and naval success – from prematurely optimistic accounts of Burgoyne's campaigns in America to the Battles of Salamanca and Waterloo – sit alongside elegiac reflections on the personal cost of national conflict as it affects readers and their communities.

The *Lady's Magazine* was particularly invested in exploring the local effects of war on individuals both on the battlefield and, more often, on the home front. Epitaphs for, elegies to and petitions from soldiers were common fare in its poetry section. A number of these poems reference particular individuals, such as Jane Porter's 'Lines on the death of lieutenant John Cochran', a solider in the 39th Regiment of Foot, who was killed during the attack on Guadeloupe in September 1794. Porter's poem, which was published in the February 1795 issue, laments the loss of her 'lovely' friend and seeks consolation for the living. The poem's anger is palpable. Knowing that Cochran 'fell, his country's weal to save' is insufficient to assuage the author's grief, so Porter looks to poetry for reparation for her senseless loss:

> THE sympathising sigh my sorrows seek
> The heart that weeps to hear another morn
> O'er a far distant friend's untimely urn. (96)

Ultimately, though, Porter finds words inadequate to the task for which she attempts to mobilise them. 'Cold is that heart which glow'd with valour's flame', she writes. The cold heart evoked here seems not only to refer to that of the deceased Cochran, but also to that of the poet herself. The warm pride once inspired in her by military heroism has been cooled by the appalling reality of her friend's sacrifice. As Porter knew at the time of submitting the poem to the magazine, within three months of Cochran's death, the battered British garrison had been forced to capitulate to the French and to leave Guadeloupe. His death had been entirely in vain.

Porter's poem, while not explicitly anti-war, is representative of a significant body of material in the magazine that emphasised war's human cost and questioned the price of patriotism. Much of this work – much but not all of it poetry – focused not on named figures like Cochran, but on generic soldier figures from whose viewpoint events are told. For these unknown soldiers, there is even less consolation in valour or death than for Porter. Death holds no answers, for instance, for the eponymous solider in G.'s 'The Dying Soldier. A Fragment' (July 1798), who expires unable to answer the question with which he begins:

> – AH me! –
> Why did I wander from my native vale
> And leave my cottage where Contentment smil'd?

Like so many of his compatriots in arms, the solider regrets the guilelessness of youth that led them to be duped into entering what John Webb, in 'The Wounded Soldier's Petition' (May 1806), referred to as 'the sanguinary trade' of war (37: 273).[41] Poem's like Porter's, G.'s and Webb's make clear that kind of heroism for which the Nelson was celebrated held no romance or posthumous glory for the ordinary men who were the loved ones of the magazine's readers.

Much of the magazine's fiction in the 1800s and 1810s elaborated on this theme, often meditating on the psychological effects of war. Take, for instance, Margaret B.'s 'The Young Officer. A Tale' (May–July 1810). Centred around a love triangle involving the titular officer, Anna (the woman he loves) and Ellen, who is tragically infatuated with him, the tale anatomises the physical and mental toll of war on its casualties on and off the battlefield. A 'remnant of his former self', Edward initially cannot be drawn on his experiences of fighting in the desert, but persistent questioning forces him to recount his troop's attempts to hide from the enemy in sand cots that are subsequently repurposed as graves for the slaughtered. Edward is transformed by these horrific experiences and his subsequent rehabilitation is difficult. Eventually he marries Anna, and Ellen dies of a broken heart. The story concludes not with an image of conjugal felicity, but with Edward silently weeping by the buried Ellen's grave (31 (July 1810): 301). Like the sand bunkers-cum-graves by which the former officer's disturbed mind is haunted, the churchyard symbolises both the promise of life and the inevitability of death. The pain and trauma of war, as so many of the magazine's tales verified, are not confined to the battlefield; they travel home.

The question of how to live with the realities of war and conflict was almost obsessively revisited by *Lady's Magazine* contributors, often in tales that focused not on soldiers but on their wives, sisters and daughters. The compensatory fictions these contributors penned frequently attempted to mitigate the horrors of war through implausibly serendipitous resolutions in which loved ones believed lost are brought back from the brink at the critical moment. The 'Reward of Filial Piety' (August 1801) is representative. The unsigned story follows the effects of the capture and presumed death of a British naval officer in the West Indies, whose wife and daughter become destitute (32: 595). The officer's daughter narrowly avoids sexual ruin at the hands of a 'youth of fortune' before the surprise arrival of the naval officer, who describes his imprisonment, eventual escape and the reward of significant prize money that will alleviate the family's financial troubles forever (595). The plot is hackneyed but represents a popular type of tale that from the mid-1780s is often found in the magazine's opening pages. Other examples include: T. Lacey's 'The Soldier's Return' (March 1797), in which a solider parted from his wife by the 'necessity of war' returns in time to prevent her rape; and 'The Distressed Mother' (July 1788), in which the wife of a soldier feared dead in the American Revolution finally returns home just in time to prevent his spouse's suicide.

A more disturbing variation on this theme can be found in 'The Victim of War' (Supp 1803) by regular contributor Catharine Bremen Yeames (1784–1817).[42] In this tale, too, an officer is brought back from the brink of captivity and near death, but there is no happy ending to console readers. The tale centres on Claudia Hadlier, who accompanies her naval father on a last voyage to France before his retirement, only for them to be kidnapped and imprisoned by French troops. Descriptions of the terror of Claudia's captivity and the sexual threats she endures at the hands of her male captors form the bulk of the tale, which concludes shortly after Claudia takes her own life when threatened with permanent separation from her father. Her devasted parent is subsequently freed by her horrified captors in a prisoner exchange so that he can live out his days with his grief in the 'land of blooming liberty' (34: 706). Unlike 'The Reward of Filial Piety', there is no narrative compensation to offset the horrors of war, which mark the female body with fatal violence in Yeames's bleak narrative. Civilian life for Claudia's devastated father, as for Edward in 'The Young Officer', is yet another form of unbearable internal conflict between gratitude for his own life and despair for his daughter's. It was a conflict that Yeames was living through at the time her tale was published. Like Claudia, the author was the oldest of seven siblings and a naval daughter. A brief prefatory note to the tale explains that it is 'inscribed to the author's father, brother, and kinsman; who unfortunately are detained as prisoners of war by the Batavian republic' (701). Although her brother was subsequently released, Catherine's father was to remain in captivity for another decade when, in the dire winter of January 1814, he died of fatigue as a prisoner of war ('Correspondents' (July 1814): n.p.). In life as in fiction, there was no happy ending for the Yeames family.

Within the pages of the *Lady's Magazine* the personal and political regularly collide. In 'The Victims of War', as in all the poems and tales discussed above, the news events consigned to the back pages of the *Lady's Magazine* meet readers' lives in multiple and unsettling ways. Although some of the periodical's content indulgently celebrated figures including Nelson, many other contributions worried away at these commemorations by depicting war as ungallant and heroism as a far cry from the posturing masculinity that dupes Webb's soldier into the military. Through their meditations on the irreparable physical and psychological damage to those on the front line of conflict and the loved ones left behind, such contributions interrogate whether war and nation are worth the sacrifices paid in their name. In the questioning, fictions such as 'The Victims of War' or 'The Young Officer' and poems by the likes of Porter and Webb reveal the inadequacy of the magazine's official news coverage and supplement and remediate that coverage by registering how the abstractions of news shaped the reality of readers' lives. By publishing these contributions, the *Lady's Magazine* made history's under-plots one of its central narratives.

Part 2: Advice and Education – An Introduction

The world that the *Lady's Magazine* presented, then, was a far cry from the apolitical vision of stability described by Poovey. We have already seen how the periodical provided a space for readers to register how global and domestic uncertainty affected them. In the final part of this chapter, I turn to the periodical's related claim that learning to read its eclectic contents effectively (that is: associatively, critically and pragmatically) would equip these same readers to better navigate these challenges in their daily lives. This was a claim that was visually reinforced in dozens of the magazine's annual frontispieces, which commonly imagined readers walking on a path compromised by insidious forces (Figure 3.3) or havering at a symbolic crossroads under the watchful gaze of the goddess Minerva (Figure 3.4). Enabling readers to choose the correct path or to make the appropriate turn was, as we saw in Chapter 2, the self-declared objective of the *Lady's Magazine*. It was with these objectives in mind that the magazine declared that it had 'no other end in view than to cherish *Female* Ingenuity and to conduce to *Female* Improvement' ('Address', 12 (January 1781): iv). The miscellany format and the discriminatory form of 'mental exercise' called upon to make sense of its eclectic contents were, the periodical claimed, uniquely adapted to this aim.

My account below builds on the case I have been making in this and the previous chapter to illuminate how the *Lady's* insistently projects magazine reading as a distinctive kind of labour that was a vital asset to women in the world beyond its pages. As Eve Tavor Bannet has demonstrated, 'miscellenarian genres' – manuals, jest books, miscellanies, newspapers, periodicals, romances – dominated the eighteenth-century market for print and promoted 'discontinuous' reading practices long marginalised in histories of reading and the book.[43] The *Lady's Magazine* actively modelled and invited similar practices. More importantly, the periodical forcefully asserted the epistemological value of these critical, adjudicatory habits of thinking for women readers in particular. I return to how the forms of 'mental exercise' the magazine encouraged were foundational to the publication's views on women's education in the final section of this chapter. First, I consider how the

Figure 3.3   Frontispiece to the *Lady's Magazine* for 1773. Bayerische Staatsbibliothek München, Per. 123 m-4. Urn:nbn:de:bvb:12-bsb10613825-6.

Modes, Media and Miscellaneity 107

Figure 3.4 Frontispiece to the *Lady's Magazine* for 1780. Bayerische Staatsbibliothek München, Per. 123 m-11. Urn:nbn:de:bvb:12-bsb10613832-5.

periodical's promotion of critical reading habits operates even in its most ostensibly prescriptive content: advice literature.

Authority and the Advice Column: Dr Cook and the Matron

Advice is in ready supply in the *Lady's Magazine*, and comes in many forms. Excerpts from well-known conduct books by the likes of Jacques du Bosc, James Fordyce, John Gregory, William Kenrick, Hannah More, Jean-Jacques Rousseau and George Savile (Marquis of Halifax) resurface throughout its run.[44] The magazine also published original conduct books written expressly for it, most notably Ann Thicknesse's 'Mrs. T— ss's Advice to her Daughter' (June 1775–October 1776), Thos and Mary D—n's 'Advice to the Fair Sex' (February–May 1778) and 'Domestic Lessons for the use of Female Readers (Supp 1786–March 1790). As we saw in this book's Introduction, the presence of these prescriptive and often conservative texts has dominated thinking about the gender politics of the *Lady's Magazine*. But in isolation, such extracts tell us little about a periodical that also gave generous page space to anti-conduct books, including Wollstonecraft's *Vindication of the Rights of Woman* (1792), or that placed conduct book excerpts such as Fordyce's *Sermons to Young Women* (1765) alongside more morally ambiguous material like the magazine's sympathetic account of the Duchess of Kingston's bigamy trial (7 (April 1776): 176–7). Moreover, the dominance of conduct books in the magazine has been exaggerated. Conduct book extracts constitute only a small percentage of the advice literature that the magazine contains, and the typically monologic mode of texts such as Fordyce's *Sermons* or Gregory's *A Father's Legacy to his Daughters* (1774) – in which an authority figure speaks to or corresponds with a silent advisee – is not how advice is generally transmitted in the *Lady's Magazine*.[45]

The magazine's advice modes and genres are as diverse as the subjects on which its commentators pronounce. One of the most important of these modes is the advice column, a genre that is prescriptive, but crucially also dialogic. This dialogic quality, as we will see, manifests itself in various ways. It exists in the literal conversation between advice seeker and advisor staged in the column itself and in the subsequent conversations that these exchanges spark between readers who reflect on the appropriateness of the published advice in relation to external evidence. Just as the magazine invited readers to flesh out and critique its news coverage in their contributions, it provided a forum in which readers were encouraged to check and rethink the pronouncements of advice givers in light of both other material in the magazine and their own lived experience.

The advice column was a prominent feature of the *Lady's Magazine* from its inception. After tentative beginnings with the 'Female Rambler' and 'The Lady's Counsellor' in the early 1770s, such columns steadily grew in number. The subjects they covered were varied but coalesced most often around: manners and moral conundrums; household management and childrearing; reading and intellectual pursuits; and spiritual matters. Some columns lasted only a few months, while others endured for over a decade. By the 1780s, several competed for readers' attention in a single issue of the magazine. In 1783, for instance, readers had the benefit of the collective wisdom of six: 'The Budget' by Thomas R—n (likely Thomas Robertson); 'The Essayist' by Castalio (William Mugliston); 'Female Reformer, by the petulant Bob Short Junior' (George Wright); Martha Grey's 'The Matron' (identity unknown); Dr William Turnbull's 'Lady's Physician'; and 'The Wanderer' by Plummericus (Thomas Harpley). The list is indicative: a small number of the periodical's advice columns were authored by named individuals, like Turnbull, whose credentials as advice givers rested on reputations established outside the magazine; the majority were led by pseudonymous personas, whose authority was established within periodical itself. Neither breed of columnist, however, was guaranteed the unwavering respect of their readers, who were given ample space within the magazine to mediate or refute its authorities' pronouncements.

Some of the most prominent of the magazine's named columnists were medical professionals. One of the most long-serving of these advisors was Dr John Cook (1704–77) of Leigh, Essex. Inspired to write for the magazine after seeing an advertisement for the periodical in the *Ipswich Journal* (1720–1902), Cook published his first essay on 'Convulsions in Children' in the September 1774 issue. Two months later, he was given a regular column entitled 'The Lady's Physician', which ran until November 1777. (Cook had died a few months earlier on 13 June, an event that the magazine marked in the July issue with a poem and 'tearful' editorial.[46]) The physician was no newcomer to publication when he started writing for the *Lady's Magazine*. A prefatory letter accompanying his first column notes that he had authored several books, as well as dozens of magazine essays (5 (September 1774): 464).[47] Now in his seventies, incapacitated by gout and confined to a 'wheeled chair', Cook was looking for ways to exercise his active mind and fill his days. He recognised in the *Lady's Magazine* an opportunity to make himself 'useful to the last' by imparting his medical expertise to a wide, predominantly female audience (464).[48]

As Roy Porter has demonstrated, periodicals had established themselves as one of the 'polyphonous voices of lay medicine' long before the *Lady's Magazine*'s launch.[49] Yet as Cook recognised, few had carried medical columns responsive to the specific concerns of women readers, and those concerns were legion. As he declared in the second 'Lady's Physician': 'MISERABLE women are by nature not only subject to almost all the diseases common with men, but to 200 others peculiar to their own sex besides, from their state of virginity, gestation, child-bed, births, giving suck, &c.' (6 (May 1775): 256). Cook's column principally addressed ailments commonly associated with women (such as thrush, menstrual pain and mastitis) and their children (croup, teething, newborn jaundice and so forth). His descriptions of these ailments and their root causes are sometimes eccentric and sporadically pathologise femininity. The pernicious effects of the health, habits and morality of wet-nurses on their charges are recurrent causes for complaint. Mothers of 'a weak, relaxed habit' are identified as a potential risk factor for children developing rickets in infancy (8 (November 1777): 580). Red-headed readers, meanwhile, are accorded the dubious privilege of being declared 'the best breeders of the nation' (6 (June 1775): 316). For the most part, however, Cook devoted himself to practical cures rather than moral judgements. His prescriptions – some of which are not for the faint-hearted – occasionally included efforts to persuade women to accept surgical intervention, as with severe cases of mastitis.[50] More often than surgery, though, Cook prescribed home-made curatives, the recipes for which he commonly adapted from medical textbooks. For instance, when recommending a poultice first devised by Dutch physician Herman Boerhaave (1668–1738) for blocked milk ducts and made from chamomile flowers, Venice soap, sea salt and boiled milk, Cook pays careful attention to what Boerhaave ignored: the process of making the cataplasm, including the precise quantities of, and methods for, combining ingredients; and potential mistakes in the course of preparation that compromise the effectiveness of the cure (6 (May 1775): 256–7).[51]

Cook's column sought to make medical wisdom accessible to a non-professional female audience who were so eager for affordable cures that they might otherwise seek quack remedies for relief.[52] His efforts were appreciated by the 'numerous correspondents among the sex' who frequently solicited advice for particular complaints (8 (July 1777): 338). Many of these requests were printed in the periodical along with Cook's replies, but crucially, it was readers, rather than Cook, who usually had the last word. In May 1775, for example, E. M. R. wrote to the magazine to request for a cure for a condition that Cook had not yet addressed: the removal of 'superfluous hair' (6 (November 1775): 599).

The physician responded the following month with several recipes to assist her, but this did not end the matter. The exchange generated a slew of further letters about the problem and its putative cures, all of which were written by, and directed to, other readers, and all of which bypassed Cook entirely. The exchange concludes in the December issue, when Cecilia writes to ask E. M. R. if she has attempted any of the cures Cook had suggested and to request that she report to fellow readers on their efficacy (6 (December 1775): 633). The correspondence has significance beyond its ostensible subject matter, indicating as it does that while the doctor's expertise was sought and appreciated, readers ultimately looked to the rival authority of subscribers to authenticate or dispute the physician's claims. In affording such discussions page space, the magazine validates the collective wisdom of readers as much as that of is editorial professionals.

Just as any reader could be a contributor of fiction or poetry to the magazine, any subscriber could, in theory, become one of its 'medical correspondents': an often-used phrase that tellingly elides the distinction between professional and lay knowledge that the magazine allowed. Dozens of 'Cards' – brief notices that requested or offered recipes for conditions such as pimples, cramp, dental problems, coughs, corns, headaches, nervous complaints and burns – appeared regularly after the termination of the 'Lady's Physician', despite the magazine commissioning further columns in the same line by the likes of Turnbull. Some readers, like E. H., tried to facilitate the mutual traffic in medical knowledge among readers by offering to exchange a trusted solution for one condition – such as warts – for another – such as removing freckles (14 (December 1783): 653).[53] Cards like E. H.'s, which requested and/or offered medical receipts, reveal readers' appetite for home-made cures by other readers trusted on the basis of mutual subscription. On medical as on other advisory matters, subscribers were encouraged to mind attentively, and to police actively, the potential gap between advice derived from theory and that based upon real-world application.

A similar dynamic to what we see in and around 'The Lady's Physician' operates in relation to the magazine's most enduring and prominent advice column, Mrs Grey's 'The Matron' (January 1774–April 1791).[54] Like 'The Lady's Physician', 'The Matron' is founded upon a dialogue between the columnist and her readers. Mrs Grey claimed that she received dozens and sometimes hundreds of items of reader correspondence every month, and most instalments of her column featured one or sometimes several letters to which she replied in the same or subsequent issues. Yet for all the respect the Matron commanded and the wealth of life-knowledge upon which she claimed to draw for correspondents' benefit, readers did not see her verdicts as definitive, and regularly submitted letters that weighed in on the conundrums presented to Mrs Grey by offering alternative perspectives to that of the agony aunt.[55] Those perspectives could be drawn from real-life experience or, as we will see, could be vicariously arrived at by reading the magazine's contents, especially the ubiquitous moral tales alongside which the Matron was placed, and the heroines of which frequently navigating similar moral dilemmas to those articulated by Mrs Grey's correspondents. The tensions between Mrs Grey's pronouncements and readers' viewpoints reveal the inadequacy of conduct book wisdom to accommodate the realities of readers' lives and the social, cultural and economic pressures that determine them.

Correspondents sought advice from the Matron on a bewildering array of ethical and logistical personal dilemmas. Of these problems, the navigation of marital discord dominated. The picture of marriage that the column paints is decidedly unappealing. For someone who claims to have enjoyed a contented married life prior to an admittedly much more contented widowhood, Mrs Grey is sanguine about the prospect of marital felicity for others. In response to Miss Singleton – a thirty-one-year-old spinster who writes to the Matron to express dismay at some women having had 'two husbands before another can get one' (13 (Supp 1783): 702) – Mrs Grey expresses a doubt about second attachments that exceeds Marianne Dashwood's, and an even more deep-seated reservation about whether any woman could expect contentment in married life. Miss Singleton, she advises, should console herself with the knowledge that a 'second marriage is frequently the foundation of more unhappiness than felicity', and that even among first matches there are 'more unhappy than happy ones' (14 (January 1783): 9). The sometimes comic, but often excruciating, insights that such letters provide into eighteenth-century married life build up an unflattering picture that proves the Matron's assertion that while matrimony is 'rationally ... desired by many females', many women would have a much 'fairer chance for felicity in the single state' (Supp 1777: 687).

Resigned to the necessity of marriage, yet unconvinced by the prospect of wedded bliss, Mrs Grey's advice in matters of marital conflict is characterised by an uneasy pragmatism that did not always sit well with readers or even with Mrs Grey herself. Her response to a livid Harriot Hurricane of St James's Street is characteristic (5: February 1774). Harriot's letter was occasioned by the revelation that her husband kept a mistress. She claims to know exactly what to do with the 'impudent creature' who had taken her husband from her – she wants to tear her eyes out – but seeks the Matron's advice on the trickier issue of how to deal with her husband (72). The response received is not one that Harriot wants. Mrs Grey advises Mrs Hurricane to 'neither see, hear, nor speak of any thing which may occasion the smallest disquiet', and to 'be particularly careful not to let Mr Hurricane discover any suspicions in her regard to constancy' (72). Mrs Grey counsels silence, not to exonerate the husband, but in recognition that it will not help Harriot to confront her spouse. 'Roving husbands are never domesticated by reproaches', she rues, so remaining 'quite silent about this business' is the surest way to ensure that the wronged Harriot can enjoy a modicum of the peace she deserves (72).

Though the Matron's reply suggests a rather conservative or even anti-feminist outlook, her advice reads differently to habitual readers of the magazine, the content and form of which presented a much more contingent and disputed view of the world than the Matron's missive suggests. As we saw in the W— G— exchange earlier in this chapter, the frequent time-lags in Mrs Grey's responses to correspondents allowed readers to adjudicate on problems before her official response was issued and readers also knew that her verdicts, when they came, might always be retrospectively advised. Indeed, the Matron openly invited correspondents to reflect on and dispute her counsel. She not only accepted that subscribers might 'entertain different sentiments from her's', but actively encouraged dissent. By 'throwing new light upon subjects under consideration', she announced, 'difference of opinion' generated 'beneficial consequences' for everyone, including seasoned advice givers such as herself (13: 191). Contributors proved receptive to her invitation to disagreement, and were quick to dispute the Matron's judgements, as did Miss Careless, who in the March 1782 issue responded angrily to Mrs Grey's reply to a man who had the misfortune to be loved by a woman for whom he had no affection. Miss Careless's unsparing criticism of the vanity of the male correspondent is addressed sympathetically by the Matron in the April issue.

Difference of opinion is not only expressed internally within the Matron column. It is evident also in the myriad juxtapositions of viewpoints articulated within her column and those in the content that flanks it. The most effective of these juxtapositions are those that emerge when the advice column is read alongside its fictional counterpart, the moral tale. The scores of young women who wrote to the Matron asking for her sanction to reject their parents' demands to enter into financially advantageous but loveless marriages were usually met by Mrs Grey with regretful, yet circumspect, reminders of the necessity of filial duty.[56] These same readers would, however, have found plenty of alternative answers to their queries in the periodical's fiction. 'The Rape of the

Marriage-Contract' (Wheble 3 (September 1772)) is one of many tales in the magazine in which a young woman escapes the threat of mercenary marriage by a fortuitous recovery of the family fortune or other life-changing event. In this particular case, the heroine manufactures her own solution to the predicament in which she finds herself via a daring act of rebellion when her avaricious mother coerces her into signing a marriage contract with an 'exceedingly rich' octogenarian (413–14).[57] Unappeased by her mother's assurances that her prospective husband 'could not live long' after the marriage ceremony, and distraught that in becoming his wife she will defraud a close female friend who is her future's husband's current heir, the heroine poses as a highwayman, holds up her suitor's carriage at gunpoint and destroys the only copy of the signed contract in existence (413). Precisely because it is a work of fiction, 'The Rape of the Marriage-Contract' can openly endorse behaviour that the magazine's official moral arbiters, like the Matron or Lady's Counsellor, cannot, and that endorsement is unequivocal. While the tale expresses some disbelief at the 'extraordinary' lengths to which the heroine went to secure her victory, it applauds her triumph and the necessity of her action: 'how nauseous to such a one is the husband of four-score years, and what will she not attempt, in order to get rid of him!' (415).[58]

The heroines of tales such as 'The Rape of the Marriage-Contract' enjoy lucky escapes as improbably serendipitous as that occasioned by the presumed-dead father in 'The Reward of Filial Piety' and its ilk. Many more heroines are less fortunate and suffer various kinds of trauma as they are forced to endure unhappy marriages to unsuitable or abusive spouses. One of the most disturbing of these fictions is 'The Assault' (April 1798), a tale purportedly based on a true story. 'The Assault' recounts the years of physical and mental abuse inflicted upon Clara Irwin by her husband, whom she eventually leaves for the sanctuary of her brother's house (29: 149). The husband locates Clara and orders a servant to abduct her during a snowstorm in a violent scene graphically depicted in an accompanying engraving (147). Mrs Irwin is returned to the marital home 'more dead than alive', whereupon she falls unconscious. The wife's physical decline, coupled with a chance discovery of 'some circumstances' that prove the 'absurdity' of her husband's jealousy, prompts her spouse's remorse (149). The story concludes with Mr Irwin declaring 'the most ardent vows of unchangeable affection' (149). At the end of so unremittingly shocking a tale, it is hard to believe that the author, let alone any of her readers, would have accepted the about-turn with which the story ends as we leave the couple with 'love and joy reign[ing] in full perfection in their hearts' (149).

At first glance, the triumphs over marital adversity in which these tales trade seem to offer consolation to those living through the nuptial strife that filled the 'Matron' column by offering fictional realisations of the kinds of outcomes sought by Mrs Grey's correspondents. Reading dozens of these tales over time – and in conversation with the advice column – has a different effect, though. Fantastic tales like 'The Rape of the Marriage-Contract' pointedly draw attention to the contrived nature of their happy endings and, in the process, advertise how remote the chances of resolution were for most readers. They model ways out of the dilemmas faced by some of the magazine's subscribers and, at the same time, close down these alternatives as realistic options. Fictions like 'The Assault', by contrast, are all too realistic in their laying bare of the psychological and physical costs paid by women who play by the rules of right conduct in the pursuit of the fantasy of marital contentment. Literary criticism has generally been unforgiving in its response to short tales like these. Robert D. Mayo overlooks them entirely in his account of eighteenth-century magazine fiction in favour of 'longer' and 'more interesting' serialised novels, while T. O. Beachcroft's study of the short story describes magazine tales as 'stories of an almost incredible degree of silliness'.[59] Both scholars find it hard to take these short fictions seriously because of their melodrama, their superficial didacticism, their brevity and, above all, their formulaic plots. Yet as with magazine's fictional depictions of the oriental enslaved women discussed earlier in this chapter, the force of repetition with difference exerted by these tales generates effects that reading any one of them alone does not. The very fact that these fictions are formulaic is precisely their point, allowing readers to reflect critically on the intractability of the problems they faced as they navigated courtship and marriage markets that failed to acknowledge – let alone respect – women's wishes, desires, health or even their lives.

Reading the tales in conversation with the advice column makes more explicit what the Matron much more subtly intimates in the decade and a half over which her column ran: that conduct book advice is poorly equipped to enable women to navigate the complex and frequently unpalatable realities of marriage and certainly ill-calculated to make women content with their lot. Within their day-to-day lives, the Harriot Hurricanes of the periodical's readership often had little room to manoeuvre, but within the magazine's pages a host of alternative routes opened up before them. Some of these alternative routes were practical – cures that could be applied or action that could be taken – while other routes were purely fictional and aspirational. Ultimately, neither avenue was privileged above the other. The best advice that the magazine extended to readers was not a particular prescription for health or happiness, but an insistence that women develop the intellectual resourcefulness to test the dictates of authority against the kind of real-world applications evidenced in other of the magazine's contents. When it comes to taking advice, readers of the *Lady's Magazine* were always encouraged to be fiercely critical.

Conversing about Education: Form as Method

The critical reflection that the *Lady's Magazine* encouraged in response to its advice literature – and to its news and current affairs coverage – was part of its broader commitment to women's education. As the editor asserted in the 1778 reader 'Address'– and some fourteen years before Wollstonecraft used the phrase more famously – the periodical aimed to generate a 'revolution in female manners' that would result in women 'excell[ing] each other' in intellectual pursuits and 'scientific studies' rather than the 'trifling' arts of femininity (9 (January 1778): 3). The magazine waged this self-declared revolution on two fronts: content and form. In terms of content, it printed copious extracts from rival educational theorists and commentators such as Maria and Richard Lovell Edgeworth, Elizabeth Hamilton, Catharine Macaulay, Hannah More, Jean-Jacques Rousseau, Sarah Trimmer and Mary Wollstonecraft. The periodical's reprinted and originally authored content additionally exposed readers to a wide range of what we would now recognise as academic disciplines.[60] Through such diverse coverage, the *Lady's Magazine* more than earned its credentials as 'a repository of female learning' (7 (January 1776): n.p.). Yet the periodical aspired less to be a purveyor or container than a facilitator of knowledge. The miscellany format and the active reading practices required to make sense of its heterogeneous content were inextricably yoked to these pedagogical aspirations.

While the magazine's commitment to female learning is unequivocal, the revolutionary language used to describe its educational agenda is somewhat exaggerated. Contributors and columnists were often scathingly critical of the all-too-common cultural elision of accomplishments and learning in the 'fashionable mode of education' adopted by a certain class of boarding school, for instance ('The Matron', 19 (October 1788): 532). And yet the magazine knew that it was reliant on subscriptions from these academies as well as content from their pupils, and frequently advertised its willingness to attend to 'hints' from 'governesses of the most celebrated boarding schools . . . with the greatest punctuality' ('Correspondents', 5 (January 1774): n.p.). These were not lone concessions. One of the most striking and consistent contradictions in the magazine's treatment of women's education is that despite containing hundreds of biographies, anecdotes and essays celebrating the achievements of learned women, many of these contributions were careful to present these same women as notable exceptions to the general rules that should govern female ambition. Even outspoken columnists such as the 'Friend to the Fair Sex' were prone to tempering arguments for women's intellectual equality by conceding that the likes of Émilie du Châtelet or Madame Dacier 'ought rather to be admired than imitated' *en masse* ('Of the Studies proper to the Sex', 4 (August 1773): 401). In the words of the openly misogynist 'The Trifler' (1788–9), few men would encourage their wives or daughters to prefer 'a sedulous pursuit of intricate points in Epictetus, to a prudent management of domestic affairs' ('On Female Authorship', 20 (July 1789): 297). The nod to Elizabeth Carter – a favourite of the magazine – is revealing. Carter can be celebrated despite her 'sedulous pursuit of intricate points in Epictetus' because, as Samuel Johnson famously remarked, she could make a pudding as well as she could translate ancient Greek. Carter, critically, did 'not esteem' herself 'above the ordinary duties of domestic life'.[61]

Yet for all these caveats, the magazine was no apologist for, or training guide in, domesticity. The 'arts of femininity' with which Kathryn Shevelow identifies the magazine were explicitly rejected by editors and contributors as the objectives of its readers' lives.[62] Although the periodical regularly published content tailored to the concerns of the domestic sphere – essays on household management and domestic life, as well as the song sheets, needlework patterns and fashion plates I discuss in Chapter 5 – the publication presented itself above all as a vehicle for 'disseminating instruction' ('Address', 13 (January 1792): iii). That instruction was drawn widely from various disciplines, including 'History, Geography, Antiquities, Criticism, and the whole circle of Polite Literature', the latter catch-all encompassing essays, prose fiction and belles-lettres, philosophy, anthropology, astronomy, natural history, botany and chemistry (iv). Printing extracts from already published works in these fields helped the magazine to fulfil its promise to disperse the 'discoveries and observations of the learned and ingenious ... which might otherwise be confined within a narrow circle' (iii). Original contributions on the same subjects made good on this promise in different, and more valuable, ways by promoting self-reflexive and critical dialogue upon the scope, limits and utility of female learning.

History was deemed a particularly important and suitable area of study for the magazine's readers. For some contributors, as Jacqueline

Pearson observes, history's utility was strictly demarcated along gendered lines. Whereas its study prepared boys for '"active" (i.e. public) life', it fitted girls and young women for 'domestic life' by making them more interesting companions and conversationalists.[63] Not all of the magazine's arguments about women's pursuit of history were so conservative. Philalethia, who extracted material for a two-part series on the Gunpowder Plot (November–December 1780), introduces her contribution with a letter in which she encourages the magazine's readers not to look to history to 'amuse a leisure moment' or to store 'their minds with matter for conversation' suitable for 'the circles of politeness', but to enable them to grasp the 'grand events' that shaped the formation of their 'own nation' (11 (November 1780): 571). Like more famous commentators on the subject, such as Anna Barbauld, Philalethia contends that women's reading of history and consequent ability to take the long view of contemporary political crises – her own contribution was prompted by the outbreak of the Gordon Riots – provided 'a means of fostering women's sense of belonging to a civic and Protestant public sphere'.[64] This sense of belonging, she cautioned, could not be achieved by simply taking historians at their word. Philalethia's source material is drawn from three rival accounts: one by Parliamentarian Arthur Wilson; another by Jacobite Thomas Carte; and a final account by republican, and 'favourite of the historic Muse', Catharine Macaulay, whose words are offered as a 'proper conclusion' to the two-part series.[65] Philalethia's strategy of seeming inclusion is one designed to draw attention to history's mediation by 'various writers' who view 'the same object in a different light' because of the time in which they lived, their politics and their gender (571). In so doing, she demonstrates that learning to read history effectively develops skills that exceed the bounds of the discipline. In requiring the same 'mental exercise' needed to read the magazine well – an ability to read across texts and between the lines – the study of history honed women readers' critical and reasoning skills and gave them real-world application.

Philosophy was presented as worthy of subject of subscribers' attention for similar reasons. 'Correspondence between a Gentleman and a Lady' (Supp 1785), for example, advocated female study of 'true philosophy' via the works of Descartes, Fontenelle, Locke, Gassendi and Newton in order to comprehend 'the history of mankind' and cast off the narrow 'prejudices' cultivated by women's insufficient educations (26 (Supp 1785): 685).[66] In order to advance this aim, the magazine made frequent allusion to the works of French, Scottish and English Enlightenment philosophers (especially Montesquieu and Voltaire, Hugh Blair, David Hume and Locke), and documented the scientific discoveries of Newton and his successors in news items, occasional lectures and extracts from the transactions of the Royal Society. The magazine's investments in these philosophical and scientific questions dovetailed in the publication's abiding interest in natural history. The most notable example of its commitment to the subject was 'The Moral Zoologist' (January 1800–November 1805), a long-running and beautifully illustrated serial written by royal tutor and educationalist Ann Murry (1750–1812). As Murry explained in the first instalment of the serial, 'a moral investigation of the regular gradations, instincts, and other relative traits, which eminently distinguish the various orders of animals' was 'useful knowledge' for women and men. It drew 'ideas to their proper uses – the contemplation of the great Author of Nature' and of man (31 (January 1800): 9–10). Like 'Correspondence between a Gentleman and a Lady', Murry's serial delivered its material via the familiar format: an epistolary conversation between two parties, in this case a teacher and her resistant, though intellectually curious, female pupil. The familiar format, as Ann Shteir has demonstrated, was instrumental in helping women 'exercise their intellectual voices', in the late eighteenth and nineteenth centuries especially in more abstract fields of intellectual enquiry.[67] Its dialogic structure is germane to the series' pedagogical aspirations. As in Philalethia's account of the Gunpowder Plot, the 'knowledge' the 'Moral Zoologist' seeks to impart is not to be taken passively on trust by readers, but is to be acquired through the intellectual labour of meditating upon different positions and arguments.

If such arguments were pursued in individual items of content, then they were more emphatically advanced by the miscellany format in which they appeared and which was central to the vision of female learning that the *Lady's Magazine* imagined. The periodical did not offer a coherent curriculum for its women readers, but this was not its objective. Ultimately, it was less interested in where a woman acquired her education and of what that education should consist than in the method of instruction to which it hoped her mind would become habituated. An early and provocative contribution to the magazine's ongoing dialogue about how women might best acquire knowledge appeared in an extract from poet and educationalist Samuel Whyte's *The Shamrock: or, Hibernian Cresses* (1772), entitled 'Thoughts on Education'.[68] The essay opens with a searing condemnation of the arrogation of 'a superiority of intellect' by the 'imperious Lords of the creation', before turning an impassioned protest against 'the neither just nor rational' because purely 'mechanical' nature of girls' and young women's education (Wheble 3 (October 1772): 470–1). Objecting to an educational system that teaches girls and young women to imbibe social graces and affect scant knowledge '[w]ithout idea, without sentiment', Whyte warns passionately against the kind of mental passivity so commonly yet erroneously associated with eighteenth-century readers of women's magazines (472).

Whyte's sentiment aligned with the ethos of the periodical in which his work was excerpted. The *Lady's Magazine* was committed to cultivating active reasoning and reflection, and understood its dialogic, conversational form as germane to this objective. If education is understood, as it is by the author of 'Letters from a Brother to his Sister at a Boarding School' (January, Supp 1788), as 'the communication of knowledge, or the cultivation of the understanding', then the magazine format was the ideal vehicle to deliver its ambition (19 (July 1788): 337).[69] Some contributions to the magazine communicated discrete items of information, whether lessons from history or biography, news of scientific discoveries or current events or pieces of medical or moral advice offered in response to individual circumstance. Other items of content capitalised on the magazine's periodicity in the form of interactive content that cultivated readers' understanding in the form of solicited responses to, for instance, the enigmas and rebuses the magazine printed for decades in its back pages, or in the French passages offered up for readers' translation in the 1770s and 1780s discussed in the previous chapter. More creatively, such engagement was cultivated through the publication of the needlework map patterns of Great Britain, Africa and the Americas that the magazine issued alongside essays on this history and flora and fauna of these regions in order to instil knowledge through material practice (Figure 3.5).[70]

Interactive genres represent only one example of the open invitation that the *Lady's Magazine* extended to readers to engage intellectually, morally and politically with its contents. Readers who submitted material to the magazine did so knowing, and in many cases expecting, that their contributions would elicit further responses from other readers. Editors, for their part, encouraged readers to enter into this kind of dialogue with its published material, especially material on the subject of women's education. Differences of opinion on this subject were more explicitly encouraged than on any other in the periodical because readers' ability to navigate these differences and arrive at their own conclusions provided incontrovertible proof both of women's intellectual competence and of the magazine's effectiveness as an improving print format. One example must stand for many. Debates about women's right to, and fitness for, intellectual pursuits bubbled away throughout the magazine's run, but they reached boiling point during the first half of 1780. The war of words begins in the February issue with a contribution by Sukey Foresight. Intending to settle the discussion once and for

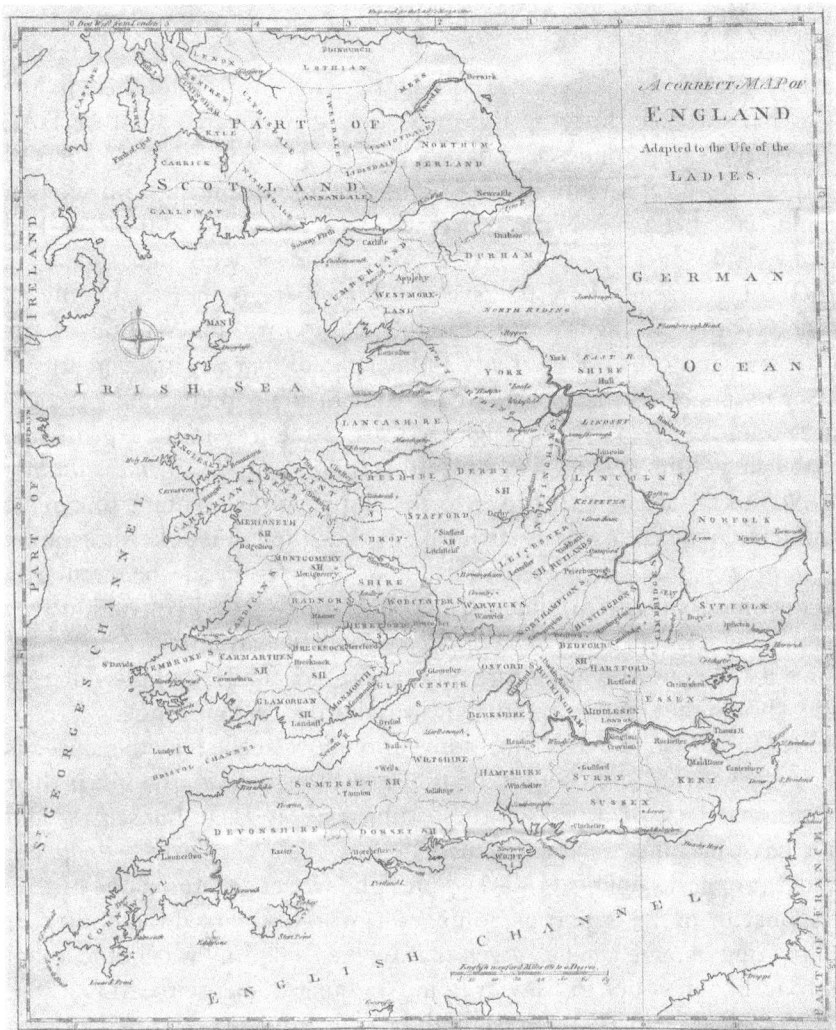

Figure 3.5 *A Correct Map of England Adapted to the Use of the Ladies*. Map sampler pattern from the *Lady's Magazine* for October 1776. Special Collections and Archives, University of Cardiff.

all, Foresight proposes that the magazine hosts a 'public discussion' on 'whether the all bountiful Creator has been more liberal to the male than the female part of the human race, in bestowing on the former a larger share of mental endowments' (11: 70). She forcefully argues that man's supposed intellectual superiority over women is an 'advantage ... acquired by study and application' rather than 'any natural or innate [sic] advantage', and invites other readers 'better calculated for such an undertaking, to stand forth in support of the mental endowments of our sex' (70–1).

Two lengthy responses to Foresight's letter were published in the March issue. The first, by the misleadingly monikered 'IMPARTIAL COMBATANT', condescendingly acknowledges women's '*quickness* of parts', before repeatedly driving home his conviction that 'no woman could have been a Newton' no matter how much education she had received (154). The second, by a correspondent who signs herself a 'FRIEND', defends Foresight's claim that there is 'not a shadow of a doubt' that women 'are as capable of oratory and writing as the male sex' and calls for the *Lady's Magazine* to 'bar . . . male creatures' from its pages so that women can exercise their intellectual prerogatives unmolested (125). Foresight returns to the fray in the April issue, mobilising John Locke's *Essay Concerning Human Understanding* (1690) in an attempt to prove to the Impartial Combatant that male and female minds are each 'as fertile as the other, and alike susceptible of *improvement and cultivation*'. In an attempt to break the circularity of her interlocutor's arguments, Foresight reinforces a conviction that female contributors had been vociferously articulating in the magazine since its inception: that culture and nature are fundamentally different and should not be confused.[71] It was hardly 'astonishing', she concluded, that women had not conventionally excelled in the pursuits of '*mathematics, philosophy*, or the science of *astronomy*' given their traditional lack of access to these subjects: 'Sir Isaac himself' would not have become 'a Newton' had he not been 'regularly trained up, under proper discipline' (180–1). Foresight's letter generated one further response from the Impartial Combatant, who questioned the 'utility' of cultivating 'female genius', given that women's destiny was not to roam abroad like men but to 'stay at home' in quiet domesticity (May 1780: 235; original emphasis). Foresight did not dignify the essay with a reply, perhaps because she, and presumably many of the magazine's readers, recognised that in resorting to questioning the usefulness of education for women who might not have opportunities to apply their acquired knowledge, the Impartial Combatant had implicitly ceded the original point of women's intellectual capability (May 1780: 235). Her work and the magazine's had been done.

The Foresight/Impartial Combatant's verbal parrying – one of dozens of such skirmishes about women's education in the magazine – has its formal counterpoint in the multiple juxtapositions of genres, media and viewpoints upon which this chapter has focused. In the *Lady's Magazine*, individual items of content, the juxtapositions and remediations produced by the miscellany format, coupled with the periodical's extension of a right of reply to any item of content it printed, were tailored to generate critical reflection. The periodical's contents are not closed, but associative and open-ended. Knowledge is divined not by reading discrete essays, letters, advice columns or tales but via the work of interactive and discontinuous reading demanded by the miscellany format. The magazine, in other words, did not present itself as a monologic instructive guide, but as a vehicle for learning. In its own words, it business was not to teach, but rather to 'habituate the [reader's] mind to *think on paper*', a process that combined critical arbitration, adjudication and the kinds of associative linking necessary to draw conclusions about the magazine's heterogeneous coverage of the wide variety of subjects and debates it presented to readers ('Advertisement', 7 (January 1776): n.p.). Able to mediate upon different viewpoints and ways of knowing allowed readers to cultivate an 'independency of intellect' that could provide aid to navigate the difficult and often unsatisfactory world beyond the magazine's pages (22 (Supp 1781): 710). The conversational, interactive and re/remediated miscellany form and the particular 'Exercise' it presents to readers' 'Ingenuity' were foundational to the aspirations of the *Lady's Magazine* ('Address', 17 (January 1786): 4). The lack of a coherent curriculum, like the absence of a stable or self-evident political position, was not the periodical's failing but its guiding rationale.

Chapter 4

Authors, Readers, Writing Cultures

If any praise, if any encouragement be due, it must concenter only in our Female Correspondents. They have abundantly convinced the world that no *Salique* law can be introduced in the *Republic of Letters* . . . We are therefore to express our gratitude to the Sex, not only for their patronage, but likewise for their literary productions . . . [The *Lady's Magazine*] is supplied entirely by *Female Pens*, and has no other end in view, than to cherish *Female* ingenuity, and to conduce to *Female* improvement.
'Address to the Public', *Lady's Magazine* 12 (1781)

Were novel writing confined to women of education and genius, holding an independent rank in life, there is no doubt but their works would obtain due celebrity, the morals of the younger branches of the community be less in danger, and the occupation itself be held up as respectable. But unhappily, it is now far otherwise. . . . [T]he rage for scribbling knows no bounds . . .
'The Matron's Society', *Lady's Magazine* 46 (August 1815): 354

Who read the *Lady's Magazine*? This is a difficult question to answer. One of several reasons why the Charlotte Brontë letter with which this book opened is so important is its exceptionality: a rare, first-hand account of an individual's experience of owning and reading the periodical. Brontë's letter is not a wholly unique document, however. The correspondence and accounts of George Washington indicate that in 1772 at least one issue or volume of the magazine – whether Wheble's or Robinson's is unclear – was dispatched to Mount Vernon in a trunk of gifts including a prayer book, thread, pins, laces and silk stockings for his stepdaughter, Patsy.[1] Evidence of a less renowned readership for the magazine has been uncovered by Jan Fergus. Her analysis of the records of 1770s Midlands booksellers illuminates the vibrancy of the periodical's provincial sales not just among women, but also among men: labourers, schoolmasters and curates whose lower to lower-middling status may well have 'afforded . . . some sense of identification with women'.[2] Four decades later and a few counties to the north, Lancashirebased governess and diarist Ellen Weeton confirmed her readership of the magazine by corresponding with a friend about needing 'patterns for fancy work' that she kept bundled up with copies of the magazine and items of clothing in a drawer at home.³

Tantalising though these glimpses of the magazine's mixed-sex, socially diverse and transatlantic readerships are, they generate only anecdotal impressions from which it is hazardous to draw broad conclusions. Additional information about the magazine's readers must, therefore, be intuited from its own pages. As we saw in the previous chapter, the magazine's content and form give a clear sense of the intellectual expectations it harboured for readers. The fact that the periodical survived for so long suggests strongly that it found at least some who lived up to these ideals, even if concluding as much does not get us much closer to pinpointing the identities or demographic profiles of subscribers. We might feel we get nearer to establishing the magazine's audience by scouring its 'Correspondents' pages, many of which engage directly with subscribers' praise, criticism or queries. Yet few of the correspondents cited in the columns are named or identifiable, and some are likely to have been editorially manufactured. The best way, then, to determine who read the *Lady's Magazine* is to pose what for other publications might be an entirely different question: Who wrote the *Lady's Magazine*?

When the magazine addressed its 'Public', it commonly used phrases such as 'Female Correspondents' or 'Fair Patronesses', expressions that conflate author and reader in a single figure. (The fact that many of the magazine's patrons were men was not reflected in its vocabulary.) An individual could favour the magazine by purchasing and reading it, or she could patronise it by using her 'ingenuity' to pen original content for it. Ideally, she would exercise both forms of 'patronage'. Authors were not always readers, though. Particularly after 1820, when the periodical began consistently to pay for copy, there is little reason to assume that its contributors were also subscribers. Mary Russell Mitford, to whom I return below, was a voracious reader of all kinds of literature including various monthly and quarterly periodicals and magazines. She does not, however, seem to have taken the *Lady's* even occasionally before she was persuaded by her friend, advisor and fellow contributor, Thomas Noon Talfourd, to submit prose sketches to it in late 1822.⁴ Even before the payment for copy that Mitford enjoyed became routine, there was no guarantee that contributors were the loyal 'friends' of the magazine that their valedictory sign-offs implied. Periodical editors had been fabricating readers, massaging circulation figures and passing off staff as contributor copy since the medium's inception. There is no reason to assume that the *Lady's Magazine* operated any differently. Identifying whether the periodical's authors are genuine contributors – and therefore likely readers – or paid writers masquerading as reader-contributors is often impossible. The problem is further complicated by the magazine's culture of anonymity and pseudonymity, a culture that masks the identities of readers, contributors, staff writers and editors alike.

Despite these challenges, it is nonetheless possible to piece together various kinds of internal and external evidence to establish key information about, and sometimes substantial biographies for, many dozens of the magazine's contributors. Reconstructing the writing lives that are the focus of this chapter's second half builds the most comprehensive picture possible of the magazine's readership, its day-to-day operation and its appeal. As we will see, there is no single typical profile for *Lady's Magazine* contributors, and the opportunities the publication afforded authors evolved over time. Some contributors submitted only one-off or occasional pieces to the periodical. Others sent in material regularly for months, years or decades. Some of its authors were aspiring literary professionals and, with varying success, used the magazine to launch careers or to revitalise flagging ones. Many seemingly had no end in view other than publication within the *Lady's Magazine* itself. A significant number submitted material to several periodicals simultaneously and most seemed never to have received or expected payment for their 'favours'. Others – especially after 1810 when the magazine started to pay some contributors – sought to secure a modest living or to supplement their income by writing for the magazine. Although many of these writers are little known or obscure today, their contributions sit in the magazine's pages alongside excerpts taken from works by the era's leading poets, novelists, travel writers and essayists, and they reached readerships far more extensive than most would have achieved by volume publication.

Collectively, these authors' stories reveal a culture of unRomantic authorship that literary history has largely misunderstood or ignored. This culture is unRomantic in at least two ways. It is unromantic, in part, because it is characterised by the realities of precarity, graft and, in many cases, lack of posthumous recognition. It is unRomantic also because it fails to align with the myth of Romantic authorship (that of the named solitary male composer of works of original genius) and the associated hierarchies of literary value and labour alongside which that myth developed and around which literary history is still largely understood.[5] As we will see, at precisely the moment that literature and the author were being professionalised in relation to these categories, the *Lady's Magazine* presented aspiring authors with an alternative mass-media outlet that was eagerly exploited by hundreds of writers.

Scrutinising the opportunities that the *Lady's Magazine* presented to writers, and by whom and on what terms these opportunities were seized, dispels several longstanding and erroneous assumptions about the periodical. As Brontë hinted, such an exercise also forces us to interrogate assumptions about authorship, gender and genre that have underpinned and distorted women's literary history by obscuring the rich contributions that hundreds of named and pseudonymous, paid and unpaid translators, poets, essayists and novelists made to it.

Amateurs, Professionals and Payment

Before examining the magazine's writers in detail, it is important to address the single greatest reason why they have not been taken seriously in the past: their presumed status as amateurs. The *Lady's Magazine* wore its debts to its volunteer correspondents proudly. The warmest expressions of editorial gratitude are found in the periodical's annual subscriber addresses in which the number and quality of contributions received are cited as proof both of the periodical's success in 'cherish[ing] *Female* ingenuity' and of women's ascendancy within the republic of letters. Some twentieth-century scholarship celebrates the periodical in similar terms, locating its success in its responsiveness to women's reading pleasure and authorial aspirations. Cynthia White's pioneering *Women's Magazines, 1693–1968* (1970) praised the *Lady's Magazine* as 'the first objective and professional effort to create a magazine acceptable to women', while Alison Adburgham, in *Women in Print* (1972), attributed the periodical's popularity to its reliance upon a form of 'reader participation' that bound subscribers together in a convivial, energetic print community.[6] Yet such views are in the minority. Even at the height of the magazine's success, a number of professional authors made the periodical's large community of poets, essayists and fiction writers a butt of their satire. Mary Charlton's novel *Rosella, or Modern Occurrences* (1799), for example, poked fun at the 'sublime effusions' of 'poor' Mrs Cressy's mother, who capitalises on her daughter's misfortunes by writing sonnets about them for the *Lady's Magazine*.[7] Similarly, Charlotte Smith's *The Young Philosopher* (1798) mocks the minor character Louy, who pens copious derivative riddles, eastern tales and poems 'under the name of Parnassia' for the periodical.[8]

Charlton's and Smith's efforts to distance their authorial practices from those of talentless periodical scribblers were noticed and regularly refuted by *Lady's Magazine*. This chapter's second epigraph is representative. Here, the 'Matron's Society' – a column in which fictional, unmarried women debate different topics each month – sets out to answer whether 'the cultivation of female talent [is] beneficial to society' (36 (August 1815): 352). The conclusion is only a qualified affirmative. The Society notes that an unfortunate by-product of attempting to cultivate women's writing talent is that such efforts might encourage those with no natural bent for composition to pick up their pens when their hands would be better employed in less intellectually demanding activities. Yet the Society does not disavow its sister periodicalists. The paltry missives produced by 'shameful' scribblers are evoked in order to dissociate their activities from the superior efforts of Society members and the magazine in which the fictional Society's conversations appeared. There was, the *Lady's Magazine* insistently maintained, a palpable distinction between its volunteer correspondents and amateur hacks.

Such distinctions have not universally convinced, however. For the majority of literary historians – legatees as we are of the exclusionary notions of professional authorship that consolidated within the Romantic period – the publication's 'amateur and unpaid', pseudonymous contributors are a source of 'embarrassment'.[9] In the words of Robert D. Mayo, the *Lady's Magazine* was the 'seat of [a] new amateurism' in the periodical marketplace, an amateurism signalled by the publication's unrivalled dependency upon 'gratuitous contributions' from readers.[10] Whether or not the *Lady's Magazine* was in fact more reliant on reader copy than its competitors is unclear, tied as any such verdict would have to be to non-existent data on the ratio of reprinted to original material in these magazines. Mayo, nevertheless, concludes that *Lady's Magazine* contributors were more 'unprofessional' than those who sent material to other periodicals, and that their collective amateurism was a kind of virus that 'infected' all who came into contact with the magazine, including its editors, 'who regularly mislaid manuscripts, miscopied titles and authors' names, misnumbered essay-series, printed instalments in the wrong order, wrote "To be Continued" at the end of stories already completed, and sometimes published the same story twice'.[11] Mistakes of this kind – usually apologised for retrospectively – were certainly made by the editors of the *Lady's Magazine*, as they were by many of their brethren, although not as consistently as Mayo's 'regularly' implies.

The accusations that Mayo levels against *Lady's Magazine* contributors' lack of professionalism are not entirely groundless. A long-running altercation between the magazine's editor and 'J. L—gg' of Market Lavington, Wiltshire, illustrates the point. Amateur ornithologist and naturalist John Legg (c. 1765–1802) was the author of the anonymously published *A Discourse on the Emigration of British Birds* (1780) and, like his sister Elizabeth, was a regular contributor to the periodical between the 1770s and 1780s.[12] Legg's contributions included essays on philosophical and religious subjects, nature writing, poetry, advice literature and a single-serial novel, 'The Treacherous Husband', seven instalments of which appeared sporadically between August 1779 and May 1782. By February 1780, the magazine's editor had grown weary of dealing with Legg, who, in his failure to send in monthly batches of the novel, had proved to be as unreliable as his eponymous anti-hero. The editor explained to readers awaiting the next part of the serial that the magazine had 'published every syllable of that tale that ever came into our hands' and used the 'Correspondents' column to 'call upon' Legg for 'the *continuation*, that our readers may not be disappointed' (11: 58). He then accused Legg of deliberately withholding future instalments that he suspected had already been drafted, by way of complaint that other 'pieces' by 'him [and] his friends' – possibly his sister – had not been printed in the magazine. Tactics like these, the editor warned, would not 'intimidate' him: 'The sex at large are our patronesses', he continued, and 'we have no occasion, no grounds for predilection, and while it is both our duty and our interest to oblige *all*, it would be highest absurdity to reserve our favours only for *one*' (58). The editor concluded with a final request that his 'angry friend' complete the serial to avoid the 'slander of not performing the obligation he has entered into with respect to the public' (58). 'The Treacherous Husband' eventually wound up in May 1782. A gap of thirteen months separates the serial's penultimate and final instalments, an irritation to readers but one that the editor claimed was the result of the author's ill health. Other original pieces by Legg did, however, appear in the magazine during the hiatus.

Legg's was not the only fractious relationship between a *Lady's Magazine* contributor and editor. Colchester-based novelist, poet, literary historian and bluestocking Clare Reeve (1729–1807) famously sparred with the magazine over several years. In November 1773, she wrote to its editor both to express the sense of 'honour' she felt after 'some of [its] correspondents' had praised her talents in a 'catalogue' of respected women of letters and to object to the magazine's inaccurate reprinting of some of her verse in the previous month's issue. Reeve asked the editor to correct the lines – a poetic 'paraphrase' of a French song – and sent a copy of the original text with the suggestion that it might be a useful 'exercise' for the magazine's monthly translation competition. Reeve concluded by declaring that she would be 'tempt[ed]' to become a 'correspondent' for the magazine if it did not already have 'too many' volunteers already. Whether Reeve expresses genuine admiration, here, or disdain for the magazine's army of contributors is unclear. Unsurprisingly, the editor embraced the former interpretation. An editorial note accompanying Reeve's letter assured her that 'however numerous [the magazine's] friends are, we shall endeavour to make room for her favours' (4: 568).

Reeve did not respond, and did not contribute to the magazine for five years. She was pulled back into its pages when it published an unauthorised extract of her gothic novel, *The Old English Baron* (1777). The extract was followed by a note from the magazine's 'compiler', who claimed to be an acquaintance of Reeve's and who asked the author to consider submitting to him any 'fugitive or periodical piece' she had to hand. Reeve responded with a lengthy letter containing various unspecified complaints, to which the June 1778 'Correspondents' column elliptically alluded. Mayo speculates that these grievances aired in Reeve's correspondence were likely triggered by the magazine's 'extraordinary public invitation' to a professional 'author of reputation' to 'write *gratis* for a very lucrative publishing enterprise'.[13] But if the author was so affronted, it is hard to make sense of the conciliatory offers she evidently made in the same letter. Reeve not only consented to the publication of other extracts from her novel, but also submitted in the same packet 'two ... letters' translated from Ignace Hugary de Lamarche-Courmont's *Lettres d'Aza* (1748), part of an ongoing translation project that she had temporarily 'laid aside' but to which she hoped to return ('Correspondents', 9 (June 1778): n.p.). The editor gratefully printed the letters, but no further material from Reeve followed despite editorial pleas. Perhaps, as Mayo surmises, Reeve submitted material from her translation expecting recompense that she never received. Or perhaps she was stung by the public airing of her epistolary dispute with the magazine's editor. Whatever the circumstances, the fact that Reeve seriously considered becoming a contributor to the magazine, despite its not always fair dealings with her, suggests that she did not see writing for the publication *per se* as being at odds with her professional reputation.[14]

The question of payment remains a sticking point, however. If amateur is code for unpaid, then for most of its history the majority of *Lady's Magazine* contributors were, indeed, amateurs. The same could also be said of the majority of magazine authors in this period. Successive *Lady's Magazine* editors were unambiguous about the issue of non-payment and frequently reminded potential contributors that they would not even pay potential authors postage for submissions. The weariness with which the editor complained in October 1783 of the 'enormous expence' incurred by the unnamed yet shamed author of '*Solutions to the Charms of Nature*' is typical ('Correspondents', 14: n.p.). Prior to 1810, payment for contributor copy seems to have been rarer even than payment for postage. A sole surviving ledger – which admittedly represents only a small percentage of the publications of the vast Robinson publishing empire – provides only a single example of a writer being paid for *Lady's Magazine* copy, and then only indirectly. On 18 February 1791, Joseph Trapp was paid twelve guineas for his translation 'Alexis, or the Cottage in the Woods' (serialised March 1791–July 1793). The fact that the work is described as a four-volume novel in the publisher's receipt suggests that its inclusion in the magazine was not Robinson's original intention, and explains why Trapp was paid for his work.[15]

In the early 1810s, and after the deaths of George Robinson senior (in 1801) and junior (in 1811), the culture of non-payment began to change, at least for some. The August 1811 'Correspondents' column noted that 'On the subject of "Payment," in answer to A.B.'s inquiry, we have to observe, that, although the contributions to Magazines are usually gratuitous, we shall feel no objection to allow him a moderate remuneration for his productions, provided that we approve them' (42: n.p.). Other hints of occasional payment surface in this decade. The 'Author's Portfolio' (June 1814–June 1816), for instance, is a delightfully metafictional serial about the hazards of periodical authorship. The serial's framing conceit is that its contents are transcriptions of manuscripts by an unnamed 'Author', whose death is reported in its first instalment. The narrative frame opens with the titular writer taking lodgings in the house of a Mrs Stubbs, who mistakenly understands the gentleman's repeated assertions that he carries significant sums of money in his portfolio as a sign that he is a man of means. Only following his premature death does she learn that her lodger is insolvent, and that the papers in his possession are not banknotes, but literary manuscripts from which he had hoped to secure an income. Succeeding where the deceased writer had failed, Stubbs sends these unpublished papers to 'Messsrs Robinson, for publication in the "*Lady's Magazine*"– not doubting that they would consent to pay a reasonable sum for the copyright'. These same Messrs Robinsons – at this point in the magazine's history, George Robinson the third and his brother, Samuel – pay for and publish the manuscripts, which allows Stubbs to cover the author's funeral expenses (35 (June 1814): 251).

'The Author's Portfolio' is almost certainly a fabrication. Yet it is unlikely that the magazine would signal the possibility that contributors might be paid for their work for the periodical if this never happened. Indeed, the fictional payment given to Stubbs cannot have been unique given what we know of the straitened financial circumstances faced by many real-life contributors at the time that 'The Author's Portfolio' was published. Work by novelist, poet, children's writer and biographer Mary Pilkington (1761–1825) first appeared in the *Lady's Magazine* in late 1809 (Figure 4.1).[16] Mary Hopkins, as she was born, was a surgeon's daughter who had lived her youth 'under the prospect of enjoying an Independent if not an Affluent Fortune'.[17] Her father's death dramatically altered those prospects. Defrauded of a paternal inheritance by her uncle, Mary and her mother – whose mental health deteriorated to such an extent that she was committed to Bethlem Hospital for a time – lived off an annuity from Mary's grandfather until she married John Pilkington in 1786. Her husband – also a surgeon – managed his affairs poorly and was forced to take up a post in the navy while Pilkington became a governess. After eight years, 'Ill-health' compelled her to resign from this 'comfortable Situation', and she was compelled to attempt 'to convert those Talents which had been cultivated for Amusement, into the mean's [sic] of Support'.[18] Her first project, *Miscellaneous Poems*, was published by Cadell and Davies in 1796, and was followed, in 1797, by three works for children published by Elizabeth Newbery. Pilkington's industry was as acute as her financial need, especially following her husband's death in 1798. The next decade saw her publish an impressive range and volume of educational works for children, both original and abridged, as well as her ambitious biographical work, *Memoirs of Female Characters* (1804), and three novels: *Parental Duplicity* (1797); *The Child of Hope* (1800); and *Crimes and Characters* (1805).[19] From 1809, when she published *Sinclair; or, the Mysterious Orphan* (1809), Pilkington began a working relationship with A. K. Newman at the Minerva Press that lasted until the publication of her novel *Celebrity* (1815).

Pilkington supplemented her income from volume publication with periodical writing. Her best-known work in this line was for one of the *Lady's Magazine*'s most tenacious rivals, and eventual partners, Vernor and Hood's *Lady's Monthly Museum* (1798–1828). Pilkington wrote numerous articles and essays under various signatures (M., P., M. P. and possibly M. S.) for the *Museum* in addition to undertaking unspecified editorial work for Vernor and Hood, who had been involved in the publication of some of her works for children and *The Child of Hope*. In early 1810, however, Pilkington confronted Vernor and Hood about the inadequacy of the payment she received for her editorial work. Challenging her publishers was not simply a matter of principle, but also of acute need following the double blow of the bankruptcy of one of her publishers, a Mr Hughes, and her cherished companion and supporter, Lady Gertrude Cromie, in 1808.[20]

Writing to Vernor on 22 January 1810, Pilkington documented that she earned 'two Guineas a month' for providing a 'certain <u>number of</u>

Authors, Readers, Writing Cultures 133

Figure 4.1 James Hopwood after George Slater, *Mary Pilkington* (1812).
National Portrait Gallery.

Pages' for the *Museum*, a publication that she referred to 'as the Child of my Adoption'. She had, however, been led to expect more, and in the same letter implored her publishers 'to raise the Salary to thirty Pounds, or Guineas' a year.[21] In the months prior to contacting Vernor, she had been looking to George Robinson junior and the *Lady's Magazine* to compensate for the shortfall. The October 1809 issue of the periodical published two pieces by Pilkington. The first – 'The Shipwreck' – is an extract from *The Ill-Fated Mariner* (1809), an adventure novel 'lately published' by George Robinson junior that was evidently placed in the magazine to whet readers' appetite and boost sales. The second was the two-part moral tale entitled 'The Resuscitated Mariner', published under the signature 'Mrs. Pilkington'. Their publication marked the beginning of a more than six-year relationship between Pilkington and the *Lady's Magazine* in which she was 'a constant contributor' and 'amusement' to readers.[22]

In November 1809, Pilkington's first original fiction for the magazine appeared in the form of 'Benedict: A True History', a first-person serial inspired by Hannah More's *Coelebs in Search of a Wife* (1809). A few months later, in February 1810, Pilkington submitted a second serial novel, 'Fleet Prison', to the periodical. Neither 'Benedict' nor 'Fleet Prison' was published under Pilkington's name, perhaps to conceal her work for the *Lady's Magazine* from Vernor and Hood, from whom she was simultaneously seeking better terms. Both serials were evidently written in batches, despite the editor's avowed preference for novels to be submitted as complete manuscripts. Presumably, he was happy to enter into this arrangement because the established, yet financially distressed, Pilkington was paid for her work and could ill afford to forgo income by failing to produce future instalments. Poor health compromised the arrangement, however, and a prolonged illness from the spring of 1810 until late 1811 meant that both serials were suspended while Pilkington recovered. The desperation of her situation led her to make the first of fifteen years' worth of applications to the benevolence of the Royal Literary Fund – a charity for impoverished writers and their dependents – in January 1810.

Once restored to health, Pilkington finished the serials. The hero of 'Benedict' winds his way through the trials resulting from a disputed inheritance and marries his first love, while 'Fleet Prison' similarly – if with forced rapidity – concludes with the hero resolving the economic and associated moral difficulties that arise from his father not leaving a will, a painful situation that the author had herself experienced some four decades earlier. Over the next three years, Pilkington moved away from serial fiction to produce occasional tales, moral essays and biographies for the periodical. Her most sustained contribution to the *Lady's Magazine* at this time was 'The Old Woman' (February 1812–May 1813). Its title nodded to the long-running and sometimes abrasive agony aunt column of the same name in the *Lady's Monthly Museum*. The *Lady's Magazine*'s 'Old Woman' featured occasional reader letters, but functioned primarily as an advice column on matters including marriage, childrearing, filial responsibility, female celibacy and the perniciousness of modern novels. The general tone is conservative, although the Old Woman is intolerant of abuses of power – especially the tyranny of husbands who do not deserve their wives' respect – and of cultural strictures against female learning or spinsterhood that sought to deny women value outside of marriage. Pilkington's contributions continue until at least 1815, during which time she also wrote tales and educational works for children published by John Harris (Newbery's successor at the Juvenile Library) and novels for the Minerva Press.[23] In the final decade of her life (the last six years of which she spent as a carer to her terminally ill friend Louisa West, the daughter of Cromie), Pilkington was able to write only a few 'Communications' presented to the proprietor of an unnamed 'Periodical Work', perhaps the *Lady's Magazine*.[24] Resourceful and indefatigable to the last, Pilkington was a determinedly professional writer, yet her 'Income', as she noted disappointedly, was 'confined, & Periodical'.[25] There is no definitive proof that Pilkington was paid for her work for the *Lady's Magazine*, but altruism and authorial vanity were luxuries she could not afford.

Norfolk-based contributor Elizabeth Yeames (1787–1837), who wrote numerous works of fiction, essays and occasional pieces in other genres for the magazine between 1803 and 1818, endured similar financial difficulties to Pilkington, although in other respects her case was quite different. There is no evidence that Yeames, whose sister Catherine Bremen was discussed in Chapter 3, was ever paid for her contributions. Yet when in 1814 Yeames was 'reduced to the painful necessity' of soliciting a public subscription for the relief of her family, which included her widowed mother, disabled brother and three other siblings, the magazine rallied in support. In an extraordinary 'Correspondents' notice, the editor explained that in 1803 – the year that Yeames started writing for the magazine – her father, the master of 'his Majesty's packet, Earl of Leicester', had been taken prisoner of war by Napoleon's troops. After more than a decade's incarceration, Peter Yeames died while being forcibly marched to Blois as the allied troops approached ('Correspondents', 45 (July 1814): n.p.). An appeal was launched for charitable donations for his family's support, and the Robinsons' Paternoster Row establishment was given as a location where 'Subscriptions' for the family's support could be received. What monies were raised is unknown, but Yeames temporarily ceased writing for the magazine at this time. Three months later she married, which seems to have alleviated some of her financial difficulties. Shortly afterwards she resumed writing for the magazine and published in it under her married, Mrs R. (Robert) Clabon, until 1818.[26]

Yeames's case is similar to that of her contemporary Sophia Troughton, later Sophia Hendry (c.1777–1856), another long-serving contributor forced to appeal for charity.[27] In 1813 Troughton wrote to well-known benefactress Lady Margaret Spencer requesting support to publish a volume of 'Tales', which had been 'honoured with applause' by readers of the *Lady's Magazine* since 1807. For many years honour and applause had been enough: 'praise' had been Troughton's sole motivation, 'nor', she wrote, 'did [she] expect or need pecuniary aid' from the magazine. Following her husband's death, however, Troughton's situation altered and, like Pilkington, she looked to support herself by the writing she had formerly undertaken recreationally.[28] Spencer declined Troughton's application and the planned volume was not published. Happily, though, Troughton's financial and personal situation improved owing to a second marriage to a Thomas Hendry. In 1817 she resumed writing for the *Lady's Magazine,* and continued to do so until the end of 1820 when the magazine launched its new series and its policy on reader-authored fiction changed. At her death in 1856, Hendry was in a position to leave modest sums of money and annuities, as well as gifts of her possessions, to a number of her relatives, but she had not always been so comfortable.[29] Like Yeames, we can be fairly certain that Troughton/Hendry was never paid by the magazine. More tellingly, perhaps, it seems not to have occurred to her to request payment even when her need was acute.

By 1820, however, payment was routinely expected by contributors, even if some lamented the terms offered. Writing in 1836, James Grant noted that while '[m]ost of the articles' in the *Lady's Magazine* were 'furnished gratuitously' 'a small rate of remuneration' was 'allowed' for others. Indeed, Grant claimed that Robinson's was 'the first among the *Lady's Magazine*s to pay for contributions', typically offering 'four guineas per sheet for poetry, and three guineas and a-half for prose' in the 1820s.[30] The fees seem not to have been as low as Grant surmised, but were modest when compared to various competitors. In April 1821, Mitford noted that the *London Magazine* was offering '15 guineas' a sheet, a sum that was 'well up' on most of its rivals.[31] Just eighteen months later in November 1822, Mitford accepted the 'seven Guineas per sheet' offered for the sketches that would become *Our Village* by the printer-turned-editor of the *Lady's Magazine*, Samuel Hamilton (1778–c.1850). To add insult to injury, Hamilton conceded the smallness of the sum when brokering the arrangement with Talfourd on Mitford's behalf.[32] Hamilton intimated that Mitford might enjoy greater remuneration for future copy if the magazine's sales improved, although subsequent correspondence between Mitford and Talfourd indicates that Hamilton was already paying some contributors rather more than he was her.[33] Yet Mitford reluctantly accepted the terms. Her sketches had already been rejected by the *London* and *New Monthly Magazines*, and she found the 'drudgery' of periodical writing was 'heaven' compared to the caprice- and ego-driven world of the theatre. The *Lady's Magazine* seemed like a safe bet to a woman author who wrote 'not [for] fame or praise' but for 'the power of assisting my dearest and kindest Father'.[34] When she started submitting work to the magazine under the signature M., she had every reason to believe that she was placing her work in 'something certain'.[35]

Mitford was soon disabused when, in 1823, Hamilton went bankrupt and absconded to France owing Mitford 'upwards of forty pounds'. She hoped that Thomas Davison, then printer of the magazine, would take on its editorship – 'for he is sure pay' – but it was Hamilton's brother-in-law, artist and engraver Charles Heath, who assumed the role.[36] Heath was either unable or unwilling to pay debts owed by Hamilton, but he did give authors the right to republish elsewhere material previously printed in the magazine. By the time that *Our Village* was published as a standalone volume in 1824, the working relationship between Mitford and the *Lady's Magazine* had irreparably soured.[37] Heath promised payment for future submissions at the reduced rate of 'six guineas a sheet . . . little enough God knows'.[38] Heath additionally demanded that Mitford concede the copyright to any future submissions and grant him permission to publish in volume form any previously printed sketches that had not already appeared in *Our Village* as well as any new ones she might write. Mitford could not agree. Her last original piece for the *Lady's Magazine*, 'Lucy Re-visited', appeared in the August 1824 issue.

None of these cases, with the possible exceptions of Pilkington's and Yeames's, do particular credit to the magazine. Yet the glimpses these examples provide into its financial dealings with authors give ample grounds to question the presumed synonymy of payment and professionalism that, from the mid-nineteenth century onwards, has so clouded perceptions of the *Lady's Magazine*. Unpaid writers for the periodical, such as Legg, could and sometimes did behave unprofessionally, although the 'Treacherous Husband' is an uncharacteristic altercation in an otherwise longstanding relationship with the publication. Others, including Troughton/Hendry and Yeames, wrote for the magazine with what might seem like inexplicable diligence given that they were apparently never paid for their efforts. We can only speculate why. But consider this: Yeames's work was widely appreciated by readers and her editors, judging by the magazine's 'Correspondents' columns. Her work reached thousands every month and, moreover, it travelled, popping up in reprints in North American periodicals such as the Savannah Georgia *Ladies Magazine*.[39] Amateur though we might brand her, more people in 1811 would likely have been reading and talking about the now obscure Yeames, who published in the magazine using her legal name, than the anonymous literary professional who authored *Sense and Sensibility* in a print run of 750 copies.

No one doubts that Jane Austen's acquaintance Mitford, like Pilkington before her, was a literary professional, even if she was not always treated with equally professional behaviour by the *Lady's Magazine*. These women were not professionals simply because they were paid for their periodical work anymore than Hendry and Yeames were amateurs because they were not. 'Amateur and unpaid' does not mean 'amateur because unpaid' although we have tended to assume as much. Ethical arguments about writers meriting financial compensation for their intellectual labour should not be ignored. But setting aside these important issues for a moment, it is not the case that authors who are unpaid for their work are inevitably poor writers, any more than that those who are paid are necessarily good. If this is true today, it was truer still in an eighteenth-century magazine publishing context in which non-payment for copy was standard and in which, though we frequently forget this, it was difficult in any publishing arena for authors to support themselves solely by writing, as the archives of the Royal Literary Fund multiply attest.

The problem with labelling the majority of contributors to the *Lady's Magazine* amateurs is not primarily the presumption that they were unpaid for their work. Bigger problems are the linked assumptions: first, that these authors' work must have been so poor that it did not deserve remuneration or the prestige of volume publication (several works in the *Lady's Magazine* were subsequently published in this way as I discuss below); and second, that writers themselves failed to take the work they submitted to the magazine seriously. When we have described writers of the past as professionals, we tend to mean more than that they were simply paid for their work. Professionalism was, as Paul Keen and Clifford Siskin have shown, a term that became increasingly tied to notions of Romantic authorship in the last decades of the eighteenth century; it signalled both intellectual labour as well as the possession of a particular kind of work ethic and a set of writerly aspirations.[40] Non-payment does not necessarily preclude the possession of these behaviours and hopes, yet is commonly assumed to do so when applied to writers for publications such as the *Lady's Magazine* as opposed to the professional journalists who wrote for the Reviews and literary magazines that thrived in the early nineteenth century and played such an instrumental role in defining the new literary professionalism. It is even more commonly assumed to preclude them when the unpaid writers in question are women, and their medium is a publication aimed at women readers. As Siskin notes, the professionalised model of Romantic authorship that emerged at the beginning of the nineteenth century was an implicitly gendered one. The very language of professionalism, like the traditional 'professions' themselves, was hostile to women writers. As Brontë's nostalgic recuperation of the *Lady's Magazine* in the age of *Blackwood's* intimated, and as the case studies below illustrate, in many instances, assumptions that writers for the periodical were amateurish in their approach to and ambitions for their writing fail to hold up to scrutiny. In many cases, their long, varied, if admittedly precarious careers force us to nuance traditional and triumphalist accounts of the rise of professional authorship, which as Margaret J. M. Ezell cautions, have often 'distracted us from considering the lived, material conditions of reading and writing', especially but not exclusively for women, in the long eighteenth century.[41]

Anonymity, Pseudonymity and the 'Doubtful' Gender

One of the most pervasive, yet misunderstood, aspects of this 'reading and writing' culture is the practice of anonymous or pseudonymous publication. 'The Age of Authors', to borrow Samuel Johnson's famous coinage, was not one in which named authorship was the default position either in the world of serial publications or beyond it. Michel Foucault's influential assertion that the 'author-function' – that is, the set of discourses that circulate around the author and bestow him with explanatory power – was born in the seventeenth or eighteenth century is at least partly misleading.[42] As Robert J. Griffin observes, 'anonymity' was 'a dominant form' and 'perhaps the norm' throughout these centuries.[43] Griffin's claim is supported by James Raven's statistical analysis of novels published between 1750 and 1800, during which decades a clear majority of new works of fiction were published without authors' legal names.[44] Even allowing for cases where an author's identity was an open secret or divined by association, these figures should prompt reassessment of the assumption that anonymity and pseudonymity were deviations from established practice.[45] And what was widespread in the world of novel publishing was ubiquitous in the realm of periodicals, where 'onymity' was rare and usually a matter of choice.[46]

Recent scholarship is ensuring that anonymity, and to a lesser extent pseudonymity, are better understood than they once were, but much work remains to be done, especially in relation to how gender inflected these practices.[47] When it comes to women writers, old habits of thinking around these issues die especially hard. Virginia Woolf famously saw in the examples of women writers who adopted male pseudonyms capitulation to the notion 'that publicity in women is detestable'.[48] Such perceptions remain doggedly persistent.[49] It is certainly true, as Jacqueline M. Labbe has argued, that 'the last twenty-five years of scholarship and textual recovery have overturned the convention that women wrote unambitiously, mostly anonymously, and concentrated on "feminine" concerns like the family and home'.[50] Yet the claim that feminist scholars have successfully challenged the problem of anonymity and the unambitious feminine writing with which we associate it is problematic, not least because in claiming as much we ironically consolidate the very links we are supposed to have overturned. The *Lady's Magazine* gives ample reasons to unyoke unsigned or pseudonymous female authorship from its associations with the deferential, domestic and unambitious, associations that – like non-payment – have consolidated perceptions that periodical contributors were amateurish, non-serious scribblers.

Various degrees and types of anonymity were practised by authors for the *Lady's Magazine* and for a host of mundane, practical and creative reasons. A significant number of contributors eschewed any signature or populated the space below their submissions with typographical features, such as a teasing long dash or chain of asterisks. 'Anonymous', which oddly functions in the magazine as a kind of pseudonym, was used by numerous contributors, and the Burneyesque 'Nobody' was also occasionally used. Uncovering the people behind these signature types is often impossible, but sometimes traces of an identity can be detected. Some writers left clues for friends or family to recognise them by, even if most readers of the magazine could not. This is particularly common in poetry directed at named individuals such the 'Verses to Miss E— S—, at B— in Surrey', authored by a 'Nobody' who was presumably a somebody to the titular 'Miss E— S—' if to no one else (Wheble 2 (November 1771): 233). Other contributors concede a tell-tale geographical location, such as the poet 'Anonymous' of N. Petherton, who published in the magazine between 1810 and 1812, and whose decision to disclose his place of residence in his dateline enabled readers to disambiguate his works from those penned by the many others who adopted the same signature.[51]

Some now recently identified contributors published under partially concealed versions of their legal name, such as the aforementioned J. L./J. L—g (John Legg). Others used their initials such as B. G. (Scottish writer Beatrice Grant), J. M. L. (poet James Murray Lacey) or M. (Mitford), who adopted her pseudonym partly to avoid friends and neighbours reading themselves into her fictional sketches of provincial life.[52] Thomas Newby, author of a host of strident opinion pieces, essays and poetry between 1805 and 1809, rang the changes by adopting the final letters of his first and last names (S. Y.) for his pseudonym, while Thomas Harpley went by 'Plummericus', a variant of his wife's maiden name, Plummer, for his column 'The Wanderer'.[53] George Crabbe published under multiple signatures that played with his legal name, including variants of his initials (G. C. and C.) as well as anagrams or near anagrams of his surname (Ebbarc, G. Ebarre, and G. Ebbaac). Other contributor pseudonyms eschew personal referents entirely, however, to follow established precedents. These included: patterned initials unlikely to relate to legal names (A. Z. or A. B. C, for instance); pastoral characters (such as Myrtilla, Strephon or Delia) and parodies (including Reuben Rustic or Philly Nettletop); citational pseudonyms that alluded to fictional heroines and heroes (Eloisa, Emily Montague or Tom Jones and so forth); pseudonyms that contain self-deprecating or satirical allusions to an author's age, gender, marital, occupational status or educational background (for example, An Old Man, A Spinster, the grocer Artichoke Pulse or Oxoniensis); and that most ubiquitous of pseudonyms, 'A Lady', the first signature ever to appear in the magazine under the title of 'A Sentimental Journey'. Such pseudonyms seem mostly to have concealed a single author's identity, but they sometimes masked collaborative authorship, as in the case of Asaphides, the signature used for poems co-authored by Thomas Chatterton and John Lockstone.

While the majority of these pseudonym types seem banal, writers often selected them with care and a strong sense of affiliation. Authors whose submissions were inadvertently published without their assumed signature were often quick to object, as one contributor did in May 1799 when s/he requested that 'W. M.' be 'affixed to the Epistle of Maria to Henry inserted last month' (Wheble 2 (November 1771): 233). Those who used generic signatures sometimes objected vociferously when others utilised the same one. Such 'delinquent' behaviour was condemned by '*Leonora*', for instance, who wrote to the magazine in January 1775 to complain that 'some lady has borrowed her signature, page 661, Vol. V, and has added the name of a street, by way of distinction' ('Correspondents', 6 (January 1775): 2). Meanwhile, some authors self-consciously adopted a different signature for work in different genres. The unidentified Constantia Maria, who wrote many moral essays on love and friendship as well as translations and historical anecdotes, used HISTORICUS for the historical, political and anthropological essays she penned, a strategy that was unmasked when she once accidentally switched between the two in a single series.[54]

Constantia Maria's identity is not known for sure, but there is no evidence that her gender had a material bearing on her decision to publish pseudonymously. As we have already seen, male contributors to the *Lady's Magazine* published 'under a borrowed name[s]' with similar enthusiasm and creativity.[55] Yet few would describe Crabbe or Chatterton, Legg or Lacey as demure, any more than they would view Daniel Defoe's or Samuel Richardson's authorial masquerades earlier in the century as signs of timorousness. Whether male contributors to the *Lady's Magazine* turned to anonymity or aliases as frequently as women contributors is hard to determine because of the textual gender-bending permitted by the publication's culture of pseudonymity. Editors themselves were often in the dark about the sex of their authors and were frequently forced to address correspondents as '*him, or her*', as the editor did when addressing Elfrida, translator of Alain-René Lesage's *Le Diable Boiteux* (1707) (7 (January 1776): 29). Readers were no better informed. Respondents to specific articles in the magazine often expressed doubt about whether they were addressing female or male contributors: some of the pieces published 'under the signatures of *ladies*' seemed so '*masculine*', and 'those under the signature of *gentlemen*' appeared 'so feminine' (3 (November 1772): 517). They might have assumed, as modern readers might similarly conclude, that anti-feminist essays on women's conduct bearing female signatures were the product of male pens. But it would be as foolish to presume that men have a monopoly on misogyny as it would be to divine sex on the basis of solidarity.[56] The Matron, as we saw in the previous chapter, offered nuanced reflections on the predicament and potential of women. But the question of whether 'Mrs. Grey was a woman' was a debating point that periodically resurfaced throughout the column's run and that remains unresolved to this day.[57]

Such questions prompted some confusion among readers, yet they also presented opportunities for writers. Indeed, several contributors characterised pseudonymity as a way of writing beyond the constraints of gender. The phrase 'the doubtful gender' first appears in the *Lady's Magazine* for December 1774 (5: 626). It appeared several more times before its adoption, in May 1781, by 'A Friend to Merit', author of 'A Comparative View of the Virtues and Abilities of Men and Women. Or a Modest Defence of the Female Sex'. The 'Friend' explicitly links their affiliation with the 'doubtful gender' to the subject of their essay: how assumptions about sexual difference shape culture. In a society in which 'the masculine is more worthy than the feminine, and the feminine only worthier than the neuter', stepping outside of authorial gender is the only way, the 'Friend' continues, to challenge the status quo and restore the 'dignity and deserts' of both sexes (12 (May 1781): 254–6).

The cases of the 'Friend', Constantia Maria, M., Anon. and their fellow correspondents to the *Lady's Magazine* force us to abandon the crutch – or straitjacket – of the author-function and point to the flexibility and diversity of pseudonymity as a writing practice. Undoubtedly, some writers for the magazine embraced anonymity or pseudonymity for the purposes of concealment. Readers who sought cures for the kind of intimate medical or personal problems discussed in the previous chapter had obvious reasons for obscuring their identity, as did Mary Pilkington when she determined to conceal her move to the *Lady's Magazine* from her employers on the *Lady's Monthly Museum*. But the blanket association of pseudonymity and anonymity with peculiarly female forms of modesty, deference, amateurism or authorial embarrassment breaks down under the weight of evidence gathered by paying close attention to the authors who carved out careers for themselves in and beyond the *Lady's Magazine*. Representative examples of these varied unnamed and named writers and the divergent writing lives they formed within and beyond the magazine are the subject of rest of this chapter.

The Case of R.

One of the most reliable and important early contributors to the *Lady's Magazine* went by the pseudonym R., or the variants R— and R. R. Her career writing for the periodical began with its inaugural issue with the sentimental tale 'Happiness the Effect of Misfortune' (Wheble 1: August 1770), discussed briefly in Chapter 3. This was followed in the next issue by 'The Generous Prince', a tale translated from Denis Dominique Cardonne's *Mêlanges de Littérature Orientale* (1769). R.'s last appearance in Wheble's magazine was as the author of 'Reflections on the Duty of a Sponsor for Infants' in the April 1771 issue, at which point the signature disappears until the 1771 Supplement issue of Robinson and Roberts's *Lady's Magazine*. Between August 1770 until the mid-1780s, when her contributions cease, R. produced dozens of prose works for the periodical, the majority translated moral tales set in geographically and historically distant locations. Despite their diverse settings – which include China, Spain and Lapland – most originate in French sources, although 'The Generous Friend' (June 1772) was said to be 'translated from the German' (Robinson 3: 249). That R. was a valued contributor to the magazine is evidenced by the editorial presentation of her work. Several of her tales feature prominently in individual issues, often succeeding the headline 'A Sentimental Journey', and many are accompanied by specially commissioned engravings, taken from the designs of 'great' or 'eminent' masters (Figure 4.2).

R. is never directly addressed by editors in the magazine's 'Correspondents' columns, and her contributions give few clues to her identity. We might therefore assume that she was directly employed by the magazine to produce regular copy, and that the R. signature served to connect pieces of a similar type by either a single or multiple staff writers. Yet 'R.' seems not have been not an employee of the periodical but a volunteer contributor who published notable works outside the magazine for many years and who was connected to various literary and publisher networks. While she remains a shadowy figure, and the attribution problems she presents may never be fully resolved, her example shines a light on a prominent type of *Lady's Magazine* contributor: a figure who is barely a footnote in literary history; who existed – literally in R.'s case – on the periphery of the book trade; and who was a hard-working, talented writer who was serious about their work both for the magazine and beyond it.

E. W. Pitcher first speculated that R. was the 'minor "lady of letters"', Miss R. Roberts, in 1980.[58] His article offers little biographical information about the author beyond the fact that she was the sister of the 'highmaster' of St Paul's School. He does, however, acknowledge her as the first English translator of Marmontel's *Contes Moraux* (published as *Select Moral Tales . . . by a lady* in Gloucester in 1763). She was also the author of: *Elements of the History of France* (1771), an abridged translation of Claude-François-Xavier Millot's work of the same name (1771); *Peruvian Letters* (1774), based on Françoise de Graffigny's *Lettres d'une péruvienne* (1747); and *The Triumph of Truth: or Memoirs of Mr. De la Villette* (1775), a translation of Jeanne-Marie Leprince de Beaumont's *Le Triomphe de la Vérité* (1748). Roberts was also the author of what Pitcher describes as various 'ephemeral works of her own invention': *Sermons Written by a Lady* (1770), an extract from which appeared in the *Lady's Magazine* in October 1770; the unperformed blank-verse tragedy *Malcolm* (1779); and a verse tale collection

Figure 4.2 Engraving after Hubert-François Gravelot for R—'s 'Don Carlos', from the *Lady's Magazine* for June 1775. Private collection.

entitled *Albert, Edward and Laura* (1783).⁵⁹ While Pitcher concludes that it is 'impossible to insist ... "R." is Miss Roberts', he mobilises compelling circumstantial evidence to suggest that she was 'one of the most prolific of contributors to the *Lady's Magazine*' in the 1770s and early 1780s.⁶⁰ Principal among this evidence are the facts that: the majority of pieces by R. are skilled translations from the French; R. is regularly identified in the magazine as a woman; and that R. also used the signature R. R., which implies that both her first and surname begin with the initial. To support Pitcher's case, we might add that R.'s work for the magazine includes several translations of tales from Marmontel beyond those that appeared in Roberts's *Select Moral Tales*, as if to form a continuation of that earlier project, and that R. stops writing for the magazine at around the same time that her final identified standalone published work, *Albert, Edward and Laura*, appeared.

Yet there is some evidence that pulls against Pitcher's attribution. First, it is unclear whether every item signed R./R—/R. R. is by the same author. While it seems safe to attribute the moral tales and translations published under these variants to the same writer, some items published under the R— signature, in particular, exhibit marked generic and thematic departures.⁶¹ These items include biographies of members of the royal family, anecdotes, essays on Tahitian burial practices, and extracts from already published works. Of course, these departures do not disprove R.'s authorship. *Lady's Magazine* contributors typically ranged across several genres. However, the misogynist tone of some of these contributions is hard to reconcile. These tonal differences are especially apparent in two series with which the R./R—signature is associated. In both 'On the Education of the Fair Sex' and 'The Friend to the Fair Sex', R./R— is explicitly identified as a man, and one who expresses a much more conservative worldview than that imagined by the R./R— of the tales and translations. Her works, by contrast, routinely exhibit sympathy for wives who take lovers outside of marriage because they have been forced to accept husbands they do not love or deserve.

Even after disambiguating the two Rs, two problems remain with identifying R. as 'R. Roberts'. One is the designation 'young lady' that appears in several of the tales and translations associated with the signature. According to the *ODNB*, 'Miss R. Roberts' was born in or around 1728.⁶² By no stretch of the eighteenth-century imagination could she have been called young in the 1770s or 1780s, although she may have strategically adopted the guise of youth. Another layer of confusion arises from the odd occasions when other signatures appear in a contribution linked to R., such as that of Miss Georgiana H—t, 'a young lady between 16 and 17', whose name appears alongside R.'s translation of Marmontel's 'The Sylph Husband' (December 1780–February 1781). Clearly, Georgiana H—t cannot be a second alias of R., who appeared in the magazine some ten years earlier (when Georgiana would have been six).[63] While these contraindications are puzzling, none refutes the theory that 'Miss R. Roberts' was R. Like 'Miss R. Roberts', the *Lady's Magazine*'s R. was a highly skilled translator; 'Miss R. Roberts' and R. were drawn to the same the types of stories and to the same French sources; moreover, R.'s industrious career writing for the magazine fills the long gaps in Miss Roberts's known publication history.

But who was 'Miss R. Roberts', an obscure writer whose entry in the *ODNB* lacks detail and even a Christian name? And what light can the identification shed on the kinds of contributor who were drawn to the *Lady's Magazine*? Many aspects of Roberts's life and career remain unknown, but various bibliographical and genealogical sources can be pieced together to reconstruct a biography. Radagunda (or Radegunda/Radiganda) Roberts was born in the 1720s, probably in Bristol. She was one of at least four siblings, including the poet and barrister William Roberts (1726–1807), the aforementioned Reverend Dr Richard Roberts of St Paul's School (c.1729–1823), and the younger Elizabeth Beata Roberts (d. 1823). She lived most of her early life in Gloucestershire, and it was while living there that Roberts authored *Select Moral Tales*, published in Gloucester by Robert Raikes. The translation, which was dedicated to bluestocking Elizabeth Montagu, began as 'an exercise in the French language', which she was 'induced' by the 'partiality of ... friends' to publish.[64] In 1769, when her brother became High Master of St Paul's, Roberts moved with him to London. A stone's throw from Paternoster Row and London's publishing centre, St Paul's School educated the children of various writers as well as the sons of booksellers including John Wilkie and Thomas Lowndes.[65]

Shortly after moving to London, Roberts published *Sermons* and, thereafter, the three-volume *Elements of the History of France*. This latter ambitious work opens with a 'Translator's Preface' that outlines Roberts's understanding of her authorial responsibilities, asserts the importance of 'history' to 'female education', and acknowledges a recent translation of Millot's *Elements of the History of England* (1771) by 'the ingenious' novelist, playwright and periodicalist 'Mrs. [Frances] Brooke'.[66] Roberts, in fact, was well – although not always cordially – acquainted with this ingenious woman via Brooke's sister, Sarah Moore, and their mutual friend Jane Collier.[67] Brooke's son, John Moore Brooke, was a St Paul's pupil, and Frances Brooke wrote about Radagunda and disparaged her rival translation efforts in her correspondence.[68] It would be another three years before Roberts published her most significant work, *Peruvian Letters*, a translation of Graffigny's bestseller for which Roberts produced an original continuation.[69] This was the first publication issued under the name 'R. Roberts' rather than 'by a Lady' or 'by the author of ...', a move that perhaps suggests new-found authorial confidence. It might also reflect Roberts's sense of the uniqueness of this literary endeavour. If the translator's role, as Roberts explained in the preface to *Elements*, was to 'convert [the feelings] of another', then this was a different project altogether: a 'novel kind of writing' in which the feelings of author and translator jostled for supremacy. Roberts's continuation alters Graffigny's work by making the 'Indian Princess', Zilia, a 'convert to Christianity by conviction' (68). It was an audacious move, as was Roberts's fulsome dedication of *Peruvian Letters* to her 'friend', John Hawkesworth, who had corrected the 'first sheets' of the work before he passed away in November 1773 (68). In the months leading up to Hawkesworth's death, his reputation had been famously damaged by his editorship of Cook's *Voyages* (1773). Roberts's unambiguous endorsement in her preface of so publicly maligned a figure was as pointed as it was bold.

Even after his death, Hawkesworth remained a significant figure in Roberts's life and career. The preface to *The Triumph of Truth*, for instance, notes that Roberts only undertook the project because 'this exalted Genius' had recommended it to her some years previously.[70] The closeness of the friends' relationship is confirmed by Roberts's will (proved June 1788), which opens with a plea that her 'friends [would] kindly indulge me in the last piece of human weakness' and allow her to be 'privately buried at Bromley in the same grave with Dr. Hawkesworth'.[71] Anticipating the objection of Hawkesworth's wife, Mary, 'who may chuse to lie on his right', Roberts requested to lie 'on his left'. The concession did nothing to appease Mrs Hawkesworth and Roberts was buried with her parents instead. Treasured possessions related to Hawkesworth appear in Roberts's will, including some china he had given her and which she bequeathed to her brother, Robert, and her copy of Hawkesworth's translation of François Fénelon's *The Adventures of Telemachus* (1768), which was left to her nephew, Alfred William Roberts. Other of the few named books in Roberts's will include her copy of Brooke's *Emily Montague* (1769), which was left to Alfred's sister, Mary, a good friend of Hannah More, whose *Sir Eldred of the Bower* had inspired Roberts's *Albert, Edward and Laura*.[72]

Whatever the nature of Roberts's relationship with Hawkesworth, it was clearly of great importance to her personally and professionally. When the two met is unknown, although a surviving letter reveals that they knew each other by New Year's Day of January 1759 and thus before the publication of both *Telemachus* and Hawkesworth's glowing, unsigned reviews of two of Roberts's works in the *Gentleman's Magazine*.[73] Hawkesworth had a significant impact on Roberts's career as a translator. We can only speculate how his career as a periodical founder, editor and contributor might also have influenced Roberts. It is certainly plausible that a man whose own literary career began with the submission of a poem to the *Gentleman's Magazine* in 1741 might have encouraged Roberts to submit work to the *Lady's Magazine*, a periodical that was published just yards from her home in St Paul's.

R./R—/R.R. is an easy figure to dismiss. The difficulties of attribution, coupled with the fact that the majority of her works are translations rather than original compositions, have licensed her marginalisation. Radagunda Roberts may not have pursued her literary career with the same obvious determination as Brooke, despite sharing the publishers James Dodsley and Thomas Cadell and inhabiting overlapping social and literary networks.[74] Yet Roberts was a professional and original author, and it is only right that the significance of her volume translations is now starting to be acknowledged in eighteenth-century scholarship, particularly translation studies.[75] Her prolific work for the *Lady's Magazine* deserves to be part of this emerging conversation. Writing for the periodical was no apprenticeship for Roberts, who had already published the impressive three-volume *Elements* before her first appearance in the magazine. Nonetheless, her work for it provided opportunities: to hone the translation skills that deployed to such great effect in *Peruvian Letters*; to develop her talent for storytelling; and to pave the way for a host of subsequent female translators published by the magazine.[76] As importantly, it enabled her to fulfil the ambition she articulated in the prefaces to her standalone works: to serve the cause of 'female education' and 'facilitat[e] the accomplishment of her sex' by bringing foreign language moral tales from leading French authors and periodicals, to a British audience.[77]

Living in Periodicals: Poetry as social media

If literary history has, until recently, failed to take translators like R— seriously, then the hundreds of the magazine's poets from this period have fared little better. Poetry is one of the Romantic magazine's most enduring and ubiquitous genres, and periodicals were one of the era's most important media for the mass dissemination of poetry by men, women and juvenile writers, both celebrated and little known. Yet the terms 'magazine poetry' and 'magazine poet' are often deployed as accusations rather than as descriptions. Magazine verse is frequently overlooked in periodicals and literary scholarship – its omission in the otherwise indispensable *Wellesley Index to Victorian Periodicals* is indicative – and where it has received critical attention, it has generally been dismissed as occasional, unashamedly populist or mawkishly sentimental.[78] This holds especially true for poetry in magazines that targeted female readerships. As Kathryn Ledbetter documents, until very recently the critical reputations of magazine poetry and of women's magazines have been inextricably and damagingly intertwined, so that the presumed 'inauthentic, non-serious status' of each is used to confirm that of the other.[79] Thanks to the work of Ledbetter and others, the critical tide of opinion on magazine poetry is turning, a development that invites us to reconsider the contributions and careers of individual writers. Here I focus on a single, representative poet who, for many years, submitted original verse to the *Lady's Magazine*, and to other periodicals besides. Charlotte Caroline Richardson (1795–1854) is no longer a household name. Her verse, like that of so many of her fellow contributors, was often occasional and almost always autobiographical. Yet like the Victorian magazine poetry that Ledbetter foregrounds, Richardson's work offers us 'a short-track to ideology': a 'window through which we may view important cultural notions, lifestyles, historical details, and perspectives of and about women'.[80] As importantly, her example reveals how the *Lady's Magazine* provided a space in which the professional and personal aspirations of authors could intersect and thrive.

Richardson, or C. C. R., as she often appeared to magazine readers, lived her life in periodicals. A poet, children's writer and (belatedly) novelist, Richardson's first poem in the *Lady's Magazine*, 'Lines by C. C. R.', appeared in August 1810 when she was just fifteen. Her place of residence, as documented in the poem's dateline, was Hinderwell, North Yorkshire. Richardson continued to write for the magazine until December 1818, when it published a 'Hymn on the Death of her Majesty', Queen Charlotte, the last of three poems on the royal family she penned for periodical.[81] Earlier that year, Richardson had self-published her second book of verse, the anti-war *Harvest, A Poem, in Two Parts; with Other Poems*.[82] Those 'other poems' included several that first appeared in the *Lady's Magazine* and others from the long-running annual the *Ladies' Diary* (1704–1841), then edited by *Harvest*'s dedicatee, mathematician Charles Hutton. A favourable review of *Harvest* appeared in the May 1818 *Lady's Magazine*. It proudly noted that many of the poems in Richardson's work had been originally published in its pages, and promised that future excerpts would be printed in subsequent issues. Later in her career, Richardson published *Ludolph, or, the Light of Nature. A Poem* (1823), and the novel, *The Soldier's Child, or Virtue Triumphant* (also 1823), published by George Robinson senior's nephew, John Robinson (dates unknown). Richardson continued to write poetry for serial publications such as *Pawsey's Ladies' Fashionable Repository* (1809–76) for a further two decades.

As for so many of its poets, the *Lady's Magazine* did not command Richardson's absolute loyalty. Her relationship with the *Ladies' Diary* (1704–1841) was, in fact, of much longer duration and more central to her existence in a literal sense. Richardson's parents had, in fact, 'met' in the pages of the eclectic annual, with its strange blend of taxing mathematical problems, enigmas and poetry. In the 1780s, Robert Richardson, a longstanding *Diary* contributor, became intrigued by the verse of Yorkshire enigmatist and poet Elizabeth (Betty) Smales. After a short correspondence, they married in Hinderwell in 1788. Charlotte was the couple's third daughter and their first to be born after the couple relocated to London. Her older sisters Elizabeth (later Baker) and Eleanor (later Long) also became poets. At least one poem by Eleanor, 'Hope' (October 1815), appeared in the *Lady's Magazine*, printed on the same page as verse by Charlotte. Charlotte and Elizabeth later worked together on a volume of their deceased mother's poetry (published 1846).[83]

Charlotte's relationship with her family was not an easy one. For reasons that are not entirely clear, but may have been connected to the family's financial insecurity and Charlotte's 'delicate health', the youngest of the Richardson daughters was sent to live with an aunt in Hinderwell following her father's death in 1804, while her mother moved to Vauxhall, London, to set up a school.[84] Biographical accounts suggest that Charlotte's separation from her family was never intended to be more than a temporary arrangement, but it became prolonged. Not until late 1815 did Charlotte finally reconcile with her mother and move to live with her siblings in the capital. The catalyst was a contribution published in the *Ladies' Diary* for 1815 entitled 'The Redbreast's Fate, a Fact: by Miss Charlotte Caroline Richardson of Hinderwell, Yorkshire; youngest daughter of Mrs. R. Formerly Betty Smales'.[85] In the poem, a 'shivering' robin is caught in a storm and nurtured by the poet before being killed by a cat. The symbolism is unsophisticated, but contributes to a recurrent strain that animated so much of Richardson's poetry for the *Ladies' Diary* and *Lady's Magazine*: that life is predictable only in its precarity and cruelty. Perhaps it was these lines that so affected Elizabeth:

> So oft in life's uneven way,
> Some stroke may intervene,
> *Sweep* all our fancied joys away
> And change the once-lov'd scene.[86]

In the following year's *Diary*, Elizabeth responded to her daughter in a poem that hails her daughter's literary talent and mourns the loss of her spouse. Touched by Charlotte's words, Elizabeth vowed to 'clasp' her daughter to her 'aching heart' once again.[87]

This poignant exchange is presented in all of the very few accounts of Richardson's life that we have as pivotal to the mother–daughter reunion. Yet Richardson's poetry for the *Lady's Magazine* qualifies this account in various ways, not least because its monthly publication schedule provides a more nuanced timeline than the sweeping transformations documented in the annual *Diary*. Richardson's early poetry for the *Lady's Magazine*, written while separated from her parents and siblings, offers little hint of domestic disquiet. Her debut, 'Lines', begins with a preface in which she addresses the editor, expresses apology for her 'worthless' verse 'trifle', and her hope that her 'humble name' might be 'plac'd in your crowd / Of Correspondents' before introducing one her 'favourite' early themes: the 'love, peace, and friendship' to be found in retirement (41 (August 1810): 375). Richardson frequently returned to the subject of the consolations of friendship in her poetry for the magazine, including in stanzas dedicated to her absent friend, Ann Harrison. Occasional poetry of this kind – written to commemorate personal attachments, losses and celebrations rather than matters of public concern – was, as Stephen C. Behrendt describes, 'the most numerous type in the eighteenth century', and a staple of 'annuals and "keepsake" anthologies'.[88] It was also a mainstay of monthly periodicals, including the *Lady's Magazine*, where it reveals the periodical's function as an early form of social media that consolidated existing networks between individuals and provided an infrastructure for the formation of new relationships and affiliations.[89]

Richardson recognised as much when, as a young woman, she submitted verse to the magazine addressing fellow poet Joanna Squire (1776–1851). Squire had begun writing for the magazine in 1808, two years before Richardson. Over the next seven, she produced dozens of poems for publication, including sonnets on the changing seasons, *bouts-rimés*, charades, retellings of Greek myths and a series of poems about Bonaparte, most notably 'Address to Fortune', written 'extempore' on reading that he 'had delivered his repudiated Josephine of the title of Empress' (41 (October 1810): 470). The fickleness of fortune – the theme of this as so many of Squire's poems for the magazine – may well have been what arrested the attention of the teenage Charlotte, who wrote an 'Acrostic to Miss Squire' published in the January 1811 issue.

Richardson's career shares several similarities with Squire's. Both women wrote poetry for more than one periodical. Squire's verse was published under her maiden and then married name, Carey, in publications including the *Gentleman's Magazine*, the *Lady's Monthly Museum* and the *Literary Chronicle* (1819–28) as well as the *Lady's Magazine*.[90] Both submitted verse addressed to other correspondents to the *Lady's Magazine*: Squire to the poets C. T. and James Murray Lacey, who had previously addressed admiring verse to her. Both also wrote political poetry about the effects of war on the women left to live with its consequences, whether those women were the Empress Josephine, as in Squire's poem, or the 'parents, virgins, wives and friends', whose pride and despair for their loved ones are recorded in Richardson's *Waterloo, A Poem, On the Late Victory* (1817).[91] Finally, both turned at the end of their careers to novel writing: Joanna Carey's *Lasting Impressions* appeared in 1824, one year after Richardson's *Soldier's Child* was published.

Yet when Richardson first addressed Squire in the poetry section of the *Lady's Magazine*, the differences between the women were pronounced. Squire lived in London, was Richardson's senior by two decades and wrote with an archness and self-assurance that eluded the younger poet. Squire's 1809 'Lines to the Editor' on the magazine's failure to print a poem that she had submitted – the editor claimed to have lost it – is characteristically masterful in its blend of sarcasm and calculated self-deprecation. Neither were traits that endeared Squire to the magazine, despite her popularity with readers. In 1815, matters came to a head. A decisive break was forced after Squire sent the editor an 'angry epistle' full of 'petulant remarks' (46 (February 1815): n.p.). The cause of the dispute is unknown, but Squire's poetry did not grace the magazine again. A review of *Lasting Impressions* appeared in the magazine in November 1824, but no reference is made to the author having been a previous contributor. It is possible that the editor did not know that Carey and Squire were the same person.

Despite being at very different career stages, Richardson stated that she was compelled to write to Squire as she embarked on her own. Moreover, she declared that she felt emboldened to 'claim' Squire's 'friendship', because the magazine and the print community it sustained had already made Squire feel 'like an acquaintance', with whom she was '[o]n an intimate footing' (42 (January 1811): 37). It was eight months before Squire's response to the young poet – 'Lines to Miss Richardson' – was published. The poem, which presents the older poet as 'crush'd' by unspecified 'sorrow', apologises for the 'late' reply but shows mutual respect and friendship for her poetic correspondent:

> And if the friendship of a soul sincere
> Will to thy gen'rous heart indeed be dear,
> From me to accept, what you so kindly claim;
> And on your chosen list inscribe my name. (42 (September 1811): 429)

Whether the friendship between Squire and Richardson extended beyond this correspondence is unknown. Regardless, Squire's gesture of friendship was important to Richardson as she embarked on her life as a writer and as a young woman, living apart from her mother and siblings, 'not knowing on whom to depend' (42 (January 1811): 37).

The connection seems to have emboldened Richardson in her future verse for the magazine, which, like the poetry of Charlotte Smith, uses autobiographical references to various and powerful effects. The personal and the political are intertwined throughout this later work. The autobiographical resonances of 'Jepthah' (September 1814), a retelling of the Israelite judge's sacrifice of his daughter's life for personal gain, imbue the poem with a pathos and depth of feeling against cruelty to women that would be absent without knowledge of the author's life. Richardson's compulsive return to the subject of personal trauma as a self-styled child of 'despair' similarly underlines her 'Lines on hearing a Friend Play on the Psaltery', a poem that contests the gendered aesthetics of Samuel Taylor Coleridge's 'The Eolian Harp' (1817).

That this poem post-dates Richardson's reconciliation with her mother and siblings by two years does not rule out a biographical reading. Indeed, despair continues to be a running thread of Richardson's poetry long after the supposedly happy reunion. 'Lines on Leaving Hinderwell' (December 1815), published just months after she moved to London, paints the poet's return to her family as a journey of loss for one 'driv'n by sorrow from thy blest abodes, / To seek contentment on my native plains' (568). Yorkshire and the life she left behind remained palpable presences in her future compositions. One of Richardson's last poems for the magazine, 'To a Friend, on Being Solicited to Return Back to Yorkshire', expresses the 'pang' of 'regret' that she feels in being forced to recollect the landscape and, most especially the people – her deceased aunt, Anna, and an unidentified former lover – that she has been forced to leave behind (49 (October 1818): 477).

Yet for all its focus on injustice and isolation, Richardson's poetry also demonstrates forcefully how the periodical served as a mechanism for reparation. Lives could be remade both through poetic retelling and the forms of print community that the magazine facilitated. Richardson lived her life in, and, indeed, owed her very existence to periodicals. Yet for all the particularities of her relationship to the form, the way that she engaged with the *Lady's Magazine* as a contributor was more broadly representative. Many poets for the *Lady's Magazine* – such as John Webb, Mary of Coleshill (Mary Dodwell) discussed in the previous chapter – similarly commemorated familial dramas and milestones in their verse and approached the magazine as a vehicle to forge friendships and connections with fellow correspondents. This is poetry as social media, for which the magazine, with its regular publication schedule and ability to bring together readers across the country, served as a professionally and personally useful platform.

'First Published Periodically': Novelists in the *Lady's Magazine*

The *Lady's Magazine* served as a different kind of platform for the authors of its popular serial fiction. When Henry D. Symonds published the two-volume epistolary novel *Derwent Priory* in 1798, it did not bear its author's name. A short preface offers scant biographical detail beyond the facts that it had been penned by an 'Authoress', and one whose life had forced her to become 'inured to the pressures of disappointment'.[92] The title page offers little more information, signalling only that the novel was 'By the Author of the Castle of the Rock', a three-volume Gothic fiction that Symonds published the same year under the circular ascription 'By the Author of Derwent Priory'. *Derwent Priory*'s subtitle, however, gives important clues to its author's identity when it notes that this was a novel that was '*First Published Periodically*'. The *Lady's Magazine* is not cited as the periodical in question, perhaps because Symonds assumed he could take readers' knowledge of this fact as read. 'Derwent Priory', recalled over forty years later by Charlotte Brontë in the letter to Hartley Coleridge, ran in twenty-two parts in the *Lady's Magazine* from January 1796 to September 1797, and appears to have been one of its most popular serial fictions. Before it appeared in volume form (in forty-two 'Letters'), it was also reprinted, likely without its author's knowledge, in at least two further periodicals including the *Hibernian* (April–November 1797; and November–December 1801); and the *Aberdeen Magazine* (June 1796–March 1798).

'Derwent Priory' was published anonymously in the *Lady's Magazine*. Attentive readers would, however, have been able to divine at least its author's initials. The September 1797 issue in which 'Derwent Priory' concludes also features a poem entitled 'The Endowments of Farren. By the Author of Derwent Priory', signed A. K. of Isleworth. No further original work seems to have been submitted by A. K. to the *Lady's Magazine*, although an extract from her second novel, *The Castle on the Rock*, appears in the May 1798 issue. Work by 'A. K. of Isleworth' appears in a handful of other contemporary periodicals, however. The three-part educational tale, 'The School for Parents', was published in Symonds's *Monthly Visitor* (1797–1804) before being republished as a standalone volume, while the poem, 'Lines to a Sleeping Infant Composed During a Storm' by 'Ann Kendall' of Isleworth, was published in the September 1804 *Lady's Monthly Museum*.[93] By 1804, Kendall, had produced at least one other novel, *Tales of the Abbey* (1800), ascribed to 'A. Kendall, Author of Derwent Priory, The Castle of the Rock, &c. &c.'. She went on to write *Moreland Manor* (1806) for Longman and Company, this time going by 'Mrs. Kendall'. Beyond knowing that Mrs Kendall authored these works and that she lived in Isleworth, at least for a time, we have little secure biographical information about this once popular author, and it is possible that she wrote more poems and fictions for periodicals than those cited above. Even this glimpse into her career, however, is instructive for the light it sheds on another important type of *Lady's Magazine* author: a writer whose work for the magazine was deemed sufficiently commercial to be republished in volume form, and who used their supposedly 'amateur' writing for the periodical to launch a professional career outside it.[94]

A number of these writers authored Gothic fiction. The magazine's close association with the Gothic was a hallmark of its innovation and aligned with the Robinsons' broader publishing priorities. Mayo, for instance, notes that of 118 periodicals that published fiction between 1770 and 1820, only around twenty published Gothic fiction, and some only sporadically. By some considerable margin, the *Lady's Magazine* published 'more new Gothic fiction and a greater variety of it than any other miscellany of its day'.[95] One of the most successful of its Gothic serials was 'Grasville Abbey, a Romance', by G. M., which appeared in forty-seven instalments between March 1793 and August 1797. A page-turner in the spirit of Ann Radcliffe's *The Romance of the Forest* (1792), 'Grasville Abbey' is a multi-generational tale of familial betrayal, usurped inheritances and murder, set in England and France during the reign of Louis XIV. The serial was an immediate hit. The Dublin *Sentimental and Masonic Magazine* (founded 1792), again likely without the author's knowledge, reprinted a little over half of the instalments of G. M.'s romance a few months after they appeared in Robinson's periodical. In 1797, 'Grasville Abbey' was reissued as a triple-decker novel by the Robinsons themselves. A note appended to the final instalment of the serial in the *Lady's Magazine* advertised the forthcoming volume republication: 'At the request of several of our readers, this much-admired romance is now reprinted in volumes by G. G. and J. Robinson, Paternoster-row' (38 (September 1797): 356). The publishers' collective hunch about *Grasville Abbey*'s commercial viability proved sound. While it is hard to corroborate Maurice Lévy's assertion that the novel was the most popular Gothic fiction of the late eighteenth century, it certainly captivated readers in Britain and beyond.[96] A second edition followed swiftly in the spring of 1798, the same year that a two-volume Irish edition and a French edition also appeared, the latter widely presumed to be a translation of a Radcliffe novel.[97] An American edition, published in Salem, Massachusetts, followed in 1799 and later reprints were published in London for the Minerva Press.

Unlike *Derwent Priory*, *Grasville Abbey* did not advertise its periodical origins. Reviewers, however, were quick to point out the novel's inauspicious beginnings. The *Monthly Mirror* is typical in its contempt for the 'ill-calculated' 'medium' in which the novel first appeared, yet was forced to concede that *Grasville Abbey* was a good read that gave 'considerable satisfaction' with the exception of a handful of 'digressions' attributed to 'its having been written at various and distant intervals'.[98] The *Critical Review* (1756–1817), a publication never inclined to give praise to novels where it was not merited – and sometimes when it was – was more appreciative. With grudging admiration, the reviewer noted that while the request of subscribers to the *Lady's Magazine* to have the serial issued as a standalone publication would not ordinarily 'indicate merit', *Grasville Abbey* had proved 'an exception': a 'new and striking' Gothic novel 'superior' to most of its kind.[99]

The identity of the novel's author was seemingly unknown to reviewers. Readers of the *Lady's Magazine* were better informed. They knew that G. M. was the author of several other items in the periodical, including poems on subjects as various as liberty (February 1795) and an 'Epitaph on a Favourite Little Dog' (June 1796). In March 1800, G. M.'s 'Lines to the Memory of Miss Sarah Bland of Kensington' appeared in the magazine for the first time under the author's full legal name: 'George Moore. Author of "Grasville Abbey"'. Moore's name also appears under 'The First Navigator' (February–June 1801) – a translation via the French of Salomon Gessner's *Der Erste Schiffer* (1762) – and under an 'Impromptu' published in September 1801. Thereafter, Moore disappears from the magazine, but becomes much more visible outside it. In 1802, George Robinson junior and his uncle John published Moore's *Theodosius de Zulvin*, a novel that provided a source of inspiration for Charlotte Dacre's *Zofloya* (1806).[100] Other of Moore's works included: the unperformed play, *Montbar; or the Buccaneer* (1804); the biographical *Lives of Cardinal Alberoni, the Duke of Ripperda, and Marquis of Pombal* (1806), which Jane Porter acknowledged as an important source for *The Pastor's Fire-side* (1817); and *Tales of the Passions* (1808–11), a prose work inspired by Joanna Bailey's *Plays on the Passions* (1798).

Beyond this bibliography of works, Moore has remained mysterious. Mayo, following James Foster, speculates that he was a clergyman, a Reverend George Moore who had published an unspecified novel prior to the publication of 'Grasville Abbey'.[101] *Eighteenth-Century Collections Online* suggests, by contrast, that the George Moore who wrote *Grasville Abbey* was the same Irish 'barrister at law' who wrote an *Essay on the Rights of the Prince of Wales, Relative to the Dutchy of Cornwall* (1795) and the pro-Union *Observations on the Union, Orange Associations and Other Subjects of Domestic Policy* (1799). Determining Moore's identity, profession, prior publication history and whether or not he was paid for his magazine serial is, according to Mayo, the only way to resolve the critical question of whether or not 'Grasville Abbey' counts as a professional or amateur endeavour.[102] Mayo needs Moore to be 'Rev. George Moore' – although George Moore, barrister at law, would also have served his purposes – to justify his serial's enthusiastic critical and popular reception. The Reverend George Moore may be obscure today, but the mere fact of prior publication is enough to confirm Mayo's view of Moore's status as a literary professional and the success of his novel despite its inferior, periodical origins. Yet the attribution is spurious. George Robinson senior's scant surviving business records identify Moore as neither a clergyman nor a barrister. A memorandum of agreement dated 6 July 1802 between Moore and Robinson confirming the purchase of the copyright of *Theodosius de Zulvin* for fifty guineas describes the author as a surveyor and builder who lived in Tottenham Court Road.[103] No further biographical details have been established with certainty, but Moore was no literary amateur whatever his prior publication history or other professional credentials were. 'Grasville Abbey' was popular and successful in both serial and volume forms. It was widely translated; it influenced other authors, particularly women writers, in the first decades of the early nineteenth century; and, as with Kendall's 'Derwent Priory', it paved the way to the longer career that Moore conducted both within and beyond the pages of the magazine.

Kendall's and Moore's serials were not alone in finding an afterlife in volume form. Another notable example is the uneven and occasionally baffling gothic romance, *The Monks and the Robbers. A Tale of* the Fifteenth Century. Published in two volumes by George Robinson junior, the Monks and the Robbers (1808) was first published in the Lady's Magazine in fifty-two much-interrupted instalments between 1794 and 1805, and was the work of at least two authors.[104] A less well-known example is 'Memoirs of a Young Lady. In a Series of Letters' (April 1783–November 1786), a serial later published as Vicissitudes of Life, Exemplified in the Interesting Memoirs of a Young Lady (1815) and commonly attributed to Jane West.[105] The periodical also published some serials that originated as novels. These included Royall Tyler's The Algerine Captive (first published in America in 1797) and Catherine Cuthbertson's Romance of the Pyrenees (1803), both of which were published in their entirety in instalments in the Lady's Magazine after a warehouse fire in February 1803 largely destroyed the print runs of the volume publications. The Irish-born Cuthbertson, another successful novelist in the Radcliffean tradition, went on to publish a further four novels for two generations of the Robinson family, several of which were enthusiastically puffed in the Lady's Magazine in subsequent years.[106]

A different serial-novel trajectory can be tracked via the example of the popular gothic fiction writer, Catherine Day Haynes (1793–1851), later Catherine Golland. Haynes/Golland is relatively well known in Gothic studies and features prominently in studies of the Minerva Press, which published the six novels she authored between 1818 and 1841. The first of these, The Foundling of Devonshire; or, What is She? (1818), ascribes the work to 'Miss C. D. Haynes, "Author of the Castle of Le Blanc, &c &c"'.[107] The Castle of Le Blanc is mentioned on the title pages of several of Haynes'/Golland's later works, and is frequently presumed to be a lost text because there is no surviving volume publication. 'The Castle of Le Blanc' very much exists, however, in the sole form of its original publication: the nineteen instalments that appeared in the Lady's Magazine between October 1816 and the Supplement issue for 1818. The identity of its author, C. D. H., was an open secret to a handful of the periodical's readers able to decipher the thinly veiled references to her identity in the earlier noted poems, songs and rebuses that she also contributed to the magazine. It was not until January 1821, however, that the periodical retrospectively attributed the serial to Haynes in an announcement of her marriage: 'At St. Bride's, Mr John Golland, of the New Kent Road, to Miss C. D. Haynes, author of the Castle of Le Blanc, Foundling of Devonshire, and several other works' (52: 56).

As Symonds did with Kendall's Derwent Priory and The Castle on the Rock, A. K. Newman marketed The Foundling of Devonshire via its link to a magazine serial, the title of which he assumed readers would recognise and attract those readers eager to devour its author's next production. In using the serial to sell the novel, Newman perhaps took the lead from Haynes herself, who had successfully leveraged her success as a magazine writer to sell the copyrights of her new work. However, when she attempted the reverse by trading on her success with Minerva to place another serial in the *Lady's Magazine*, her efforts proved fruitless. Shortly after the birth of her first child in 1822 – one of several of Haynes/Golland's life events documented in the births, marriages and deaths columns of the *Lady's Magazine* – she went back to the periodical that had launched her career to place a new serial novel 'called the "Single Gentleman, or a Flight of Fancy"'. The editor rejected the manuscript on the grounds that it did not suit his publication's 'present system'. The reason for the rejection is not articulated, although it was likely related to the magazine's marginalisation of original fiction following the new series in 1820, a move I document in the following chapter. Regardless, the incident is instructive for the light it sheds on how authors understood the relationship between periodical and volume publication. Haynes/Golland did not see volume publication as the objective of her career and, like Pilkington, she refused to identify herself with a single publishing outlet even when her publishers encouraged her to do so. As DiPlacidi contends, Haynes/Golland saw her professional work writing multi-volume novels for the Minerva Press as contiguous with a career writing for the *Lady's Magazine*, even if the *Lady's Magazine* ultimately took a different view when it closed the door on the 'Single Gentleman'.[108]

In tracking writers who published serial fiction in the *Lady's Magazine* and multi-decker novels outside it, my intention has not been to privilege volume publication as the benchmark of literary professionalism, although such an exercise effectively disproves claims that serial fiction in the *Lady's Magazine* was not good enough to appear in this more conventionally respected print format. More importantly for the concerns of this chapter, the exercise gives further and compelling reasons to interrogate related assumptions about what constitutes Romantic authorship. Haynes/Golland, Kendall, Moore, Legg, Reeve, Richardson, Roberts, Mitford, Pilkington, Troughton and Yeames all led very different lives, enjoyed very different writing careers and harboured different aspirations, and the *Lady's Magazine* played very different roles in shaping those lives, careers and aspirations. Any survey of the periodical's authors is necessarily partial: partial because many of their identities are irrecoverable or obscure; and partial also because even those that have been identified are so numerous that their stories would merit a book of their own. My objective in this chapter, however, has been to avoid another kind of partiality that has long overdetermined how it has been possible to view these writers and the magazine to which they contributed: their association with amateurism and shameless popularism supposedly confirmed by the often inaccurate assumption that they could not secure more payment or prestigious outlets for their work or that they sought to conceal their identities behind pseudonyms out of modesty or embarrassment. Certainly, there are writers for the magazine whose example could be mobilised to confirm either or both of these pejorative assumptions. Yet there is no typical *Lady's Magazine* contributor, any more than there is a single motive or set of motives that drew writers to provide content for its pages, to publish under their full legal name or to hide behind a pseudonym.

Kathryn King, in an important essay on the intersection between scribal and print publication in the early eighteenth century, argues that 'the accomplishments of our female forebears' can only be fully recognised by a 'higher order of attentiveness ... to the nuanced spectrum of often overlapping publication possibilities' open to women and the 'astonishing variety of actual writing and publishing choices exercised by actual women in the eighteenth century'.[109] In the last decades of the eighteenth century and before the emergence of the professional journalist in the early decades of the nineteenth, magazine publishing presented a unique and, as I explore in more detail in Chapter 6, a putatively more democratic and accessible medium and outlet for writers of both sexes. Thousands of women and men took advantage of this possibility, yet the practice of 'publish[ing] periodically' has been largely ignored in histories of eighteenth-century and Romantic authorship and has been often misunderstood on the rare occasions when it has been taken into account. Publishing within the pages of the *Lady's Magazine* meant many different things to the periodical's many different writers. It could serve as: a repository for fugitive pieces; a place in which to serve a literary apprenticeship; a mechanism to launch or relaunch a career; a place to commemorate personal and national losses or to build friendships and repair familial bonds; and, in its later years, it formed a vital lifeline in times of economic difficulty. Many writing lives and careers began in this magazine. Some ended there too. The models of authorship I have outlined in this chapter are unromantic and unRomantic: they are messy, not always appealing to modern sensibilities and, as we have seen, challenge a number of the defining characteristics of literary professionalism as they were being codified. Taking note of the extraordinary range and influence of the essayists, fiction writers, poets and translators who wrote for the *Lady's Magazine* can only refine this sense further and bring us closer to the complex and diverse realities of being an author in this period.

Chapter 5

Rivals: The Changing Face of the Women's Magazine

We are sensible that in ushering this NEW LADY's MAGAZINE into the world, we have some Foes to contend with, who may think it their interest to oppose our Publication; and would only remind those who pretend to monopolize Wit and Learning, and to set Bounds to other people's Knowledge and Industry, that the fate of those that once flourished, and are now forgotten, should convince them that Time and Chance happen to all Things; and that as we invade no Man's Property, we certainly have as much right to oblige and entertain the Public as others. We have heard the complaints of the Ladies, we have seen the imperfections of those who have gone before us. . . . THE PUBLISHER and EDITOR.
    'Address to the Ladies', *The New Lady's Magazine*, 1 (February 1786)

The *Lady's Magazine* for 1786 marked the periodical's seventeenth year of publication in typically ebullient fashion by boasting its 'unrivalled Popularity and Fame' in 'every Quarter of the Kingdom' ('Address', 17 (January 1786): 4). Editorial confidence was shaken just a few weeks later, however, when one of George Robinson senior's Paternoster Row neighbours, Alexander Hogg (1752–1809), launched a direct rival: the *New Lady's Magazine; or Polite and Entertaining Companion for the Fair Sex*. Under the editorship of the almost certainly fictional 'Rev. Mr. Charles Stanhope', the *New Lady's Magazine* went head-to-head with Robinson's *Lady's Magazine* for eleven years.[1] Hogg's campaign began with a public declaration that the women's magazine would die without the transfusion of new blood that the *New Lady's Magazine* intended to supply. '[S]everal attempts', he noted, had been made to establish 'a Monthly Magazine appropriated solely to the use and amusement of the FAIR SEX', but most had 'sunk into oblivion'. Defunct periodicals and those, like the *Lady's Magazine*, that had not yet had the decency to retire, had 'degenerated' almost to the point of no return (4). Hogg and his editor promised to reinvigorate the form through strenuous efforts to 'surpass every other publication of its kind'. The *New Lady's Magazine* boasted publication by royal licence and claimed 'superior[ity]' in terms of its 'Print, and Copper-Plates' and 'improved, liberal and extensive plan' (5). The periodical's second issue reported that within a few short weeks it had received 'applause in every part of the town and country' and achieved sales of nearly twenty thousand copies (1 (March 1786): 82). A glorious future for the *New Lady's Magazine* was predicted with a degree of hyperbole that makes the self-congratulatory editors of the *Lady's Magazine* seem positively humble by comparison.

The subsequent war of words between Hogg and Robinson quickly became ugly in ways that are reminiscent of the Robinson/Roberts–Wheble altercation of the early 1770s. Indeed, Hogg invited comparison with the earlier dispute in a series of public attacks launched in the pages of his periodical. The *New Lady's Magazine*'s inaugural issue printed a 'Caution' to readers urging them to recognise 'that the *New Lady's Magazine*' was 'an entire New Work' and not a continuation of any old publication whatever of a similar nature' (1: 5). In a pre-emptive shot against Robinson's objections to this periodical incursion, Hogg denied that his publication invaded any 'Man's Property'. Leaning on the same language that Lord Mansfield had used in his summing up at the 1771 trial, Hogg presented his periodical as a legitimate rival publication to Robinson's *Lady's Magazine*, asserting that the long-term viability of the two publications could only be determined by the 'Public' (4).

Robinson responded angrily in a spat that spilled out into the newspaper columns and onto the streets in and around Paternoster Row. According to an anonymous pamphlet addressed 'to the Booksellers of London, Westminster, &c', and reprinted in the *New Lady's Magazine* for March 1786, Robinson resorted to a host of 'unfair' measures to prevent the sale and distribution of Hogg's magazine. These included Robinson 'skulking' his hefty six-foot frame into booksellers' shops; ripping out advertisements for Hogg's periodical from titles on display in shop windows; attempting to 'poison the minds' of provincial booksellers against the *New Lady's Magazine*; and hosting a breakfast at which Robinson attempted to persuade wholesalers against supplying it (1: 83). While the allegations in the pamphlet cannot be verified over two centuries later, Robinson was undoubtedly angered by the launch of Hogg's journal.[2] Moreover, the pamphlet's claim that Robinson was a hypocrite for objecting to Hogg's venture has more than a kernel of truth to it. What right did Robinson, the publisher of 'the NEW ANNUAL REGISTER, in Opposition to Mr. *Dodsley* – The NEW DAILY JOURNAL, in Opposition to Mr. *Baldwin*, – The NEW DISPENSATORY, in Opposition to Mr. *Nourse*, – NEW LADIES POCKET-BOOKS, in Opposition to Mr *Baldwin and others*' and 'the NEW ALMANACKS – in Opposition to the whole *Company of Stationers*', have to be 'offended' by Hogg's 'new' enterprise (83)?[3]

The answer to this question lies in Robinson's and Hogg's rather different understandings of the word 'new'. As the question above implies in its repetition of 'in Opposition to', the 'new' in Robinson's titles was intended to signal works that offered political or otherwise meaningful alternatives to their namesakes. (The *New Annual Register* was a radical rejoinder to the conservative *Annual Register*, and so on.) Hogg's application of the term was less oppositional than parasitic. When he launched the *New Lady's Magazine*, he was already well known for attempting to boost sales by disingenuously repackaging old works as 'new', 'revised' or 'corrected' editions when they were nothing of the kind.[4] In the words of Michael Harris, Hogg made a career of 'skirt[ing] the main interests of the respectable London booksellers'.[5] The *New Lady's Magazine* did nothing to improve his reputation in this regard. While his periodical grew its readership and increased its original contributions over time, it flagrantly reprinted copious essays, tales, serials and even song sheets first published in the *Lady's Magazine*. Reprinting on this scale and for this duration went far beyond the culture of scissors-and-paste recycling that was customary in the trade. The wholesale, unacknowledged lifting of swathes of content from *Lady's Magazine*, an established publication with a near identical title sold out of the same street as Hogg's, crossed a line. There was little that was new about the *New Lady's Magazine* (Figure 5.1). Robinson may have found some small consolation in the fact that Hogg was considerably inconvenienced by his publication's close emulation of its namesake. The June 1788 *New Lady's Magazine*, for instance, adverted to the 'unnecessary Trouble' occasioned by confused readers who sent them correspondence intended for Robinson's periodical or by authors who hedged their publication bets by submitting contributions for consideration by both magazines in a single packet ('Correspondents', 29 (June 1788): 3). It might perturb both Robinson and Hogg to learn that the *Lady's Magazine* and the *New Lady's Magazine* are regularly mistaken for one another to this day.

Yet the fates of these two ladies' magazines were very different. Hogg outlived Robinson by nearly a decade and was one of the Paternoster Row's oldest residents when he died. The magazine was much less long-lived, however, though its demise was protracted. For several years before the magazine finally ceased publication in 1797, the *New Lady's Magazine* was struggling to source copy and was forced to pad out issues with a serialisation of Samuel Richardson's *Pamela* (1740). Robinson's *Lady's Magazine*, by contrast, survived not only its publisher's death in 1801, but also that of his son (in 1811), in addition to weathering

Rivals: The Changing Face of the Women's Magazine 165

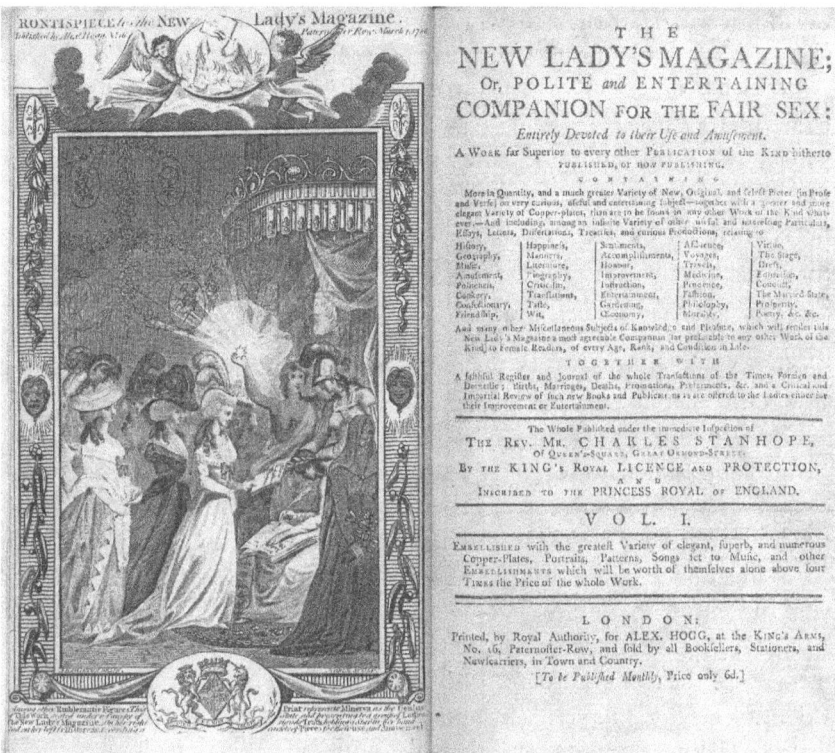

Figure 5.1 Frontispiece to and title page for the first volume of Alexander Hogg's *New Lady's Magazine* (1786). Special Collections and Archives, University of Cardiff.

the storms of a financially devastating warehouse fire, several publisher bankruptcies and the financial mismanagement and desertion of the periodical's printer and later editor, Samuel Hamilton (1778–c.1850).[6] Hogg's tenacity was simply no match for the might of the Robinson firm and the loyalty of the *Lady's Magazine*'s readers.

As this chapter documents, Hogg's was just one of 'a great number' of 'rivals' that reared up against the *Lady's Magazine* and whose competition it navigated with care and determination ('Address', 37 (January 1806): n.p.). Two of the most important of these competitors, the *Lady's Monthly Museum* (1798–1828) and John Bell's *La Belle Assemblée* (1806–32), eventually merged with the *Lady's Magazine*, thereby ensuring all three publications' survival until the mid-nineteenth century. The fate of the *Lady's Magazine*, as we will see, was intimately bound up with these and others of its rivals. While the periodical maintained a clear brand identity for much of its history, it was always responsive to shifts and changes in the marketplace and in readers' sensibilities. The magazine was successful, its editors claimed, partly because they had 'never ... departed from' the 'original Plan of the LADY'S MAGAZINE' (33 (January 1802): 3). Yet it could not afford to be 'merely passive' (6 (January 1775): iii). At critical moments, the periodical's publishers and editors proactively set about extending its plan to keep readers engaged and to ensure its survival. The 'Rivalship' of the magazine's many 'Antagonists' forced numerous changes in the *Lady's Magazine*'s contents, its organisation, as well as its look and feel (17 (Supp 1786): 1786). Here I track the most significant of the changes the magazine instituted between 1800 and 1830, namely: changes in the periodical's appearance, layout and organisation; the addition of new multi-media content (especially its fashion plates and reviews); and the jettisoning of older content (such as needlework patterns, and fiction and poetry authored by reader-contributors). Each of these evolutions reveals how successive generations of the magazine's editors and publishers attempted to move with the times while not losing the core of the magazine's identity or readership. The resulting balancing acts were difficult to maintain, however, and while the magazine's ability to survive during six decades of change, expansion and professionalisation in the periodical marketplace undoubtedly renders it a success story, it was not – as we will see – an unqualified one, as the magazine became distanced from the content, structure and tone that had long secured readers' loyalty.

Designing Women: Format, Illustrations and Illustrators

When it launched in August 1770, the *Lady's Magazine* looked reassuringly familiar. With the exceptions of its embroidery patterns and song sheets, there is little to distinguish the periodical's initial design from that of contemporaries such as the *European*, *Gentleman's*, *London* and *Universal Magazine*s. In April 1771, when they bought the periodical from Coote, Robinson and Roberts introduced only a few layout changes, mostly to align the periodical's typesetting conventions with those of the *Town and Country Magazine* (1769–96). For much of the next thirty years, formatting and organisational changes were rarities. The January 1778 issue announced with much fanfare that the publisher had 'had *a new letter cast* at an immense expence', but the typeface looks no different in 1778 (or in 1798 for that matter) than it did in 1770, and any improvement in print quality generated by a new casting is not discernible. As the magazine entered a new century, however, and as it attempted to fend off stiff competition from an ever-growing number of new and elegant periodical competitors, more marked changes were instituted with greater frequency.

In 1800, when the magazine's cover price rose to a shilling and the hand-coloured fashion plates discussed in the next section of this chapter were introduced, a new typeface was adopted. The vertical line separating the magazine's twin columns was also removed to give text pages a less cluttered appearance (Figure 5.2). These innovations heralded further production changes in the 1810s. Design refreshes, as we will see below, typically went hand in hand with changes in the magazine's content and organisation and, although it is not always self-evident, seem often to have coincided with changes in editorial personnel. The most significant of these developments came at a cost for readers, although the magazine vowed to keep its cover price as low as practicable to ensure value for money. Its second price hike (to one shilling and sixpence) in 1811 – the year that the magazine passed to George Robinson III (dates unknown) and Samuel Robinson (1785–1834) – was occasioned by the use of 'superior quality' paper stock and the launch of a new page 'arrangement', which consisted of minimising blank spaces around the text and abridging serial instalments to accommodate a more diverse range of monthly contents ('Advertisement', 42 (January 1811): n.p.).

More sweeping changes followed in 1820 when, to celebrate fifty years of publication, the magazine launched a new series at two shillings an issue.[7] Now under the proprietorship of its former printer, Samuel Hamilton (1778–c.1850), the periodical ceased issuing needlework patterns and dropped the annual Supplement.[8] Just three years later, the magazine's design was updated again. In addition to a reorganisation of contents into newly retitled sections, the font size was reduced to increase further the number of articles the magazine could publish. These changes were so significant that Hamilton contemplated launching a second new series to make them, but instead settled on an overhauled subtitle. The *Lady's Magazine; or, Entertaining Companion for the Fair Sex* became the *Lady's Magazine; or, Mirror of the Belles-Lettres, Fashions, Fine Arts, Music, Drama &c*. Introducing these innovations in a triumphant address to readers in the January 1823 issue, Hamilton boasted that the magazine could survive 'comparison with any other periodical publication of a similar nature that ever existed' ('Address', 1st new ser. 4: n.p.). Underpinning his editorial pride was his confidence in the 'unrivaled beauty' of the magazine's 'embellishments', which had not only improved in quality by this date, but had also grown in number so that an extra half sheet per issue was required to accommodate them ('Address', 1st new ser. 4: n.p.). A further half sheet was added in 1825, and an additional sixpence was levied on the cover price to help defray

168   The Lady's Magazine and the Making of Literary History

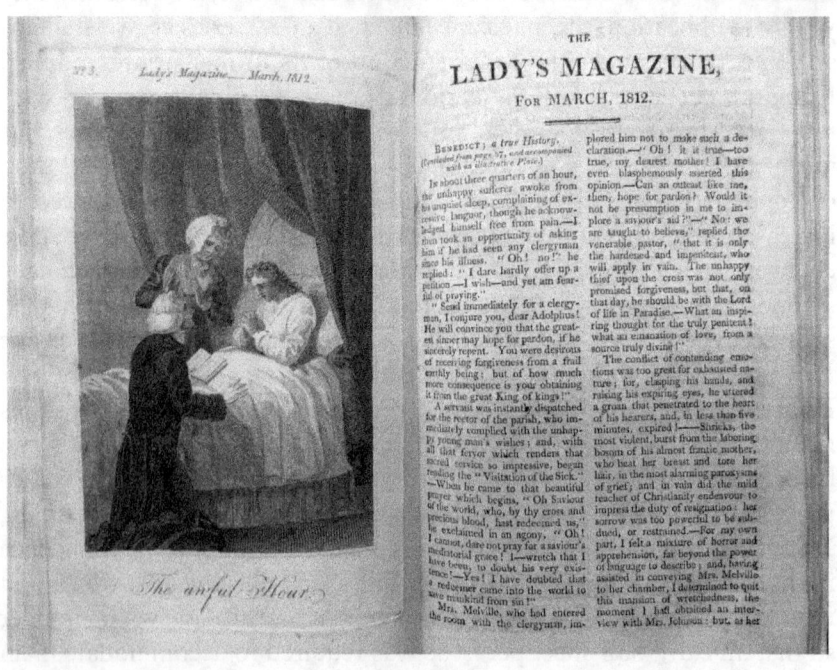

Figure 5.2   Comparison of layout changes in the *Lady's Magazine* for April 1778 (top) and March 1812 (bottom). Private collection.

the expenses and to satisfy readers' growing appetite for more illustrations and plates.

Illustrations had always been an integral part of the *Lady's Magazine* and a key element of its appeal, even though the majority of monthly issues published in the first three decades of its run contained only a single engraving because of the production costs involved. January issues from 1770 to 1820 featured some of the most elaborate of these images in the form of the periodical's annual frontispieces.[9] The majority were variations on a single theme: the goddess Minerva (substituted by Britannia in the nineteenth century) ushers female readers away from the temptations and distractions of the world into a temple of fame or wisdom symbolised by the copies of the magazine the readers carry in their hands. The iconography was hardly novel. As James Raven notes, Minerva was a 'crucial emblem' in transatlantic Enlightenment iconography. Connoting the civilising effects of reading through acts of 'bibliographical benevolence', the goddess appeared on library bookplates, on the title pages of educational works, and in frontispieces to titles such as the *European, London, Universal* and *Westminster* magazines, in which she commonly directs the magazine's male representative towards immortality.[10] As I have argued elsewhere, the *Lady's Magazine* took this conventional iconography and re-visioned it to recuperate the ubiquitous Minerva as a symbol of the magazine's aspirations and the individual and cultural benefits of women's reading and writing.[11]

Most of the magazine's engravings were less allegorical and more straightforwardly illustrative. These 'embellishments' predominantly depicted dramatic or otherwise affecting moments in the periodical's moral tales. Some accompanied biographical sketches or domestic or international travel writing. Others illustrated topical news items, such as the assassination of Prime Minister, Spencer Perceval (June 1812), the bigamy trial of the Duchess of Kingston (April 1776) or the conviction of 'The Monster', Renwick (or Rynwick) Williams (Figure 5.3), whose crimes against London women the magazine followed with horrified fascination. Almost all of these images have captions indicating that they were produced 'for the *Lady's Magazine*', but some were engraved after previously published designs. The illustrations for the magazine's serialisation of Cook's third voyages, for instance, reproduced images that had appeared in the official account of the voyages published the same year (1784). Other engravings, however, were commissioned to order, an act that seems to be indicative of the esteem in which the accompanying content and/or its author was held. As we saw in the previous chapter, several of Radagunda Roberts's moral tales featured commissioned illustrations as did Ann Murry's popular natural history serial,

Figure 5.3 Rynwick Williams Commonly called The Monster from the Lady's Magazine for July 1790. Private collection.

'The Moral Zoologist' (1800–5). Occasionally contributors submitted sketches of their own composition with their written copy, which were subsequently executed by professional engravers. Even more rarely, contributors gave the magazine permission to reproduce engravings that they owned or had self-commissioned, such as when Philip Thicknesse provided the editor with an 'elegant engraving' to accompany a short article on the memorial he and his wife, Ann, had raised for the poet Thomas Chatterton (15 (February 1784): 62).[12]

Until 1820, all of these illustration types were proudly listed along with other non-text media in a dedicated section of the monthly contents page, and the subjects of future engravings were trailed in both the 'Correspondents' columns in the periodical itself and in newspaper advertisements. The inclusion of engravings was no mere marketing tactic, however. The 'utility' of the engravings, the magazine argued in 1827, lay in 'utilising the productions of the painter, and transferring even to the habitations of the lower classes the rare embellishments of princely and lordly mansions' ('Remarks on Beauty, in the Fine Arts', 58 (December 1827): 659). Illustrations were not mere ornaments, but a material articulation of the magazine's democratic impulse to bring culture and the arts to a wide readership who could afford its comparatively low cover price.

Despite such claims about the importance of illustrations to the magazine and to its readers, little scholarly attention has been paid to the periodical's engravings. This is partly because illustrations, like other extra-textual materials, were frequently removed by owners of the magazine prior to binding or cut out by collectors and print-sellers post-binding. A further obstacle to study is that, like the magazine's text contributions, its engravings are frequently unattributed. Some accompanying captions gesture to the credentials of the 'celebrated' artists, Royal Academicians, and French and Italian masters whose works inspired the engravings. Rarely, however, are these artists or engravers identified before the1800s. The appearance of Joseph Collyer's (1748–1827) name under the magazine's annual frontispieces for the volumes for 1774 to 1776 and 1778 is so unusual as to be worthy of comment (Figure 5.5). Only in the nineteenth century were the periodical's illustrators more routinely named, although the practice was still followed idiosyncratically.

The gradual move to the consistent crediting of artists and engravers coincided with the magazine's growing self-consciousness about the need to be 'pleasing to the eye of Taste' if it were to compete successfully against titles such as the *Lady's Monthly Museum*, Rudolph Ackermann's *Repository of Arts* (1809–28) and especially *La Belle Assemblée*, which espoused higher production values and had raised

Figure 5.4 *Falcon* from 'The Moral Zoologist' in the *Lady's Magazine* for June 1803. Private collection.

Figure 5.5 Joseph Collyer after Angelica Kauffman. Frontispiece to the *Lady's Magazine* for 1775. Private collection.

periodical readers' expectations ('Advertisement', 42 (January 1811): n.p.). As a consequence, from 1810, the editors entered into a protracted conversation with readers about the quality of its illustrations. In May 1812, for instance, the editor assured subscribers that they could in future rely fully on the 'neatness and accuracy' of the colouring of the periodical's fashion plates ('Notices', 43: n.p.). The following year, he explained that a commissioned engraving of the actress Mrs Smith had proved unsatisfactory, been rejected and another ordered in its place ('Notice', 44 (March 1813): n.p.). The name of the offending engraver was omitted, but the magazine quickly lost its coyness in such matters. In February 1817 a dispute broke out between the editor and painter and engraver, G. M. Brighty (fl. 1809–27), whose designs had been the source of frontispieces and occasional engravings in the magazine for the best part of a decade. The editor terminated the magazine's relationship with Brighty citing the '[g]reat disappointment' of 'subscribers to the Lady's Magazine'. In 'subsequent numbers', the editor reassured readers, the magazine would admit 'no embellishments by the above designer and would only commission 'engravings by the most eminent artists; from the designs only of Messrs. Burney, Corbold [sic], Stothard, and Westall' ('Notice to Correspondents', 48: n.p.).[13] Precisely what Brighty did to disappointment Lady's Magazine readers is unclear, but his public dismissal was presented as evidence of the seriousness of the periodical's commitment to professional production values.

Of the aforementioned list of 'eminent artists', Royal Academician Thomas Stothard (1755–1834) enjoyed the most important and long-standing connection with the magazine. Stothard, as Shelley M. Bennett documents, was 'probably the most prolific illustrator of his times'. He produced hundreds of designs for various periodicals including: the British Magazine (1782–3), the Lady's Poetical Magazine; or Beauties of British Poetry (1781–2), the New Novelist's Magazine (1786–7) and the Town and Country Magazine.[14] In the early nineteenth century, he also produced designs for La Belle Assemblée and annuals including The Amulet (1826–36), Friendship's Offering (1824–44) and The Keepsake (1828–57). A. C. Coxhead's painstaking work on the Stothard archives held by the British and Victoria and Albert Museums concludes that over ninety unsigned illustrations published in the Lady's Magazine between 1780 and 1797 were engraved after the artist's designs. Yet the actual total will have been significantly higher given that Stothard's association with the magazine extended a further two decades into the 1820s.[15] Those illustrations that we can conclusively identify as Stothard's demonstrate his incredible versatility and include: frontispieces; portraits; illustrations of news items such as Margaret Nicholson's attempt to assassinate George III in 1786 and the 1794 Ratcliffe Highway fire; and, most prominently, illustrations for moral tales (Figure 5.6) and serial fiction such as 'Charlotte Bateman; A Tale' (1782–3).

Many of Stothard's designs were engraved for the magazine by James Heath (1757–1834), Stothard's Newman Street neighbour and friend, and an artist whose connection with the Robinsons and the *Lady's Magazine* was of a similarly long duration. Heath was made associate engraver of the Royal Academy in 1791 and, three years later, was appointed historical engraver to George III. His career began two decades earlier in 1771: the year that Robinson and Roberts bought the *Lady's Magazine* and the same year that Heath was apprenticed to one of the periodical's earliest illustrators, Collyer. Various sources suggest that George Robinson senior funded Heath's apprenticeship to Collyer, although Sir John Heath, the family's biographer, has cast doubt upon the assertion.[16] Whatever the precise nature of their business relationship, the Robinson and Heath families enjoyed close personal and business associations for at least half a century, with James serving as one of the executors of George Robinson junior's will in 1811. It is not known precisely when James Heath started producing engravings for the *Lady's Magazine*, but it was likely before the Supplement issue of 1784 when his signature first appeared underneath 'A Woman of Unanlashka', one of a series of illustrations the artist produced to accompany the magazine's serialisation of Cook's voyages (June 1784–February 1789). He produced dozens more engravings for the magazine over the next four decades, including portraits for biographies of the likes of William Pitt, the Prince Regent, Nelson, Wellington, the Empress Josephine and Lucien Buonaparte and, from the late 1810s, engravings to illustrate the new review section to which I return below (Figure 5.7).[17]

The Heath family's relationship with the magazine was consolidated further via two of James's children: his daughter, Caroline (c.1789–1880), who married the magazine's former printer-turned-editor Hamilton; and his engraver, illustrator, entrepreneur and publisher son, Charles Heath (1785–1848). Like his father, Charles produced many engravings for the periodical, especially illustrations for reviews (Figure 5.8). Heath's pioneering work with Jacob Perkins, the inventor of siderography, was enthusiastically embraced by the *Lady's Magazine* in 1823 when it introduced steel-plate engravings for the first time.[18] The year is doubly significant, coinciding as it does with Heath's assumption of editorial responsibility for the *Lady's Magazine* after Hamilton went bankrupt and absconded. Although it is unclear how long Heath served in this role, the likely overlap of his editorship with his work on the *Forget Me Not*, the *Literary Souvenir*, and *The Amulet* is significant, and may

Figure 5.6 Thomas Stothard, *The Remonstrance*, from the *Lady's Magazine* for October 1780. Private collection.

Figure 5.7 James Heath after Henry Corbould, *The Abbot*. This engraving, which accompanied a review/extract of Sir Walter Scott's 1820 novel of the same name appeared in the *Lady's Magazine* for January 1821. Private collection.

Figure 5.8 Charles Heath after Robert Smirke, *The Light of the Haram*, an engraving to accompany a serialised review-extract of Thomas Moore's *Lalla Rookh* (1817), from the *Lady's Magazine* for December 1822. Private collection.

help to explain the magazine's direction-changing preoccupation with this new periodical form at the time. From the 1820s into the 1830s, the *Lady's Magazine* started to appropriate ever more content from the annuals, eventually rebranding itself a 'companion' to these stylish and more costly publications. This development, to which I return below, altered the magazine in fundamental ways. When he attempted to clear up the mess left by his brother-in-law, Hamilton, Heath prevented the premature demise of the magazine, but he also irrevocably changed its future. By the mid-1820s, the magazine was starting to feel and look like a very different proposition to its readers.

Fashioning the Reader, Restyling the Magazine

The engravings most associated today with the *Lady's Magazine* were late additions. Among the most obvious differences between the magazine before and after 1800 are the regularity and extent of its fashion coverage. To many modern readers, the periodical is still best known for the elegant, hand-coloured fashion plates and associated reports on the latest London and Parisian styles that finally became regular features at the turn of the nineteenth century. Scholarship on the *Lady's Magazine* has tended also to privilege fashion content above the rest of the magazine's diverse textual offerings. Edward Copeland has gone so far as to argue that 'fashion' was not merely a preoccupation of the periodical, but its 'operative language', adding that to 'make any sense of it at all', readers needed to be fashion literate.[19] Likening the experience of reading the *Lady's Magazine* to 'window-shopping', Copeland imagines its ideal subscriber as a consumer who 'turns rapidly through the pages to glance at the illustration of the month's story, skips to the end [to] see if there is perhaps an illustration of a Paris Dress or some sheet music or a pattern for an apron', after which the reader is 'free to turn to the tale and peruse its columns through the decoding lens of fashion'.[20] The magazine, according to his influential account, was a print arena in which readers were forced to navigate the Scylla and Charybdis of morals and modishness and substance and style.

Dress and fashion were indeed central to the *Lady's Magazine* from its inception (Figure 5.9). These interrelated topics played important roles in the periodical's ongoing conversation about women's place in society and feature heavily in many items that, on first glance, seem to have little to do with these subjects. Descriptions and discussions of dress feature prominently in diverse content types, from anthropological accounts of the peoples and customs of the Pacific, Japan and Tartary, to

Figure 5.9 *A Lady in Full Dress* from the *Lady's Magazine* for August 1770. Bayerische Staatsbibliothek München, Per. 123 m-1. urn:nbn:de:bvb:12-bsb10613821-5.

antiquarian essays on sumptuary laws under the Tudors and Stuarts. The folly or wisdom of fashion – a fine line drawn differently depending on the wearer's age or socio-economic position – is frequently raised in the periodical's moral essays, 'The Matron' and other advice columns. And a significant percentage of the magazine's fiction – like contemporary fiction outside it – uses dress as a vehicle to debate wider concerns about morality and economics. Yet fashion journalism, as we would now call it, was conspicuously thin on the ground in the magazine for at least the first thirty years of its publication, despite the promise made to readers in the inaugural issue that 'sartorial intelligence' would be one of several editorial priorities.[21] The changes wrought by the eventual introduction of this content were material, but not in the ways we might initially imagine. The difficulty presented by the magazine's inclusion of more extensive fashion coverage was not – as is conventionally argued – that this coverage conflicted with an editorial commitment to women's intellectual improvement. The problem, as we will see, was that the nature of this coverage undermined the agency and authority it once accorded readers around matters of self-fashioning and self-presentation.

Until regular fashion reports and plates appeared in the magazine in 1800, the most reliable and practical sources of sartorial information the periodical provided were the embroidery patterns for embellishing garments, accessories and household objects that it issued every month between August 1770 and December 1819 (Figure 5.10). These hundreds of needlework patterns have received little critical attention largely because of the inserts' low survival rate.[22] Intended to be removed for use and designed to be transferred to fabrics in ways that would not necessarily facilitate reuse, the patterns were not meant to be bound up in annual volumes of the magazine. Although each issue of the periodical lists the subject of the month's pattern on its contents page, the 'Directions to the Binder' published at the end of the year's Supplement issue to instruct on the placement of engravings usually omit the patterns entirely or specifically instruct excision. Surviving examples of the around 650 patterns that were published in the magazine and found scattered now in bound volumes in libraries and private collections are, therefore, accidents of posterity.

Scarcity is not the only reason why the patterns have fallen below the scholarly radar. A further problem, as Chloe Wigston Smith elaborates, is posed by their failure to align with long-held assumptions about the magazine. The decline-into-domesticity thesis challenged throughout this book is further complicated by the magazine's needlework designs. While Shevelow identified 'needlework and fashion' as two of the consumer-oriented, passive and insidiously feminine interests that the

Figure 5.10   A New Pattern for a Winter Shawl from the Lady's Magazine for December 1796. Private collection.

Lady's Magazine promoted at the expense of women's minds, the patterns themselves tell a different story.[23] Printed without accompanying instruction or guidance on colours or stitches, they assume a high level of 'material literacy' from readers, whom the magazine could expect to have the requisite skills and taste to scale, transfer and competently execute the designs in aesthetically pleasing ways.[24] The patterns additionally qualify formerly dominant accounts of Georgian needlework as a form of female oppression by affording women makers affordable access to fashionable embellishment and allowing them, in Smith's words, to 'develop forms of agency outside traditional domestic and commercial institutions'.[25] They also, as editors recognised, encouraged brand loyalty. Subscribers who worked up the patterns could literally wear their allegiance to the magazine, outfitting themselves in gowns, shawls, veils, caps and even shoes that served 'as material evidence of the periodical's readership, their needlework practices, and a sociable community of craft'.[26]

How extensively the patterns were used is difficult to gauge, although their rarity is suggestive and their popularity was regularly confirmed in the periodical's pages. Anecdotal evidence, such as Ellen Weeton's journal entry discussed in Chapter 3, demonstrates that at least some readers relied on the magazine's patterns to update their wardrobes stylishly yet thriftily, and we are beginning to track surviving artefacts embroidered with the periodical's designs (Figure 5.11).[27] A further

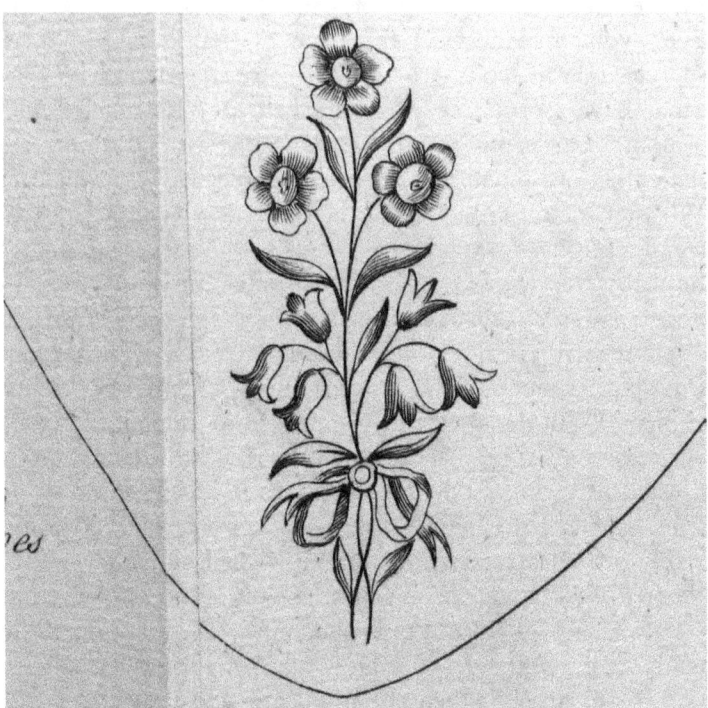

Figure 5.11 (Top) Embroidered shoes held by the Victoria and Albert Museum (Accession No. T.476–1913). Copyright Victoria and Albert Museum, London. (Bottom) Pattern (detail) for a pair of shoes from the *Lady's Magazine* for April 1775. Private collection.

indicator of the patterns' popularity is the enthusiasm with which rival periodicals quickly started issuing their own. The *Lady's Magazine* seems to have been the earliest periodical to include regular needlework patterns.[28] It was undoubtedly the first to make them integral to the women's magazine format, much to the 'alarm' of commercial pattern-drawers whose trade was threatened by the magazine's mass production and circulation of such designs.[29] Other periodicals oriented to female readerships were led by the *Lady's Magazine*'s example. Hogg's *New Lady's Magazine* printed monthly patterns from its first issue, as did the *Fashionable Magazine* (1786), which commissioned the French pattern-drawer, Charles Styart, for the task. In the early nineteenth century, competitor journals, including *La Belle Assemblée* and the *Repository of Arts*, followed suit.[30] And it was not only explicitly female-oriented magazines that included needlework patterns. Some, like the Dublin-based *Hibernian Magazine*, later Walker's *Hibernian Magazine* (1771–1812), used the designs to widen their readership by enticing women subscribers. According to Geraldine Meaney, Mary O'Dowd and Bernadette Whelan, the *Hibernian* owed a good deal of its success 'to the attention it paid to women readers' in the form of 'music scores', 'serialised fiction' and 'embroidery inserts'.[31] Few of these inserts have survived. Those that have reproduce originals that were published usually one or two months earlier in the *Lady's Magazine*, a trend mirrored in the *Hibernian*'s fiction, much of which originated in Robinson's periodical.[32] Whether the reproduction of the patterns was an act of piracy or evidence of a business arrangement between the titles is undocumented.

If the *Lady's Magazine* led in the production and circulation of embroidery patterns, in other aspects of its fashion coverage it was a late adopter. Early promises of assiduous attention to fashion quickly turned to apathy, much to the consternation of some readers. As early as November 1770, the magazine was forced to attempt to appease the disappointed by assuring them that it had 'lost sight of [its] promise to the Fair Sex, of giving them the most early intelligence of the revolutions which shall be made in fashions', by offering them a plate of the fashionably attired actress Ann Catley on stage in *Love in A Village* (Wheble 1: 170). The magazine's first fashion report – 'Undress for the Month of February' – was not published until 1773. Printed without an accompanying plate, the description is typical of the genre in its elliptical and staccato prose, which communicates most effectively to those already in the fashion know: 'The hair in front, with small puff curls; a close cap, made with wings; narrow ribbon, in small puffs; double row of lace; ditto lapelled, doubled and puffed' (4: 72). The following month, the magazine followed with two one-sentence reports on full dress and undress for March, which suggested that fashion's progress, even from month to month, was rapid: the 'Hair front' was now 'lower' than a few weeks earlier and 'puff curls' suddenly negotiable where they had not been just weeks earlier (152).

Perpetuating the sense of fashion's relentless march enabled the magazine to present itself as an essential guide, uniquely privileged by the regularity of its publication to enable readers to navigate fashion's unceasing progress. Its efforts were nevertheless impeded by the magazine's volunteer reporters, who proved as impermanent as the quickly outmoded styles they described. Readers in 1773 who wanted to know if hair fronts would plunge even lower after March had to wait until September for the next update, and thereafter for another four issues for further bulletins. The problem deteriorated before it got better. Charlotte Stanley was by far the most reliable of the *Lady's Magazine*'s fashion reporters, although this is no great compliment. Her career of fashion reporting for the periodical began in March 1774. She wrote three more reports that year but did not resume her column until March 1776 following a barrage of reader complaints. Stanley produced only one more dispatch that year. As late as June 1782, following sporadic reports over the previous two years, regular contributor Henrietta C—p—r, begged Stanley to again bestow her 'elegant favours' upon her readers (13: 312). The plea was in vain, and Stanley's name does not appear in the magazine thereafter.

Beyond annual catalogues of the court 'dresses' worn on the Queen's and King's birthdays, fashion reports became consistent features in the magazine only in the late 1790s and a permanent fixture from 1800, when the magazine finally committed to hand-coloured monthly fashion plates (Figure 5.12). Until this time, fashion plates were rarer items of content than fashion reports, and usually printed with editorial commentary emphasising the cost of their inclusion. The black-and-white plate commissioned for the May 1775 issue to accompany a depiction of the fashions worn at Ranelagh Gardens by Patronessa R— (Figure 5.13) was ordered only because the verbal report itself was too 'obscure' to make sense of in isolation (6: 233). It was a gesture that the editors were not moved to repeat regularly until their hand was forced.

This was despite the fact that fashion had long been a feature of serial publications marketed at women readers. Annual pocket or memorandum books – including the Robinsons' *Ladies Own Memorandum Book* (1769–1803) – had been issuing fashion plates since the 1750s, although the fact that they were published in the autumn prior to the year for which they were designed ensured that the plates' function was more decorative than useful. Some monthlies attempted to introduce

Figure 5.12 *London Walking and Evening Dresses.* Typical hand-coloured fashion plate from the *Lady's Magazine* for March 1812. Private collection.

Rivals: The Changing Face of the Women's Magazine

Figure 5.13 *Two Ladies in the newest Dress From Drawings taken at Ranelagh* from the *Lady's Magazine* for May 1775. Private collection.

plates, including Stanhope's *Lady's Magazine* (1759–63), the December 1759 issue of which, as we saw in Chapter 1, features an engraving of the 'Habit of a Lady' intended to purvey city fashion to provincial subscribers. From the 1770s, plates appeared more regularly in titles including the *Magazine à la Mode, or Fashionable Miscellany* (1776–7), and the *Fashionable Magazine*. French periodicals dedicated to fashion started appearing in the 1780s following the success of the elegant *Les Cabinet des Modes* (1785–93), which was the source of several of the plates in *The Fashionable Magazine*.[33] By the 1790s, the fashion magazine was firmly established, spawning titles such as the British *Gallery of Fashion* (1794–1803), by Niklaus Wilhelm von Heideloff, and the French monthly *Le Journal des Dames et des Modes* (1797–1837), upon which the *Lady's Magazine* kept a watchful and appropriative eye.[34] *Le Journal des Dames* provided originals for many of the *Lady's Magazine*'s earliest Parisian plates in the 1800s.

The periodical's London fashion coverage was urged by two publications closer to home. The first of these was the *Magazine of Female Fashions of London and Paris* (1798–1806), which contained several coloured plates per month and was considerably more affordable than Heideloff's *Gallery*.[35] 1798 also, and more importantly, saw the launch of the *Lady's Monthly Museum* by Thomas Vernor and Thomas Hood. Although this self-declared 'elegant and useful publication for the fair sex' did not explicitly market itself as a rival to the *Lady's Magazine* in the way that Hogg's *New Lady's Magazine* did, its 'Prospectus' (1798) made clear that there would be considerable crossover with Robinson's publication. The periodicals' business models were similar. The *Museum*, like the *Lady's Magazine* relied heavily upon volunteer contributors, although we know that the 'Society of Ladies', who authored it, included at least some regularly paid contributors such as Mary Pilkington. Moreover, the kinds of submissions the *Museum* encouraged were nearly identical to those of the *Lady's Magazine*. The *Museum* promised: 'Novels, Tales, and Romances'; 'Poetry original and selected'; short pieces in French; and 'Charades and Enigmas'.[36] Here the similarities end. The *Museum* deliberately set out to look very different from its predecessor. It dropped the traditional twin-columned eighteenth-century magazine format, was considerably smaller – a 'convenient size for the pocket' – and was 'fancifully done up in coloured paper'. It also promised departures in content. Biographies were made headline features and a substantial reviews section was instituted. Subscribers were also informed that they would not be 'taxed by the necessity of pursuing unending narratives' (2), a thinly veiled dig at the several *Lady's Magazine* serials that were left unfinished by contributors. But it was in its fashion coverage that the *Museum* claimed to be most innovative. Acknowledging that it was 'not the fortune of every one to move in a sphere or to occupy a station where the prevalent state can be caught by the eye and copied in the dress', Vernor and Hood's periodical boasted 'not only a verbal description' of monthly fashions, but also a 'COLOURED plate of fashionable modes' in every issue ('Prospectus', 2). The 'Cabinet of Fashion' section launched in the periodical's inaugural July 1798 issue with a plate of two figures adorned in a Sutton wrap and curricle respectively. Just two sentences of text accompany the image, but the magazine promised to 'excel . . . any similar production' with respect to fashion coverage in future months (1: 60). It lived up to expectations, but its excellence came at a price. The *Museum* offered its readers less text content than the more densely printed and larger *Lady's Magazine* for a higher cover price.

For many readers, the *Lady's Monthly Museum* was worth the additional expense. Recognising as much, within eighteen months, the *Lady's Magazine* also became a shilling monthly so that it too could publish fashion plates and reports. Less than a decade later, both publications revised their fashion coverage following the launch of *La Belle Assemblée*. This stylish royal octavo publication reflected the high production values of its influential publisher, John Bell (1745–1831). *La Belle Assemblée* launched in February 1806 with a grandiose announcement that its editors were 'laying the foundation of a Work that, in the comprehensiveness of its instruction, the variety of its amusements, and the elegance of its embellishment, has had no parallel in the history of periodical publications'.[37] The periodical's original and reprinted contents were, indeed, rich and varied. Rather like the *Lady's Magazine*, however, the magazine remains best known today for its dedicated and substantial multi-page monthly fashion section, which in the first issue alone included the reports 'London Fashions for the Present Month'; 'Parisian Fashions, for February'; 'General Observations on Fashions and Fashionables'; 'Three whole length Portraits, and four Head Dresses of the London Fashions'; 'Five whole length Portraits of Parisian Fashions'; and four embroidery patterns. At this point, the plates were black-and-white engravings, but this changed ten months later. According to Bell's biographer, Stanley Morison, the publisher's hand was forced to make the change because of competition from his son, John Browne Bell's (1779–1855), *Le Beau Monde, and Monthly Register* (1806–9). By December 1806, *La Belle Assemblée* was issued in two formats: one with uncoloured engravings costing two shillings and sixpence per issue; and another with coloured plates costing a shilling an issue more.[38] Even at its lowest price point, *La Belle Assemblée* commanded more than double the fee per issue of the *Lady's Magazine,* and we must assume that the periodicals' readerships were different even if they shared some contributors.[39] Nonetheless, *La Belle Assemblée* and successors, such as Rudolph Ackermann's *Repository of Arts,* undoubtedly raised periodical readers' expectations – particularly about the quality and quantity of fashion plates – to which the *Lady's Magazine* had to pay heed.

One further and critical innovation to which the *Lady's Magazine* had to respond was *La Belle Assemblée*'s emphasis on named authorities for its sartorial intelligence. Rather than relying upon fashion-conscious correspondents like Charlotte Stanley, *La Belle Assemblée* and the *Repository of Arts* affiliated themselves with a succession of individual dressmakers in the capital. In one of the earliest examples of this kind, the May 1806 *Belle Assemblée* contained a 'Plate containing whole length Figures of the Fashionable Spring Dresses, drawn by Mr. Devis, from the elegant Designs of Madame Lanchester'.[40] Madame (Margaret) Lanchester was previously the editor of the lavish but short-lived *Le Miroir de la Mode* (1803). As the *Repository* later notes, her 'taste' and authority 'in the department of ladies' dress and female ornaments' was 'so well known' as to 'render any eulogium unnecessary'.[41] In 1809, Lanchester was replaced by Mrs Bell, who ran her famous millinery, dress- and corset-making establishment out of a succession of establishments in Bloomsbury and St James's. Mary Anne Bell (*née* Millard), was John Bell's daughter-in-law via her marriage to the aforementioned John Browne Bell, with whom she would collaborate on the *World of Fashion and Continental Feuilletons* (1824–51). Fashions devised by this celebrated 'Inventress' appeared in column after column and plate after plate in *La Belle Assemblée* for nearly a decade, while advertisements for her latest inventions, including the Circassian, Royal and Armenian Divorce and pregnancy corsets for which she was especially known, frequently headed the periodical's monthly advertising sheets.

The *Lady's Monthly Museum* quickly responded to *La Belle Assemblée*'s move by adopting its own named fashion authorities. After dragging its heels for some time, the *Lady's Magazine* eventually did the same. In July 1818, the periodical declared itself 'indebted to the taste of Miss Macdonald' of 50 South Moulton Street, Bond Street, for information about a new style of 'dinner dress', and suggested that it had 'more than once [before] received patterns of elegant dresses' from her in the past. (The *Museum* had been showcasing Miss Macdonald's gowns for several months prior to this.) Miss Macdonald was soon replaced in the *Lady's Magazine* by Mrs W. Smith of 15 Old Burlington Street, 'whose suite of apartments' had recently 'opened with a selection of very elegant

Rivals: The Changing Face of the Women's Magazine

Figure 5.14 *Evening Dress* designed by Mrs Smith from the *Lady's Magazine* for April 1819. Private collection.

novelties' (49 (November 1818): 529) (Figure 5.14). She was eventually superseded in 1823 by Miss Pierpoint, of 12 Edward Street, Portman Square, to whom the *Lady's Monthly Museum* had looked since 1819, and who remained a continuous presence until 1828 when the *Museum* and *Lady's Magazine* merged.

The precise nature of these magazines' relationship with the dressmakers to whom they turned for sartorial guidance is unclear. Whether the women who wrote the copy that accompanied plates illustrating their gowns and accessories were remunerated for their advice, or whether they paid to advertise their businesses in the magazines, has been impossible to determine. Regardless, the implications for readers of bringing professional dressmakers into the pages of the *Lady's Magazine* were varied and profound. As Laura Engel observes, fashion reports and images that linked specific garments and accessories to '"real" women and actual shops' functioned as 'ideological and material advertisements for idealised forms of femininity'.[42] On the one hand, they made fashion seem attainable, literally directing readers to the fashionable London streets from which the latest styles could be ordered and purchased; on the other hand, these fashionable Bloomsbury and St James's addresses made clear just how geographically and financially out of reach these fashions were for the majority of *Lady's Magazine* subscribers. More importantly, the move to cite named dressmakers and milliners signalled a new commitment on the periodical's part to professionalisation and to the re-siting of authority with established authorities rather than the personal expertise of readers.

Dress historians continue to debate whether fashion plates accurately reflect what real people wore, although Hilary Davidson's recent description of such images as primarily 'aspirational' is undoubtedly accurate, perhaps especially for the *Lady's Magazine*, which attracted a middling and lower-middling sort of readership.[43] In the field of literary history, this same aspirational quality is conventionally interpreted as evidence of the impossibly contradictory demands that magazines make of women readers. Fashion plates have been charged with various offences, from fuelling desires incompatible with the middle-class socio-economic and moral values historic that women's magazines claimed to uphold, to undermining the intellectual ambitions that periodical editors formerly harboured for their readers.[44] The inclusion of regular fashion plates undoubtedly changed the appearance of the *Lady's Magazine*. Yet at first, they did little to alter the periodical's philosophy and tone. Like the annual descriptions of court dresses that had been part of the magazine since its inception, the images and the longer fashion reports merely presented readers with an image of a fashionable world of which many subscribers would have no first-hand experience. Within two decades, however, the picture changed.

The termination of the needlework patterns in 1820 coupled with the rise of the authorised fashion plate and report marked a shift in direction for the magazine that was of much wider significance. The patterns were more than the Georgian equivalent of a free gift. They were a material acknowledgement of readers' skill and – like the magazine's text-based contents – required makers actively to exercise their taste and judgement as they worked with the designs to adorn and fashion their public selves. Moreover, as Smith contends, the patterns acknowledged the sartorial know-how of readers and 'undermined the authority of the professional dress and tailoring trades'.[45] Observers of fashion plates – the passive window-shoppers, in Copeland's phrase, of goods that few could afford regularly or even at all – occupied a very different relation to the magazine's contents than women like Weeton, who removed and used its patterns to embellish and update their clothing. The magazine's granting of authority to named professionals such as Miss Macdonald, Mrs Smith and Miss Pierpoint, rather than to subscribers – the makers of its patterns and the readers and authors of its contents – was an unavoidable move in light of periodical competition, but as we will see in the following section, it was more broadly indicative of a shift in the magazine's priorities, which fundamentally changed the periodical's character and its relationship to its readers.

Reviews, Fiction, Poetry and the Professionalisation of the *Lady's Magazine*

Beyond the design evolutions discussed above, the magazine's change of direction is most evident in the shifts in content type after 1800. As with the periodical's fashion coverage, much of the 'new' content that the magazine introduced in the nineteenth century marked less of an editorial departure than a reconsideration and re-weighting of longstanding preoccupations, which combined to produce a very different magazine. The magazine's critical appraisal of recently published works is a case in point. Like fashion journalism, reviews had always been an occasional interest of the *Lady's Magazine*, but they came to prominence only after 1810. As we saw in Chapter 2, theatrical journalism had a presence in the periodical from its launch. The September 1770 issue featured the first of the many hundreds of 'Accounts' of plays and theatrical entertainments to appear across the periodical's run, in this instance a description of a 'New Burletta' entitled 'The Madman' performed at Marylebone

Gardens (Wheble 1: 76). Over the next few months, Wheble's *Lady's Magazine* devoted ever more column inches to all things theatrical, from further 'Accounts', to biographies and anecdotes, occasional engravings of actors and transcriptions of prologues and epilogues. September 1772 saw an increased commitment to this aspect of the magazine's coverage with the launch of 'The Theatrical Intelligencer, or Female Guide to the Play-houses'. Quite what made the column's intelligence 'Female' is not clarified by reading the column, which died with Wheble's magazine in December 1772. Robinson's periodical was not as committed to theatrical matters initially, although 'Accounts' of tragedies, comedies, pantomimes, puppet shows, ballets and operas were present from the outset. Like the aforementioned 'Account of the Madman', most of these pieces seem to originate in newspapers and appear simultaneously or near simultaneously in several magazines.[46] Largely synoptic rather than critical, the accounts provide cast lists, plot summaries and conclude with a brief paragraph of evaluative commentary.

Reviews of prose and poetry volumes are much rarer in the magazine before 1800. Extracts from previously published works of literary criticism, such as Joseph Addison's essays on Milton and appraisals of the works and careers of Alexander Pope, Elizabeth Rowe and Elizabeth Griffith, are certainly present in the magazine's early years. Yet reviews, as we would recognise them today, are absent until the late 1810s. This is surprising, not least because refusing to publish reviews for so long put the periodical unusually out of step with its competitors. As Antonia Forster documents, following the launch of the *Monthly Review* (founded 1749) and the *Critical Review* (founded 1756), it was 'an accepted fact' that new magazines would include lists and critical accounts of new publications.[47] These expectations intensified with the founding of the influential *Edinburgh Review* (in 1802) and *Quarterly Review* (in 1809). From the mid-eighteenth century, short reviews were introduced into several periodicals including the *Gentleman's*, *London* and *British Magazines*. In one of its few departures from its namesake, the *New Lady's Magazine* also included 'a Critical and Impartial Review of such new Books and Publications as are offered to the Ladies either for their Improvement or Entertainment'. It was an innovation that the *Lady's Magazine* declined to emulate. Nor did the magazine respond a decade later to the *Lady's Monthly Museum*'s substantial 'Review' section. The *Lady's Magazine*'s decision not to cater to periodical readers' taste for reviews is seems all the more surprising when we consider that the *Town and Country* had provided capsule reviews – and therefore potential shared copy – since its launch in 1769. The matter becomes curiouser still when we consider that George Robinson had a stake in the *Critical Review* from around the time that he bought the *Lady's Magazine*.

Why the *Lady's Magazine* so frequently mined the back catalogue of the *Critical* and other Reviews for material it could excerpt yet declined for so long to commission reviews of its own is a puzzle. It is possible that the decision was linked to the magazine's determination to maintain its identity as a reader-oriented and reader-created print community that imagined itself in opposition to the 'corporate' monolithic periodical identities that Jon Klancher associates with many early nineteenth-century literary magazines and Reviews.[48] This is certainly the impression generated by the 'pseudo-reviews', for want of a better phrase, that the magazine occasionally printed in its first half-century of publication, and that died a death in 1820, by which time its review section was fully established.[49] Reader-authored appraisals of recently published works occupy a corner of most mid- to late-century periodicals and even some Reviews.[50] Those in the *Lady's Magazine* usually take the form of excerpted extracts with a prefatory note or short essay. Where a genuine reader review begins and a shameless puff ends is not always easy to discern. It cannot be coincidence that several such appraisals in the *Lady's Magazine* showcase works from the Robinson catalogue. Take, for instance, 'Remarks on Mrs. Inchbald's Novel, entitled *Nature and Art*' signed Eliz. L— (April and July 1796). Eliz. L— recommends Inchbald's novel, published by the Robinsons earlier that year, to 'such of [the magazine's] readers who seek rational amusement' in novel reading, and goes on to elaborate how this superficially 'simple' fable is, in fact, a cleverly satirical fiction 'peculiarly adapted to the dangerous errors of the present times' (27 (April 1796): 168). The account features lengthy extracts from *Nature and Art* and takes several opportunities to condemn the critical reception of the controversial novel by attacking the ignorance and hypocrisy of professional reviewers who 'call themselves *British*' and yet 'reverence' the abuses of the power of which Inchbald's novel is scathingly critical (168). Whether Eliz. L— is a genuine reader or a staff writer covertly promoting the work of Inchbald – a woman who called George Robinson her 'best friend on earth' – is difficult to determine.[51]

Puff or not, within twenty years, such appraisals fell out of favour. In January 1814, the periodical finally launched a list of 'Books Recently Published' in its back pages, supplemented – from October of that year – by notices of 'Literary Intelligence' that catalogued books in production. Three years later, the *Lady's Magazine* instituted a significant shift of approach to its reviewing practices and with it inaugurated one of the most important changes in the magazine's history: the introduction of a dedicated and beautifully illustrated section entitled 'Review of New Publications'. The move coincided with a redesign of the magazine's layout that brought it more in line its nearest competitors. Until this point, the magazine's structure was – to put it politely – informal. Subscribers knew that they could find the poetry section at the back of the magazine, where it was followed by lists of births, marriages and deaths and the news section. By the early 1800s, readers keenly interested in fashion would know to flick to just before the poetry section, where their fingers would meet the heavier paper stock used for the fashion plates, opposite which they could locate information on the latest London and Paris styles. The rest of the magazine's content was printed more indiscriminately and with no differentiation between what *La Belle Assemblée* termed 'Original Communications' (written by correspondents for the publication) and 'Miscellanies' (that is, excerpted content). This changed in February 1817 – the same issue that saw the launch of the 'Reviews' section and the dispute about Brighty's engravings. The *Lady's Magazine* finally adopted the section heads used by Bell's publication: 'Original Communications', 'Miscellanies', 'Poetry', 'Fashions', 'Dramatic Intelligence', the 'Chronicle' (the renamed news section) and lists of births, marriages and deaths. This was more than a cosmetic change; the new 'Review' section headed the brave, new and ordered periodical world the *Lady's Magazine* sought to present to its readers.

The first official review that the magazine published was of Lord Byron's *The Prisoner of Chillon, and other Poems* (1816). From 1812, the year in which Byron notoriously remarked that he had woken up to find himself famous, the *Lady's Magazine* enthusiastically played its part in what Nicholas Mason describes as 'Building Brand Byron'.[52] Dozens of his poems are reprinted in the magazine, as well as poetic epistles and imitations from readers, several biographical accounts, a portrait and an extraordinary two-part dialogue between the deceased Byron and Buonaparte, which appeared in June and July 1828. The magazine's characteristically fascinated yet cautious view of Byron's life and work infuses the two-page unsigned review of *The Prisoner of Chillon*, which acknowledges how 'highly wrought' Byron's poetry is but laments the 'gloomy tincture of misanthropy' that infuses the 'slight performance'. The review concludes that Byron would be a better poet if he showed as much 'respect' to his 'merited reputation' as he did to his 'public' (28 (February 1817): 51–2).[53] Poetry continues to dominate the reviews section for the rest of the year in the form of a multi-part illustrated review of Thomas Moore's *Lalla Rookh* (1817). Other featured works include novels – such as Anne Ker's *Edric the Forester* (1817), Jane

Porter's *The Pastor's Fire-Side* (1815) and Sir Walter Scott's *Tales of My Landlord* (from 1816) – travel writing and non-fiction volumes on grammar, music, medicine, cosmetics and even butchery. Of the sixteen works reviewed in total from February to the end of 1817, ten were authored by men, three by women and three were anonymous. Male-authored works continued to dominate the reviews section for years to come, but women poets and particularly women novelists were well-represented and reviews of their work played an important role in the periodical's ongoing project – to which I return in Chapter 6 – to accord women authors their rightful place in literary history and curate their reputations for posterity.

The magazine undoubtedly had its favourite authors and often these preferences – such as the periodical's warm appreciation of Scott and Porter – fell in line with broader critical consensus. But the *Lady's Magazine* was not always of a mind with the Reviews and literary magazines, both of which forms were themselves subject to sustained criticism in the periodical. Occasionally the magazine recommended Reviews and literary journals for the edification of its female readers, as it did in the June 1798 'Thoughts on the Propriety of young Ladies reading Criticisms in the different Reviews', which enjoined governesses to allow their charges to read 'works of fancy' alongside a review 'article, in one, or more literary journals, where that work is commented on' (29 (June 1798): 261). More frequently, though, the *Lady's Magazine* lambasted Reviews and literary magazines for their self-serving and unsparing criticisms, especially their criticisms of women writers and popular genres. According to Mr Playfair, the pseudonymous author of an 1815 article 'On Reviewers', the profession sorely needed 'regulation'. 'The reviewers', he wrote, formed 'a considerable literary phalanx, whether estimated by their numbers, or by their talents, or by the mode they have of distributing their works'. The old-boy networks concealed by reviewers' anonymity needed exposing, he continued, and reviewers' propensity to compliment only those who were already 'favourite[s]' of those 'connected with themselves' had to be challenged, even if regulation of the reviewing profession did not seem 'practicable' at first glance (46 (Supp 1815): 594–5).

Playfair's criticism was playing to the gallery of readers all too aware of the animosity levelled by the Reviews at the *Lady's Magazine* and its contributors. The measure of the Reviews' collective disdain is amply demonstrated by the dismissive notices of novels such as *Derwent Priory* (1798) and *Grasville Abbey* (1797) discussed in the previous chapter. It is evident also in their general disparagement of the popular print forms with which the *Lady's Magazine* was most closely associated. As the anonymous author of 'On Criticism' (November 1804) intimated, the Reviews' habit of 'damning in the lump' the kinds of writing published in the *Lady's Magazine*, along with novels published by the Minerva Press or written for the circulating libraries, evidenced an insidious and transparently gendered disdain for women's writing and reading habits. Quite how the *Lady's Magazine* felt about being thus lumped with novels published by the author of 'On Criticism' is undocumented, although its editors were surely aware that Minerva novels and novelists were sometimes less than complimentary.[54] Despite this, the *Lady's Magazine* publicly endorsed many of the Press's writers and championed their work in the form of excerpts, advertisements and laudatory critical notices (Figure 5.15).[55] Such endorsements partly reflect the fact that the *Lady's Magazine* shared several authors with Minerva, including Mary Pilkington, Catherine Day Haynes/Golland, Barbara Hofland and Amelia Opie. They also serve as a polemical gesture for a publication that, by the 1820s, was actively styling itself as an alternative to the Reviews. A 'Letter to the Editor' (April 1823), signed Jane Fisher, was one of several items published around this time to praise the periodical in these terms when it praised the *Lady's Magazine* for being 'as universally read as these sterner works of criticism' and much more conducive to readers' 'pleasure' (54: 215).

Literary journals and magazines were not flattered by such comparisons and were still more displeased when the *Lady's Magazine*'s emulation extended to appropriations of their contents. A bitter exchange broke out in 1819 when the *Lady's Magazine* began reprinting original works that had originally appeared in *Blackwood's* (founded in April 1817) despite its much-repeated objections that the Edinburgh periodical was 'too erudite' and 'too local' to interest the majority of its readers. In the October 1819 issue, the editor of the *Lady's Magazine* devoted much of the month's 'Correspondents' column to refuting claims that he had, '"without alteration, abridgement, or acknowledgement"', reprinted works by Samuel Taylor Coleridge and John Wilson previously published by 'the respectable Proprietor of *Blackwood's*'. Harking back to the debates aired at the 1771 trial about the *Lady's Magazine*'s ownership, the editor was forced to address the question of whether or not such a thing as '"invasion of property"' existed in the realm of periodical publication. Unsurprising, the *Lady's Magazine* denied that it did, and assured *Blackwood's* that any mimicry of its contents was meant only as a 'compliment to [*Blackwood's*] excellence' ('Correspondents'). Within a decade, the continuing altercation had become so acrimonious that even the veneer of civility was abandoned. The *Lady's Magazine* branded *Blackwood's* a bad-tempered, 'snarling cur' and dismissed the

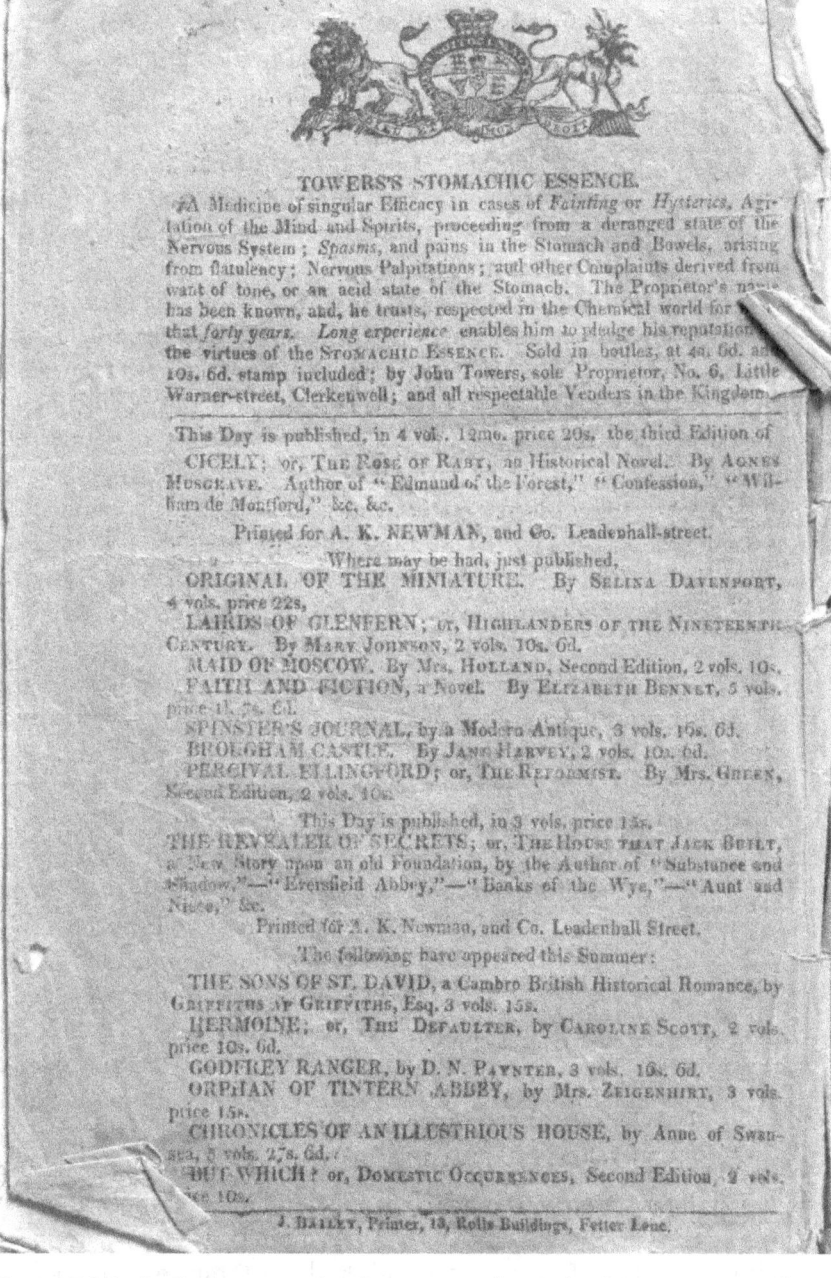

Figure 5.15 Back wrapper with advertisements for medical preparations and Minerva Press novels from the *Lady's Magazine* for September 1816. Private collection.

latter's declaration that Robinson's periodical 'ha[d] no business, and should not interfere with its masculine contemporaries' as jealous and misogynist raving. The editor of the *Lady's Magazine* pointed out that women readers were vital to the commercial success of 'nine ... out of ten' journals and presented its own contents, especially its reviews, as key to its utility as a publication that further helped refine women's understanding by directing their 'attention' to such works 'as they may, in this age of degeneracy and immortality, safely peruse' (2nd new ser. 2 (November–December 1830): 306).

In isolation, the addition of the reviews section might seem of limited import. Critical notices had, as already noted, been a feature of eighteenth-century magazines for many decades before they were introduced in the *Lady's Magazine*. The timing and nature of the move indicates otherwise, however. Many of the 'reviews' that the magazine published, especially its multi-part appraisals of Moore's poetry and Scott's novels, are ostensibly serialised abridgements that contain little to no evaluative commentary. This alone might seem unimportant given that many Reviews often resorted to printing lengthy excerpts bookended with minimal critical commentary. Yet in the context of the magazine, it marked a decisive shift as these extended excerpts of recently published novels and poetry coincided precisely with a sharp decline in the volume of original fiction and verse contributions by correspondents with which the magazine had been so long associated.

From Patrick Brontë's objections to its 'foolish love stories' to Robert D. Mayo's accusations of amateurism, the reputation of the *Lady's Magazine* has long been inextricably and problematically bound up with its fiction. The association is misleading on at least two counts. First, as I have argued throughout this book, the assumptions that underpin blanket dismissals of the quality of the writing do not hold up to scrutiny.[56] Second, fiction – while always a vital part of the magazine's appeal – only ever represented a relatively modest proportion of the periodical's overall content. A survey of mid-year issues from the magazine's first three decades shows that after a peak in 1770, the total page count devoted to fiction (defined generously to include moral tales, translated fiction and original serials) ranged between around 10 and 25 per cent.[57] Moreover, at various points in its first decades of publication, the magazine's editors sought to streamline its fictional content via attempts to limit the number of parts any given serial novel ran to. Even before the first instalment of the epistolary serial 'Seymour Abbey' (December 1785–November 1787) was published, the editor warned its anonymous author against prolixity. Fearing that the long, yet unfinished, manuscript he had received would either take up too many pages per issue or run for too many months to maintain readers' interest, he politely requested 'a winding up in the next packet', and warned other would-be contributors that 'no *Novel* of similar length would be countenanced in future ('Correspondents', 16 (October 1785): n.p.). Like so many of the magazine's policies, this was an agreement that editors were content to overlook either to fill pages or to draw in readers. At around 60,000 words, readers' favourite 'Derwent Priory' (January 1796–September 1797) was more than twice as long as the approximately 27,000-word 'Seymour Abbey'. 'The Monks and the Robbers' (August 1794–May 1805) was longer still at a hefty 86,500 words.

In the 1810s, attempts to police the length of all but the most successful serials gave way to a concerted effort to reduce the number of original serials that the magazine published at any one time. The May 1812 'Correspondents' column informed readers that 'it is not from choice that we have of late devoted so large a portion of our Magazine to Novels, but from an unpleasant temporary necessity accidentally imposed on us'. The nature of this 'unpleasant . . . necessity' is unspecified, but in 1812 the magazine was certainly publishing more serial fiction – about 50 per cent of the overall content – than it ever had ever done before.[58] This was a temporary aberration, and by 1820 the magazine's commitment to the kinds of reader-authored fiction that Charlotte Brontë nostalgically recalled had dramatically diminished. Contributors had been warned. In March 1819, the editor announced that no 'Occasional Tales' would be admitted to the magazine if they exceeded three or four instalments in order to allow other editorial plans 'to mature' ('Correspondents', 50: n.p.). Three months later, authors were warned that longer serials already in train had to conclude within the calendar year to make way for the 'new series' and its new plan ('Correspondents', 50 (July 1819): n.p.). When that new series launched in 1820, the magazine included no original serialised novels. Only three novellas in instalments appeared across the entire year: the anonymous 'Antonia de Cordova' (likely a translation); G. S.'s three-part 'Stranger Night'; and 'Don Pelajo', the last offering by long-term contributor Sophia Hendry (née Troughton).

Short fiction, which continued to be a mainstay of the magazine in the nineteenth century, weathered changes in editorial policy more successfully by evolving with the times. While the once-dominant gothic, oriental and historical tales, so popular in the magazine's first decades, never entirely disappeared from the magazine, the periodical's preference was increasingly for short works that privileged the local, the particular and the probable. Mitford's 'Our Village' sketches set the tone for the magazine's fictional sensibilities in the years to come. The first of these, which appeared in December 1822, just one month after Catherine Golland's manuscript novel 'A Single Gentleman' was rejected, encapsulates the magazine's changed attitude to original fiction: 'in books I like a confined locality . . . Nothing is so tiresome as to be whirled half over Europe at the chariot-wheels of a hero' (1st new ser. 1: 646). Other short fiction writers followed Mitford's restraint by modifying the length, scope and tone of their imaginative prose. At precisely the same moment that the volume and focus of the magazine's original fiction became much more tightly constrained, the *Lady's Magazine* was increasing the page space it devoted to review extracts of recently published work by established and emerging professional novelists. By this sleight of hand, the periodical was able to maintain that imaginative prose remained an editorial priority, even as it culled original fiction by the contributors who had, for so long, been integral to the magazine's identity and appeal.

Tracking changes in magazine's poetic content from the early nineteenth century exposes a similar trajectory. The periodical's poetry section was one of its most stable components throughout its history. Located for over fifty years in the same place in the periodical's back pages, the poetry section looks virtually the same in 1822 as it does in 1772. Yet in later decades, the magazine's poetic content, like its fiction, evolved in ways that reflected a growing squeamishness about amateurism in the new 'age of periodical publications' as verse penned by contributors was side-lined in favour of already published works ('Address', 52 (January 1821): i). Discerning precisely how much of the *Lady's Magazine*'s poetry is original at any point in its history is difficult. For much of the eighteenth century and the Romantic period, poetry circulated promiscuously among many types of serial publications. Identical copies of the same ode, elegy or sonnet often appeared near simultaneously in multiple journals and newspapers, while other poems reappeared with no or slight variations and sometimes variant signatures for decades. As the previous chapter demonstrated, the magazine undoubtedly provided an important publication venue for a number of poets – such as George Crabbe, Mary Dodwell, James Murray Lacey, Thomas Newby, Charlotte Caroline Richardson, Joanna Squire, John Webb – many of whose works first or exclusively appeared in its pages. From the late 1810s, these poets, like their fellow fiction writers, found ever fewer publishing opportunities in the *Lady's Magazine*. Around this time, a distinct shift in editorial sensibility is detectable as 'Correspondents' columns started to foreshadow twentieth-century criticisms of the slightness and aesthetic demerits of periodical verse. Volunteer contributors working across all genres had always been vulnerable to criticism from the magazine's editors, who claimed they were forced to reject hundreds of readers' 'favours' each month for want of room. Poets had never been immune to such criticisms, but they were now actively dissuaded from sending in any material. In February 1819 the editor wrote to dissuade readers from submitting work to its 'POETICAL department' on the grounds that amateur verse was damaging to the publication's reputation. 'Magazine poetry', he continued, had 'fallen intro discredit', a phenomenon for which he accepted partial blame as he had '*occasionally*' admitted verses 'of little comparative merit' out of 'a wish to oblige Correspondents'. Times had changed, and the magazine aspired to a 'high character' ('Correspondents', 50: n.p.).

Subsequent rejections of poetic contributions continued to be civil for a short while. The March 1819 'Correspondents' column, for instance, pointed out that while T. L.'s poems were not 'sufficiently finished' for a magazine that could publish only the 'most beautiful specimens of fugitive poetry', they were nevertheless 'remarkable for a young lady of fifteen' ('Correspondents', 50: n.p.). Editorial politeness soon evaporated, however, and the barbed comments that had always been directed at a handful of individual contributors were issued more indiscriminately. Sarcasm began to erode the relationships between the magazine and its reader-contributors and many editorial compliments came with a sting in the tale. The magazine's criticism of 'Sappho' is typical. Her poem was so 'beautifully *written*', the editor wrote, that it could not 'appear to greater advantage to print it – *reading* it is out of the question' (53 (June 1822): 336). The only consolation for Sappho was that she one of an increasingly large company of would-be poets who fell victim to the magazine's efforts to hold its own in the reputational line by lampooning individuals before its readership at large.

As with the decline in reader-authored fiction at this time, the periodical's ever more insistent rejections of original fugitive poetry coincided with a marked increase in the magazine's reliance on extracts from already published poetic works by established writers, including John Clare, Samuel Taylor Coleridge, Felicia Hemans, Letitia Elizabeth Landon, Mary Russell Mitford and William Wordsworth. By 1823, fugitive poetry was a negligible presence in the magazine and the poetry section was accordingly dismantled in favour of a small number of largely reprinted verses or verse extracts scattered throughout individual issues. Within twelve months, almost all of this poetic content originated in annuals including the *Amulet*, the *Keepsake* and the *Forget Me Not*. Short prose works from the same were also enthusiastically reprinted. The magazine first started looking to the annuals in October 1824 when it published a review of the *Forget Me Not* for 1825. The notice was universally complimentary and lavishly praised the entrepreneurial insight of Ackermann, who was credited as the 'introducer' of this new periodical form (1st new ser. 5: 544). The 1825 *Forget Me Not* was reviewed the following autumn, as, two years later, was the first volume of the *Amulet*. The November 1827 issue contained a reprint of the *Amulet*'s 'Sir Edgar and His Falcon', which was followed by a review of the 1828 *Forget Me Not*, an annual that the *Lady's Magazine* deemed the superior of the two publications. Nevertheless, the magazine continued to mine the *Amulet* for content, and in December reprinted 'The Last Voyage', a 'True Story' by a long-time favourite of the *Lady's Magazine*, Opie. Poetry and tales taken from these and other annuals by the likes of Hofland, Landon, Mitford, Percy Shelley and Susanna Strickland became an all-year round feature of the *Lady's Magazine* over the next decade. In July 1831 issue, the magazine's debt to the form was acknowledged when it declared itself 'The Companion to the Annuals'. Whether this rebranding captures a formal business relationship between the magazine and the publishers of the annuals or simply commercial opportunism is unknown. Regardless, the companionship was presumably intended to be of mutual benefit. The magazine's extensive reviews of the annuals and reprintings of their contents both advertised and made accessible these elegant publications to a wider audience, while the inclusion of content from the annuals in the periodical made the *Lady's Magazine* a more attractive proposition to readers for whom the annuals were prohibitively expensive. Yet the strategy seems not to have worked and, in conjunction with the other developments documented in this chapter, reimagined the magazine in ways that alienated its traditional readership.

The introduction of reviews and review extracts, coupled with an increased reliance upon reprinted fiction and poetry excerpted from already published sources such as the annuals, constituted radical changes in the *Lady's Magazine*'s format and its relationship to subscribers. These developments were tied to the periodical's bid to be taken seriously as a rival to the Reviews and literary magazines that proliferated from the early nineteenth century even if, as we have seen, the magazine remained deeply sceptical about the credentials, professionalism and objectives of these journals. The magazine never stopped printing original contributions, and some of the best known and highly regarded of the magazine's contributors – like Mitford and Opie – only began writing for it in the 1820s. Nonetheless, the ratio of repurposed to original contributions had shifted markedly this time. Arguably, by being more selective about the nature and volume of original material it published, the mean quality of fictional and poetic content in the *Lady's Magazine* was raised. Yet by closing the door on many dozens of volunteer contributors who had formerly published with the magazine over long periods of time, these innovations ultimately made the periodical more derivative. As the *Lady's*

Magazine attempted to become more and more like its rivals – importing not only their content but also their organisation and layout – it became much less recognisable, as we will see, even to its own staff.

Closing Down the Conversation

In 1830 the *Lady's Magazine, or Mirror of the Belles-Lettres, Fine Arts, Music, Drama, Fashion &c.* launched a second 'improved' series. Although the magazine's title page still bore 'Paternoster Row' and a Robinson on its imprint (now George Robinson senior's grandson, Samuel), this was a very different publication from that sold by Coote to Robinson and Roberts six decades earlier. Material changes to the magazine's paper quality and typeface are the most immediately obvious of these changes, followed by structural changes that moved communications with correspondents and contents lists to the back pages of each issue. Staples of the magazine for the majority of its run – including its serial fiction, dedicated poetry section, embroidery patterns and annual Supplement – had vanished, while other regular features such as reviews, a drama and arts section and fashion plates had been introduced. Some constants remained. The January issue contained: essays on familiar subjects, including 'The Power and Influence of Music' and 'Metropolitan Improvements'; a biography of the recently deceased artist, Sir Thomas Lawrence; poetry reprinted from the annuals; and an oriental tale taken from the *Arabian Nights Entertainments*. Most of this and subsequent issues was repurposed from other sources and only two of the very small number of apparently original contributions – poems by Louisa Clark and John S. Clark – are signed.

Traces of the magazine's readers are present only in the new 'Correspondence' (note: 'Correspondence', not 'Correspondents') column, where they are roundly satirised. The opening letter by Julia Flyaway describes a disappointed young reader opening a copy of the periodical at the recommendation of 'an elderly lady' in the hopes of discovering an 'abundance of those "trifles, light as air," with which well-educated and fashionable female are so much delighted' only for her to find to her 'indignation ... no love-tales, no scandal, no wit, no ghost-stories, and, in short, nothing amusing' (2nd new ser. 1: 53). There is little subtlety in this presumably fabricated letter, but it is good value for the magazine in that it provides the periodical with an opportunity both to perform the seriousness of its intent in the form of joke at the expense of the Miss Flyaways of its potential readership and to signal the distance its new editor and proprietor wished to put between their priorities and those of past editors who had been only too glad to fill their pages with tales authored by another Julia, R. or C. D. H.

Flyaway's letter is further indicative of the magazine's tendency post-1820 to suppress the reader debate it once actively encouraged. Her letter's attempt to initiate a conversation that the magazine swiftly closes down is but one of numerous examples from this later period of the magazine's history that the days of discussion about women's education and reading tracked in Chapter 3 were over. The periodical had, in fact, long ceased to offer opportunities for conversation between texts and their authors, favouring editorial consensus created through the 'judicious selections' of the works it excerpted or reviewed and the original material for which it made room (1st new ser. 10 (January 1829): ii). On no subject was the twice-improved *Lady's Magazine* more certain than that of 'woman'. The periodical's once determined commitment to the 'mental cultivation' of the fair sex did not die, but in the 1820s and 1830s its understanding of the ends of this process did. To quote the despondent author of 'Woman', the essay that opens the February 1825 issue: 'The times [had] changed' and women's sights, like the magazine's, were set on determining how the female sex could 'exercise their virtues in domestic retirement'. '[W]ise' women were no longer defined by learning and habits of thinking, as they were in the magazine's first four decades, but by their resolve not to set their ambitions beyond the domestic sphere, the scope of which had significantly contracted since the periodical launched. Modern women could 'perceive the bad taste manifested in striving for mastery with man' and were 'contented' by spending their time in 'truly feminine occupations', centred around the domestic comforts of their husbands and children (1st new ser. 6: 65). As we saw in Chapters 2 and 3, when similarly conservative views on women's lives were expressed in the magazine in its first decades, they were generally met with vigorously asserted counterarguments by other readers. If the newly constrained model of womanhood to which the magazine subscribed in the 1820s and 1830s ruffled the sensibilities of readers of the Lady's Magazine, there is no internal evidence. The right of reply extended to readers for so many decades was now denied.

This was a decisive shift for the magazine. Further changes followed. In response to dwindling sales, from 1830 onwards the magazine reached out to other publications to help reverse its fortunes. In additional to becoming 'the *Companion to the Annuals*' in the summer of 1831, in November of the same year the magazine announced a 'union ... with the most elegant of the fashionable Periodicals', the French journal *Le Follet* (1829–92), which gave the *Lady's Magazine* the exclusive right to publish its fashion plates in England (Figure 5.16). In January 1832,

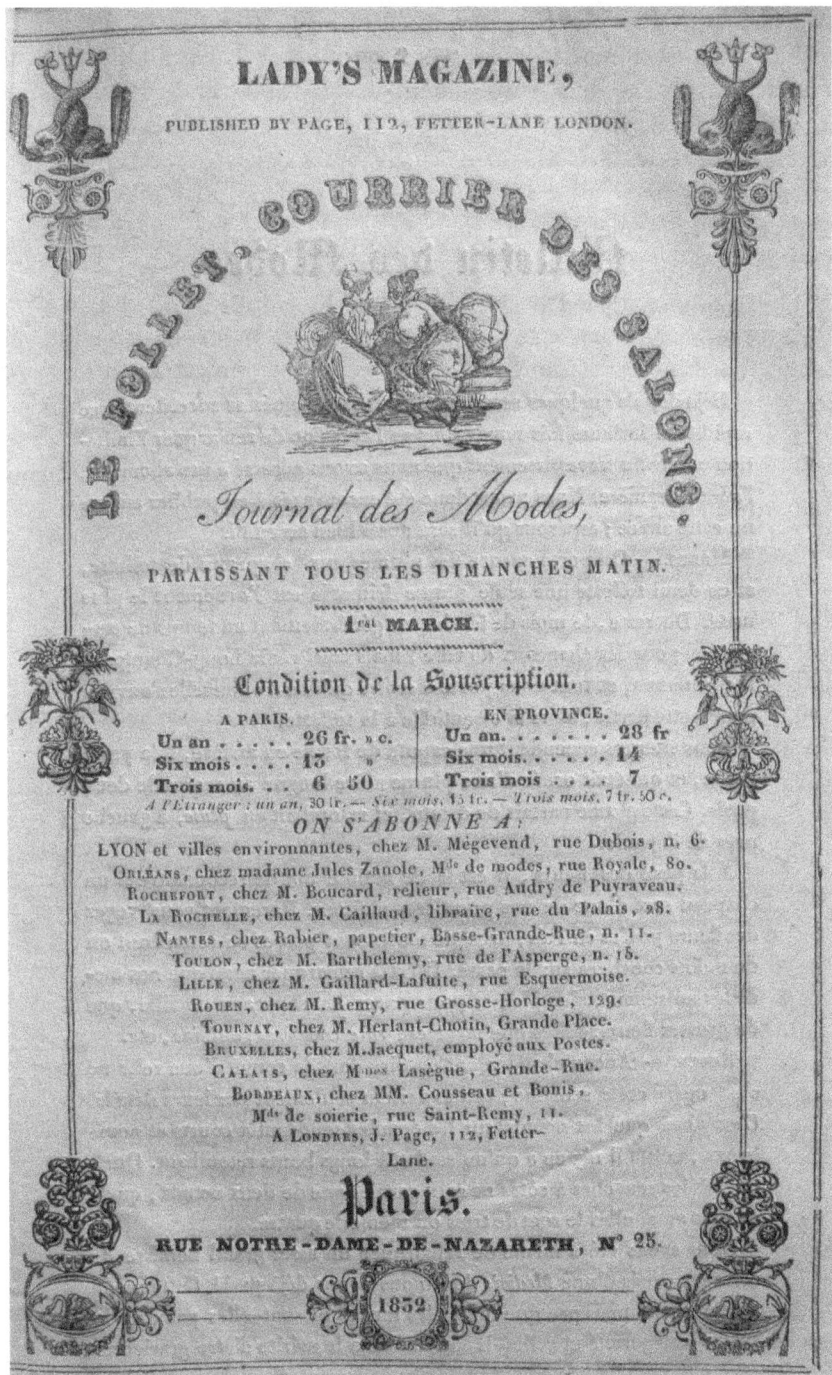

Figure 5.16 *Le Follet* insert in the *Lady's Magazine* for March 1832. Private collection.

an eight-page 'Le Follet' insert was introduced as a sort of magazine-within the magazine that looks less sure of what it was and for whom it is designed. The new arrangement was made around the time that the periodical permanently fell out of the Robinsons' hands. The new publisher of the *Lady's Magazine*'s was James Page, of 112 Fetter Lane, Paternoster Row.[59] Within months of Page taking over publication, the *Lady's Magazine* merged with the *Ladies' Museum* (formerly the *Lady's Monthly Museum*). As we have seen, the relationship between these two periodicals had always been strained, but by 1832 it was openly hostile. Only a year before the merger, the *Ladies' Museum* devoted a significant part of its 'Editorial Council Chamber' column to an altercation with its superannuated rival, which it repeatedly referred to as 'the *Old Lady's Magazine*' or the 'poor old dame'. How the *Ladies' Museum* so soon afterwards became the partner of a periodical that it had publicly accused of dirty tricks, plagiarism, dishonesty and 'intellectual sterility' is undocumented.[60] The resulting publication, the *Lady's Magazine and Museum*, presented the union as an ideal partnership between a work that was 'the accredited organ of communicating the changes which are continually taking place in *modes* and fashions' (the *Lady's Magazine*) and the much respected *Museum*, which owed its 'success' to the 'distinguished writers' who had 'favoured' it 'with their contributions'.[61] In reality, it was a marriage of convenience.

The *Lady's Magazine's* self-styling, here, as 'the accredited organ' of fashion communication indicates just how far the periodical had evolved since its inception in 1770. A further sign that the magazine was reimagining itself and dissociating itself from its previous iterations can be found on its new title page. In July 1831, the month in which Page took over the magazine's publication, the periodical's title page proudly boasted that it had commenced publication in 1756. Presumably, the confusion arose from the new editor and publisher mistaking the periodical for Stanhope's *Lady's Magazine* (founded in 1759) with which Robinson's *Lady's Magazine* had no relationship. As this chapter has shown, this was only one of many signs that the magazine was moving away from its original plan in response to the emergence of its many rivals and the changing tastes of its readership in an increasingly diversified and professionalised periodical landscape. That the *Lady's Magazine* endured six decades of change and expansion in the periodical marketplace undoubtedly marks it out as a triumph, but in its final years it was forced to break from so many of the conventions it had established and, at the same time, because something very different from, and less sure of, itself. The periodical that Charlotte Brontë recalled – one that was conducive to the voracious appetites that readers had for new content and that aspiring authors had to provide it – had transformed into a very different, less inclusive, publication by the 1820s. And yet, as I go on to document in the following chapter, despite these developments and concessions, the *Lady's Magazine* nonetheless left a number of very real and lasting legacies for individual authors, women's writing and literary history. These achievements were significant, multiple and well-remembered by readers, even if the magazine's last editor and publisher could not recall them.

Chapter 6

Achievements and Legacies: The *Lady's Magazine* in Literary History

> The utility of Miscellanies of this kind ... need not be insisted on. They collect, as it were, into a focus, the scattered rays of the literature of the times, exhibit to notice what might have been disregarded, and rescue from oblivion what might have been forgotten.
> 'Address to the Public', the *Lady's Magazine* (1793)

The Romantic-era periodical has a vexed relationship with women's literary history. No other genre did more to shape the reputations and legacies of individual women writers. Part of the 'fame machine', periodicals mediated authorial careers for the reading public through the publication of reviews and extracts, and satisfied an appetite for information about writers' private lives in the form of anecdotes, biographies and memoirs.[1] But if periodicals and magazines made literary careers, they also broke them. Clifford Siskin's work has been particularly instructive in revealing how journals – especially the Reviews – were instrumental in one of the most extraordinary sleights of hand that literary history has performed: the 'Great Forgetting' of women writers. Siskin detects periodicals' collective efforts to professionalise and masculinise the literary at the beginning of the nineteenth century in a multitude of 'exclusionary practices' that disproportionally affected female authors. It was a process, he continues, that was 'neither causal nor natural' but systematic, an inevitable consequence of decisions about 'whose texts, read or *even unread*, did get talked about and reproduced and whose texts, unread or *even read*, slipped into silence and out of production'.[2]

My account in Chapter 5 of the *Lady's Magazine*'s change of editorial direction in its final decade and a half of production might seem to offer yet more evidence in support of such claims. In responding to shifts and changes in periodical print culture at the beginning of the nineteenth century, the magazine conceded many of the impulses and practices that were once integral to its brand and appeal so that, eventually, it became unrecognisable even to its own staff. Less page space and less authority were given to original works by, and conversations between, reader-contributors, and ever more attention was devoted to recirculating the work of established writers in now canonical genres. Yet the contribution that the *Lady's Magazine* made to literary history is not defined by the last fifteen troubled years of its more than six-decade run, and its long-term impact on women's writing and on women writers was much more affirmative than its eventual capitulation to prevailing trends suggests. The periodical's self-appointed role as a promoter of women's writing talent and of women's reading pleasure was, as we will see, much more effective and enduringly influential than literary history has recognised.

In this concluding chapter, I return to the book's Introduction and to the arguments put forward in Charlotte Brontë's letter to Hartley Coleridge both to assess the most significant of the *Lady's Magazine*'s achievements and legacies and to position it centrally within Romantic literary history. These achievements and legacies are multiple and coalesce around the notion of print community. This community was both manufactured and organic. Already published authors were passively gathered into the magazine when their printed works were excerpted or their lives were documented in its pages. Reader-contributors and paid correspondents, by contrast, entered the magazine's community of their own accord and actively shaped its conversations and identity. Who was drawn into or actively sought access to this community, how the community was theorised by members, and how it influenced writers who published outside it are the focus of this chapter. As we will see, the *Lady's Magazine* created a unique set of conditions for writers and readers that do not always map easily onto conventional literary-historical models. Many authors and subscribers nonetheless found these conditions compelling. Determining why eighteenth- and nineteenth-century readers and writers found the opportunities offered by the *Lady's Magazine* so attractive a proposition and literary-historical scholarship has not is the central aim of this final chapter.

Manufacturing Community, Remembering Women Writers

The *Lady's Magazine*'s legacies to women's literary history are intimately bound up with its recollections of writers from the past and its commemorations of the living. The nature and implications of these commitments come into sharp focus in the periodical's October 1777 issue, for which the editor hastily ordered an engraving to replace a planned illustration for one of the month's moral tales. The engraving's subject is the author, educationalist and historian Catharine Macaulay, a controversial marble statue of whom had been erected just weeks earlier in St Stephen Church, Walbrook (Figure 6.1). The sculpture, created by J. F. Moore at the commission of the writer's champion and admirer, the Reverend Thomas Wilson, envisions Macaulay as History. But she is figured as more than mere muse. Leaning on a stack of five volumes of her *History of England* (1763–93) and holding a quill in one hand and a scroll bearing the admonishment 'Government is a power adopted for the happiness of mankind' in the other, Macaulay is emphatically envisioned as both a writer and a thinker. This was a Macaulay who was fully recognisable to readers of the *Lady's Magazine*. An extract from the first volume of her *History* had already appeared in the issue for March of that year, and Macaulay's name had for some time been a recurrent presence in the lists of celebrated women writers that frequently appeared in the periodical.[3]

The magazine partly commissioned the engraving and its two-page accompanying essay to justify Macaulay's continued presence in these lists in the face of the increasingly hostile debate about her reputation that was reanimated by the statue. As the periodical documents in detail, the sculpture had generated considerable scandal and several calls for its removal in the weeks after its installation on the grounds that its subject was living and, moreover, was a woman whose republican politics rendered her a controversial subject for commemoration.[4] The *Lady's Magazine* vigorously contested both objections. The unknown author of 'On the Statue of Mrs Macaulay' notes with incredulity how 'puerile and malicious' detractors had slandered Wilson by falsely accusing him of 'prostituting the church' and 'giving rise to idolatry' (8 (October 1777): 510). S/he continues that the 'most civilised states of antiquity ... erected no less than a hundred statues to a living hero' and, in any case, Macaulay would not live forever.[5] Upon her death, the monument would rightly 'be looked upon as justice, that she is paid that veneration which her distinguished merit [can] demand' (510).

The periodical's defence of the statue and the writer whose achievements it memorialises is unusually confrontational.[6] Biographies and short essays commemorating the achievements of notable 'ancient' and 'modern' women, as we saw in previous chapters, had always been a feature of the *Lady's Magazine*, where they had served as proof of the individual and cultural benefits of women's education. In one sense, 'On the Statue of Mrs. Macaulay' is simply another example of this content type. Yet the facts that Macaulay was alive at the time of this memorialisation and that the magazine knew it was courting controversy in wading in on the debate sparked by the statue render this intervention distinctive.

Achievements and Legacies 213

Figure 6.1 *The Statue of Mrs. Macaulay* from the *Lady's Magazine* for October 1777. Bayerische Staatsbibliothek München, Per. 123 m-8. urn:nbn:de:bvb:12-bsb10613829-2.

We might dismiss the magazine's coverage as a cynical attempt to capitalise on Wilson's extraordinary and controversial memorial, which had 'set such an edge on masculine and female curiosity' ('Correspondents' (October 1777): n.p.). But while this explanation could account for the decision to commission the engraving, it does not fully explain the editorial commentary that mediates the image. The essay's defence of Wilson's and Macaulay's reputations transforms mere description into a polemic that spills out into a further two lengthy and impassioned paragraphs, also devoted to the subject of the Macaulay statue, which appear in the 'Correspondents' columns for October and November. These texts collectively function as verbal equivalents of the statue: they celebrate Macaulay's 'merits' in the here and now and set out to capture her achievements for future generations long after the writer herself has 'mould[e]red into dust' (October 1777: 510). The interventions were warmly appreciated by readers. The November 1777 'Correspondents' column continued the conversation by thanking subscribers for their 'numerous' correspondence in support of the magazine's 'tribute' to this rightly celebrated figure (8: n.p.)

As the author of 'On the Statue' was well aware, the conversation his or her piece initiated had implications beyond the historian's own case. While the essay celebrates Macaulay's particular virtues as a woman, a writer and an historian, it also styles her as a figurehead for women in general. She is both exceptional – 'a kind of prodigy' we would wish 'once in every age' would 'appear' – and 'proof' of a truth too often masked by custom: 'that genius is not confined to sex' (8 (October 1777): 509).[7] Macaulay, in other words, embodies the aspirations the *Lady's Magazine* harboured for its readers, a fact emphasised by the striking similarities between the writer's appearance as 'History' in the statue/engraving and the established iconography of the periodical's annual frontispieces. The statue specifically imagines Macaulay as Clio. Yet as Claire Gilbride Fox observes, its 'total effect' is to transform the image of the 'young and attractive muse of history' into the 'formidable Minerva, goddess of war and wisdom'.[8] Minerva's owl, which adorns the brooch that the classically draped Macaulay wears, is not discernible in the scaled-down engraving, but Macaulay's resemblance to the goddess at whose feet the *Lady's Magazine* worshipped is unmistakable. The magazine's defence of Macaulay-as-Minerva is simultaneously a defence of the cultural values and pedagogical ambitions for which the periodical stood.

'On the Statue of Mrs. Macaulay' clarifies the stakes for which the *Lady's Magazine* played when it commented on the achievements of women writers – living or deceased – and drew them into its print community. The periodical consistently performed two interrelated roles: of champion of women writers and curator of their reputations. These responsibilities were intimately linked to the publication's aspirations for its readers. By becoming its contributors, these readers produced poems, essays and fictions that sat alongside work by the women whose achievements the magazine commemorated. In the process, they became part of an intergenerational, international textual community that united the unknown, aspiring and established. Gaining a 'footing' in this writerly 'inclosure' was no mean accomplishment. In the words of regular contributor Castalio (William Mugliston), the literary of efforts of 'those fair' unknowns were unlikely to be deemed 'sufficiently important to attract public notice 'as distinct works'. Yet when these works are 'combined together' with those of 'a Griffith, a Moore [sic], an Aikin, a Cowley, and a Macaulay', they provide 'amusement' and evidence that women's 'minds are capable of as great exertions as lordly man' (13: May 1782: 258).[9] Later sections of this chapter explore further how this print community served both reader-contributors who voluntarily participated in it and those writers such as Jane Austen and Charlotte Brontë who published outside it while finding inspiration in its pages. First, though, I turn in more detail to writers, including Macaulay, who never wrote specifically for the magazine, but who were drawn into its community through its publication of excerpts from their works and reflections on their life and achievements.[10] Scrutinising those whom the magazine remembered and celebrated – and on what terms – reveals a literary history that is only partially recognisable. Tracing the contours of this unfamiliar literary landscape additionally complicates standard literary histories by exposing what we have forgotten about how eighteenth- and nineteenth-century readers thought about writers of their and previous generations.

Catharine Macaulay remained a presence in the *Lady's Magazine* for a little over a decade after the publication of 'On the Statue'. A handful of further extracts from her *History of England* were reprinted over the following years, as were excerpts from her *Letters on Education* (1790), which featured in the magazine in 1790 and early 1791, just months before the July issue published notice of Macaulay's death on 22 June of that year. Throughout this period, and in spite of the well-documented scandal generated by her marriage to William Graham in November 1778, Macaulay continued to occupy a place in the magazine's lists of notable women who did 'honour' to the 'sex' by their 'richly cultivated minds' ('The Matron', 6 (June 1775): 315). Her companions in these lists were many and various; writers working in and across different genres, eras and nations were well represented. Among the most frequently celebrated were the aforementioned Elizabeth Carter, Anna Barbauld, Hannah Cowley and Hannah More. They were joined by a significant company of recurring figures including: Frances Brooke, Frances Burney, Hester Chapone, Catherine Cockburn, Anne Dacier, Elizabeth Griffith, Charlotte Lennox, Elizabeth Montagu, Katherine Philips, Clara Reeve, Elizabeth Rowe, Françoise-Marguerite de Sévigné, Catherine Talbot and Lady Mary Wortley Montagu. Other women moved in and out of the lists over time.

Citation was not always a recommendation, however, and not all women writers whose names feature in these lists are equals. The 'Scale of Female Literary Merit' in the June 1792 issue brings this matter into sharp focus in a table that evaluates the virtues of sentiment, imagery, animation, strength, harmony, feeling and originality – none of which criteria is glossed – in the work of fourteen women novelists, playwrights, travel writers and poets, several of whom are found to be lacking in one of more of these categories (23: 290).[11] The table gives predictably high scores for popular authors such as Burney, as well as for those like Barbauld and Carter, who featured prominently in the magazine, and/or those such as Cowley, Charlotte Smith and Helen Maria Williams, who had professional connections with the Robinson firm. The abysmally low score awarded to the playwright and travel writer Lady Craven (who scores eleven out of a possible seventy in the merit scale) is equally unsurprising given the modest success of many of her early works and the scandal of her first marriage. Less explicable is the ranking of More, who was as highly lauded as Barbauld throughout the magazine's history, but who fares little better than Craven in the published rankings. The editor's disavowal of responsibility for 'every particular estimate' made by the scale's author goes some way to resolving the implied contradiction (290). Yet there is a larger point made here and one with which regular readers of the *Lady's Magazine* were intimate: assessments of literary merit, and especially 'female literary merit', are often subjective, opaque or unjustifiable. Worrying away at the prejudices that underpin these assessments to position women at the centre of the republic of letters was one of the periodical's key objectives.

Such catalogues of female literary excellence were no mere inventories. Their potential – both individually and collectively – to write women into literary history was clearly recognised by the magazine's editors and contributors alike. It was a project taken to heart by Pratilia, author of a deliciously satirical essay published in January 1778. Possessing a curious double title – the running head 'A Dream' morphs into 'A List of Female Writers' two pages in – Pratilia's essay revises *Spectator* no. 37, popularly known as the 'Lady's Library'. In the original, Mr Spectator delivers a letter to widow and beauty Leonora, and is invited to wait for her in her library. As he does so, Mr Spectator takes down a catalogue of the works he sees on the shelves until interrupted by Leonora's arrival. Reflecting on the widow's collection – which comprises a combination of works of science and philosophy, conduct books and romances ornamented with oriental curiosities – Mr Spectator views Leonora 'with a Mixture of Admiration' for her devotion to reading 'and Pity' provoked by material evidence or baser reading pleasures. This evidence includes the patches he finds in her copy of Locke's *Essay Concerning Human Understanding* (1690); the ease with which her copy of Madeleine de Scudéry's *Clelia* (trans. 1656–61) opens at 'the Place that describes two Lovers in a Bower'; and the revealing presence of Delariver Manley's *New Atalantis* on one of her shelves (1709).[12]

As Kathleen Lubey observes, while Mr Spectator 'praises the spectrum of taste represented by her library, he yet chides Leonora' for her unruly tastes and feminine tendency to get 'stuck in the quagmire of erotic scenes'.[13] Pratilia's imaginative return to this scene more than half a century later in the pages of the *Lady's Magazine* tells a very different story about women's reading and writing, in which Mr Spectator's 'Pity' is supplanted by pride. The essay opens with Pratilia reminding readers of an exchange between her and George Robinson senior published in the December 1777 issue, in which she had requested less news coverage in the magazine and the introduction of a review section specifically tailored to the interests of women readers. Both requests were rejected in an editorial note. This follow-up essay takes up the cause to bring the achievements of writers to female readers' notice in a novel way. Pratilia, who explains that she intends to build her own library using the proceeds of a recent lottery win, falls asleep while reading *Spectator* no. 37, and dreams of visiting a now considerably older, but still graceful, Leonora, who shows her visitor her collection of books and artefacts.

At first glance, the scene that greets Pratilia – 'books . . . intermixed with china vases' – seems to replicate what 'the Spectator describes' in the earlier periodical (9 (January 1778): 21). In fact, everything has changed. Pratilia's attention is immediately arrested by 'Mrs. Macaulay's bust', taken from the 'statue at Wallbrook church', which, by drawing attention to the dispute over the historian's reputation, serves as a vivid rejection of Mr Spectator's views on women's writing and reading. Leonora's book collection further emphasises the point. She has not only discarded 'most' of the romances to which Mr Spectator objected, but she has also, and more importantly, rid her library of 'all' works by 'male authors', barring a handful of conduct books and copies of periodicals including the *Guardian*, the *Tatler* and, of course, the *Spectator*

(21). Leonora takes Pratilia's astonishment at this information to indicate fear that in showcasing women's writing, her collection would be reduced to such a 'small compass' that there would be little for her to see, a misconception that the remaining half of the essay meticulously corrects as Leonora lists the achievements and genius of the more than forty women novelists, literary critics, essayists, historians, periodicalists and translators, from antiquity to the present across Britain, Europe and America.

The list, which begins with Macaulay, includes a familiar cast of characters (Sappho, Hypatia, Queen Elizabeth, Philips, the bluestockings), but has several surprises, too. Novelists are represented in the form of Sarah Fielding (referred to as 'Sally'), along with the Miss Minifies and Lennox, whose Shakespeare criticism, rather than fiction, generally attracted more of the magazine's attention. Among the poets represented in the collection are Anna Williams, the 'blind poetess', and 'the humble Phillis Wheatley', 'a poor uninstructed negro girl, whose genius broke out superior to all the disadvantages of slavery and ignorance' and whose example is offered up by Pratilia as convincing proof of the 'natural strength of female capacity' (22). Equally surprising is the representation of the works of the now virtually unknown 'Miss Roberts', likely Radagunda Roberts, whose contributions to the *Lady's Magazine* are discussed in Chapter 4.[14] The *Lady's Magazine* itself takes pride of place alongside Stanhope's earlier title of the same name (1759–63) and a set of ladies' pocket-books.

The dream abruptly terminates shortly after the periodicals section of the library is scanned when the bust of Macaulay ominously crashes to the floor, waking Pratilia from her reverie. Pratilia's women's library remains a 'dream', but her 'vision' of the prodigious achievements of so many women writers and the cultural value of the 'labours of female pens' remain potent (22–3). Robinson might previously have rejected its contributor's suggestions for better helping women readers navigate the world of new publications, but its printing of Pratilia's second essay shows that it accepted the important work that it could do in advocating for women's literary history through its memorialisation of women writers. In its pages, as in Leonora's reimagined library, the famed and the forgotten, women of antiquity and the present, authors of multi-volume histories or novels and contributors of single essays to women's periodicals proudly sit side by side.

The *Lady's Magazine*'s efforts to memorialise women's literary achievements took other forms beyond its cataloguing of women's achievements in the kinds of lists of female worthies found in Pratilia's 'Dream'. Biographies played their part. So too, eventually, did obituaries.¹⁵ The periodical's practice of excerpting constitutes a less obvious act of memorialisation, but was its most persistent, and arguably most effective, strategy for writing women into literary history. As the magazine's inaugural 'Address' makes clear, identifying and bringing to readers' notice extracts of works it felt were deserving of their attention had always been part of the *Lady's Magazine*'s design. Excerpting is always a double-edged act. If, on the one hand, the practice impugns the integrity of the original textual whole, on the other, it is an act of preservation. As we saw in Chapters 2 and 3, the import of particular extracts changes when they are divorced from their original context and remediated by the periodical format. Nonetheless, the simple fact that this text, rather than another, was chosen for reprinting intimates noteworthiness and confers status upon the chosen extract, the work from which it is taken and its author. Over the course of its history, the magazine published thousands of extracts from the works of individual writers. Some were extracted by staff writers or copied from other publications where the excerpting work had already been done; some were strategically placed by the Robinsons to puff items on their wider list or seem to have been inserted at the behest of other publishers for the same reasons. Some were commonplaced and submitted by correspondents. The sheer number and miscellaneity of these thousands of excerpts makes any attempt to synthesise their impact on readers difficult to gauge, although the proliferation of extracts from particular writers (such as Lord Byron, Sir Walter Scott, Helen Maria Williams and Mary Wollstonecraft) at particular historical moments, or of specific writers over a long period of time (such as Carter, More, Stéphanie Félicité de Genlis and Madame de Staël) tells its own stories.

Easier to situate in terms of the magazine's overall design are the many extract series it published. Some of these series were devoted to particular authors such as Joseph Addison, William Shakespeare and Mary Wollstonecraft, but the majority were devoted to collections of extracts, maxims or reflections by multiple writers. Women writers featured heavily in these series and one of the longest running, 'Select Pieces of Literature of Literature of Various Kinds, in Prose and Verse' (1775–81), featured work exclusively authored by 'Female Hands'. Appearing under frequently manufactured titles, such as 'Reflections on Liberty of Conscience' (7 (April 1776): 186) or 'the Connection Between the Body and the Soul' (April 1776: 187), these extracts were recommended to readers as prompts to engage with particular philosophical or moral questions and as testimony to the perspicacity of female intellect. Writers familiar from the lists of notable women such as Barbauld, Brooke, Carter, Chapone, Griffith, Lennox, More and Lady

Mary Wortley Montagu are well represented, but writers the magazine noticed less consistently, such as Anne Finch, Mary Chandler and Mary Jones also make appearances. Cumulatively, the lists and the extract series that elucidate and justify them create a repository or canon of women writers and women's writing across various genres, including periodicals, correspondence, poetry, essays and literary criticism, that the magazine identifies as worthy of preservation and deserving of its readers' continued notice and recollection.

The facts that few of these once popularly celebrated women writers are widely read today outside specialist academic circles and that some – like Chandler and Jones – are little read or written about even within them should give pause to those of us committed to literary history. That the visibility and popularity of authors and works were widely celebrated in periodicals such as the *Lady's Magazine* and yet are barely known today should, at the very least, remind us that the feminist recovery project is still a work in progress and one for which periodicals offer a rich and still barely tapped resource. The visibility in individual excerpts and extract series of women writers who, according to conventional literary histories, were considered unfashionable, disreputable, redundant or even entirely forgotten at certain moments in time relates another cautionary tale. On many occasions, the magazine attests to the enduring legacy of writers commonly understood in later scholarship to have fallen out of fashion. For more than five decades after Eliza Haywood's death in 1756, for instance, the *Lady's Magazine* was remembering her work in the form of extracts from her translation *La Belle Assemblée* (1724), *Epistles for the Ladies* (1748–50) and her periodicals *The Parrot* (1746) and *Female Spectator* (1744–6). These were, of course, among Haywood's more polite publications, although *La Belle Assemblée* belonged to the part of Haywood's career that Sophronia, in Clara Reeve's *Progress of Romance* (1785), declared should be 'forgotten'.[16]

Still more striking is the notice the magazine paid to Haywood's contemporary, Manley. Manley may have been excised from Leonora's library in Pratilia's dream, but she is very visible elsewhere in the *Lady's Magazine*. In March 1781, the magazine printed 'Miscellaneous Observations by the Celebrated Mrs. Manley', which carried three twin-columned pages of extracts taken from *The New Atalantis* (1709). The redaction of Manley's text transforms this topical political satire into a universal modern moral guide on such matters as covetousness, luxury, modesty and the perils of gambling. But this is no bowdlerisation. As the magazine recognised, excerpting was a political act. And while the practice could serve writers well it could also – and especially in the case of women writers – serve them poorly. This latter was a subject discussed at length in 'A Defence of Mrs Wollstonecraft Godwin', published in the magazine for February 1805 and written by Richard Allchin, a Unitarian master of a dissenting charity school in Maidstone, Kent. Allchin explains that he has been provoked to write his vindication of Wollstonecraft's life and writings after reading an essay calculated to 'prejudice the minds of its readers' against the author, which had recently appeared in the *Ladies Select Pocket Remembrancer* for 1805 (36: 80). Allchin's strategy is to fight fire with fire, countering the original author's attack on sections of Wollstonecraft's publications with 'passages' of his own selection designed 'as an antidote to that prejudice which has probably been excited in the minds of many readers against a meritorious character' (79). Read via Allchin's later essay, the magazine's redaction of Manley's *New Atalantis* seems less clearly an attempt to sanitise the original than a recuperation of her reputation as a writer and as a woman at precisely the moment when literary history tells us it was beyond the pale. At the very least, it reveals that the assertion just four years later in Reeve's *Progress of Romance* that Manley's novel was 'almost forgotten' and her works in general 'sinking gradually into oblivion' was wishful thinking rather than fact.[17]

As its attitude to the *New Atalantis* suggests, when it comes to women's writing the *Lady's Magazine*'s default mode was one of remembrance rather than the forgetting with which Romantic-era periodicals are commonly associated. Like the Reviews, the magazine presented itself as a navigation aid in an ever more diffuse publishing world and as a gatekeeper of what was worth reading and remembering. Unlike the Reviews, however, it primarily sought to realise these goals not through strategies of exclusion or dismissal, but through acts of inclusion and recuperation that kept the woman reader and writer in sight at all times. This was work to which the miscellany form – one that could bring together multiple texts by various authors from different periods – was particularly well suited, as the January 1793 'Address' with which this chapter began makes clear. In their capacity to capture the bewildering diversity and proliferation of print, 'Miscellanies ... collect, as it were, into a focus, the scattered rays of the literature of the times'. Looking to past and present with an eye to futurity, they 'exhibit to notice' what otherwise 'might have been disregarded, and rescue from oblivion what might have been forgotten (24: [iii]). The editor's words are as unwittingly ironic as they are polemical. The *Lady's Magazine*'s own posthumous reputation, largely eclipsed as it has been by unfavourable comparisons with the literary Reviews and periodicals against which Victorian readers and Romantic scholarship have traditionally defined it, reveals that its fate was even more complexly intertwined with the women writers and women's writing it championed than its editors could have imagined. Acknowledging this gives yet further reason to remember the magazine, the multiple and sometimes surprising acts of commemoration and celebration of women's writers' careers in which it engages and the alternative textual genealogies to conventional literary histories it maps. Reviews may well have played a crucial role in 'how we forgot', but the *Lady's Magazine* played a vital and unjustly unacknowledged role in what, who and how readers remembered women writers.

Theorising Community

It is difficult to know how already published and living authors, such as Macaulay, felt about being drawn into the *Lady's Magazine*'s textual community through the biographical accounts, anecdotes, critical essays about, and extracts from, their works that the periodical printed. Aside from notable exceptions such as Clara Reeve's correspondence with the magazine's editor – discussed in Chapter 4 – documentary evidence is scant. The thoughts of the magazine's volunteer correspondents are, by contrast, much easier to substantiate because they so frequently expressed these thoughts within the magazine itself. Part of the appeal that the magazine held for such contributors was the pleasure of proximity: that a 'Nobody' could publish work that sat alongside that of a somebody such as a Carter, a Sévigné or a Macaulay. In the magazine, as in the dream-conjured lady's library on which Pratilia reflects, 'space and time' are 'annihilated'; the old and the new, the domestic and foreign, are collected into a single, if heterogeneous, whole (29 (January 1778): 21). But there were other pleasures besides the metaphorical rubbing of textual shoulders. The personal satisfaction of reaching large and appreciative audiences, as the likes of Elizabeth Yeames and Sophia Troughton did, could also be considerable. The magazine's editors, however, suggested that the principal incentive to publish in, or subscribe to, the periodical was not the possibility of appearing in print so much as the pleasure of being part of a sociable print community of individuals with common aspirations.

Since the nineteenth century, the question of community has both dominated the reception of the *Lady's Magazine* and divided its critics. Alison Adburgham, for instance, locates the periodical's extraordinary popularity and success in its editors' efforts to cultivate 'feeling of friendship' and a 'sense of belonging' among its contributors and readers.[18] Robert D. Mayo and Gillian Hughes take a very different view, casting the same community-based model of reader participation as a sign of parasitic editorial dependency upon subscribers' questionable talents.[19] Setting aside for a moment reader-contributors' thoughts on the matter, it is worth pausing to consider why community formation is so central to the scant scholarship on the *Lady's Magazine* given how integral the practice was to *so many* periodical ventures of the time. Appeals to readers' desire to be part of a virtual community or, in Jürgen Habermas's formulation, a 'public' of like-minded individuals had, after all, been a key strategy of the periodical press from the late seventeenth century.[20] Yet there are key differences between community formation as achieved in a magazine as opposed to an essay-periodical, and these differences have framed perceptions of the *Lady's Magazine*'s integrity and professionalism. Principal among these differences is the magazine's polyphony. As we saw in Chapter 2, essay-periodicals manufacture community partly through the publication of contributor letters, which evidence readership while also subordinating the views of individual readers to the unifying perspective of the periodical eidolon who mediates the correspondence. The magazine, as we saw in Chapter 3, presents a more unstable and dynamic print ecosystem, in which consensus is counterintuitively achieved through the proliferation of different and often dissenting voices speaking within the same textual space.[21]

According to successive generations of the *Lady's Magazine*'s editors, what bound this disparate community of individuals together and prevented a descent into textual anarchy were feelings of friendship and mutual obligation. The magazine's 'correspondents', 'friends' and 'patronesses' benefited from the magazine's efforts to entertain and improve them, a debt they repaid through continued subscription, fan mail and the 'favours' (i.e. textual contributions) upon which the magazine relied for copy. These favours, in turn, obliged the magazine to respond in kind with an 'assiduous' commitment 'to omit nothing which could store the heart with moral acquisitions, or refine the understanding with intellectual improvements'. In reality, though, the magazine could not 'balance [its] accounts' with readers. The fact that so 'many a thousand favours' were purportedly received at Paternoster Row each month left the editor with a surfeit of material that he had neither the 'power' nor the pages 'to oblige' with publication (12 (March 1781): 114). Editorial selectivity diminished what Jon P. Klancher terms the 'aura of the democratic and communal' that eighteenth-century periodicals sought to conjure.[22] The magazine was democratic by impulse, but it was meritocratic of necessity, and at the point of publication, the fiction of inclusivity eroded. Although anyone might gain a footing in the magazine, to return to Castalio's metaphor, in practice contributors had to meet certain and not always transparent standards or face rejection or ridicule in the 'Correspondents' columns. Yet for all these disincentives, thousands of individuals sought access to the *Lady's Magazine*'s 'inclosure'. Although many contributors struggled to find the right language to describe this community, most were in agreement with editors that this community offered them something distinctive and enticing.

This distinctiveness comes most clearly into view via the language that contributors used, and the discursive models on which they leaned, as they attempted to capture the magazine's reading and writing culture. Finding an appropriate vocabulary or analogy for the magazine's community vexed many of its subscribers, just as it continues to tax modern readers. The chief difficulty lies in the community's failure to correspond precisely with the prototypes it most nearly resembles. Markman Ellis, for instance, has argued that the *Lady's Magazine* was the '"feminine" equivalent of the club and coffee-house where women might converse with each other (and even some men) in a decorous and virtuous setting', a space 'that existed in no physical place outside the imaginary realm' of the periodical.[23] The equivalence is not entirely convincing, however. In fact, homocentric models of sociability – as epitomised by the coffee-house or club – and the garrulous or opinionated grandstanding they encouraged were roundly and regularly criticised by the magazine's contributors.[24] Equally, all-female clubs, which become a regular object of satire in the 1810s and 1820s, were frequently viewed with suspicion, and their members satirised for their vacuity and loquaciousness.[25] While the *Lady's Magazine* was unapologetically feminocentric in outlook, it viewed a 'mixed company' of 'both sexes' as the only 'eligible' means to produce the 'considerable advantages' it sought for its readers ('Matron', 20 (September 1789): 485).

The debating society was considered a nearer approximation of the magazine's project according to some, at least before the 1790s when organisations became intensely politicised.[26] Yet while the *Lady's Magazine*'s editors were happy to acknowledge the 'beneficial consequences' generated by the expression of 'difference of opinion', neither they nor the majority of their contributors embraced the attempt to suggest an exact equivalence between the periodical and the debating house (13 (April 1782): 191). J. H—T, the author of an essay, 'On Female Oratory', which was offered up as a late intervention into the Sukey Foresight/Impartial Combatant skirmish discussed in Chapter 3, is typical in his view that the 'rage of debating' destroyed 'the blush of innocence' in women. For all the apparent misogyny of his argument, J. H—T claimed not to be motivated by a wish to 'abridg[e women's] natural prerogatives', but by his belief that the public and performative environment of the debating society destroyed its own aim. Noting that speakers at the recently formed, all-female debating society, La Belle Assemblée, wore masks to conceal their identity from onlookers, he concluded that the debating society privileged performance over principles, show over substance, and calculated wit over the genuine 'wisdom' the magazine sought to promote (11 (May 1780): 251).[27]

The only physically realised prototype for the magazine's textual community that had any lasting purchase for contributors was the literary coterie, a term that appears regularly, and in different contexts, throughout the magazine's history. Sometimes, as in the January 1780 'Correspondents' column, 'Coterie' is used as an alternative to 'female committee' or 'female parliament', phrases used to describe the periodical's editorial board (11 (January 1780): n.p.). On other occasions, it is used – admiringly or disparagingly – to characterise the literary gatherings of 'blue-stockings' and 'witlings' ('Memoir of Mr. Gifford', 58 (January 1827): 32), or to distinguish between the legitimate productions and printed conversations of *Lady's Magazine* authors and the indecorous public activities of women in various other societies, such as the probably fictitious Matrimonial Society, a '*new Coterie*' that acted like a modern day dating agency (Wheble 3 (November 1772): 512), and the infamous 'Female Coterie' debating society.

Yet it is less as a word than as an idea and set of principles that facilitate and regulate social relationships, that the 'coterie' had its greatest resonance for editors of, and subscribers to, the *Lady's Magazine*. Traces of coterie culture are visible throughout the magazine's history. They are present, for instance, in the frequent references to prominent literary circles and their members, such as Carter, Montagu and Talbot. They are evident in the type and diversity of textual forms – letters, poetry, prose and interactive genres such as enigmas and rebuses – that fill the periodical's pages and that were characteristic of coterie culture. They are also present in the widespread adoption of pseudonymity that characterises both magazine and coterie culture. These traces are visible finally, if more obliquely, in the hundreds of references made to manuscript production and circulation within the magazine, often by contributors who claimed that their submissions originated in manuscripts authored long ago by themselves or accidentally found following the original author's death or relocation.

These persistent, self-conscious nods to scribal culture should not be surprising. A friendly, yet critical and dynamic mixed-sex community of readers and writers bound by mutual interest and intellectual conversation consolidated through the reciprocal exchange of texts in different genres, the early modern coterie was a precursor to the first miscellany periodicals. As Margaret J. M. Ezell observes in her reappraisal of the *Gentleman's Journal* (1692–4), the innovation of Peter Anthony Motteux's periodical miscellany lay in its integration of the practices of mixed-sex scribal coterie culture into a commercial print genre.[28] Ezell's argument is an important corollary to the vital work she has done more broadly to document how early modern women and men entered literary culture as writers and readers, work that has successfully challenged the overarching critical narratives that once shaped studies of literature and authorship in the seventeenth and early eighteenth centuries.[29] Recent scholarship on coterie culture and the co-existence and interdependence of scribal and print forms throughout the eighteenth century and Romantic period, particularly by Betty A. Schellenberg and Michele Levy, has developed these claims further to counter triumphalist accounts of the indomitable rise of print culture and the professional author, as well as the literary histories that have been constructed around these axes.[30] At the same time that they acknowledge the persistence of scribal and coterie culture, these scholars observe the 'developing discursive dichotomy between the professional, "masculine" author, on the one hand, and the feminised coterie amateur, on the other' that became deeply entrenched in the last third of the eighteenth century and eventually led to the former's marginalisation and attempted obfuscation of the latter.[31] The consequences of these processes for the long-term reception of the *Lady's Magazine*, which continued to encourage these discursively marginalised writing cultures will, by now, be familiar to readers of this book.

As many readers of the *Lady's Magazine* recognised, its hybrid format reflected what Schellenberg describes as the 'pluralist' media ecology of the time in the printed-yet-coterie-style community it created.[32] Just as the magazine's editors saw the periodical's role as both recuperative and future oriented – as collecting what might otherwise be forgotten for posterity – its contributors understood that the magazine was reimagining traditional scribal practices in the world of print. At the precise moment that coterie-style practices were being most intensely challenged by the discursive chasm opening up between professional and amateur, masculine and feminine, these historically valued reading and writing cultures continued to thrive within the periodical form and worked to create unique opportunities for writers. Coterie membership afforded opportunities for both sexes, of course, but as Ezell and Schellenberg demonstrate, the benefits could be especially important for women, some of whom saw in this environment a possible conduit to fame or publication, but the majority of whom seem to have found confidence, an inspiration to 'composition and innovation' and the opportunity to create 'authorial identities with a status, and respectability difficult to achieve by an unknown author moving directly into print'.[33] The print community of the *Lady's Magazine* claimed to afford similar opportunities to those opened up by the physically realised mixed-sex coteries that Schellenberg analyses. Not only that, but it expanded those opportunities by providing a large, demographically diverse and geographically disparate virtual writing environment for those who had no access to a network of individuals to encourage, interact with or sustain their literary activities.

In its adaptation of the practices and ethos of the coterie to the form of the printed miscellany, the *Lady's Magazine* acknowledged what eighteenth-century scholarship had long forgotten: the special importance of scribal culture to women's literary activity and ambitions. And like Motteux's *Gentleman's Journal* nearly a century earlier, it mobilised this recognition for its own ends. These ends were undoubtedly commercial, a fact confirmed by the *Lady's Magazine*'s abandonment of these values towards the end of its run when they ceased to be economically viable. Yet these ends were also consonant with the periodical's broader ambition 'to cherish and direct the developement [sic] of Female Genius' ('Address' (January 1809): n.p.), and to convince the 'world that no '*Salique* law can be introduced in the *Republic of Letters*' ('Address' 12 (January 1781): iii). The reality of participation within the magazine's 'inclosure', as we saw in Chapter 4, could be more exploitative and less convivial than this community-based rhetoric suggests. The periodical was no textual utopia or print democracy. However, readers' embracing of the language of community that was such an indelible part of the magazine's identity for so many years, coupled with their repeated allusions to scribal practices, suggests that the coterie ideal and the communitarian values for which the magazine claimed to stand had considerable and enduring appeal, especially for women readers who, like Brontë, took the periodical's distinctive 'encouragement' of female 'literary aspirations' as their 'due'.[34]

Communities of Influence: The Case of Jane Austen

Brontë's claims for the enduring legacies of the *Lady's Magazine*'s community for writers who published outside it are arresting. Verifying her assertions presents challenges, however. As Simon Eliot notes, evidence of magazine readership in the eighteenth and nineteenth centuries is obscured by the ubiquity of the form: periodicals were simply 'too much a part of the fabric of everyday life' to be widely documented in the correspondence, diaries and printed records of the individuals who read them.[35] Pursuing lines of potential influence between individual items of content in any given magazine on the works of writers who did not publish in it is certainly possible, and, as Jenny DiPlacidi has shown in her work on *Lady's Magazine* serial fiction, can prove surprisingly suggestive.[36] In the absence of external evidence to corroborate these connections, however, any conclusions we might draw about a periodical's direct impact on particular authors or genres remain necessarily speculative. In the case of the *Lady's Magazine*, there are nonetheless various instances where the intertextual evidence is sufficiently persuasive to make a more sustained interrogation possible. Among the most striking of these are the multi-directional lines of topical and linguistic influence that lead from the periodical to the work of Jane Austen and back again.

Austen is not known to have published any original material in the *Lady's Magazine*. The same holds true for most major women novelists of her generation, including Burney, Maria Edgeworth and Susan Ferrier. Yet only Austen's non-appearance in the magazine has drawn scholarly comment. Clifford Siskin argues that Austen's 'turn' away from the periodical form is significant for two reasons: first, because this was a medium that gave cultural value to, and generated a mass audience for, fiction, and thus created the condition for the making of 'a "Jane Austen"'; and second, because periodicals would have provided a ready outlet for her work during the long hiatus between her initial attempts at novel writing in the 1790s and *Sense and Sensibility*'s eventual publication in 1811.[37] According to Siskin's reading, Austen's 'staying out of the periodicals' helped shore up the 'hierarchical system of what we now know as high versus low culture'. Opting out of magazines, as much as opting into the novel, in other words, helped Austen to define a new category of 'Literature' that gained cultural recognition partly through the strategic devaluation of lesser print forms such as the periodical.[38] Austen's engagement with the *Lady's Magazine* gives considerable grounds for reassessing this argument. As we will see, her relationship with the *Lady's Magazine* was intimate rather than dismissive, and its influence on her creative practice was more facilitative than this account implies. Individual essays and short fictions in the *Lady's Magazine* have long since been acknowledged as key, if ambivalent, intertexts of Austen's novels, although periodicals in general have not been subjected to the kind of sustained engagement that Austen scholars have devoted to the influence of drama and the novel upon the development of her plots and narrative style.[39] No less important, though less well known, is the active role that the *Lady's Magazine* assumed in the curation of Austen's reputation.

Austen's extant correspondence makes no mention of the *Lady's Magazine*. Yet we know that she could have accessed – and likely did access – the periodical either by subscription, by loan from one the circulating libraries she patronised in Bath, Southampton or London, or via the excerpts from it that appeared in the *Hampshire Chronicle* (founded 1772).[40] There are many reasons why the magazine might have captured Austen's notice, not least of which is the publication's extensive coverage in April 1800 of the trial of her aunt, Jane Leigh Perrot, at the Taunton Assizes for stealing a card of lace from haberdasher, Elizabeth Gregory. The trial proceedings, which unfold over six densely printed pages, are accompanied by what seems to have been a specially commissioned portrait of Leigh Perrot as she appeared in court (Figure 6.2), soberly dressed and sadly, yet defiantly, holding the viewer's gaze.[41]

The *Lady's Magazine*'s account is often cited in Austen scholarship and its engraving of Austen's aunt has been frequently reprinted.[42] Yet the pressing question of why the periodical devoted any attention, let alone six pages, to the proceedings is never posed. Notorious court cases, such as the Duchess of Kingston's bigamy trial, the trial of William Renwick ('The Monster'), the years-long proceedings against Warren Hastings, and the sedition trials of John Horne Tooke and Thomas Paine, received coverage in the magazine. Yet the reporting of court cases was a comparatively rare gesture, so rare in fact, that such accounts are usually prefaced by an editorial justifying the extraordinary coverage. Intriguingly, no such caveat accompanies the report on the 'Trial of Mrs. Leigh Perrot'. Why, what or who prompted the editor to publish the account and to take on the commission for the portrait are unknown. Nor do we have evidence of the Austen family's response to the trial report, although it is hard to believe that they did not know of its existence. If the Austens did read the report, they would likely have been reassured by its tone and treatment of their relative's plight. At no point in the account is there any room to doubt the not-guilty verdict that the jury arrived at after a mere fifteen-minute adjournment. The article's author extends unqualified sympathy for the 'distress' caused to Leigh Perrot, a genteel woman of 'exemplary character' who had been maligned by unscrupulous tradespeople (31: 176).

If Austen read the account of her aunt's trial, this was almost certainly not her first encounter with the *Lady's Magazine*.[43] Evidence that the young writer was accessing copies of the periodical in the 1780s and 1790s can be found in at least four of her novels. Sayre Greenfield has made a convincing case for the influence of Abraham Thrifty's letter, 'On the Prevalence of Acting Plays in Private Families', from the June 1789 *Lady's Magazine,* on both 'Love and Freindship' (1790) and *Mansfield*

Figure 6.2 *Mrs Leigh Perrot* from the *Lady's Magazine* for April 1800. Bayerische Staatsbibliothek München, Per. 123 m-31. urn:nbn:de:bvb:12-bsb10613852-6.

Park (1814).⁴⁴ Further, and still more compelling, evidence that Austen was reading the *Lady's Magazine* in and beyond her teenage years can be found in *Sense Sensibility*, a novel that Austen began drafting in the 1790s. As Janine Barchas acknowledges, the names of Marianne's rival suitors, Willoughby and Brandon, 'have robust, and multiple, historic associations' with other novels from this period – such as Burney's *Evelina* (1778) – and also conjure specific real-life referents.⁴⁵ To my knowledge, however, only one work of fiction from this period contains both names: 'The Shipwreck', an unsigned moral tale from the *Lady's Magazine*'s Supplement for 1794.

The plot of the 'The Shipwreck' is sentimental and melodramatic. Like much of the periodical's short fiction, it is unsparingly critical of the devastating consequences of mercenary marriages. Its heroine, Charlotte Brandon, is the daughter of a wealthy gentleman from the west country. A composite-before-the-fact of Elinor Dashwood, Marianne Dashwood and Anne Elliot, Miss Brandon is 'beautiful and accomplished', and in possession of the 'valuable endowments of good sense, generosity, and sensibility' (25: 678). She loves the 'financially embarrassed', yet 'constant' and 'heroic', Frederick Willoughby, a possible prototype for *Persuasion*'s (1818) Captain Wentworth and the son of a formerly wealthy friend of Charlotte's father. When Brandon urges his daughter to pursue a more advantageous match to the son of an Irish peer, she attempts to suppress her feelings for the sake of her father's interest (679; 680). '[R]ent by conflicting passions', yet bound by the 'fondest filial affection' (680), Charlotte reluctantly travels with her father to meet her prospective suitor. Soon after setting sail, a storm erupts and Charlotte is thrown overboard whereupon she is rescued by a young man who nearly dies in the attempt to save her. Few readers would have been surprised to learn that Miss Brandon's saviour is 'the generous, the constant Frederick Willoughby', who has disguised himself as a passenger in the hopes of prompting a reconciliation (680). In the tale's typically hasty conclusion, the grateful and humbled Brandon laments his former pursuit of 'useless wealth and tinsel honours' and gives his consent for Charlotte to marry Willoughby (680).

There are many differences between this compressed and unsophisticated tale and the plots, tone and language of Austen's novels, of which the former's sensationalist description of the heroine's 'loose undress' as she is rescued by the hero is only the most obvious (680). Yet the similarities – not only the identical character names, but also the texts' shared interest in love thwarted by money and paternal interference, as well as their common episodes of near death and rescue – are too arresting to be ignored. Edward Copeland first acknowledged 'The Shipwreck' as an intertext for *Sense and Sensibility* in 1989.[46] (The faint but discernible traces of 'The Shipwreck' in *Persuasion* have gone unremarked.)[47] Yet the import of the connection continues to vex Austen scholarship, which typically reasserts Copeland's conclusion that the 'purpose of an allusion so thoroughly buried in the oblivion of the *Lady's Magazine*' is so obscure that it can only be 'guessed at'.[48]

The functions of Austen's explicit allusions to another of the periodical's tales in *Emma* (1816) have seemed more explicable. 'Guilt Pursued by Conscience' (November 1802) revolves around a distressing encounter between a young woman, Clara, who is walking with her infant when she is accosted by 'a man in dirty and tattered clothes, . . . [with] a long beard, and naked legs and feet; who seemed to have a wild kind of stare' (33: 563). Frightened by the 'signs of a disturbed mind' that she detects in the man's appearance, Clara attempts to 'hasten her pace' and flee, whereupon the man offers to explain himself (563). There are no gypsies here, nor is there any suing for charity or gallant rescue, but the parallels between this scene and that in which Harriet Smith is accosted in *Emma* are self-evident. Like Harriet, Clara is a 'deserted orphan' of suspect origins, who has been raised at a country 'boarding school' (563). 'Amiable' and virtuous, Clara 'despise[s] ambition' and seeks 'only the genuine enjoyments of domestic happiness', which she finds with Mr Knightley, a 'country gentleman' who endures 'censure and sneers' when he prioritises love above advantage and marries Clara (563). The testimony of the stranger, Valory, reveals Clara to be the orphaned child of a wealthy French couple. Entrusted to Valory's care upon her parents' death, her unscrupulous guardian had placed her in a boarding school and absconded with her inheritance to the continent. Years later and plagued by guilt over his actions, Valory gives away all of his ill-gotten gains and goes in search of Clara. Following his serendipitous encounter with his former charge, Mr Knightley takes pity on the repentant former guardian of his wife and enables Valory to live out the rest of his days in a convent.

According to Copeland, *Emma* 'pointedly rejects' the *story* it evokes and rewrites. Austen's novel satirises its intertext by implicitly likening the notoriously self-deluded Emma Woodhouse to the romantic-minded 'tradesman's daughters' who subscribed to the *Lady's Magazine* and insatiably devoured horrid novels along with Catherine Morland and Isabella Thorpe. Like the reader of 'Guilt Pursued by Conscience', Emma wants to believe that the humble, boarding-school-raised orphan is, in fact, a somebody. Yet Austen's novel closes down this possibility when it reveals Harriet Smith to be a nobody and, in the process, exposes '[c]heap fiction' like that published in the *Lady's Magazine* as 'an untrustworthy system for interpreting social signs'.⁴⁹ Copeland's account of Austen's engagement with 'Guilt Pursued by Conscience' dovetails here with Siskin's claim about Austen's 'staying out' of the magazine in that both arguments present Austen's novels as strategically rewriting or overwriting the print forms that preceded them.⁵⁰ By absorbing and reconfiguring popular periodical fiction's plots and forms, so the argument goes, Austen immunised her novels from the taint of association and established her literary labour's superiority and primacy through the strategic displacement of its inferior, periodical other. This a recognisable Jane Austen, the same Jane Austen whom some have suspected of posturing as the frivolous, self-absorbed Sophia Sentiment in a letter from her brothers' periodical, *The Loiterer* (1789–90), which satirises female magazine readers and the hopelessly romantic fictional content they craved. Yet as those who have questioned the *Loiterer* attribution contend, this is a difficult Jane Austen to square with the author of the novels, an author whose indebtedness to, and subversion of, literary genres and traditions are not straightforwardly dismissive, but complex, playful and creative.⁵¹ If this holds true for the multiple nods in Austen's fiction to specific novels and poems, then it is even more true of her novels' largely overlooked allusions to periodicals and, specifically, to the *Lady's Magazine*.

Sense and Sensibility's echoes of 'The Shipwreck' – not just its borrowed character names but the phrasing imported from the original tale for the later novel's title – suggest that Austen might have had access to the *Lady's Magazine* during her initial composition of 'Elinor and Marianne' in the 1790s as well as when the novel was reworked and retitled prior to publication in 1811. Similarly, if Austen read 'Guilt Pursued by Conscience' in 1802 when it was first published, she likely also had it to hand more than a decade later when composing *Emma*. Austen could have remembered Mr Knightley's name or a plot involving a surprise confrontation between a humble orphan and a vagrant years after reading the tale, but it seems unlikely that she would have been able to recall the specific language she repurposes from the magazine fiction in her novel. It is the 'sneers' directed at both the *Lady's Magazine*'s and Austen's Mr Knightley that unlock the relationship between these two texts. The Knightley of 'Guilt Pursued by Conscience' successfully brushes off the 'sneers' he endures after marrying his obscure bride, yet those that Emma Woodhouse imagines Mr Knightley experiencing should he marry Harriet Smith are too awful even to contemplate:

> It was horrible to Emma to think how it must sink him in the general opinion, to foresee the smiles, the sneers, the merriment it would prompt at his expense; the mortification and disdain of his brother, the thousand inconveniences to himself. – Could it be? – No; it was impossible.⁵²

Emma's 'horrible' imaginings of the consequences of a putative marriage between Mr Knightley and the obscure Harriet might be read as further evidence of Austen's determination to debunk magazine fiction and its improbably romantic plots as 'impossible' in the context of the real world or the world of the realist novel. Yet such a reading is undermined by the heroine's unreliability. The fact that these thoughts about the inadmissibility of Mr Knightley's marrying beneath him are expressed by Emma, not by a less self-interested character or by the narrator, is significant. By this point in the novel, readers understand the heroine as a narcissistic interpreter of reality, and they recognise that the fears Emma articulates here are not felt solely or primarily for Mr Knightley's sake, but for her own. Emma Woodhouse needs to believe that a match between Mr Knightley and Harriet is 'impossible', even though she privately acknowledges that it is 'far, very far from impossible', to keep alive the hope that she might marry him herself.[53] Her concerns for Mr Knightley mask her dawning sense of culpability in facilitating a match between him and Harriet. The threat to the 'hierarchical order' posed by such a union is ultimately less important to the novel, as Karl Kroeber argues, than 'Emma's awareness . . . that she is personally responsible for the threat'.[54] 'Guilt Pursued by Conscience' does not need *Emma* to neutralise the threat to the social order that is posed if momentarily. The tale itself is highly effective in neutralising the threat of cross-class marriage it moots when it reveals that Clara – unlike Harriet Smith – has precisely the socio-economic credentials required of the wife of Mr Knightley. *Emma* draws readers' attention to this fact when it allows the heroine to recollect the 'sneers' directed at the Mr Knightley of 'Guilt Pursued by Conscience' and to reflect on Emma's culpability in making what is 'impossible' in the pages of the *Lady's Magazine* a potential reality in Highbury. In recalling the earlier tale, *Emma* does not condemn popular magazine fiction, but rebukes her novel's heroine. The moral tale serves as the textual 'conscience' that proves Emma's own 'guilt'.

A final, and arguably more striking, example of the *Lady's Magazine*'s influence upon Austen can be found in a non-fiction serial that appeared in the periodical in instalments in the early 1810s. Elenir Irwin's 'A Defence of Women' (November 1810–August 1811) is an unabridged, original translation of Benedictine monk Benito Jerónimo Feijoo's, *Defensa de las Mujeres* (1726).[55] 'Defence of Women' was an important contribution to the magazine's ongoing debate about women's education that eloquently challenged philosophical, medical and cultural myths of sex and gender through its careful elaboration of the intellectual, political and artistic achievements of a catalogue of European women.[56] The 'great point' of this endeavour is clearly articulated in the Supplement issue for 1810: to settle, once and for all, the 'question of [women's] understanding' by asserting their capacity for rational thought and behaviour. Here the 'Defence' attempts to end debates about women's intellectual capabilities via a fable that originally appeared in Carducio's dialogues on painting. The fable concerns a man and a lion discoursing on the respective merits of their species. The man finds what he believes to be conclusive proof of humankind's superiority in the form of a sculpture of a lion lying prostrate under the foot of a triumphant conqueror. The lion is unconvinced and responds that the artwork proves nothing beyond the arrogance of the male sculptor: 'I assure thee, that, if a lion had been the sculptor, he would have turned the tables, and placed the lion over the man, making a hash of him for his own dinner' (41: 595).

The magazine translation proceeds to give the fable a real-world application, using it as a way to think through the systemic marginalisation of women's contribution to the cultural, intellectual and political life of various nations and cultures: '*Men* were the writers of these books in which the understanding of women is stigmatised as inferior to ours. If *women* had penned them, we [men] ourselves might have been brought low' (595). This parsing of the fable is not found in two of the three identified earlier English translations of Feijoo's work, although it does appear in a third from 1778, where the text runs in the following, slightly different form: 'The case is, they were men who wrote those books, in which the understanding of the women are held so cheap; had they been written by women, the men would have been placed in an inferior class.'[57] The closeness of this text to the *Lady's Magazine* translation is clear, but the addition of the language of women's pens in Irwin's text brings hers much closer to the more famous articulation of the near identical sentiment in Austen's *Persuasion* when Anne Elliot has the final word on women's emotional and intellectual capacities in her conversation with Captain Harville: 'Men have had every advantage of us in telling their own story. Education has been theirs in so much higher a degree; the pen has been in their hands. I will not allow books to prove any thing.'[58] Various editions of *Persuasion* offer up different source texts for this passage, but none is as close in language or conviction as Irwin's 'Defence of Women'. Unlike the complex allusions to *Lady's Magazine* fiction in *Sense and Sensibility* and *Emma*, identifying this reference to 'Defence of Women' in *Persuasion* might not change how we view Austen's novel. Readers do not have to recognise the textual debt to be won by Anne's Elliot's claim, although those who do can find ample further evidence in the original in support of the heroine's contention. In some ways, not recognising the reference to Elenir Irwin's translation hammers home Anne's point more forcefully by signalling our collective failure to acknowledge those instances when women have had the pen in their hands and wielded it effectively. The forgetting of texts like Irwin's is yet another example of men's 'advantage' both over women and over the popular women's reading epitomised by the *Lady's Magazine*.

As the above examples demonstrate, books – the novels, plays and poetry collections that are the focus of most work on Austen and intertextuality – provide only a partial story of literary influence in the eighteenth and early nineteenth centuries. Moreover, books provide only limited insights into how authors were received in and beyond their lifetimes. Periodicals – not just literary magazines and the Reviews – played an important role in the curation of Austen's reputation, and the *Lady's Magazine* was no exception. During her lifetime, Austen featured only rarely within the periodical and under the same cover of anonymity as her novel-writing career. The few paragraphs extracted from the *Pride and Prejudice* (1813) – dubbed 'Match in Embryo' in the August 1813 issue – could not have been attributed to Austen even if the editor had wanted to cite the author's name. Only after her death, when her authorial identity was more widely known, does Austen enter the periodical more regularly. All but one of these appearances come via Mary Russell Mitford's 'Our Village' sketches. The first of these appeared in the opening paragraph of the series' inaugural instalment:

> Even in books I like a confined locality, and so do the critics when they talk of the unities. Nothing is so tiresome as to be whirled half over Europe at the chariot-wheels of a hero, to go to sleep at [Vienna] and awaken at Madrid; it produces a real fatigue, a weariness of spirit. On the other hand, nothing is so delightful as to sit down in a country village in one of Miss Austen's delicious novels, quite sure before we leave it to become intimate with every spot and every person it contains ... (53 (December 1822): 644)

This well-known passage has long been recognised as marking 'a later (and more sentimental)' shift in Romantic-era 'epistemological and aesthetic values' centred around 'a conception of place as a specific kind of locality'.[59] 'Our Village' also, as we saw in Chapter 5, marks an important shift in the fictional sensibility of the magazine in which it first appeared. Although Mitford likely never intended it as such, her sketch effectively serves both as a manifesto for the new direction in which the magazine was travelling from the 1820s onwards and as a sign of a new editorial intolerance of the enthusiastic flouting of the classical unities once so common in the geographically expansive novels and melodramatic short stories that the periodical had published for decades.

If Mitford initiated that shift, then 'Our Village' makes it clear that she could do so only because Austen had set the precedent. The aforementioned passage reasserts what, by 1822, was an already established critical view about Austen's fiction that associated her writing with the virtues and comforts of immersion in the local, the particular and the familiar. Yet Mitford goes beyond these established views by additionally asserting Austen's ambition and talent. The geographical and temporal scope of Austen's novels were circumscribed, but her achievements were not. As Katie Halsey observes, Mitford's references to Austen, here and throughout *Our Village,* perform double work in 'simultaneously claiming literary authority for Austen and providing herself with a legitimate literary ancestress' worthy of a 'critical recognition' more lasting and deeper than that reflected in the Reviews.[60] Mitford's magazine sketch participates in a critical act of remembering, one that both popularises familiar critical orthodoxies about Austen's fiction established in the Reviews and presents the author as a model for a new generation of not just novelists (the way this passage is conventionally read), but also and more specifically for periodical writers such as Mitford. In publishing Mitford's sketch, the *Lady's Magazine* participates in the creation of a particular version of Austen and uses this Austen to project a new version of the periodical to its subscribers. Austen's fiction, which had knowingly appropriated and creatively developed material from the magazine, is subsequently assimilated into, and curated by, the *Lady's Magazine* as part of the magazine's evolving aesthetic after its new series launched in 1820.

This was but one dimension of the magazine's curation of Austen's posthumous reputation. An entirely different, if also uncannily familiar, Austen is presented to the reader in a long, curious and wickedly funny 'Letter to the Editor' published in April 1823. The letter, signed Jane Fisher of Little Chatterton, opens by discussing the competition between those 'useful and elegant publications' called magazines and the 'Reviews', which Fisher describes as 'a kind of intellectual Bastille, erected for the slavery of the free-born sons of genius' (54: 214). These framing reflections quickly segue into a long, humorous account of Fisher's recent election to a local reading group, pretentiously known as the 'Intellectual Club'. The club, which meets weekly in members' houses, sets itself up as a literary gatekeeper, with members 'reading aloud' and arbitrating on the virtues and demerits of recently published works 'before they descend into the hands of the generality' (216). Entrance to the society, we learn, is strictly policed by members, who require new entrants to have 'added to the general stock of literature' through print publications that might 'deserve the approbation of, and reflect honor [sic] on, the association' (216). Fisher explains that her own entrance to the club was secured by the publication of a poetic enigma of the kind that had formerly filled the back pages of the *Lady's Magazine*, for which she received payment of four red Morocco pocket-books. Fisher's 'Letter to the Editor', we learn, is prompted by her ambition to become the society's next president. This particular aspiration is fuelled by her infatuation with *Northanger Abbey* (1818) – 'what virtues!– what talents!–what singular excellence' – a novel that Fisher and club members had read for a recent meeting (217). '[P]anting to attain such a reputation … and to deserve such a eulogium' as the 'meritorious' author of that novel, the young woman becomes consumed by desires to be both the new Austen and the next president of the Intellectual Club. The deluded Fisher recognises deep down that she lacks the life experience and natural genius to succeed in her endeavours, but takes heart from two good omens. The first is a dream in which Austen touches her on the lips with a copy of *Persuasion*. The second is her sister's serendipitous meeting with an acquaintance of the deceased Austen, which presents an opportunity to mine for 'materially useful' biographical information on the deceased novelist (218). Jane immediately purchases some blue muslin, and then learns that Austen wore a gown of the same with 'a lace cap and pink ribbons' when writing, and also manages to secure a likeness of the author. When the latter arrives, Fisher is 'somewhat disappointed in the turn of face and features, which had more of a plump roundness, and less of expression, than her works had led [her] to expect', but she is nevertheless delighted to find 'a certain air of genius in the nose' and an uncanny similarity between Austen's chin and her own (218).

Dressed in her replica Austen gown, and wearing the miniature around her neck, Fisher sits at her desk with sheets of blank paper and pens in an attempt to channel Austen's genius. '[S]everal hours' later, and in 'floods of tears', Fisher has nothing to show for her efforts, and wails that she has 'no ideas' (218–19). Fisher's second attempt yields nothing more than a draft title of the sort familiar to long-time readers of the magazine's fiction: 'Adelaide, or the Distressed Damsel' (219). Eventually, Fisher's aunt comes to the rescue. Gently pointing out to her niece that literary genius is 'a gift only bestowed on a few', she gives Fisher a near-complete autobiographical narrative by her friend, 'Mrs T—', taken 'in her own words', and invites the aspiring author to devise a conclusion. Fisher completes the task but fears that her efforts will be insufficient to secure her presidency, especially given the Intellectual Club's recent treatment of another of its members, Miss Bluett. Bluett's rival candidacy, Fisher explains, had been scuppered when her recently published seven-decker novel had been excoriated in the Reviews. The Reviews' criticism causes Club members who were formerly enthusiastic in their praise for Bluett's novel retrospectively to declare their indifference, to block her nomination and to decree that 'no work, however popular, shall give reputation to its author till the critical works shall have sanctioned the work of the public' (221). Fisher concludes her letter by pleading with the magazine's editor to publish an approving notice of her work in the hopes that it will win Club members to her cause. She signs off by noting that the *Lady's Magazine* is 'the idol of our community' and that its approval will surely secure her presidency (221).

The Fisher satire is wonderful, multi-layered and every bit as knowing as Austen's famous defence of the novel in Chapter 5 of *Northanger Abbey*. Her letter – which eerily seems to predict a peculiarly modern kind of Austen fandom – is strewn with in-jokes designed to be recognised by devotees of Austen's novels: the connection between the names of the Fisher sisters and two of the Bennet siblings; the sound of Club members' clinking pattens walking past Fisher's house as they do in *Persuasion*'s Bath; and the Fishers' decision not to attend a particular Club meeting for fear that walking in the rain might make them ill.[61] Yet while the letter indulges what we might think of as fannish responses to Austen, it also pokes fun at them by underlining Fisher's naivety and inferiority. The satire works only when readers recognise the gap between the true 'genius' of the author of *Northanger Abbey* and the dullness of the Fishers of the world (216). Yet this distinction is not leveraged to reinforce a division between high and low literary culture. Indeed, like Austen's novel, Fisher's letter is unsparingly critical of the Reviews and their self-appointed role in policing this division. In Fisher's account, it is the *Lady's Magazine*, not the Reviews, that has the more legitimate claim to cultural authority and that does greater service to women's writing and reading.

If Chapter 5 of *Northanger Abbey* vindicates the novel, then Fisher's contribution cleverly celebrates and champions the women's magazine, another popular print form as 'universally read' as it was commonly derided by its foes (214). In addition to the playful allusions to Austen's novels, Fisher's letter is saturated with references to the *Lady's Magazine*'s history to indulge regular readers. These include references to 'Mrs T—', whose memoir Fisher completes and who shares a name with the magazine's popular advice series, Ann Thicknesse's 'Mrs T—'s Advice to her Daughter' (June 1775–Supp 1775). They also include the nod to Miss Bluett, a name shared with the doggedly insistent 'Bessy Bluitt' who, as we saw in Chapter 3, continued to bother the magazine's editor for a recipe for how to melt butter without flour while he was understandably more preoccupied with the unfolding Gordon Riots. Then there is the allusion to Fisher's poetic enigma, a form ubiquitous in the periodical's poetry section until the new series launched in 1820. And finally, there is the title of Fisher's abandoned-before-started 'Adelaide or the Distressed Damsel', which seems to stand in metonymically for the sensational fiction with which the magazine was popularly associated, and may even refer to specific novels and short stories in the magazine's earlier history that had very similar titles.[62] We might read these gestures to the magazine's history as Copeland reads allusions to *Lady's Magazine* fiction in Austen's novels: that is, as acts of absorption and displacement. However, Fisher's letter ultimately frustrates any such attempt. Her satire has two heroines: one is Austen; the other is the *Lady's Magazine*. The butts of its joke are Fisher and, more particularly, the Reviews, whose tyranny and indifference to the talents of women writers and pleasures of women readers are exemplified by the Intellectual Club members' vicious turn against Bluett and the novel they had previously loved. Like the Reviews, the women's magazine establishes its credentials as an arbiter of literary taste through editorial practice. Yet in opposition to these 'sterner works of criticism', the *Lady's Magazine* exercises these credentials via editorial generosity not 'despotism' (215). Like the novel, the women's magazine takes seriously the talent of women writers and the 'pleasure' of women readers (215).[63]

Fisher's letter is a witty contribution that plays with, in order to subvert, prejudices against the magazine, its writers and its readers. Fisher herself is not a talented writer, of course, and is, as the comparison to the 'genius' Austen indicates, a poor figurehead for the *Lady's Magazine*. The humour of her letter turns on readers' recognition of these facts. Yet Fisher's unwitting reading of the periodical's value is astute and her vindication of its aspirations and achievements is powerful. Her co-opting of Austen and of *Northanger Abbey* is critical to the letter's effects and its efforts to vindicate the magazine at a time when, as we saw in the previous chapter, its continuation was threatened by various commercial and cultural pressures. It is tempting to speculate whether the author of the Fisher letter, an unidentified correspondent who might have known Austen and might even have been Mitford herself, used the author of *Northanger Abbey* in these ways because she knew Austen had herself used the *Lady's Magazine* so creatively in *Sense and Sensibility*, *Emma*, *Mansfield Park* and *Persuasion*.[64] We may never discover whether this is the case or not. What is clear is that despite what literary history has told us, Jane Austen did not turn away from the *Lady's Magazine*, nor did the periodical forget her.

Recognising how entangled the women's magazine was with other contemporary print forms such as the novel and the Reviews, as the Fisher letter invites us to do, suggests new and necessary ways to think about literary history in the eighteenth and early nineteenth centuries. It reminds us that periodical publication was not a parallel, alternative or second-tier literary culture to that represented by volume publication, but a practice that was deeply enmeshed within that culture. As we saw in Chapter 4, writers such as Radagunda Roberts, Mary Pilkington, Catharine Day Haynes, Ann Kendall and Mitford moved between periodical and volume publication throughout their careers and, in several cases, traded on their success in each sphere to buttress it in the other. And even those, like Austen, who attempted to 'stay out' of periodicals could, nonetheless, be creatively moved by their contents in ways that the *Lady's Magazine* recognised and to which it responded in kind.

But of course, no writer of this period, even those who did not expressly or purposefully write for journals, operates entirely outside of periodicals, so deeply invested as the form is via anecdotes, biographies, reviews and its culture of reprinting in the lives of works of authors past and present. If this is an important point to make in general terms, then it is an especially significant one to make in the history of women's writing. As this book has contended, a women's literary history that does not recognise the centrality of periodical print culture or the particular contribution of individual titles such as the *Lady's Magazine* is a distorted and impoverished one. It is also one that participates in a politics of forgetting that the magazine and its intergenerational communities of authors and readers not only rejected, but also actively sought to counter.

Afterword

In their co-edited collection, *Romantic Periodicals in the Twenty-First Century: Eleven Case Studies from* Blackwood's Edinburgh Magazine (2020), Nicholas Mason and Tom Mole argue that 'however large periodicals may have loomed in the consciousnesses of the era's writers and readers, they have never occupied more than a marginal place in the academic study of the Romantic period'.[1] If this is true of the Romantic periodical in general, then it is doubly the case for the *Lady's Magazine*, a periodical that, as we have seen, has been little more than a footnote both in Romantic studies and in the evolving and dynamic field of Romantic periodical studies. In writing this book, my aim has been to bring the *Lady's Magazine* from the periphery to the centre of our conversations about literary and cultural life in the sixty-two turbulent and extraordinary years the publication spanned. Much of my work on the periodical beyond the confines of this book – particularly my collaboration with Adam Matthew Digital on a digitisation of the magazine, and the work I conducted with Dr Koenraad Claes and Dr Jenny DiPlacidi for the University of Kent's Leverhulme-funded *Lady's Magazine* project – has been devoted to making the magazine's rich and varied contents and its authors accessible to researchers, teachers and the general public. This book, however, has attempted to move beyond recovery to offer an intervention: to see what Romantic-era literature, authorship and literary history look like if we view them anew through the lens of one of the period's most long-running and popular publications.

The answers I have been presented with at every turn as I researched these questions can be summed upon in one word: they look 'unRomantic'. In using the term, I mean that some of the realities the magazine exposes are not entirely pleasant or palatable, such as the cynicism about love and marriage copiously evidenced in the magazine's short and serial fiction and the precarious, challenging writing lives that some of the magazine's contributors led. I use it also, to refer to the ways in which the magazine challenges, interrogates or otherwise exposes the limits of various of the taxonomies and hierarchies that have historically shaped Romantic scholarship and literary history more broadly. In so doing, I deploy the term 'unRomantic' advisedly, and not – of course – to imply that Romanticism is, or ever was, a stable or coherent moment, movement or ideology. Over the last few decades, Romantic studies has become a much more inclusive and diverse field (particularly in terms of canon, genre, gender, race and nation), and many of its once central concepts and myths have been successfully dislodged. Nevertheless, the ghosts of Romanticism's pasts continue to haunt literary-historical scholarship in the form of the normative (Romantic) analytical categories of the author, the reader and the literary that have structured such histories from the early nineteenth century onwards. One of the principal reasons why the *Lady's Magazine* has not been integrated into these histories until now is because it is hard to accommodate to these structures. My contention has been that it is these challenges – historically misconstrued as its messiness, lack of seriousness or amateurism – that make the effort of integration all the more important and instructional.

In the preceding chapters, I have attempted to reveal some of the myriad ways in which close attention to the *Lady's Magazine*'s form, content and authors worried away at these norms at the very moment that they were being formulated by various writers and critics and, indeed, by other by periodicals. In so doing, the book has sought to contribute to the growing body of articles and monographs that examine the critical role that periodicals played in shaping and contesting British Romanticism. In taking seriously the magazine's popularity, format and the distinctive writing cultures it fostered and the reading practices it demanded, it is indebted to and has aimed to complement recent work on miscellaneity and on the histories of reading and the book.[2] Though itself a partial history – a book about one, albeit long-lived, publication – its goal has been to expand our understanding of what constituted women's writing and women's reading in this period by placing – as the magazine itself did – the works of Elizabeth Yeames, C. D. Haynes and countless 'anons' alongside those of Jane Austen, and the likes of C. C. R. alongside Byron.

In doing as much, this book does not claim to offer a new way of doing literary history, although I hope that its methods and insights might pave the way for more, and much-needed, work on other eighteenth-century and Romantic women's magazines. It is, nonetheless, a book that has sought to keep the 'making of literary history' as much as the *Lady's Magazine* itself in its sights. This seems as natural a move to me as it did to Charlotte Brontë when she evoked the periodical in her epistolary war of words with Hartley Coleridge. As we saw in Chapter 6, the *Lady's Magazine*'s editors and contributors were all too aware that literary history has its own history, a history that has been construed in particular ways to serve particular ends, and that continues to engage in strategic acts of forgetting so that other things can be remembered. In its own acts of remembrance and curation, in its championing of women's education, women's reading and writing and in its promotion of the readerly community in and across time, the *Lady's Magazine* ambitiously presented itself as an agent and agitant in literary history. Its efforts did not always hit the mark and did not serve all members of its community well all of the time. Yet the magazine's achievements never lagged far behind even its loftiest aspirations and its legacies were multiple and lastingly significant. Recalling these achievements forces us to remember how much histories of Romantic literature, authorship and readership have forgotten when the extraordinary contribution of the *Lady's Magazine* to the making of literary history has been overlooked or marginalised. As importantly, the exercise invites us – as Brontë invited Coleridge and this book invites its readers – to account for the reasons why we did. If this book makes it harder for future literary histories to dismiss the periodical and, indeed, other Romantic-era magazines for women, it will have done what it set out to do.

Notes

Introduction

1. Charlotte Brontë to Hartley Coleridge, 10 December 1840. In Margaret Smith, edn, *The Letters of Charlotte Brontë with a selection of letters by her family and friends, Vol. 1 1829–47* (Oxford: Clarendon Press, 1995), p. 240.
2. On the juvenilia see, for instance, Judith E. Pike and Lucy Morrison, eds, *Charlotte Brontë from the Beginnings: New Essays from the Juvenilia to the Major Works* (London: Routledge, 2017).
3. Letter from Robert Southey to Hartley Coleridge, 12 March 1837, in Margaret Smith, ed., *The Letters of Charlotte Brontë*, pp. 166–7.
4. Quoted in Fannie Elizabeth Ratchford, *The Brontës' Web of Childhood* (New York: Columbia University Press, 1941), p. 108.
5. The signature 'C T' was adopted by several contributors to the *Lady's Magazine*. It was used, for instance, by the authors of 'Verses on the Power of Love over Adversity' (9 (August 1788): 432); 'The Emblematical Rose' (39 (October 1808): 463); and 'The Farewell' (39 (September 1808): 414).
6. In 1823 the magazine's title changed to the *Lady's Magazine; or, Mirror of the Belles-Lettres, Fashions, Fine Arts, Music, Drama &c.*
7. Coote's and Wheble's respective roles in establishing the magazine are documented in Chapter 2.
8. The fictions she recalls are: 'Derwent Priory' (January 1796–September 1797); 'Grasville Abbey' (March 1793–August 1797) and the single instalment tale 'Athelwold and Ethelinda' (March 1797).
9. Coote's sale of his interest in the magazine to George Robinson and his partner John Roberts in July 1771 is discussed in Chapter 2. Roberts died six months later, hence my subsequent references to Robinson's magazine.
10. Exceptions are the issues for 1819, in which year the magazine appeared – at least for a time – under the imprint of Baldwin, Craddock and Joy at 47 Paternoster Row, the address from which George Robinson (the third) published the magazine in 1818, and those for 1832, which appeared under the imprint of J. Page, 112 Fetter Lane.
11. In July of 1832 the magazine merged with the *Lady's Monthly Museum*. This continuation was entitled the *Lady's Magazine and Museum of Belles-Lettres* (1832–7). In 1838 the magazine incorporated the *Court Magazine*

and *Belle Assemblée* (formerly *La Belle Assemblée, or Bell's Court and Fashionable Magazine*). This final title was published as the *Court Magazine and Monthly Critic, and Ladies' Magazine and Museum of Belles-Lettres*, and ran until 1847.
12. See, for example, Robert D. Mayo, *The English Novel in the Magazines, 1740–1815* (London: Oxford University Press; and Evanston: Northwestern University Press, 1962), p. 421n75.
13. In addition to twelve monthly issues a year, the magazine also produced an annual Supplement issue from 1772 to 1819. The Supplement was dropped when a new series was launched in 1820.
14. The influence of the magazine on Austen's fiction is discussed in Chapter 6.
15. Edward Copeland, *Women Writing about Money: Women's Fiction in England, 1790–1820* (Cambridge: Cambridge University Press, 1995), p. 119.
16. Individual volumes of the magazine held by the New York Public Library and University of Chicago Library have been digitised and made available via HathiTrust. The longer run (1770–1802) held by the Bayerische Staatsbibliotek has also been digitised. *Eighteenth-Century Journals V* provides digital surrogates of volumes held by the Library of Birmingham (formerly Birmingham Central Library), the Bodleian Library and Cambridge University Library.
17. Surviving business papers and correspondence of John Nichols, whose printing house owned and edited the *Gentleman's Magazine* from 1778 to 1856, are being archived by Julian Pooley. For more information on the in-progress Nichols Archive Project, contact jpooley@surreycc.gov.uk.
18. Data from the University of Kent's project, 'The Lady's Magazine (1770–1818): Understanding the Emergence of a Genre', suggest that in the period from 1770 to 1818 at least a fifth of the magazine's contents was repurposed from other sources. See <https://research.kent.ac.uk/the-ladys-magazine/index/> (last accessed 8 October 2020).
19. Sean Latham and Robert Scholes, 'The Rise of Periodical Studies', *PMLA* 121. 2 (2006): 517–31.
20. See Mayo, *The English Novel in the Magazines* (1962); Ros Ballaster, Margaret Beetham, Elizabeth Frazer and Sandra Hebron's important *Women's Worlds: Ideology, Femininity and the Woman's Magazine* (Basingstoke: Macmillan, 1992); Copeland, *Women Writing about Money* (1995); Jacqueline Pearson, *Women's Reading in Britain 1750–1834: a Dangerous Recreation* (Cambridge: Cambridge University Press, 1999); Richard de Ritter, *Imagining Women Readers, 1789–1820: Well-regulated Minds* (Manchester: Manchester University Press, 2014); Jan Fergus, *Provincial Readers in Eighteenth-Century England* (Oxford: Oxford University Press, 2006), pp. 199–209; Cynthia White, *Women's Magazines, 1693–1968* (London: Michael Joseph, 1970); Alison Adburgham, *Women in Print: Writing Women and Women's Magazines from the Restoration to the Accession of Victoria* (London: George Allen & Unwin, 1972).
21. See, for example, Anthony D. Barker, 'Edward Cave, Samuel Johnson and the *Gentleman's Magazine* (unpublished PhD thesis, University of Oxford, 1981); Emily De Montluzin, *Attributions of Authorship in the Gentleman's Magazine, 1731–1868: An Electronic Union List* <http://bs

uva.org/bsuva/gm2/GMintro.html> (last accessed 8 October 2020); and Gillian Williamson, *British Masculinity in the Gentleman's Magazine, 1731–1815* (Basingstoke: Palgrave Macmillan, 2016).
22. I am thinking here of books including David Higgins's important monograph *Romantic Genius and the Literary Marketplace: Biography, Celebrity Politics* (London: Routledge, 2005). Throughout the book, I follow the convention of referring to review journals as 'Reviews' and use 'reviews' to signal critical appraisals of published works.
23. David Stewart, *Romantic Magazines and Metropolitan Literary Culture* (Basingstoke: Palgrave Macmillan, 2011), pp. 32–3. Kim Wheatley's special issue on *Romantic Periodicals and Print Culture* for *Prose Studies: History, Theory, Criticism* 25:1 (2002) devotes no attention to periodicals specifically marketed at women readers.
24. Kathryn Shevelow, *Women and Print Culture: The Construction of Femininity in the Early Periodical* (London: Routledge, 1989), pp. 188–9.
25. See, for example, Iona Italia, *The Rise of Literary Journalism in the Eighteenth Century: Anxious Employment* (London and New York: Routledge, 2005) and Shawn Lisa Maurer, *Proposing Men: Dialectics of Gender and Class in the Eighteenth-Century English Periodical* (Stanford: Stanford University Press, 1998).
26. Margaret Beetham, *A Magazine of her Own? Domesticity and Desire in the Woman's Magazine 1800–1914* (London and New York: Routledge, 1994), p. 21.
27. For a thorough reappraisal of ephemera, see Gillian Russell, *The Ephemeral Eighteenth Century* (Cambridge: Cambridge University Press, 2020).

Chapter 1

1. I use the gender pronoun 'he' advisedly. The editor's identity is unknown, but for at least some of the time under Wheble's tenure, seems to have been carried out by poet, essayist and editor John Huddlestone Wynne (bap. 1742–88). All of the few editors of the magazine who have been identified are men.
2. Manushag N. Powell, *Performing Authorship in Eighteenth-Century English Periodicals* (Lewisburg, PA: Bucknell University Press, 2012), p. 133.
3. The patterns, which I discuss in Chapter 5, were dropped when the magazine launched its new series in 1820. The magazine also issued monthly song sheets throughout much of its run. These were not mentioned in the opening 'Address'.
4. Shawn Lisa Maurer, *Proposing Men: Dialectics of Gender and Class in the Eighteenth-Century English Periodical* (Stanford, CA: Stanford University Press, 1998), p. 54.
5. Powell, *Performing Authorship*, p. 133.
6. Powell, *Performing Authorship*, p. 60.
7. On Manley's editorship of the *Examiner* see Rachel Carnell, 'Protesting the Exclusivity of the Public Sphere: Delarivier Manley's *Examiner*', in *Women's Periodicals and Print Culture in Britain, 1690–1820s: The*

Long Eighteenth Century, eds Jennie Batchelor and Manushag N. Powell (Edinburgh: Edinburgh University Press, 2018), pp. 153–64. On Montagu's editorship of *Nonsense of Common-Sense* see Isobel Grundy, '"A moral paper! And how do you expect to get money by it?" Lady Mary Wortley Montagu and Journalism', in *Women's Periodicals and Print Culture*, pp. 165–77; and Manushag N. Powell, 'Women Readers and the Rise of the Periodical Essay', *A Companion to British Literature, Vol. III: Eighteenth-Century Literature 1660–1837*, eds Robert DeMaria, Jr, Heesok Chang and Samantha Zacher (Chichester: Wiley-Blackwell, 2014), pp. 78–94.

8. As Powell notes, specifically with reference to essay periodicals of the first half of the century, 'the designation "female" may have nothing at all to do with the sex of the actual author, or of the presumed reader either'. *Performing Authorship*, p. 58.
9. Kathryn Shevelow, *Women and Print Culture: The Construction of Femininity in the Early Periodical* (London: Routledge, 1989), pp. 188–9.
10. Although Robinson was neither the first nor the last publisher of the periodical, I use 'Robinson's magazine' throughout this chapter to distinguish between this *Lady's Magazine* (1770–1832) and the other *Lady's/Ladies'* magazines discussed below.
11. On the history of the use of the term eidolon to describe periodical personas, see Powell, *Performing Authorship*, pp. 23–9.
12. Powell terms such publications – in the main 'collections of essays that falsely purported to be bound versions of earlier essay series' – 'pseudo-periodicals'. 'Eliza Haywood, Periodicalist(?)', *Journal for Early Modern Cultural Studies*, 14.4 (2014): 163–86 (175).
13. Iona Italia, *The Rise of Literary Journalism in the Eighteenth Century: Anxious Employment* (London and New York: Routledge, 2005), p. 21.
14. Italia, *The Rise of Literary Journalism*, p. 22. An exception in Romantic periodical studies is the 'literary magazine', the adjective 'literary' serving here not only as a way of describing these publications' contents, but also as a marker of aesthetic and scholarly respectability.
15. Susan Carlile, *Charlotte Lennox: An Independent Mind* (Toronto: University of Toronto Press, 2018), p. 188. The original title of the *Lady's Museum*, as evidenced by a November 1759 petition for its royal licence, was *The Female Magazine; or Lady's Polite Companion*. Whether Lennox or her publishers, Newberry and Coote, were responsible for the title change is unknown. See Barbara Laning Fitzpatrick, 'Physical Evidence for John Coote's Eighteenth-Century Periodical Proprietorships: The Example of Coote's *Royal Magazine* (1759–71) and Smollett's *British Magazine* (1760–7)', *Analytical and Enumerative Bibliography* (new ser.) 11 (2000): 211–58 (256n70).
16. Samuel Johnson, *A Dictionary of the English Language*, 2nd edn (London: J. Knapton; C. Hitch and L. Hawes; A. Millar; R. and J. Dodsley; and M. and T. Longman, 1756).
17. Ros Ballaster, Margaret Beetham, Elizabeth Frazer and Sandra Hebron, *Women's Worlds: Ideology, Femininity and the Woman's Magazine* (Basingstoke: Macmillan, 1991), p. 7.
18. Shevelow, *Women and Print Culture*, pp. 188–9; Shawn Lisa Maurer, 'The Periodical', in *The History of British Women's Writing, vol. 4 1690–1750*,

ed. Ros Ballaster (Basingstoke: Palgrave Macmillan, 2010), pp. 156–72 (p. 166).
19. *The Lounger*, no. 60 (25 March 1786): 234–42. Subsequent references will be given in the text.
20. Barbara Benedict, 'Literary Miscellanies: The Cultural Mediation of Fragmented Feeling', *ELH* 57.2 (1990): 407–30 (424).
21. The *Ladies Mercury* (London: T. Pratt, 1693). 'Ladies and Gentlemen' were invited to send questions to the Mercurians via the 'Latin-Coffee-House in Ave-Mary-Lane'.
22. Because of its non-consecutive pagination, references to the *Ladies Mercury* will be given by volume and issue number only. For excellent accounts of the *Mercury* and its relation to Dunton's *Athenian Mercury* see Nicola Parsons, 'The *Ladies Mercury* (1693)', *Women's Periodicals and Print Culture*, pp. 315–26; and Slaney Chadwick Ross, 'John Dunton's *Ladies Mercury* and the Eighteenth-Century Female Subject', *Women's Periodicals and Print Culture*, pp. 327–41.
23. In fact, female querists continued to appear in the *Athenian Mercury* for the rest of its run.
24. Eve Tavor Bannet, 'Discontinuous Reading and Miscellaneous Instruction for British Ladies', *Women's Periodicals and Print Culture*, pp. 40–52 (p. 40).
25. *The Gentleman's Journal: or the Monthly Miscellany. By Way of a Gentleman in the Country. Consisting of News, History, Philosophy, Poetry, Musick, Translations, &c.* (1692–4).
26. An eight-page weekly bearing the title the *Ladies Journal* launched in January Dublin in 1727. The *Ladies Journal* is quite different from its namesake although it similarly adopts a hybrid eidolon-led yet miscellany form. It devoted some of its limited page count to matters of 'Love and Gallantry' (no. 1 (17 January 1727): 3), but it was primarily concerned with weightier matters, including philosophy and history. As Bannet documents, the *Journal* was intellectually challenging and assumed its female readers' capability as decipherers of allegory and parable in particular. See Bannet, 'Discontinuous Reading', p. 47.
27. These include: Aphra Behn's 'Hopes, Fears, Desires, Wild Tyrants of my Soul'; Anne Finch's 'Love! thou art the best of human joys!'; and Anne Wharton's 'Verses on the Snuff of a Candle made in Sickness'.
28. Margaret J. M. Ezell, 'The *Gentleman's Journal* and the Commercialisation of Restoration Coterie Literary Practices', *Modern Philology* 89.3 (1992): 323–40 (339).
29. Ezell, 'The *Gentleman's Journal*': 340.
30. See esp. Erin Mackie, *Market à la Mode: Fashion, Commodity, and Gender in* The Tatler *and* The Spectator (Baltimore and London: Johns Hopkins University Press, 1997); Maurer, *Proposing Men*, pp. 118–75; and Shevelow, *Women and Print Culture*, pp. 93–145.
31. *Tatler* no. 1. Richard Steele, *The Tatler*, ed. Donald F. Bond, 3 vols (Oxford: Clarendon Press, 1987), 1: 15. Subsequent references will be given in the text.
32. Shevelow, *Women and Print Culture*, p. 93.
33. Shevelow, *Women and Print Culture*, p. 93.

34. *Spectator* no. 10. Joseph Addison and Richard Steele, *The Spectator*, ed. Donald F. Bond, 5 vols (Oxford: Clarendon Press, 1965), 1: 46. Subsequent references will be given in the text.
35. Jonathan Swift, *Journal to Stella*, ed. Harold Williams, 2 vols (Oxford: Clarendon Press, 1948), 2: 482.
36. Shevelow, *Women and Print Culture*, pp. 1–2.
37. Mackie, *Market à la Mode*, p. 164.
38. Iona Italia, 'Fair-Sexing It', *Media History* 14:3 (2008): 323–35 (333).
39. Michael Suarez, 'Introduction', *The Cambridge History of the book in Britain: Vol. V, 1695–1830*, eds Michael Suarez, S. J. and Michael L. Turner (Cambridge: Cambridge University Press, 2009), pp. 1–35 (p. 11).
40. Kathryn R. King, 'Frances Brooke, Editor, and the Making of the *Old Maid* (1755–1756)', *Women's Periodicals and Print Culture*, pp. 342–56 (p. 343).
41. The *Female Spectator* was issued monthly in twenty-four instalments between April 1744 and May 1746. Its publisher was T. Gardner, with whom Haywood collaborated also on the *Parrot*, *Epistles to the Ladies* and various other of her publications in the 1740s and 1750s. It should be noted that Leah Orr has cast doubt on Haywood's authorship of the *Parrot*, *Epistles* and *Young Lady*, all three of which are attributed by association via their title pages' allusions to the *Female Spectator*. Orr points out that these attributions are problematically based on Haywood's sole authorship of the *Female Spectator*. Leah Orr, 'The Basis for Attribution in the Canon of Eliza Haywood', *The Library* 12.4 (2011): 335–75.
42. Eliza Haywood, *The Female Spectator. The Selected Works of Eliza Haywood*. Part 2. Vols. 1–2, eds Kathryn R. King and Alexander Pettit (London: Pickering and Chatto, 2001), 2, book 1, p. 17. Subsequent references will be given in the text.
43. Frances Brooke, *The Old Maid. By Mary Singleton, Spinster* (London: A. Millar, 1764); Charlotte Lennox, *The Lady's Museum* (1760–1). Subsequent references will be given in the text.
44. Eve Tavor Bannet, 'Haywood's Spectator and the Female World', in *Fair Philosopher: Eliza Haywood and the "Female Spectator"*, eds Lynn Marie Wright and Donald J. Newman (Lewisburg: Bucknell University Press, 2006), pp. 82–101 (p. 83).
45. Eloquent counterarguments to this assertion have been put forward by Bannet, 'Haywood's Spectator'; Powell, *Performing Authorship*, pp. 150–7; and Kathryn R. King, 'Patriot or Opportunist? Eliza Haywood and the Politics of *The Female Spectator*', in *Fair Philosopher*, pp. 104–21.
46. Ballaster et al., *Women's Worlds*, p. 61.
47. Italia, *The Rise of Literary Journalism*, pp. 139, 133, 139.
48. Ballaster et al., *Women's Worlds*, p. 60.
49. King, 'Patriot or Opportunist?', p. 110.
50. Catherine Ingrassia, 'Eliza Haywood's Periodicals in Wartime', *Women's Periodicals and Print Culture*, pp. 178–89 (p. 178).
51. Powell, *Performing Authorship*, p. 157.
52. King, 'Patriot or Opportunist?', p. 105.
53. Lord Orrery's contributions to the *Old Maid* are discussed by King in 'Frances Brooke, Editor', pp. 342–56.

54. Powell, *Performing Authorship*, p. 160; p. 168.
55. Harriet Guest, *Small Change: Women, Learning, Patriotism, 1750–1810* (Chicago: University of Chicago Press, 2000), p. 15.
56. *Lady's Museum* (1760–1) 1.1: 4. Subsequent references will be given in the text.
57. *London Chronicle* (19–21 February 1760).
58. Susan Carlile, 'Eyes that Eagerly "Bear the Steady Ray of Reason"': Eidolon as Activist in Charlotte Lennox's *Lady's Museum*', in *Women's Periodicals and Print Culture*, pp. 357–76 (p. 359).
59. Susan Carlile, *Charlotte Lennox*, p. 171.
60. Anna K. Sagal, 'Constructing Women's History in *The Lady's Museum*', *Women's Periodicals and Print Culture*, pp. 53–66 (p. 55).
61. Italia, *The Rise of Literary Journalism*, p. 178; p. 205.
62. 'Advertisement', *Gentleman's Magazine* 1 (January 1733): n.p.
63. See Gillian Williamson, *British Masculinity in the Gentleman's Magazine* (Basingstoke: Palgrave Macmillan, 2016), p. 17.
64. Italia, *The Rise of Literary Journalism*, p. 122.
65. Will Slauter, 'Upright Piracy: Understanding the Lack of Copyright for Journalism in Eighteenth-Century Britain', *Book History* 16. 1 (2013): 34–61 (34).
66. Ronan Deazley, *On the Origin of the Right to Copy: Charting the Movement of Copyright Law in Eighteenth Century Britain (1695–1775)* (Portland, OR: Hart Publishing, 2004), pp. 79–80. In the case of Trapp's work, the concern was that Cave was planning to serialise the original work in full in the *Gentleman's Magazine*. As Slauter notes: 'The Statute of Anne did not explicitly prohibit others from making abridgements of protected works, a fact that Cave and other magazine publishers exploited'. Slauter, *Who Owns the News?* (Stanford: Stanford University Press, 2019), p. 74.
67. Slauter, 'Upright Piracy': 34.
68. Williamson, *British Masculinity in the Gentleman's Magazine*, p. 6. On women readers of the *Gentleman's Magazine*, see particularly pp. 56–60.
69. *Universal Spectator and Weekly Journal* (7 April 1733). This John Roberts, who went on to publish Samuel Johnson's *Life of Richard Savage* (1744), is not to be confused with the John Roberts with whom George Robinson first published the *Lady's Magazine*.
70. The magazine was published by T. Dormer and was available 'at the Pamphlet-Shops in Town and Country, and by all the Hawkers that carry News'. This surviving page can be found at the British Library: 1879, c.6(4).
71. This copy is held by the Bodleian: Hope fol. 106 (154). Page numbers are given in square brackets as they are not printed in the magazine.
72. Lennox's *Lady's Museum* had the same cover price when it was founded in 1760.
73. *The Lady's Magazine; or, Polite and Entertaining Companion for the Fair Sex* was published by John Wilkie, for whom Oliver Goldsmith worked as conductor of *The Bee* (1759). Richard C. Taylor notes that in editing the *Bee* for Wilkie, Goldsmith became part of an influential group of book trade professionals of publishers, editors and printers affiliated with John Newbery. Collectively this group had a hand in many periodicals,

for more than one of which Goldsmith worked. John Coote, who went on to publish the *Lady's Museum* with Newbery and later founded the *Lady's Magazine* (1770–1832), was a 'peripheral' member of this group and employed Goldsmith to write for the *Royal Magazine, or Gentleman's Monthly Companion*. See *Goldsmith as Journalist* (Rutherford, Madison, Teaneck: Farleigh Dickinson University Press; London and Toronto: Associated University Presses, 1993), p. 87.

74. See, for instance, *London Chronicle*, 22–5 September 1759; and *Sussex Advertiser*, 17 September 1759.
75. *London Chronicle*, 22–5 September 1759.
76. *Lady's Magazine; or Polite Companion for the Fair Sex* 1 (December 1759). Subsequent references will be given in the text.
77. Shevelow, *Women and Print Culture*, p. 179; and Taylor, *Goldsmith as Journalist*, p. 87.
78. *London Chronicle*, 22–5 September 1759.
79. Shevelow, '"C— L—" to "Mrs. Stanhope": A Preview of Charlotte Lennox's *The Lady's Museum*', *Tulsa Studies in Women's Literature* 1.1 (Spring 1982): 83–6.
80. In 1759, for instance, the *Gentleman's Magazine* impugned the quality of contributions made by *Lady's Magazine*'s reader-contributors in a statement that prompted a sanguine response from Stanhope in the November issue: 'how hard it is to wry good verses, or how difficult to obtain such for a magazine' (1 (November 1759): 104).
81. Italia, for instance, sees this move as symptomatic of Stanhope's *Lady's Magazine*'s abandonment of the kind of 'clear educational programme' discernible in early periodicals. Reliant as the periodical was upon readers rather than upon the 'specialist knowledge or particular expertise' of its editor, the magazine's improvement of its readers – where this happened at all – could only be 'fortuitous, rather than planned' (*The Rise of Literary Journalism*, p. 190).

Chapter 2

1. *Middlesex Journal*, 29 September–2 October 1770. Wheble, then publisher of the *Lady's Magazine*, also published the *Middlesex Journal*.
2. Wheble, like Robinson and Roberts, worked in Paternoster Row. For a few months after the dissolution of the partnership between George Robinson's grandsons, George Robinson III and Samuel Robinson, the magazine was published by Baldwin, Craddock and Joy at number 47 in the Row. When Samuel Robinson stepped back in as publisher in December 1819, the magazine returned to its original Row address. Only in 1832, when the magazine was sold to J. Page did the address migrate from the Row to Fetter Lane, just off Fleet-Street.
3. Thomas Penant and John Wallis, *London: Being a Complete Guide to the British Capital*, 4th edn (London: Sherwood, Neely, and Jones, 1814), p. 212.
4. Raven documents that about 40 per cent of the properties on the Row were occupied by booksellers, stationers, printers and bookbinders. James

Raven, *The Business of Books: Booksellers and the English Book Trade, 1450–1850* (New Haven and London: Yale University Press, 2007), p. 168.
5. Raven, *The Business of Books*, p. 173.
6. I am thinking primarily, here, about Alexander Hogg's *New Lady's Magazine*, which is discussed in Chapter 5.
7. Readers principally associated journals with the publishers under whose imprint they were issued and to whose premises reader correspondence was directed.
8. John Nichols, *Literary Anecdotes of the Eighteenth Century*, 6 vols (London: printed for the author, 1812), 3: 719.
9. The *Lady's Museum* was one of at least twenty serial publications with which Coote has been identified, seventeen of which Barbara Laning Fitzpatrick has discovered 'he either established or controlled at some point in their existence'. 'Physical Evidence for John Coote's Eighteenth-Century Periodical Proprietorships: The Example of Coote's *Royal Magazine* (1759–71) and Smollett's *British Magazine* (1760–7)', *Analytical and Enumerative Bibliography* (new ser.) 11 (2000): 211–58 (213). Of the seventeen periodicals with which we know Coote was associated, sixteen were launched before the *Lady's Magazine* first appeared, and eight were still running in August 1770 when its inaugural issue was published.
10. Fitzpatrick, 'Physical Evidence': 238.
11. During 1771, Wheble moved again to number 24, thereby locating his business next door to Robinson and Roberts's establishment.
12. According to Charles Henry Timperley, Wilkie was a relative of Wheble's, although I have not been able to verify the familial connection. *A Dictionary of Printers and Printing with the Progress of Literature, Ancient and Modern: Bibliographical Illustrations, etc. etc.* (London: H. Johnson, 1839), p. 878.
13. Much of the biographical information we have about Wheble derives from his obituary published in the *Gentleman's Magazine* 90 (November 1820): 471–3.
14. See, for instance, Peter D. G. Thomas, 'John Wilkes and the Freedom of the Press (1771)', *Historical Research* 33 (1960): 86–98.
15. William West, 'Notice of the Robinsons', *Aldine Magazine of Biography, Criticism and the Arts* 1.9 (26 January 1839): 132–5 (132); and *Fifty Years' Recollections of an Old Bookseller* (London: printed by and for the author, 1837), pp. 92–5 (p. 92).
16. Anon., 'George Robinson, Esq.', *New, Original, and Complete Wonderful Museum and Magazine Extraordinary*, 6 (1808): 3150–6 (3151). Mary (Molly) Richardson was the widow of bookseller Joseph Richardson, who died unexpectedly on a business trip to Scarborough in September 1763. Mary took over the business on her husband's death and traded until at least 1764. Roberts had evidently worked for Joseph Richardson for some time and was called upon to verify the scribbled will found inside a book belonging to Richardson upon his death. Will of Joseph Richardson of Saint Faith, City of London (6 October 1763), PRO 11/892/324.
17. 'George Robinson, Esq': *New, Original, and Complete Wonderful Museum and Magazine Extraordinary*: 3151.
18. 'George Robinson, Esq.', *New, Original, and Complete Wonderful Museum*

and Magazine Extraordinary: 3151. Roberts appears to have been born to John and Mary Roberts in London in 1733 and was baptised on 11 April 1734 in the parish of St Botolph, Bishopsgate (London Metropolitan Archives). A death notice appeared in the *Lady's Magazine* for January 1772, though Roberts's death date is usually cited in print sources as c.1776.

19. The remaining shares were purchased by: Bedwell Law of Ave-Maria Lane; publisher and stationer Stanley Crowder of 12 Paternoster Row; and Lacey Hawes, who traded out of number 32. This information, from the Stationers Company Records, Entry Book of Copies 1774–86, is cited in Fitzpatrick, 'Physical Evidence': 251n48. In later years, the Robinson firm was involved in several further serial publications, including the *New Annual Register* (1780–1825). According to West, the firm was also 'concerned' in the newspapers the *Courier* and the *Telegraph*. West, 'Notice of the Robinsons': 133.

20. According to the *New, Original, and Complete Wonderful Museum and Magazine Extraordinary*, Archibald Hamilton senior printed 'all of [Robinson's] publications' for many years (3152). Robinson, who was one of the three executors of Archibald senior's will, had for several years prior been entrusted with funds by Hamilton senior to loan to his grandson, Archibald Hamilton III, to support his printing business. Another of Archibald senior's grandsons, Samuel Hamilton, to whom I return in Chapter 5, was the printer of the *Lady's Magazine* (with some interruptions) from at least 1799 until 1823 and also its editor in the early 1820s.

21. George Robinson Sr, his son, George, and his brothers and business partners, John and James, were called before the King's Bench in November 1793 for distributing Thomas Paine's *The Rights of Man II* (1792). George senior, junior and James were fined 50l each, and John 100l.

22. 'Notice of the Robinsons', *Aldine Magazine*: 132. On Robinson's connection with the Dublin and Edinburgh book trades, see Richard B. Sher, *The Enlightenment and the Book: Scottish Authors and Their Publishers in Eighteenth-Century Britain, Ireland, and America* (Chicago and London: University of Chicago Press, 2006), esp. 387–97.

23. Jan Fergus, *Provincial Readers in Eighteenth-Century England* (Oxford: Oxford University Press, 2006), p. 216.

24. See Jon P. Klancher, *The Making of English Reading Audiences, 1790–1832* (Madison: University of Wisconsin Press, 1987), esp. pp. 20–6.

25. Evidence of the magazine's success in this area can be found in the records Fergus has analysed, which indicate that around half of the single-title adult subscribers in the Clay archives for Daventry, Rugby and Lutterworth (or 57 out of 116, to be precise) subscribed only to the *Lady's Magazine*. Fergus, *Provincial Readers*, p. 216.

26. Ros Ballaster, Margaret Beetham, Elizabeth Frazer and Sandra Hebron, *Women's Worlds: Ideology, Femininity and the Woman's Magazine* (Basingstoke: Macmillan, 1992), p. 66.

27. Robert D. Mayo, *The English Novel in the Magazines, 1740–1815* (Evanston: Northwestern University Press and London: Oxford University Press, 1962), pp. 341–2.

28. Paul Goring, 'The Evolution of "A Sentimental Journey. By a Lady" in *The Lady's Magazine*', *The Shandean*, 39.3 (2020): 67–100.
29. Coote's likely editorship of the *British Magazine* (1760–7) from 1763 when Smollett left for the continent is discussed by Fitzpatrick 'Physical Evidence': 211–17; 224–40. Coote was also the publisher of *Sir Launcelot Greaves* when it first appeared, in two volumes, in 1762. Wheble noted Coote's proprietorship of the *Universal Museum* in the trial transcript published in his *Lady's Magazine* (1 (July 1770): 47). His role as co-publisher of the *Lady's Museum* was discussed in Chapter 1.
30. In a footnote to the November 1773 instalment of the travelogue, for instance, the serial's author issued thanks to 'Mr. C— for his communications of the alterations made in Exeter' since the publications on which she based her account of the city had appeared. She also invited other readers to 'furnish her with similar elucidations with respect to other places' that she had not visited in real life (4 (November 1773): 568).
31. JoEllen DeLucia, 'Travel Writing and Mediation in the *Lady's Magazine*: Charting "the meridian of female reading"', in *Women's Periodicals and Print Culture in Britain, 1690-1820s: The Long Eighteenth Century*, eds Jennie Batchelor and Manushag N. Powell (Edinburgh: Edinburgh University Press, 2018), pp. 205–16 (p. 206).
32. Ros Ballaster, *Fabulous Orients: Fictions of the East in England, 1662–1785* (Oxford: Oxford University Press, 2005), pp. 7–8.
33. Kamrath is writing about oriental tales in early American magazines, a good number of which previously appeared for the first time in English in British periodicals. Mark L. Kamrath, 'An "inconceivable pleasure" and the "Philadelphia Minerva": Erotic Liberalism, Oriental Tales and the Female Subject in Periodicals of the Early Republic', *American Periodicals* 14.1 (2004): 3–34 (26).
34. The *Lady's Magazine* had been silently appropriating content from this popular work even before it began using it as a translation text. The August 1770 issue contained two translated pieces from Cardonne: 'Comfort for the Afflicted' and 'The Taylor's Dream'. The identity of the tales' translator – possibly a staff writer – is unknown.
35. Margaret Cohen and Carolyn Dever, eds, *The Literary Channel: The International Invention of the Novel* (Princeton: Princeton University Press, 2002). Cohen and Dever's book is concerned with the novel as opposed to periodicals, however.
36. Gillian Dow, 'Criss-Crossing the Channel: the French Novel and English Translation', in *The Oxford Handbook of the Eighteenth-Century Novel*, ed. J. A. Downie (Oxford: Oxford University Press, 2016), pp. 88–104 (p. 99).
37. Ballaster, *Fabulous Orients*, p. 22.
38. This quotation is drawn from the epigraph for the first instalment of 'A Sentimental Journey', which is taken from Isaac Watts, *The Improvement of the Mind* (1741).
39. Edward Copeland, *Women Writing about Money: Women's Fiction in England, 1790-1820* (Cambridge: Cambridge University Press, 1995), p. 119.
40. Jean E. Hunter, '*The Lady's Magazine* and the Study of Englishwomen

in the Eighteenth Century', in *Newsletters to Newspapers: Eighteenth-Century Journalism*, eds Donavan H. Bond and W. Reynolds McLeod (Morgantown: School of Journalism, West Virginia University, 1977), pp. 103–17 (p. 109). Hunter's assertion that 'Mr. T— H— was a man and Clarissa was a woman' is disputable (p. 108).

41. Prominent male poets in Wheble's magazine include John Seally and Asaphides, the pseudonym adopted by Thomas Chatterton and John Lockstone for their collaborations. John Seally contributed poems to various periodicals in the 1760s and 1770s and was conductor of the *Universal Museum* (1762–70), in which Coote had a hand. Nine poems with the Asaphides signature appeared in Wheble's magazine between August 1770 and the end of 1772.

42. For a more detailed discussion of how marriage enters and is navigated by the *Lady's* and other magazines, see Jennie Batchelor, '"Be but a little Deaf and Blind ... and Happiness you'll Surely Find": Marriage in Eighteenth-Century Magazines for Women', in *After Marriage in the Long Eighteenth Century: Literature, Law and Society*, eds Jenny DiPlacidi and Karl Leydecker (Basingstoke: Palgrave Macmillan, 2017). pp. 107–27.

43. Katherine Sobba Green, *The Courtship Novel, 1740–1820: A Feminised Genre* (Lexington: University Press of Kentucky, 1991), p. 62.

44. Were it not for the trial transcript, Johnson's role in the magazine would be unknown. Only after 1800 were printers' names routinely listed in the magazine.

45. Although the trial transcript does not mention any editor, the scholarly consensus has been that the magazine did have an editor from its inception, and that the editor of Wheble's magazine was John Huddlestone Wynne (bap. 1742–88). Charles Wynne, John's son, notes that 'Wheble engaged' his father 'to conduct his *Lady's Magazine*, for which he received a regular monthly stipend'. Charles Edward Wynne, 'Account of Mr John Huddlestone Wynne', *Monthly Magazine* 22 (August 1806): 16–20 (18). I have found no evidence to support or refute the claim that Wynne edited the magazine from its first issue. However, in light of the trial transcript and Wynne's conspicuous absence from the courtroom discussion, it is reasonable to assume Wynne took on the role of editor for Wheble after March 1771 when Coote sold the magazine until the end of 1772 when Wheble's magazine terminated.

46. 'The Pyrenean Hermits' is a translation of Nicolas Bricaire de la Dixmerie's 'Les Solitaires Des Pyrénées; Nouvelle Espagnole et Françoise' from *Contes Philosophiques et Moraux* (1765).

47. To avoid confusion, I will use Robinson's magazine to refer to the publication originally launched by George Robinson and Roberts. John Roberts died just months after this magazine launched.

48. Establishing what percentage of collections hold only Wheble's issues for April 1771 to December 1772 is difficult, in large part because library catalogues are often unclear about which versions of the magazine they hold. The 1771 and 1772 issues held by Birmingham Central Library, the Bodleian, the British Library and Harvard University Library are Wheble's.

49. Fergus notes that Wheble's was the more popular of the two rival *Lady's*

Magazines among the Midlands customers she documents. *Provincial Readers*, p. 201n5.
50. Bound first volumes of the magazine – which include the issues for August 1770 to July 1771 – take on a bewildering array of forms. Most of those I have consulted contain only Wheble issues of the magazine. These include the copy held by the Library of Birmingham – the volume digitised for Adam Matthew's *Eighteenth-Century Journals V* – and that held by the Bodleian Library (Bodleian Library: Vet.A5 e.1986), which was digitised for *Eighteenth-Century Collections Online*. (Confusingly, however, this latter volume bears a title page identifying Robinson and Roberts as it publishers, and carries their – not Wheble's – frontispiece.) The bound first volumes of the *Lady's Magazine* held by the University of Chicago Library and one of the two copies of the 1770 volumes held by the Bayerische Staatsbibliothek München contain the same title page and frontispiece but include the first eight issues produced by Wheble followed by the first four published by Robinson and Roberts.
51. Further evidence that Coote had provided the new owners of the magazine with content originally destined for Wheble can be found in 'Moyen ingenieux d'un Visir', another translation exercise from Cardonne that appears in the April 1771 issues published by both Wheble and Robinson.
52. Robert Hudson (1732–1815) was a composer and singer. He was music master of Christ's Hospital and had a long association with St Paul's Cathedral, where he was eventually buried. In the months after Coote sold the magazine to Robinson and Roberts, the music sheets for Wheble's periodical were set by 'Mr Hook' (James Hook, 1756–1827).
53. The *Oxford Magazine* (1768–76) was sold by William Jackson at Oxford, and Samuel Bladon and John Coote in London. It is possible, indeed likely, that the theatre reviews in both magazines originated in the newspapers and circulated rather like modern syndicated copy.
54. Hannah Doherty Hudson, '"The Lady is Descended from a Good Family": Women and Biography in British Magazines, 1770–1798', in *Women's Periodicals and Print Culture*, pp. 278–93 (p. 278).
55. Musician, biographer, travel-writer and novelist Ann Thicknesse was also a contributor of original material for the *Lady's Magazine*. Her unsigned conduct book serial, 'Mrs T—ss's Advice to her Daughter', appeared in the magazine between June 1775 and October 1776.
56. *Lady's Monthly Museum* 1 (July 1798): 2.
57. *The Whole Duty of Woman* was published under the pseudonym 'a Lady', but was in fact authored by writer and satirist William Kenrick, whose profligate lifestyle suggests that this would-be physician should perhaps have attempted to heal himself first.
58. One understood marker of these serials' superiority is that they were subsequently published in volume form. As I discuss in Chapter 4, the same is true of several serial fictions published in the *Lady's Magazine*.
59. Mayo, *The English Novel in the Magazines*, p. 351, p. 242.
60. Jenny DiPlacidi, '"Full of Pretty Stories": Fiction in the *Lady's Magazine* (1770–1832)', in *Women's Periodicals and Print Culture*, pp. 263–77 (p. 266).
61. In May 1771 Thistlewaite's work appeared in both Robinson's and

Wheble's *Lady's Magazines*. Thistlewaite was not alone in hedging his bets in this way. Essayist, poet and novelist Robert Meldrum or 'Rt. M—m', to cite the most common of his various signatures, moved back and forth between both *Lady's Magazines*, apparently finding it hard to put his eggs in the Robinson and Roberts's basket until Wheble's magazine ceased publication. First appearing appeared in Wheble's magazine in July 1771, Meldrum features regularly in Robinson and Roberts's magazine after. November 1771. He briefly drifted back to Wheble's publication in January 1772 before finally nailing his colours to the mast and remaining a regular contributor to Robinson's magazine until 1775.

62. The October 1773 issue also featured an essay by Crabbe entitled 'Origin of a Macaroni'. On Crabbe's poetry for the rival *Lady's Magazines* see *Poems by George Crabbe*, ed. Adolphus William Ward, 3 vols (Cambridge: Cambridge University Press, 1905–7), 1: 1–8; and Graham Pollard, 'The Early Poems of George Crabbe and *The Lady's Magazine*', *The Bodleian Library Record*, 5: 3 (July 1955): 149–56.
63. The signed declaration of opposition to Wheble's publication appeared in the form of an advertisement printed in numerous newspapers. See, for example, the *General Evening Post*, Issue 5857 (27–30 April 1771).
64. Along with Wheble, Bell was one of the twelve original proprietors of the *Morning Post* (founded 1772), a newspaper that Wheble published.

Chapter 3

1. Margaret Beetham, 'Towards a Theory of the Periodical as a Publishing Genre', *Investigating Victorian Journalism*, eds Laurel Brake, Aled Jones and Lionel Madden (Basingstoke: Macmillan, 1990), pp. 19–32 (p. 26).
2. David Mazella, 'Temporality, Microgenres, Authorship and the *Lady's Magazine*' (unpublished; original emphasis).
3. In this, I should acknowledge that I am revising my approach to my own work. Not long after I began work on my Leverhulme Research Project, 'The *Lady's Magazine* (1770–1818): Understanding the Emergence of a Genre', I realised that the object of my enquiry was not how a genre comes into existence but the effects of the developing media ecology of the women's magazine on writers, readers and reading.
4. Christina Lupton, *Knowing Books: The Consciousness of Mediation in Eighteenth-Century Britain* (Philadelphia: University of Pennsylvania Press, 2011), p. 5.
5. Clifford Siskin and William Warner, eds, *This is Enlightenment* (Chicago and London: University of Chicago Press, 2009), p. 15.
6. Jay David Bolter and Richard Grusin, *Remediation: Understanding New Media* (Cambridge, MA: MIT Press, 1999), p. 45. On remediation, see also John Guillory, 'Enlightening Mediation', in Siskin and Warner, *This is Enlightenment*, pp. 164–72.
7. On the prevalence and politics of discontinuous print forms and reading practices across genres in the eighteenth century see Eve Tavor Bannet, *Eighteenth-Century Manners of Reading: Print Culture and Popular Instruction in the Anglophone Atlantic World* (Cambridge: Cambridge

University Press, 2017), 171–224. Christina Lupton sheds important light on the discontinuity facilitated by multiple (and/or selective) readings and readings over time in *Reading and the Making of Time in the Eighteenth Century* (Baltimore: Johns Hopkins University Press, 2018).
8. Mark Parker, *Literary Magazines and British Romanticism* (Cambridge: Cambridge University Press, 2004), p. 3.
9. Jeffrey Drouin, 'Close- and Distant-Reading Modernism: Network Analysis, Text Mining, and Teaching *The Little Review*', *Visualizing Periodical Networks*, ed. J. Stephen Murphy. Special issue of *Journal of Modern Periodical Studies* 5.1 (2014): 110–35 (115).
10. As Laurel Brake and Julie F. Codell observe of Victorian periodicals, the coherence promised by editors is usually illusory, appearing as it does to present 'a unified policy, or set of beliefs as if the journal itself were a single author' or genre when periodicals are 'fragmented, interspersed, and intertextual'. 'Introduction: Encountering the Press', in *Encounters in the Victorian Press: Editors, Authors, Readers*, eds Laurel Brake and Julie F. Codell (Basingstoke: Palgrave Macmillan, 2005), pp. 1–7 (pp. 1–3).
11. Genres and media that do not feature prominently in this chapter (including reviews, biographies, fashion coverage and illustrations) are the focus of Chapter 5, where their emergence in response to competition from the magazine's rivals is discussed in detail.
12. Mary Poovey, *The Proper Lady and the Woman Writer: Ideology as Style in the Works of Mary Wollstonecraft, Mary Shelley, and Jane Austen* (Chicago and London: University of Chicago Press, 1984), pp. 16–18.
13. Margaret Beetham, *A Magazine of her Own? Domesticity and Desire in the Woman's Magazine, 1800–1914* (London and New York: Routledge, 1994), p. 24. Beetham's view of the magazine is no doubt shaped by her concern only with its later years, by which time its news coverage had dwindled substantially.
14. See, for instance, 'On Female Beauty', part 12 of 'Essays on Several Subjects', which argued that women needed to 'be good-humoured for a complexion' rather than involve themselves in 'scandal and politics' (6 (Supp 1775): 702). This is a reprinting of an essay by Arthur Murphy from *Gray's Inn Journal* 2 (5 October 1752).
15. Koenraad Claes, 'Vindications and Reflections: The *Lady's Magazine* during the Revolution Controversy (1789–1995)', in *Women's Periodicals and Print Culture in Britain, 1690–1820s: The Long Eighteenth Century*, eds Jennie Batchelor and Manushag N. Powell (Edinburgh: Edinburgh University Press, 2018), pp. 67–81 (p. 80).
16. JoEllen DeLucia (2015) 'Radcliffe, George Robinson and Eighteenth-Century Print Culture: Beyond the Circulating Library', *Women's Writing* 22.3: 287–99 (292).
17. Quotation from *The New Annual Register . . . for the Year 1793*, repr. in *Anti-Jacobin Review* 3 (August 1799): 461–2.
18. The 'Chronicle' section resumed with the third series of the magazine only in 1830.
19. Jeremy Black, *The English Press in the Eighteenth Century* (London: Routledge, 2011), p. x.
20. Will Slauter, 'Upright Piracy: Understanding the Lack of Copyright for

Journalism in Eighteenth-Century Britain', *Book History and Print Culture* 16 (2013): 34–61 (54).
21. Slauter 'Upright Piracy': 54.
22. See, for example, 'The Dissemblers: By a Lady', signed R., a tale in Robinson's magazine (3 (August 1772): 345–54.
23. Srividhya Swaminathan and Adam R. Beach, 'Introduction: Invoking Slavery in Literature and Scholarship', *Invoking Slavery in the Eighteenth-Century British Imagination*, eds Srividhya Swaminathan and Adam R. Beach (London and New York: Routledge, 2016), pp. 1–20 (p. 1).
24. This tale is also a translation from Cardonne.
25. Moira Ferguson, 'Mary Wollstonecraft and the Problematic of Slavery', *Feminist Review* 42 (1992): 82–102 (98–9). For a nuanced discussion of how discourses of slavery function in relation to the political philosophy of writers including Mary Astell, Judith Drake and Mary Wollstonecraft, see Patricia Springbourg, *Mary Astell: Theorist of Freedom and Domination* (Cambridge: Cambridge University Press, 2005), esp. pp. 224–33.
26. On the politics of amelioration, see, for example: Markman Ellis, *The Politics of Sensibility: Race, Gender and Commerce in the Sentimental Novel* (Cambridge: Cambridge University Press, 1996), pp. 86–114; and George Boulukos, *The Grateful Slave: The Emergence of Race in Eighteenth-Century Britain and America* (Cambridge: Cambridge University Press, 2008), esp. pp. 9–10 and 201–6.
27. For a comprehensive study of this figure see Boulukos, *The Grateful Slave*.
28. Jennifer Batt, 'Poems in Magazines', *The Oxford Handbook of British Poetry, 1660–1800*, ed. Jack Lynch (Oxford: Oxford University Press, 2016), pp. 55–71 (p. 69).
29. Little is known about Frances. The only biographical information given in the magazine is in a dateline under 'Old England's Defence: A Patriotic Ode', which describes him as 'Late of St Mary Hall, Oxon' (35 (March 1804): 157). Frances was the author of the *Lady's Magazine*'s wide-ranging essay series, 'The Cursory Lucubrator' (January–December 1801). He also published several poems on various subjects for the periodical, an essay 'On the Benefits of Regularity and Virtuous Conduct' (35 (March 1803): 127), and proposed a serialised novel, the plan for which was approved in the Correspondents column of the November 1801 issue, but which seems not to have materialised. An editorial note indicates that 'The Slave' was shortly to be set to music 'composed by the author of the ballad', Henry Frances, although the ballad's existence has not been verified.
30. The mention of Sheffield in the dateline under its reprinting of 'The Common Lot' (published in the March 1806 issue under the signature Alcaeus) hints at its origins in Montgomery's radical weekly newspaper, the *Sheffield Iris* (1794–1848).
31. Anon., 'A Memoir of Mr. Montgomery; with a Portrait of that distinguished poet', *Lady's Magazine* 58 (November 1827): 615.
32. August von Kotzebue, *The Negro Slaves: A Dramatic-Historical Piece, in Three Acts, from the German of the President de Kotzebue* (London: T. Cadell, Jr and W. Davies, 1796). The play carried a dedication to William Wilberforce and was widely reprinted. See, for instance, *The Monthly Review* new ser. 20 (Appendix 1796): 544–5.

33. Swaminathan and Beach, 'Introduction', pp. 8–9.
34. John R. Oldfield, *Transatlantic Abolitionism in the Age of Revolution* (Cambridge: Cambridge University Press, 2013), p. 8.
35. Claes, 'Vindications and Reflections', p. 69.
36. The phrase is taken from an article about Irish writer, Mrs (Frances) Peck's (fl. 1808), *Napoleon; or, the Mysteries of the Hundred Days* (1826).
37. Reader poems and essays on the imprisonment and execution of the Louis XVI and Marie Antoinette were as prominent in the magazine as published accounts by the likes of Williams. A month before Mary Robinson's 'Marie Antoinette's Lamentation' appeared in the April 1793 *Lady's Magazine*, for instance, it published 'Elegiac Stanzas (To the Memory of the Unfortunate Louis XVI)', by Eliza. The timorousness that Eliza expresses about joining literary forces with 'far more able pens' who had written about the imprisonment of the King and Queen quickly subsides as she prophesies 'Vengeance' upon the 'murd'rous-minded crew' who plotted the monarch's demise (24 (March 1793): 158).
38. James Murray Lacey (1782–1841) authored an extraordinary number of poems, prose essays and fragments for the periodical between 1803. He was the author of *The Farm House, a Tale* (1809) and was a contributor to many other periodicals including the *European Magazine* and *Repository of Arts*.
39. Mary Dodwell of Coleshill (1786–1812) contributed essays and poems to the magazine until late 1810, just two years before her premature death from hydrocephalus.
40. Edward Copeland argues that much of the magazine's fiction is driven by an 'immovable fear of economic loss' that is manifest in its heroines' continual subjection 'to unpredictable and arbitrary forms of economic violence'. *Women Writing about Money* (Cambridge: Cambridge University Press, 1995), p. 155.
41. Suffolk born John Webb (1768–1840) was a journeyman weaver and the author of the loco-descriptive poem *Haverhill* (1810). Webb's poetry appeared regularly in the magazine from 1800 to 1818.
42. Catharine Bremen Yeames (1784–1817), whose sister and fellow-contributor Elizabeth is discussed in Chapter 4, was a contributor to the magazine between 1802 and 1809.
43. Bannet, *Eighteenth-Century Manners of Reading*, p. 171.
44. Jacques du Bosc's *L'Honnête Femme* (1632–6) was excerpted in 1774; James Fordyce's *Sermons to Young Women* (1765) in 1784 and 1792 and his *Character and Conduct of the Female Sex* (1776) in its year of publication; Dr John Gregory's *A Father's Legacy to his Daughters* (1774) in 1782, 1783 and 1784; William Kenrick's *Whole Duty of Woman* (1753) in 1771; Hannah More's *Strictures on the Modern System of Female Education* (1799) in its year of publication; Jean-Jacques Rousseau's *Émile* (1762) in 1778 and 1780; and George Savile, the Marquis of Halifax's *The Lady's New-Year's Gift: or, Advice to a Daughter* (1688; excerpted 1775).
45. A meaningful study of the role of conduct books in the magazine would also have to take into account their remediation by looking closely at which sections of these texts are excerpted and which are not.

46. Semandra, 'Verses to the Memory of Dr. Cook', *Lady's Magazine* 8 (July 1777): 382.
47. These books included, *Calvis Naturae, or the Mystery of Philosophy Unvail'd: in a Discourse Shewing the Prime and Efficient Physical Cause of all the Phenomena of Nature, and Singular Motions in the Whole Universe* (1733) and *The Natural History of Lac, Amber, and Myrrh: with a Plain Account of the many Excellent Virtues These Three Medicinal Substances are Naturally Possessed Of, and Well Adapted for the Cure of Various Disease Incident to the Human Body* (1770). The periodicals for which he had previously written are unspecified in the *Lady's Magazine*, but included the *London*, the *Oxford* and *Gentleman's*.
48. Around the same time that he began contributing to the *Lady's Magazine*, Cook also began writing for the *Town and Country*.
49. Roy Porter, 'Lay Medical Knowledge in the Eighteenth Century: The Evidence of the *Gentleman's Magazine*', *Medical History* 29 (1985): 138–68 (165).
50. Cook advised that the minor procedure to deal with 'suppuration' was not to be feared; it would ease 'the horror and pain' of the obstruction and save the 'time and expense' of more invasive or risky treatments if the condition further worsened (6 (May 1775): 256–7).
51. In this case, the critical issue is the temperature of the poultice, which if 'hot' rather than 'blood warm', 'would condense, rather than resolve the obstructing humour' (257).
52. In the sixth instalment of the 'Lady's Physician', for instance, Cook laments the 'surprising progress of quackery' and the spirit of 'mammon' that motivates its spread. *Lady's Magazine* 6 (September 1775): 482.
53. Also called 'The Lady's Physician', Turnbull's column ran from February 1783 to October 1786.
54. William Mugliston, a dyer from Alfreton in Derbyshire, was identified as the Matron by E. W. Pitcher via a notice in the *European Magazine* which identifies Mugliston as the author of a concurrently running monthly serial in the *Lady's*. See Pitcher, 'William Mugleston and "The Matron": Authorship of a *Lady's Magazine* Essay Serial, 1774–91', *ANQ* 12:1 (1999): 28–9. Mugliston, whose preferred signature was Castalio, was indeed a regular contributor to the *Lady's Magazine*. The column alluded to in the *European*, however, is the 'Essayist' (1782–5), not the Matron, which continued for years beyond Mugliston's death. Mugliston's authorship of the 'Essayist' is corroborated by C. Bateman, 'Descriptive and Historical Account of Alfreton' (1812), p. 29. Derbyshire Record Office, D654/A/PZ/10. The 'Matron' column ceased publication without explanation after 224 instalments in April 1791. It was resurrected three decades later in the form of 'The Matron Revived' (February 1817–June 1818) in a column supposedly authored by Grey's granddaughter.
55. In the 1780s, there are unverifiable hints that the Matron assumed an editorial role for the periodical, leading the 'Female Parliament', which decided which reader submissions were published and which were rejected. See, for example, the January 1785 'Correspondents' column.
56. See for example, Harriot Atwood's letter to the Matron in the April 1781 issue in which Harriot explains that she is in love with a man to whom her

father objects because he has insufficient wealth. The Matron is characteristically sympathetic to Harriot's plight and hopes that subtly advertising her lover's merits might change her parent's mind. If her father cannot be moved, Mrs Grey prescribes 'dutiful acquiescence' to his dictates (12: 191).
57. The tale is a free translation by Florio of a French tale published in Wheble's magazine for September 1772.
58. I examine various other tales that have similar plots to the 'Rape of the Marriage Contract' in '"Be but a little Deaf and Blind ... and Happiness you'll Surely Find": Marriage in Eighteenth-Century Magazines for Women', in *After Marriage in the Long Eighteenth Century: Literature, Law and Society*, eds Jenny DiPlacidi and Karl Leydecker (Basingstoke: Palgrave Macmillan, 2017), pp. 107–27.
59. Robert D. Mayo, *The English Novel in the Magazines, 1740–1815* (London: Oxford University Press; and Evanston: Northwestern University Press, 1962), pp. 1–2. T. O. Beachcroft, *The Modest Art: A Survey of the Short Story in English* (London: Oxford University Press, 1968), p. 94. For a more recent and appreciative survey of early short story, see Tim Killick, *British Short Fiction in the Early Nineteenth Century: The Rise of the Tale* (Aldershot: Ashgate, 2008), pp. 5–38.
60. An additional quarter sheet, which reprinted the content of an article covering a meeting at the National Society at Sion College about the Madras System from the *Morning Post* of 4 June 1813, was produced for the June 1813 *Lady's Magazine*.
61. Anon., 'The State of Female Literature in the Sixteenth Century', 22 (November 1791): 564–5. For a detailed account of the complex relationship between Carter's association with the domestic sphere and her reputation for learning, patriotism and piety, see Guest, *Small Change*, esp. pp. 111–33.
62. Kathryn Shevelow, *Women and Print Culture: The Construction of Femininity in the Early Periodical* (London: Routledge, 1989), pp. 188–9.
63. Jacqueline M. Pearson, *Women's Reading in Britain, 1750–1835: A Dangerous Recreation* (Cambridge: Cambridge University Press, 1999), p. 50.
64. Karen O'Brien, *Women and Enlightenment in Eighteenth-Century Britain* (Cambridge: Cambridge University Press, 2009), p. 205. Philalethia claims that readers would better understand the origins and implications of the current Gordon Riots through historical awareness of the Gunpowder Plot, an 'event which threatened [the nation's] religion, our laws, and property' over 150 years earlier (11 (November 1780): 571).
65. These texts are: Arthur Wilson's *History of Great Britain, being the life and reign of King James the First* (1653); Thomas Carte's *A General History of England* Vol. 3 (1747); and Catharine Macaulay's *The History of England from the accession of James I. to that of the Brunswick line* (1763), which is presented as a 'proper conclusion' to the two-part series (11 (November 1780): 571).
66. The essay appears to be an original translation from Jean-Baptiste de Boyer's *Lettres Philosophiques et Critiques* (1744).
67. Ann B. Shteir, *Cultivating Women, Cultivating Science: Flora's Daughters and Botany in England, 1760 to 1860* (Baltimore and London: Johns

Hopkins University Press, 1996), p. 103. See also Michèle Cohen, '"Familiar Conversation": The Role of the "Familiar Format" in Education in Eighteenth- and Nineteenth-Century England', in Mary Hilton and Jill Shefrin, *Educating the Child in Enlightenment Britain: Beliefs, Cultures, Practices* (Farnham: Ashgate, 2009), pp. 99–116.

68. Whyte opened an inter-denominational coeducational grammar school in Dublin in 1758. As Geraldine Meaney, Mary O'Dowd and Bernadette Whelan explain, while Whyte's subscribed to the widespread view that women should be educated primarily in order to make them better wives, his work is 'remarkable for its radical language' and arguments for women's right to literature and education. *Reading the Irish Woman: Studies in Cultural Encounter and Exchange, 1714–1960* (Liverpool: Liverpool University Press, 2013), p. 41.
69. The author's comments are part of an extended discussion in the serial of James Nelson's *Essay on the Government of Children* (1753).
70. Maps had occasionally appeared in earlier periodicals marketed at women readers including Charlotte Lennox's *Lady's Museum* (1760–1). However, the *Lady's Magazine* seems to have been one of the first publications of its kind to encourage readers to instil geographical knowledge by inviting readers to stitch the contours of nations onto fabric. On the role that map samplers played in women's education, see Judith A. Tyner, *Stitching the World: Embroidered Maps and Women's Geographical Education* (Oxford: Routledge, 2016).
71. For an early and particularly forceful iteration of these arguments, see Lucinda's 'On the Strength and Bravery of the Female Sex', in which the contributor argues that attention to the lessons of history, to the governance and 'female administration[s]' of the ancient civilizations of Lacadaemon, Athens, Assyria or, closer to home, to the court of Elizabeth I, showed clearly that 'delicacy of constitution' was not characteristic of the sex, but 'only the consequence of our bad education', in which the 'malice of man' conspired (Wheble 2 (January 1771): 261).

Chapter 4

1. Helen Bryan, *Martha Washington: First Lady of Liberty* (New York: John Wiley & Sons, 2002), pp. 170–1.
2. Jan Fergus, *Provincial Readers in Eighteenth-Century England* (Oxford: Oxford University Press, 2006), p. 204.
3. Ellen Weeton to Miss Winkley, 11 May 1810, *Journal of a Governess*, ed. Edward Hall, 2 vols (London: Oxford University Press, 1936), 1: 1807–11, p. 261.
4. Mitford's correspondence extensively documents her reading habits. A more detailed catalogue of her reading can be reconstructed from her copy of *The Literary Pocket-Book; or, Companion for the Lover of Nature and Art for 1819* (London: printed for C. and J. Ollier), in the collections of the British Library (C.60.b.7). Mitford squeezed many years of abbreviated diary entries between 1819 and 1823 into the year's pocket-book, including daily records of the books and periodicals that she read. At no

point in the period the diary covers – the same period in which she commenced writing for the *Lady's Magazine* – does she mention the journal.
5. Several recent studies that have interrogated the myth of Romantic authorship are discussed below. See also Michelle Levy, *Family Authorship and Romantic Print Culture* (Basingstoke: Palgrave Macmillan, 2008); Megan Richardson and Julian Thomas, 'Rethinking "Romantic" Authorship', in *Fashioning Intellectual Property: Exhibition, Advertising and the Press, 1789–1918* (Cambridge: Cambridge University Press, 2012), pp. 103–15; and Susan Wolfson, *Romantic Interactions: Social Being and the Turns of Literary Action* (Baltimore: Johns Hopkins University Press, 2010). The persistence of Romantic authorship as an organising structure for literary history is addressed in my *Women's Work: Labour, Gender, Authorship, 1750–1830* (Manchester: Manchester University Press, 2010).
6. Cynthia White, *Women's Magazines, 1693–1968* (London: Michael Joseph, 1970), p. 31; Alison Adburgham, *Women in Print: Writing Women and Women's Magazines from the Restoration to the Accession of Victoria* (London: George Allen & Unwin, 1972), p. 148.
7. Mary Charlton, *Rosella, or Modern Occurrences*, 4 vols (London: William Lane at the Minerva Press, 1799), 4: 306.
8. Charlotte Smith, *The Young Philosopher*, ed. Elizabeth Kraft (Lexington: University of Kentucky Press, 1999), p. 253. The Robinsons had previously published Smith's *Desmond* (1792) and extracts from her novels and poetry collections were reprinted in the *Lady's Magazine*. Smith had submitted poetry to Stanhope's *Lady Magazine* (1759–73) as a teenager. Connections between the *Lady's Magazine* and the Minerva Press were much closer than Charlton's and Smith's disavowals suggest. See Jennie Batchelor, 'UnRomantic Authorship: The Minerva Press and the *Lady's Magazine* (1770–1820)', *Romantic Textualities*, eds Elizabeth Neiman and Christina Morin, 3 (Summer 2020), 76–93 <https://doi.org/10.18573/romtext.73> (last accessed 25 November 2021).
9. Gillian Hughes, 'Fiction in the Magazines', in *English and British Fiction, 1750–1820*, eds Peter Garside and Karen O'Brien (Oxford: Oxford University Press, 2015), pp. 461–77 (p. 463).
10. Robert D. Mayo, *The English Novel in the Magazines, 1740–1815* (Evanston: Northwestern University Press and London: Oxford University Press, 1962), p. 317.
11. Mayo, *The English Novel in the Magazines*, p. 317.
12. An extract from Legg's *Discourse on the Emigration of British Birds* (Salisbury: Collins and Johnson, 1780) appeared in the *Lady's Magazine* for April 1780. It was submitted by an unnamed 'Correspondent', possibly Legg himself.
13. Mayo, *The English Novel in the Magazines*, p. 316.
14. Reeve's relationship with the magazine's publishers also continued beyond this dispute. The Robinsons were the London booksellers listed on the imprint for the Colchester-published *Progress of Romance* (1785).
15. Literary Assignments of George Robinson. Manchester Central Library. GB127.MS f 091 A2, fol. 211.
16. The date of Pilkington's death is consistently misidentified in all major biographical sources as 1839. She died in 1825 and was buried on

18 November in Hammersmith. London Parish Register, Reference Number DD/0746/03/002.
17. Letter from Mary Pilkington to the Secretary of the Literary Fund, 2 June 1810. *Archives of the Royal Literary Fund: 1790–1918*, 145 reels (London: World Microfilms Publications, 1981–4). Case 256 (M1077/7, reel 7).
18. Letter from Mary Pilkington to the Literary Fund, 2 June 1810. *Archives of the Royal Literary Fund*.
19. Of these works, Pilkington was most proud of *The Asiatic Princess* (1800), which was dedicated with permission to, and written for, Princess Charlotte.
20. Pilkington's financial negotiations are documented in her letter to Thomas Vernor, 22 January 1810. 'Original Letters Collected by William Upcott of the London Institution. Distinguished Women', ed. William Upcott. Vol. 3. British Library Add, MS. 78688. Hughes's bankruptcy lost Pilkington a thirty-guinea commission as she explained in her letter to the Secretary of the Literary Fund, 2 June 1810. Lady Gertrude Cromie, whom Pilkington attended during a long illness, had provided apartments for the author in Brook Green Hammersmith. Thomas Faulkner, *The History and Antiquities of the Parish of Hammersmith* (London: Nichols and Son; J. Weale, E. Page, T. S. Rayner; and Simpkin, Marshall & Co., 1839), pp. 163–4.
21. Mary Pilkington to Thomas Vernor, 22 January 1810. 'Original Letters Collected by William Upcott of the London Institution. Distinguished Women'.
22. This quotation is from an obituary to Pilkington's mother. *Lady's Magazine*, 48 (May 1817): 240.
23. Many of Pilkington's contributions for the magazine are unsigned and can be attributed to her only because of editorial notes and stray references made in the magazine's 'Correspondents' pages.
24. Pilkington to the Literary Fund, 4 January 1825.
25. Mary Pilkington to Thomas Vernor, 22 January 1810. 'Original Letters Collected by William Upcott of the London Institution. Distinguished Women'.
26. Yeames married Robert Bell Clabon in Norfolk on 10 October 1814. The magazine itself does not identify Mrs Clabon as Yeames. *Norfolk, England, Transcripts of Church of England Baptism, Marriage and Burial Registers, 1600–1935* <www.ancestry.co.uk> (last accessed 8 October 2020).
27. Sophia Hood was baptised on 27 May 1778 in Stepney. She married James Troughton on 23 August 1795 in St Clement, Westminster, and her second husband, Thomas Hendry, on 19 October 1815.
28. Sophia Troughton to Lady Margaret Spencer, 13 April 1813. British Library. Althorp Papers. Add MS 75727.
29. Will of Sophia Hendry, Widow of Alfred House Kensal Green (15 December 1856), PRO 11/2243/230.
30. James Grant, *The Great Metropolis*, 2 vols (London: Saunders and Otley, 1836), 2: 331.
31. Mary Russell Mitford to Sir William Elford, 4 April 1821. Reading Central Library qB/TU/MIT (vol. 4), ff 434.

32. Thomas Noon Talfourd to Mary Russell Mitford, 19 November 1822. Reading Central Library. R/TU/TAL (vol. 2). ff. 28. Talfourd authored anonymous reviews, biographical essays and articles with a literary focus for the *Lady's Magazine*. See William A. Coles, 'Magazine and Other Contributions by Mary Russell Mitford and Thomas Noon Talfourd', *Studies in Bibliography*, 12 (1959): 218–26.
33. A letter from Mitford to Talfourd dated 16 May 1823, in the aftermath of Hamilton's bankruptcy earlier that year, indicates that at this time Thomas Christopher Hofland was being paid £10 for authoring the magazine's Fine Arts column. In the same letter, Mitford expresses suspicion that her friend Barbara Hofland was concealing how much she was being paid for unspecified tales for the magazine in order to spare the feelings of Mitford who was being paid considerably less. William Allan Coles, 'The Correspondence of Mary Russell Mitford and Thomas Noon Talfourd', Unpublished PhD dissertation (Cambridge, MA: Harvard University, 1956), p. 280.
34. Mary Russell Mitford to Benjamin Robert Haydon, 9 February 1821. Reading Central Library qB/TU/MIT (vol. 4), f. 441.
35. Mary Russell Mitford to Thomas Noon Talfourd, 24 April 1823. 'The Correspondence of Mary Russell Mitford', p. 268.
36. Mary Russell Mitford to Benjamin Robert Haydon [May 1823]. Reading Central Library qB/TU/MIT (vol. 4), f. 472.
37. The publisher of *Our Village* was George Whittaker. At this time, he was also the publisher of the rival women's magazine, *La Belle Assemblée*.
38. Mary Russell Mitford to Thomas Noon Talfourd, 5 June 1823. 'The Correspondence of Mary Russell Mitford', p. 384.
39. Yeames's violent tale 'Julia and Palmira', for instance, appeared in the short-lived US weekly *Ladies Magazine* (in Savannah, Georgia) between February and August 1819.
40. See Paul Keen, *The Crisis of Literature in the 1790s: Print Culture and the Public Sphere* (Cambridge: Cambridge University Press, 1999); and Clifford Siskin, *The Work of Writing: Literature and Social Change in Britain, 1700–1830* (Baltimore and London: Johns Hopkins University Press, 1998), esp. pp. 218–25.
41. Margaret J. M. Ezell, *Social Authorship and the Advent of Print* (Baltimore and London: Johns Hopkins University Press, 1999), pp. 19–20.
42. Michel Foucault, 'What is An Author', repr. in *Modern Criticism and Theory: A Readers*, eds David Lodge and Nigel Wood, 3rd edn (London: Longman, 2008), pp. 281–93 (p. 286).
43. Robert J. Griffin, 'Introduction', *The Faces of Anonymity: Anonymous and Pseudonymous Publication from the Sixteenth to the Twentieth Century*, ed. Robert J. Griffin (New York: Palgrave Macmillan, 2003), pp. 1–17 (p. 15).
44. The figure falls from over 80 per cent between 1750 and 1790 to a still striking 62 per cent in the 1790s. James Raven, 'The Anonymous Novel in Britain and Ireland, 1750–1830', in *The Faces of Anonymity*, pp. 141–66 (p. 143).
45. I am thinking here of novels such as Frances Burney's *Camilla* (1796), which was ascribed to 'the Author of *Evelina* and *Cecilia*'.

46. Gérard Genette, *Paratexts: Thresholds of Interpretation* (Cambridge: Cambridge University Press, 1997), pp. 39–40. In Genette's words, 'onymity', the practice of publishing under one's legal name, 'is sometimes motivated by something stronger or less neutral than, say, the absence of a desire to give oneself a pseudonym ... [I]t is ... the way to put an identity, or rather a "personality", as the media call it, at the service of the book' (p. 40).
47. In addition to his *Faces of Anonymity*, see also James Griffin, 'Anonymity and Authorship', *New Literary History* 30.4 (1999): 877–95. Margaret J. M. Ezell's work on anonymity and pseudonymity includes: 'Reading Pseudonyms in Seventeenth-Century Coterie Literature', *Essays in Literature* 21 (1994): 14–25; and '"By a Lady": The Mask of the Feminine in Restoration, Early Eighteenth-Century Print Culture', in *The Faces of Anonymity*, pp. 63–79. John Mullan's *Anonymity: A Secret History of English Literature* (London: Faber & Faber, 2007) takes a long view of five centuries of the practice.
48. Virginia Woolf, *A Room of One's Own* (1929), repr. in *A Room of One's Own and Three Guineas*, ed. Anna Snaith (Oxford: Oxford World's Classics, 2015), p. 38.
49. The 2020 #ReclaimHerName campaign led by the Bailey's Women's Prize for Fiction reflects the resilience of these arguments.
50. Jacqueline M. Labbe, ed., *The History of British Women's Writing, 1750–1830. Volume 5* (Basingstoke: Palgrave Macmillan, 2010), p. 1.
51. 'Anonymous of N. Petherton' is identified as John Ayers in a death notice in the July 1812 issue, which reports that the poet had died 'in his 23d year' (33 (July 1812): 340).
52. Beatrice Grant (1761–1845) of Duthel, Scotland, was the author of several educational works. She also published tales (often Scottish), remarks and educational pieces in the *Lady's Magazine* between 1819 and 1823, at least one of which was republished in *La Belle Assemblée*. Grant scholar Rosemary Wake has discovered numerous pieces by Grant in other periodicals, including *The Cheap Magazine*, *La Belle Assemblée*, *The British Lady's Magazine* and the *New British Lady's Magazine*. Private correspondence with Rosemary Wake.
53. Stockton-based Thomas Harpley married Mary Plummer in April 1782, just months before his first appearance in the magazine in 'The Budget' column for December. Harpley also wrote in the magazine as T. H— and under his legal name.
54. In the four-part 'Life of Edgar, King of the West Saxons' (July–December 1775), the signature Constantia Maria appears under the first three instalments and HISTORICUS under the last. Contributions by HISTORICUS appear until 1781.
55. This phrase is used by a correspondent who goes by Eliza in a letter soliciting advice from the magazine's agony aunt, The Matron. Eliza, 'Letter to the Matron', *Lady's Magazine* 19 (July 1788): 365.
56. As Susan S. Lanser argues, although we might associate 'particular ideological configurations of texts with a particular sex of authorship ... anonymous authorship reminds us that there is finally no way to guarantee the sex of a real author on the basis of the text alone'. 'The

Author's Queer Clothes', in *The Faces of Anonymity*, pp. 81–102 (p. 96).
57. See for instance the letter signed by J. B., who writes that his fun-loving and dipsomaniac wife and mother of their four children is an avid reader of the magazine who is often 'heard to ask her acquaintance if the[y] really thought Mrs. Grey was a woman'. *Lady's Magazine* 18 (September 1787): 479.
58. E. W. Pitcher, 'The Miscellaneous Periodical Works and Translations of Miss R. Roberts', *Literary Research Newsletter* 5.3 (1980): 125–8 (125).
59. Pitcher, 'Miscellaneous Periodical Works': 125.
60. Pitcher, 'Miscellaneous Periodical Works': 128.
61. A significant proportion of the tales are from common sources, esp. *Le Mercure de France* (founded 1672) and N. Bricaire de la Dixmerie's *Contes Philosophiques et Moraux* (1769).
62. Arthur Sherbo, 'Roberts, R. (c.1728–1788)', *Oxford Dictionary of National Biography*, Oxford University Press, 2004 <www.oxforddnb.com/view/article/69592> (last accessed 8 October 2020).
63. Pitcher addresses this problem by asserting that R. might have been a 'collaborative' signature under which Georgiana H—t, perhaps other young women, and the more experienced R. wrote. He implies that Roberts might have been these girls' instructress. Pitcher, 'Miscellaneous Periodical Works', p. 128.
64. [Radagunda Roberts], *Select Moral Tales: Translated from the French, by a Lady* (Gloucester: R. Raikes, 1763), pp. vi–vii.
65. Reginald Gardiner, *Admission Registers of St. Paul's School, 1748–1876* (London: G. Bell and Sons, 1884).
66. [Radagunda Roberts], *Elements of the History of France, translated from the Abbé Millot*, 3 vols (London: James Dodsley and Thomas Cadell, 1771), 1: pp. v, vi. Subsequent references will be given in the text.
67. This Jane Collier is not to be confused with the author of the *Art of Ingeniously Tormenting* (1753). Letters between Collier and Sarah Moore (later Digby) contain many references to the Roberts sisters. Collier was a close friend of the elder, Radagunda. Some of her letters have been published as E. Royds, ed., 'Stubton Strong Room – Stray Notes (end Series): Moore and Knowles Families – Two Sisters', *Reports and Papers of the Architectural Societies of the County of Lincoln, York, Archdeaconries of Northampton and Oakham and County of Leicester* 38.2 (1927). Collier left several items, including a diamond ring, a picture of a woman reading and a bookcase to her 'dear friend ... Mrs Radegonda [sic] Roberts' in her will. Will of Jane Collier, Widow of Saint John, Southwark, Surrey (3 August 1785), PRO 11/1132/272.
68. Frances Brooke to Richard Gifford, n.d. Houghton Library, MS ENG1310.
69. Clara Reeve, when she offered her translation of *Lettres d'Aza* to the *Lady's Magazine*, commented on Roberts's *Peruvian Letters*, writing to the editor that the 'lady' who translated them and 'completed the story by additions of her own' made a *'pretty novel'*, but one that, in her words, one in which 'there is not a spark of *fire* which animates the *children of the sun*' ('Correspondents', 9 (June 1778): n.p.). On Roberts's translation and its departures from Graffigny's original see the 'Introduction' to Marijn

S. Kaplan's modern edition of the text, which appears in *Translations and Continuations: Riccoboni and Brooke, Graffigny and Roberts*, ed. Marijn S. Kaplan (London and New York: Routledge, 2016), pp. xi–xx. Subsequent references to the text are taken from this edition.
70. R. Roberts, *The Triumph of Truth; or, Memoirs of Mr. De La Villette, Translated from the French by R. Roberts*, 2 vols (London: [n. pub], 1775), 1: x–xi.
71. 'Will of Radagunda Roberts, Spinster of St Faith under Saint Paul's, City of London' (3 June 1788). PRO 11/1167/16.
72. On the possible influence of More's work on Roberts's see Sherbo, 'Roberts, R.' (c.1728–1788)'.
73. The letter is held in the special collection of the Houghton Library (MS Eng 1473). Hawkesworth's reviews of Roberts's work are identified in Emily Lorraine de Montluzin, 'Attributions of Authorship in the *Gentleman's Magazine*, 1731–1868: An Electronic Union List' <http://bsuva.org/bsuva/gm2/GMintro.html> (last accessed 8 October 2020).
    In addition to serving as contributor to and editor of the *Gentleman's Magazine*, Hawkesworth also founded the periodical, the *Adventurer* (1752–4), with Samuel Johnson.
74. Roberts was also a supporter of other writers. Her name appears alongside that of her brother, Richard, on subscriptions for various works, including: Sarah Fielding, *Xenophon's Memoirs of Socrates* (1762); fellow *Lady's Magazine* contributor, Ann Murry's, *Poems on Various Subjects* (1779); and Ignatius Sancho, *Letters of the Late Ignatius Sancho, an African* (1782).
75. On the significance of Roberts's *Peruvian Letters*, see Kaplan, 'Introduction', xi–xx.
76. These women include the unidentified Eleanor H— or Twickenham – who took over R.'s mantle in the 1790s to produce original translations of (mostly plays) by Gotthold Ephraim Lessing, August von Kotzebue, Jacques-Marie Boutet de Monvel, Benoît-Joseph Marsollie and Louis-Benoît Picard – and Elenir Irwin, to whom I return in Chapter 6. Eleanor H—'s translations appear regularly between 1799 and 1804.
77. [Roberts], *Elements of the History of France*, p. vi.
78. On this omission and its significance, see Linda K. Hughes, 'What the *Wellesley Index* Left Out: Why Poetry Matters to Periodical Studies', *Victorian Periodicals Review* 20 (Summer 2007): 91–125.
79. Kathryn Ledbetter, *British Victorian Women's Periodicals: Beauty, Civilization, and Poetry* (New York: Palgrave Macmillan, 2009), p. 5.
80. Ledbetter, *British Victorian Women's Periodicals*, p. 9.
81. The other two poems were: 'Lines of the Death of Princess Charlotte' (48 (November 1817): 519); and 'Ode on the birth-day of the Prince Regent' (49 (November 1818): 526).
82. A previous work, *Waterloo, a poem on the late Victory*, appeared in 1815, published by Theodore Page.
83. [Elizabeth Richardson], *Poems. By Mrs Richardson (Formerly "Betty Smales")* (London: Simpkin, Marshall & Co., 1846). Charlotte and Elizabeth's introduction to this book provides some of the biographical information on the family drawn on in this chapter.

84. *Poems. By Mrs Richardson*, p. xxi.
85. *The Ladies Diary*, 112 (1815): 21.
86. *The Ladies Diary*, 112 (1815): 21.
87. *The Ladies Diary*, 113 (1816): 20.
88. Stephen C. Behrendt, *British Women Poets and the Romantic Writing Community* (Baltimore: Johns Hopkins University Press, 2009), p. 11.
89. Occasional poetry is also a valuable attribution aid. See, for instance, Kim Simpson's 'Becoming Jane', which uncovers the identity of one of the magazine's poets through her verse. 'Becoming Jane: the Case of a *Lady's Magazine* Emigrant', *The Lady's Magazine* (1770–1818): Understanding the Emergence of a Genre' <https://blogs.kent.ac.uk/ladys-magazine/2016/06/22/becoming-jane-the-case-of-a-ladys-magazine-emigrant/> (last accessed 8 October 2020).
90. In September 1816, Squire married Irish classical scholar and translator, Dr John Carey, extracts from whose work and original contributions from whom appeared in the *Lady's Magazine* as well as the *Gentleman's* and *New Monthly* magazines.
91. Charlotte Caroline Richardson, *Waterloo, a Poem on the Late Victory ... To Which is Added Truth, A Vision, By the Same* (London: Theodore Page, 1815).
92. [Ann Kendall], *Derwent Priory; or, Memoirs of an Orphan*, 2 vols (London: H. D. Symonds, 1798), pp. vii–viii.
93. 'The School for Parents' appeared under the signature 'A. K. Author of "Derwent Priory," and of the "Castle on the Rock"' in the September, October and December 1798 issues of the *Monthly Visitor, and Entertaining Companion. By a Society of Gentleman*. The periodical was published by Symonds, as was the standalone volume *Tales and Poems* (1804).
94. Mitford's 'Our Village' is another example of this phenomenon, although she was, as already documented, paid for her work for the *Lady's Magazine*, whereas Kendall was almost certainly not.
95. Robert D. Mayo, 'Gothic Romance in the Magazines', *PMLA* 65.5 (1950): 762–89 (765, 772).
96. Quoted in Robert D. Mayo's 'Introduction' to George Moore, *Grasville Abbey* (New York: Arno Press, 1974), p. v.
97. Montague Summers, *A Gothic Bibliography* (London: The Fortune Press [1941]), p. 136.
98. *Monthly Mirror* 4 (December 1797): 346.
99. *Critical Review* 21 (September 1797): 115–16.
100. Diane Long Hoeveler, 'Prose Fiction: *Zastrozzi, St. Irvine, The Assassins, The Coliseum*', *The Oxford Handbook of Percy Bysshe Shelley*, eds Michael O'Neill and Anthony Howe, with the assistance of Madeleine Callaghan (Oxford: Oxford University Press, 2013), pp. 193–207 (p. 199).
101. Mayo, 'Gothic Romance': 781.
102. Mayo, 'Gothic Romance': 781.
103. 'Literary Assignments of George Robinson' (fol. 33). It is possible that this George Moore is the same George Moore (a stable keeper) who died in Tottenham Court Road in the summer of 1819. Will of George Moore, Stable Keeper of Saint Giles in the Fields, Middlesex (10 July 1819). PRO 11/1618/154.

104. The anonymous author of the first three parts of the serial, which were published in 1794, is sometimes identified as Mrs (Elizabeth) Meeke, though the attribution is likely spurious. The unidentified A. Percy seems to have undertaken the remaining forty-nine parts published between April 1798 to May 1805.
105. The identification of West's novel in the magazine was made by Jenny DiPlacidi. See '"Full of Pretty Stories": Fiction in the *Lady's Magazine* (1770–1832)', in *Women's Periodicals and Print Culture*, pp. 263–77 (p. 268).
106. *Romance of the Pyrenees* was serialised between February 1804 and the Supplement issue for 1806. Extracts from Cuthbertson's *Santo Sebastiano* (1806) appeared in the magazine for 1807. Extracts from *The Forest of Montalbano* (1810) appeared in the magazine in the year of its publication. Excerpts from *Adelaide; or, the Countercharm* (1813) appeared in the magazine for 1814 and 1816.
107. Her other novels were: *Augustus and Adelina; or, the Monk of St. Barnardine* (1819); *Eleanor: or, the Spectre of St Michael's* (1821); *The Ruins of Ruthvale Abbey* (1827); *The Maid of Padua, or, Past Times: A Venetian Tale* (1835); *The Witch of Aysgarth* (1841).
108. DiPlacidi, '"Full of Pretty Stories"', p. 274.
109. Kathryn R. King, 'Scribal and Print Publication', in *The History of British Women's Writing, 1690–1750. Volume 4*, ed. Ros Ballaster (Basingstoke: Palgrave Macmillan, 2010), pp. 127–44 (p. 140).

Chapter 5

1. Alexander Hogg worked out of 16 Paternoster Row. Stanhope's name also appears on *The Oxford Family Bible; or, Christian's Complete Library* (London: J. Harrison, 1779) and on the *New Polite Tutoress* (London: A. Hogg, 1786). He is not listed in the Church of England Clergy Database.
2. [William West], *Aldine Magazine of Biography, Criticism and the Arts* 1.9 (26 January 1839): 132–5 (132).
3. The pamphlet hints that the antagonism between Hogg and Robinson preceded the launch of the *New Lady's Magazine* by some years. In 1778 Robinson had allegedly travelled to Hounslow in an unsuccessful attempt to 'bully' John Hamilton Moore to break an agreement with Hogg to author *A New and Complete Collection of Voyages and Travels* (1778), a work that Robinson viewed as competition for his *New Universal Traveller* (1779), which was then in preparation. *New Lady's Magazine*, 1 (February 1786): 84.
4. C. H. Timperley, *A Dictionary of Printers and Printing, with the Progress of Literature, Ancient and Modern; Biographical Illustrations* (London: H. Johnson, 1839), p. 838.
5. Michael Harris, 'London Newspapers', in *The Cambridge History of the Book in Britain. Volume V 1695–1830*, eds Michael F. Suarez SJ, and Michael L. Turner (Cambridge: Cambridge University Press, 2009), pp. 413–33 (p. 427).
6. George Robinson junior was declared bankrupt in December 1804 in the

aftermath of the 1803 warehouse fire. His sons, George Robinson III and Samuel, were declared bankrupt in 1817 six years before the magazine's printer and sometime editor, Samuel Hamilton, was declared bankrupt in 1823.
7. Working first with his brother, George Robinson III, out of Paternoster Row (1814–17), the partnership between Samuel and George Robinson seems to have broken down with the brothers' bankruptcy in 1817. Shortly afterwards, Samuel Robinson appears as sole publisher for the firm, working out of Chapter House Passage, Paternoster Row. He was the last of three generations of the Robinson family to publish the *Lady's Magazine* before the periodical fell permanently out of their hands in 1832. According to Samuel Robinson's will (see PRO 11/1844/372), he had been ill for a long time prior to his death, but he continued to publish a new venture, the *Royal Lady's Magazine* (founded 1831) until his decease.
8. Samuel Hamilton was born in 1778 to Archibald Hamilton junior. His name first appears as the *Lady's Magazine*'s printer in August 1799, although the inconsistency with which the periodical listed its printers prior to 1800 means that his association with the publication likely predated this period. In 1803, Hamilton's Fleet Street warehouse went up in smoke. In 1804, he temporarily relocated to 38 Shoe Lane, Fleet, before moving to Holstein House in Weybridge, Surrey. Hamilton was known for his radical political leanings and was an associate of William Godwin and Percy Shelley. The evidence for Hamilton's changing roles in the magazine's production – largely drawn from newspaper advertisements and surviving prospectuses – is ambiguous. An 1820 prospectus for the magazine's new series in the John Johnson Collection of Printed Ephemera suggests that Hamilton, who listed his correspondence address as 25 Paternoster Row, became the 'Proprietor' of the magazine at this time. Thomas Davison, of whom Mitford had such high hopes, became the printer at this point. Bodleian Library, University of Oxford: John Johnson Collection, Prospectuses of Journals 32 (36). Thereafter, it seems that Hamilton lost his proprietorship, only to regain it in May 1822 when he became the magazine's editor. Hamilton and his business partner, W. H. McQueen, to whom Charles Heath had introduced Hamilton a few years earlier, were declared bankrupt in 1823. Hamilton absconded to France, and he falls out of the biographical record at this point. The marriage records of his children suggest that his death occurred sometime between 1845, when his profession is given on his daughter, Matilda's, marriage license as 'gentleman', and 1850, when his son, Sydney Doolan's, licence lists him as deceased.
9. From 1820, the frontispieces were replaced by an emblem of a woman reader, which featured on volume title pages.
10. James Raven, *London Booksellers and American Customers: Transatlantic Community and the Charleston Library Society, 1748–1811* (Columbia: University of South Carolina Press, 2002), p. 49.
11. Jennie Batchelor, 'UnRomantic Authorship: The Minerva Press and the Lady's Magazine, 1770–1820', *Romantic Textualities: Literature and Print Culture, 1780–1820*, 23 (Summer 2020), 76–93 <https://doi.org/10.18573/romtext.73> (last accessed 25 November 2021).
12. Another instance of the same occurs in January 1807 when the editor

acknowledges receipt of a 'sketch' from S. Y. (Thomas Newby) to accompany his tale 'Eugenio and Zelma'. The tale appeared in March with an engraving commissioned after Newby's design.
13. That is: Edward Francis Burney (1760–1848); Henry Corbould (1787–1844); Thomas Stothard (1755–1834); and William Westall (1781–1850).
14. Shelley M. Bennett, *The Mechanisms of Art Patronage in England circa 1800* (Colombia: University of Missouri Press, 1988), p. vii.
15. A. C. Coxhead, R. A., *Thomas Stothard: An Illustrated Monograph* (London: A. H. Bullen, 1906), pp. 42–9. Coxhead admits that the total number of designs Stothard produced for the *Lady's Magazine* is likely to be significantly higher than the quoted figure of ninety as he did not have access to a complete set of the magazine's images with which to compare the British Museum's collection of Stothard sketches and designs. In the 1810s and 1820s there are several references to engravings being taken from Stothard designs.
16. John Heath, *The Heath Family Engravers 1779–1878*, 2 vols (Aldershot: Scolar Press, 1993), I, p. 14. George Robinson's brother and sometime business partner, John Robinson (1753–1813), was an apprentice to James Heath's bookbinder father, George.
17. See Peter Garside et al., 'Illustrating Scott: A Database of Printed Illustrations to the Waverley Novels, 1814–1901' <http://illustratingscott.lib.ed.ac.uk/index.html> (last accessed 8 October 2020).
18. The first *Lady's Magazine* engraving acknowledged to have been '[e]ngraved on steel' appeared in April 1823. 'The Loves of the Angels' illustrates an extract from Thomas Moore's work of the same name and was engraved by Heath after Richard Westall. Under the engraving a note reads: 'Perkins & Heath – hardened steel plate' (54: opposite 105). On Heath's work in this line see Kathryn Ledbetter, '"The Copper and Steel Manufactory" of Charles Heath', *Victorian Review* 28: 2 (2002): 21–30.
19. Edward Copeland, *Women Writing about Money: Women's Fiction in England, 1790–1820* (Cambridge: Cambridge University Press, 1995), p. 117.
20. Copeland, *Women Writing about Money*, pp. 117–19.
21. See Jennie Batchelor, *Dress, Distress and Desire: Clothing and the Body in Eighteenth-Century Literature* (Basingstoke: Palgrave Macmillan, 2005), pp. 83–118.
22. A number of these patterns have now been made digitally available. See Jennie Batchelor, '*The Lady's Magazine* (1770–1819) Patterns of Perfection' <https://ladysmagazine.omeka.net> (last accessed 23 September 2021).
23. Kathryn Shevelow, *Women and Print Culture: The Construction of Femininity in the Early Periodical* (London: Routledge, 1989), pp. 188–9.
24. This phrase is taken from the work of Serena Dyer and Chloe Wigston Smith, eds, *Material Literacy in Eighteenth-Century Britain: A Nation of Makers* (London: Bloomsbury, 2020).
25. Chloe Wigston Smith, 'Fast Fashion: Style, Text, and Image in Late Eighteenth-Century Women's Periodicals', in *Women's Periodicals and Print Culture, 1690–1820s: The Long Eighteenth Century*, eds Jennie Batchelor and Manushag N. Powell (Edinburgh: Edinburgh University Press, 2018), pp. 440–57 (p. 442).

26. Smith, 'Fast Fashion', p. 444.
27. Alicia Kerfoot, for instance, has identified a pair of embroidered shoes held by the Victoria and Albert Museum, and provisionally dated 1770–9, as originating in a 1775 *Lady's Magazine* pattern for embroidered uppers. Alicia Kerfoot, 'Shoe Conversations; or, What the *Lady's Magazine* Stitch Off Taught me About Eighteenth-century Footwear, Embroidery, and Community' <https://blogs.kent.ac.uk/ladys-magazine/2016/03/24/shoe-conversations-or-what-the-ladys-magazine-stitch-off-taught-me-about-eighteenth-century-footwear-embroidery-and-community/> (last accessed 8 October 2020). Edward Savage's 1789 portrait of Mary Champneys and her stepdaughter, Sarah, shows the young girl holding an embroidered 'fancy pattern', which appeared in the magazine for August 1782 and was worked up into several pieces now held by the Charlestown Museum.
28. An early advertisement for Stanhope's *Lady's Magazine* (1759–63) intimates that it had planned to include 'Patterns for the Needle', but if any were printed, none have survived or are mentioned within the periodical. The advert appeared, for example, in the *Leeds Intelligencer*, 2 October 1759.
29. An early advertisement for Wheble's *Lady's Magazine* in the *Middlesex Journal* (29 September 1770–2 October 1770) protested opposition from the 'Draw-cansir of the whole fraternity of pattern-drawers' who had publicly objected to the magazine's inclusion of patterns.
30. The *Lady's Magazine*'s later namesake, the *British Lady's Magazine* (1815–19), declared in its inaugural issue that it would include fashion reports but not plates or patterns as it had 'higher views' in mind for its publication (1 [January 1815]: 6). By July 1817 and running under the title the *New British Lady's Magazine*, it capitulated to reader demand and plates and embroidery patterns were published monthly.
31. Geraldine Meaney, Mary O'Dowd and Bernadette Whelan, *Reading the Irish Woman: Studies in Cultural Encounter and Exchange, 1714–1960* (Liverpool: Liverpool University Press, 2013), p. 45.
32. For instance, the 'Pattern for a Lady's Tippet' in the January 1775 *Hibernian* replicates the same in the *Lady's Magazine* for December 1774, and the *Hibernian*'s 'Elegant Pattern for a Handkerchief or Apron' for February 1775 is a copy of the same in the January 1775 *Lady's Magazine*.
33. The *Lady's Magazine*'s rare 1789 coloured plate, 'Fashionable full Dress of Paris', for instance, originated in *Les Cabinet des Modes*.
34. Alison Adburgham credits Heideloff's publication with spurring the *Lady's Magazine* to produce regular plates of its own from the end of 1794. *Women in Print: Writing Women and Women's Magazines from the Restoration to the Accession of Victoria* (London: George Allen & Unwin, 1972), p. 205. But the *Gallery* – a very expensive, large yet slim, and visually stunning monthly that included two coloured plates per issue with generous textual commentary – was a rival of the most indirect kind.
35. This title was continued as the *Record of Fashion and Court Elegance* until 1809.
36. 'Prospectus' for the *Lady's Monthly Museum* (London: Vernor and Hood: 1798), pp. 1–2.
37. 'To the Public, Our Readers, and Correspondents', *La Belle Assemblée* (1 (February 1806): n.p.). Subsequent references will be given in the text.

38. Stanley Morison, *A Memoir of John Bell, 1745–1831* (Cambridge: Cambridge University Press, 1930; repr. 2009), p. 66.
39. Beatrice Grant was one such contributor who published regularly in both periodicals as well as others. So too was Thomas Noon Talfourd. See William A. Coles, 'Magazine and Other Contributions by Mary Russell Mitford and Thomas Noon Talfourd', *Studies in Bibliography*, 12 (1959): 218–26.
40. Portrait painter Arthur William Devis married his second wife, Margaret Lanchester, in 1806.
41. 'Fashions for Ladies and Gentlemen', *Repository of Arts* 1 (February 1809): 52.
42. Laura Engel, *Austen, Actresses and Accessories: Much Ado about Muffs* (Basingstoke: Palgrave Macmillan, 2015), p. 64.
43. Hilary Davidson, *Dress in the Age of Jane Austen* (New Haven, CT: Yale University Press, 2019), pp. 48–51.
44. Margaret Beetham, *A Magazine of her Own? Domesticity and Desire in the Woman's Magazine 1800–1914* (London and New York: Routledge, 1994), p. 31; and Shevelow, *Women and Print Culture*, pp. 188–9.
45. Smith, 'Fast Fashion', p. 452.
46. For much of the 1770s, theatrical reviews in the *Lady's Magazine* and the *Town and Country Magazine* are near identical. In the 1780s they begin to diverge.
47. Antonia Forster, ed., 'Introduction', *Index to Book Reviews in England, 1749–1774* (Carbondale and Edwardsville: Southern Illinois University Press, 1990), p. 11.
48. Jon P. Klancher, *The Making of English Reading Audiences, 1790–1832* (Madison: University of Wisconsin Press, 1987), p. 69.
49. See, for instance, the Correspondents column for July 1824, in which a reader's unsolicited review of James Hogg's *Private Memoirs and Confessions of a Justified Sinner* (1824) is rejected on the basis that the magazine only published its 'own reviews of books . . . which are communicated by friends whom we know to be impartial' (55: 398).
50. Forster, 'Introduction', pp. 7–8.
51. James Boaden, *Memoirs of Mrs. Inchbald Including her Familiar Correspondence with the Most Distinguished Persons of Her Time*, 2 vols (Cambridge: Cambridge University Press [1833] 2013), 2, p. 46. A similar review of *A Simple Story* (1791) appeared in the magazines for February and March of 1791. As well as featuring extracts and appraisals of her novels, over ten of Inchbald's plays were reviewed in the *Lady's Magazine* from 1784 to 1805, often along with epilogues, prologues and scenes from the same.
52. See Nicholas Mason, 'Building Brand Byron: Early Nineteenth-Century Advertising and the Marketing of *Childe Harold's Pilgrimage*', *MLQ*, 63 (2002): 411–40.
53. A much shorter and less evaluative version of the same review appeared in the same month in the *New Monthly Magazine* for February 1817.
54. Batchelor, 'UnRomantic Authorship'.
55. Among the Minerva novels excerpted in the novel is Eliza Parsons' *Errors of Education* (1791). Admiring reviews of Barbara Hofland's *Integrity*

(1823) and Regina Maria Roche's *Contrast* (1828) appeared in their year of publication. Other Minerva novels reviewed in the magazine include: *The Sailor Boy* (1800); *Allan M'Dougal* (1831); *The Eve of St Agnes* (1831); and *The Doomed One* (1832).

56. See also Jenny DiPlacidi, "Full of Pretty Stories": Fiction in the *Lady's Magazine* (1770–1832)', in *Women's Periodicals and Print Culture in Britain, 1690–1820s: The Long Eighteenth Century*, eds Jennie Batchelor and Manushag N. Powell (Edinburgh: Edinburgh University Press, 2018), pp. 263–77.
57. The first issue of the magazine in August 1770 contained around twenty-one pages of fiction (mostly tales) as well as an unusually long opening instalment of 'A Sentimental Journey'. In July 1780 the magazine carried about fourteen pages of serial and short fiction (25 per cent of the magazine's overall content). The July 1790 issue contained five and a half pages (around 10 per cent of the magazine's pages). The July 1800 issue contained eleven and a half pages of fiction (nearly 8 per cent).
58. Almost 50 per cent of the January 1812 issue is devoted to five concurrently running serial fictions written for the magazine: continuations of Pilkington's 'Benedict', the epistolary 'Highland Hermitage' and the magazine's translation of Paul-Jérémie Bitaubé's *The Batavians* (1797), retitled 'The Dutch Patriots', as well as the new 'Sappho, an Historic Romance' and 'Pleasures of Benevolence'.
59. Page published the *Lady's Magazine* until 1836 when he, along with A. H. Blackwood and G. Simpkin, became the publisher of *Blackwood's Lady's Magazine and Gazette of the Fashionable World* (1836–60).
60. 'The Editor's Council Chamber', *Ladies' Museum*, new ser. 1 (May 1831): 127–9.
61. 'Address to Subscribers', *The Lady's Magazine and Museum* 1 (July 1832): n.p.

Chapter 6

1. See Frank Donoghue, *The Fame Machine: Book Reviewing and Eighteenth-Century Literary Careers* (Stanford [CA]: Stanford University Press, 1996). On Romantic-era periodicals and literary celebrity see esp. David Higgins, *Romantic Genius and the Literary Magazine: Biography, Celebrity, Politics* (London: Routledge, 2005); Nicholas Mason, *Literary Advertising and the Shaping of British Romanticism* (Baltimore: Johns Hopkins University Press, 2013); Tom Mole, ed., *Romanticism and Celebrity Culture, 1750–1850* (Cambridge: Cambridge University Press, 2009).
2. Clifford Siskin, *The Work of Writing: Literature and Social Change in Britain, 1700–1830* (Baltimore: Johns Hopkins University Press, 1998), pp. 193–228, esp. p. 218.
3. Extracts from *Letters on Education* (1790) were printed in the magazine in the early 1790s.
4. See Harriet Guest, *Small Change: Women, Learning, Patriotism, 1750–1810* (Chicago and London: University of Chicago Press, 2000), esp. pp. 160–1.
5. Claire Brock has contended that the Macaulay statue was 'seen in some way

to be cheating posterity' by satisfying the modern desire of 'instantaneous' celebrity, but as the *Lady's Magazine* notes, commemoration of the achievements of the living had a venerable history. *The Feminization of Fame, 1750–1830* (Basingstoke: Palgrave Macmillan, 2006), p. 66. Kate Davies importantly notes that Macaulay was very ill when the statue was commissioned and that the sculpture therefore needs to be understood as both funerary and commemorative. *Catharine Macaulay and Mercy Ottis Warren: The Revolutionary Atlantic and the Politics of Gender* (Oxford: Oxford University Press, 2005), pp. 140–1. The blank space above the monument's inscription was presumably left so that an epitaph could be added upon Macaulay's death.

6. Along with T. Cadell and T. Davies, George Robinson and John Roberts were publishers of the first and second editions of Macaulay's *Loose Remarks on Certain Positions to be found in Mr. Hobbes's Philosophical Rudiments of Government and Society* (1767; 2nd edn, 1769).

7. These lines are taken from the inscription on the monument itself, where they are erroneously attributed to Lord Lyttleton. The magazine included the inscription in its engraving. Fearing the letters would be too small for some readers to decipher, it also printed them in the main body of the text.

8. Claire Gilbride Fox, 'Catherine Macaulay, an Eighteenth-Century Clio', *Winterthur Portfolio* 4 (1968): 129–42 (138).

9. Three of the four writers who appear in Castalio's (Mugliston's) list – Elizabeth Griffith, Hannah More, Anna Letitia Barbauld (née Aikin) and Catharine Macaulay – appear in Richard Samuel's portrait 'The Nine Living Muses of Great Britain'. Cowley, a favourite of the magazine, does not.

10. As Jacqueline Pearson, Edward Copeland and Richard de Ritter have variously documented, the *Lady's Magazine* offers up a 'treasure-house' of evidence for a wide range of hotly debated attitudes to women's writing and to the woman reader in the Romantic period. Jacqueline Pearson, *Women's Reading in Britain, 1759–1835: A Dangerous Recreation* (Cambridge: Cambridge University Press, 1999), *passim*; Edward Copeland, *Women Writing about Money: Women's Fiction in England, 1790–1820* (Cambridge: Cambridge University Press, 1995); Richard de Ritter, *Imagining Women Readers 1789–1820: Well-regulated Minds* (Manchester: Manchester University Press, 2014), *passim*. In this chapter, I am less concerned with the debates the magazine staged about what and how women should read than in what writers and texts it made available to its readers.

11. Melissa Sodeman has written about earlier examples of 'Scales' of male and female genius in newspapers such as *The Star* in *Sentimental Memorials: Women and the Novel in Literary History* (Stanford: Stanford University Press, 2015), pp. 125–7.

12. *Spectator* no. 37. Joseph Addison and Richard Steele, *The Spectator*, ed. Donald F. Bond, 5 vols (Oxford: Clarendon Press, 1965), vol. 1: 1.158, 1.156.

13. Kathleen Lubey, *Excitable Imaginations: Eroticism and Reading* (Lewisburg: Bucknell University Press, 2012), p. 94.

14. Although most of Radagunda Roberts's contributions to the *Lady's Magazine* are prose translations, she was also a poet. Some of her verse appeared in her brother William Roberts's *Poetical Attempts* (1784) and

she may also have been the same Miss Roberts whose verse appeared in the *Lady's Poetical Magazine* (1781–2). See Olivia Cox, 'The *Lady's Poetical Magazine* and the Fashioning of Women's Literary Space', in *Women's Periodicals and Print Culture, 1690–1820s: The Long Eighteenth Century*, eds Jennie Batchelor and Manushag N. Powell (Edinburgh: Edinburgh University Press, 2018), pp. 129–48 (p. 144n9).
15. Obituaries appeared for the first time in the 1820s.
16. Clara Reeve, *The Progress of Romance, through Times, Countries and Manners*, 2 vols (Colchester: W. Keymer, 1785), 1: 122. The Robinsons were London booksellers of the *Progress of Romance*.
17. Reeve, *The Progress of Romance*, 1: 119.
18. Alison Adburgham, *Women in Print: Writing Women and Women's Magazines from the Restoration to the Accession of Victoria* (London: George Allen & Unwin, 1972), p. 148.
19. See Chapter 4, p. X.
20. Jürgen Habermas, *The Structural Transformation of the Public Sphere*, trans. Thomas Burger with the assistance of Frederick Lawrence (Cambridge: Polity, 1989), p. 43.
21. Jon P. Klancher, *The Making of English Reading Audiences, 1790–1832* (Madison: University of Wisconsin Press, 1987), p. 21. See also Rachel Scarborough King's excellent account of the function of reader letters in early periodicals in *Writing to the World: Letters and the Origins of Modern Print Genres* (Baltimore: Johns Hopkins University Press, 2018), esp. pp. 55–64.
22. Klancher, *The Making of English Reading Audiences*, p. 22.
23. Markman Ellis, *The Politics of Sensibility: Race, Gender and Commerce in the Sentimental Novel* (Cambridge: Cambridge University Press, 1996), p. 42.
24. See, for example [Anon], 'Male and Female Gossips Compared', which savages 'coffee house-orators'. *Lady's Magazine* 11 (August 1780): 403.
25. See, for example, 'The Green-stocking Club' series. *Lady's Magazine*, 48 (February–May 1817).
26. On the magazine's views on mixed-sexed and female debating societies see, for instance, 'Description of a New Society of Ladies', which was decreed as 'prejudicial to the cause of virtue' (Wheble 2 (September 1771): 119); and 'The Contrast' (Wheble 2 (October 1771): 163). Anna Clark notes that 'no female [debating] societies' seem to have survived after 1788. *Scandal: The Sexual Politics of the British Constitution* (Princeton and London: Princeton University Press, 2004).
27. On the magazine's engagement with and promotion of the founding of the Belle Assemblée debating society, see Jennie Batchelor, '"Connections, which are of service . . . In a more advanced age": *The Lady's Magazine*, Community, and Women's Literary Histories', *Tulsa Studies in Women's Literature*, 30: 2 (Fall 2011): 245–67.
28. Margaret J. M. Ezell, 'The *Gentleman's Journal* and the Commercialisation of Restoration Coterie Literary Practices', *Modern Philology* 89.3 (1992): 323–40.
29. I am thinking particularly, here, of Ezell's field-defining *Writing Women's Literary History* (Baltimore: Johns Hopkins University Press, 1993).

30. See Betty A. Schellenberg, *Literary Coteries and the Making of Modern Print Culture, 1740–1990* (Cambridge: Cambridge University Press, 2016); and Michelle Levy, *Family Authorship and Romantic Print Culture* (Basingstoke: Palgrave Macmillan, 2008).
31. Schellenberg, *Literary Coteries*, p. 21.
32. Schellenberg, *Literary Coteries*, p. 6.
33. Schellenberg, *Literary Coteries*, p. 14.
34. Charlotte Brontë to Hartley Coleridge, 10 December 1840. Margaret Smith, ed., *The Letters of Charlotte Brontë with a selection of letters by her family and friends, Vol. 1 1829–47* (Oxford: Clarendon Press, 1995), p. 240.
35. Simon Eliot, 'The Reading Experience Database; or, what are we to do about the history of reading', *The Reading Experience Database*. <www.open.ac.uk/Arts/RED/redback.htm> (last accessed 8 October 2020).
36. Jenny DiPlacidi, "Full of Pretty Stories": Fiction in the *Lady's Magazine* (1770–1832)', in *Women's Periodicals and Print Culture in Britain, 1690–1820s*, pp. 263–77.
37. Siskin, *The Work of Writing*, p. 199.
38. Siskin, *The Work of Writing*, p. 200; p. 206.
39. See, for example: Olivia Murphy, *Jane Austen: The Artist as Critic* (Basingstoke: Palgrave Macmillan, 2013); and Mary Waldron, *Jane Austen and the Fiction of her Time* (Cambridge: Cambridge University Press, 1999).
40. We tend to associate circulating libraries primarily with the novel, but they stocked many kinds of print publications, of course, including journals. Surviving library catalogues and prospectuses show that the *Lady's Magazine* was widely available through such libraries, including William Lane's Minerva Library. On the *Lady's Magazine*'s presence in the *Hampshire Chronicle*, see Ruth Facer, 'A Passage of Words: The Transmission of the Novel though Select Hampshire Newspapers, 1772–1800', *Proceedings of the Hampshire Field Club Archaeological Society* 56 (2001): 254–65.
41. The publication of the trial report coincided with the publication of two pamphlets. The text of the periodical's report is different from that in both [Anon.], *The Trial of Jane Leigh Perrot at Taunton Assizes* (Bath: W. Gye [1800]); and John Pinchard, *The Trial of Jane Leigh Perrot, Wife of James Leigh Perrot, Esq* (Taunton: Thomas Norris [1800]).
42. See, for example, F. D. Mackinnon, *Grand Larceny, Being the Theft of Jane Leigh Perrot, Aunt of Jane Austen* (Oxford: Oxford University Press, 1937). For a recent and excellent discussion of the possible influence of the Leigh Perrot trial on Austen's fiction see Janine Barchas, *Matters of Fact: History, Location, and Celebrity* (Baltimore: Johns Hopkins University Press, 2012), pp. 32–43.
43. DiPlacidi notes strong thematic echoes between several fictions in the *Lady's Magazine* from the 1770s onwards in Austen's novels. "Full of Pretty Stories", pp. 268–71.
44. Sayre Greenfield, 'The Source for the Theatricals of Jane Austen's *Mansfield Park*: A Discovery', *Persuasions*, 18 (2016): 197–204. It might also be noted in support of Greenfield's arguments that the *Lady's Magazine* offered

extensive coverage of, extracts from and appreciative critical responses to plays by Elizabeth Inchbald, the translator/adaptor of *Lovers' Vows* and the author of the original *Das Kind der Liebe* (1780), August von Kotzebue.
45. Barchas, *Matters of Fact*, p. 163.
46. Edward Copeland, 'Money Talks: Jane Austen and the *Lady's Magazine*', in *Jane Austen's Beginnings: The Juvenilia and Lady Susan* (Ann Arbor: UMI Research Press, 1989), pp. 153–71.
47. There are also faint echoes of *Emma* and Jane Fairfax's refusal to travel to Ireland with the Dixons. I am grateful to Katie Halsey for this suggestion.
48. Edward Copeland, 'Introduction' to Jane Austen, *Sense and Sensibility*, ed. Edward Copeland (Cambridge: Cambridge University Press, 2006), pp. vi–lvii.
49. Edward Copeland, 'Money', *The Cambridge Companion to Jane Austen* (Cambridge: Cambridge University Press, 2010), p. 143.
50. William B. Warner uses this phrase to characterise the relationship between Samuel Richardson's *Pamela* (1740) and the amatory fictions that the author sought to absorb and displace in his new breed of sentimental fiction. *Licensing Entertainment: The Elevation of Novel Reading in Britain, 1684–1750* (Berkeley and Los Angeles: University of California Press, 1998), pp. 192–9.
51. See, for example, Katie Halsey, *Jane Austen and her Readers, 1786–1945* (London: Anthem Press, 2013); Murphy, *Jane Austen: The Artist as* Critic; and Waldron, *Jane Austen and the Fiction of her Time*.
52. Jane Austen, *Emma*, eds Richard Cronin and Dorothy McMillan (Cambridge: Cambridge University Press, 2005), p. 450.
53. Austen, *Emma*, p. 450.
54. Karl Kroeber, *Styles in Fictional Structure: Studies in the Art of Jane Austen, Charlotte Bronte, George Eliot* (Princeton: Princeton University Press, 1971), p. 78.
55. Recently, Gillian Dow has amassed a compelling body of evidence to suggest that the translator of this work was Charlotte (Francis) Barrett (1786–1870), the niece of Frances Burney (private correspondence).
56. A serialised English translation of Feijoo's work appeared the earlier *Lady's Magazine; or, Polite Companion for the Fair Sex* (1759–63). This claimed to be a direct translation 'from the original Spanish . . . Never attempted in English before' (2 (January 1760): 197). Irwin's translation in Robinson's *Lady's Magazine* differs substantially from this translation as it does from the three other English translations of *Defensa de las Mujeres* that appeared in 1765, 1774 and 1778, which have been identified by Monica Bolufer Peruga (private correspondence).
57. Anon., *Three Essays or Discourses on the Following Subjects, A Defence or Vindication of the Women, Church Music, A Comparison between Ancient and Modern Music, translated from the Spanish of Feijoo; by a Gentleman* (London: T. Becket, 1778), p. 44.
58. Jane Austen, *Persuasion*, eds Janet Todd and Antje Blank (Cambridge: Cambridge University Press, 2006), p. 255.
59. Martha Bohrer, 'Thinking locally: novelistic worlds in provincial fiction', in *The Cambridge Companion to Fiction in the Romantic Period*, eds Richard

Maxwell and Katie Trumpener (Cambridge: Cambridge University Press, 2009), pp. 89–106 (p. 89).
60. Halsey, *Jane Austen and her Readers*, pp. 164–5.
61. It is also striking that Jane Fisher shares her name with an undeveloped character in the unfinished Sanditon.
62. These include: 'The History of Adelaide' (15: May 1784); 'Adelaide, a Fragment' (37: August 1806); and 'Adelaide: or, the Triumph of Constancy' (38: July 1807).
63. Eve Tavor Bannet, 'Discontinuous Reading and Miscellaneous Instruction for British Ladies', *Women's Periodicals and Print Media*, pp. 40–52 (p. 40).
64. Various forms of anecdotal advice indicate that Mitford might be the author of the Fisher letter. Mitford wrote a number of other essays for this issue, including three pieces that would later be reprinted in *Our Village*. One of these, 'Aunt Martha', directly precedes the Fisher letter. The *Lady's Magazine* was in the habit of printing works by the same author (even when the pieces had different signatures) next to one another. It also seems likely from the detailed references to Austen's appearance (long before a likeness was made publicly available) that the author of the letter was an acquaintance of Austen or her family.

Afterword

1. Nicholas Mason and Tom Mole, eds, *Romantic Periodicals in the Twenty-First Century: Eleven Case Studies from* Blackwood's Edinburgh Magazine (Edinburgh: Edinburgh University Press, 2020).
2. In addition to the monographs and essays on these subjects cited in previous chapters, I have in mind here the groundbreaking *Digital Miscellanies Index* and the associated publications of its researchers <http://digitalmiscellaniesindex.org/> (last accessed 8 October 2020).

Select Bibliography

Periodicals

The Amulet, or Christian and Literary Remembrancer (1826–36)
The Anti-Jacobin Review (1798–1821)
The Athenian Mercury (1690–7)
La Belle Assemblée, or Bell's Court and Fashionable Magazine (1806–32)
Blackwood's Edinburgh Magazine (1817–1980)
The Critical Review; or Annals of Literature (1756–1817)
The Fashionable Magazine (1786)
The Female Spectator (1744–6)
The Forget Me Not (1822–47)
The Gallery of Fashion (1794–1803)
The Gentleman's Journal (1692–4)
The Gentleman's Magazine: or the Monthly Miscellany. By Way of a Gentleman in the Country. Consisting of News, History, Philosophy, Poetry, Musick, Translations, &c. (1731–1922)
Hibernian Magazine (1771–1811; from 1786 Walker's Hibernian Magazine)
Ladies' Diary; or, the Women's Almanack (1704–1841)
The Ladies' Journal (1727)
The Ladies Magazine; or, the Universal Entertainer (1749–53)
The Lady's Magazine; or, the Compleat Library (1738–9?)
The Lady's Magazine; or, Polite Companion for the Fair Sex (1759–63)
The Lady's Magazine; or, Entertaining Companion for the Fair Sex (1770–1832)
The Lady's Magazine; or Universal Repository (1733)
The Ladies Mercury (1693)
The Lady's Monthly Museum (1798–1828)
The Lady's Museum (1760–1)
The Lady's Poetical Magazine; or Beauties of British Poetry (1781–2)
The Lady's Weekly Magazine (1747)
London Chronicle (1757–1823)
The Lounger (1785–7)
Middlesex Journal (1769–76)
The Monthly Visitor (1797–1804)
The New Lady's Magazine (1786–95)
New Monthly (1814–42)

The Old Maid (1755–6)
The Repository of Arts (1809–28)
The Tatler (1709–11)
Town and Country Magazine; or Universal Repository of Knowledge, Instruction and Entertainment (1769–96)
Universal Spectator and Weekly Journal (1729–46)

Online Databases and Digital Editions

Eighteenth-Century Journals (London: Adam Matthew Digital, 2013).
Batchelor, Jennie The *Lady's Magazine* (1770–1819) *Patterns of Perfection* <https://ladysmagazine.omeka.net> (last accessed 23 September 2021).
Batchelor, Jennie, Koenraad Claes and Jenny DiPlacidi, *Lady's Magazine Index* <https://research.kent.ac.uk/the-ladys-magazine/index/> (last accessed 8 October 2020).
De Montluzin, Emily, *Attributions of Authorship in the Gentleman's Magazine, 1731–1868: An Electronic Union List* <http://bsuva.org/bsuva/gm2/GMintro.html> (last accessed 8 October 2020).

Archival Sources

International Collections

Houghton Library, Harvard University. MS ENG1310. Letter from Frances Brooke to Richard Gifford, n.d.

National Archives

British Library, London: Manuscripts

Add. MS 75727, Althorp papers: Sophia Troughton to Lady Margaret Spencer, 13 April 1813.
Add. MS 78688: 'Original Letters Collected by William Upcott of the London Institution. Distinguished Women', ed. William Upcott. Vol. 3.
C.60.b.7, *The Literary Pocket-Book; or, Companion for the Lover of Nature and Art for* 1819 (London: printed for C. and J. Ollier).
M1077/7, reel 7, Case 256: Mary Pilkington to the Secretary of the Literary Fund, 2 June 1810. *Archives of the Royal Literary Fund: 1790–1918*, 145 reels (London: World Microfilms Publications, 1981–4).

The National Archives, Kew

PRO 11/892/324: Will of Joseph Richardson of Saint Faith, City of London (6 October 1763).
PRO 11/974/221: Will of John Roberts, Bookseller of Pater Noster Row, City of London (22 January 1772).
PRO 11/1167/16: Will of Radagunda Roberts, Spinster of St Faith under Saint Paul's, City of London (3 June 1788).
PRO 11/1132/272: Will of Jane Collier, Widow of Saint John, Southwark, Surrey (3 August 1785).

PRO 11/1231/164: Will of Archibald Hamilton of Princes Street Bedford Row, Middlesex (17 April 1793).
PRO 11/1359/302: Will of George Robinson of Paternoster Row, City of London (26 June 1811).
PRO 11/1522/417: Will of George Robinson, Bookseller of No 25 Paternoster Row, City of London (30 May 1811).
PRO 11/1618/154: Will of George Moore, Stable Keeper of Saint Giles in the Fields, Middlesex (10 July 1819).
PRO 11/1840/102: Will of James Heath of Lewisham, Kent (19 December 1834).
PRO 11/1844/372: Will of Samuel Robinson, Bookseller of Chapter House Court, Saint Paul's City of London (27 March 1835).
PRO 11/2243/230: Will of Sophia Hendry, Widow of Alfred House Kensal Green (15 December 1856).

Regional Archives

Derbyshire Record Office

D654/A/PZ/10: C. Bateman, 'Descriptive and Historical Account of Alfreton' (1812).

Manchester Central Library

GB127.MS f 091 A2: Literary Assignments of George Robinson.

Reading Central Library

qB/TU/MIT: The Letters of Mary Russell Mitford, 1806–49, 6 vols.
R/TU/TAL: Letters from Thomas Noon Talfourd to Mary Russell Mitford, 1821–40.

Printed, Online and Unpublished Sources

Adburgham, Alison, *Women in Print: Writing Women and Women's Magazines from the Restoration to the Accession of Victoria* (London: George Allen & Unwin, 1972).
Addison, Joseph, and Richard Steele, *The Spectator*, ed. Donald F. Bond, 5 vols (Oxford: Clarendon Press, 1965).
Anon., 'George Robinson, Esq.', *New, Original, and Complete Wonderful Museum and Magazine Extraordinary*, 6 (1808): 3150–6.
Anon., *Three Essays or Discourses on the Following Subjects, A Defence or Vindication of the Women, Church Music, A Comparison between Ancient and Modern Music, translated from the Spanish of Feijoo; by a Gentleman* (London: T. Becket, 1778).
Austen, Jane, *Emma*, eds Richard Cronin and Dorothy McMillan (Cambridge: Cambridge University Press, 2005).
Austen, Jane, *Persuasion*, eds Janet Todd and Antje Blank (Cambridge: Cambridge University Press, 2006).
Austen, Jane, *Sense and Sensibility*, ed. Edward Copeland (Cambridge: Cambridge University Press, 2006).

Ballaster, Ros, *Fabulous Orients: Fictions of the East in England, 1662–1785* (Oxford: Oxford University Press, 2005).

Ballaster, Ros, Margaret Beetham, Elizabeth Frazer and Sandra Hebron, *Women's Worlds: Ideology, Femininity and the Woman's Magazine* (Basingstoke: Macmillan, 1991).

Bannet, Eve Tavor, 'Haywood's Spectator and the Female World', in *Fair Philosopher: Eliza Haywood and the "Female Spectator"*, eds Lynn Marie Wright and Donald J. Newman (Lewisburg: Bucknell University Press, 2006), 82–101.

Bannet, Eve Tavor, *Eighteenth-Century Manners of Reading: Print Culture and Popular Instruction in the Anglophone Atlantic World* (Cambridge: Cambridge University Press, 2017).

Bannet, Eve Tavor, 'Discontinuous Reading and Miscellaneous Instruction for British Ladies', *Women's Periodicals and Print Culture in Britain, 1690–1820s: The Long Eighteenth Century*, eds Jennie Batchelor and Manushag N. Powell (Edinburgh: Edinburgh University Press, 2018), 40–52.

Barchas, Janine, *Matters of Fact: History, Location, and Celebrity* (Baltimore: Johns Hopkins University Press, 2012).

Barker, Anthony D., 'Edward Cave, Samuel Johnson and the *Gentleman's Magazine*' (unpublished PhD thesis, University of Oxford, 1981).

Batchelor, Jennie, 'Anon, Pseud and "By a Lady": The Spectre of Anonymity in the *Lady's Magazine*', in *Women's Writing, 1660–1830: Feminisms and Futures*, eds Jennie Batchelor and Gillian Dow (Palgrave Macmillan, 2016), 69–86.

Batchelor, Jennie, *Dress, Distress and Desire: Clothing and the Body in Eighteenth-Century Literature* (Basingstoke: Palgrave Macmillan, 2005).

Batchelor, Jennie, *Women's Work: Labour, Gender, Authorship, 1750–1830* (Manchester: Manchester University Press, 2010).

Batchelor, Jennie, '"Connections, which are of service … In a more advanced age": The *Lady's Magazine*, Community, and Women's Literary Histories', *Tulsa Studies in Women's Literature*, 30: 2 (Fall 2011): 245–67.

Batchelor, Jennie, '"Be but a little Deaf and Blind … and Happiness you'll Surely Find": Marriage in Eighteenth-Century Magazines for Women', in *After Marriage in the Long Eighteenth Century: Literature, Law and Society*, eds Jenny DiPlacidi and Karl Leydecker (Basingstoke: Palgrave Macmillan, 2017), 107–27.

Batchelor, Jennie, 'UnRomantic Authorship: The Minerva Press and the *Lady's Magazine* (1770–1820)', *Romantic Textualities*, eds Elizabeth Neiman and Christina Morin 3 (Summer 2020): 76–93 <https://doi.org/10.18573/romtext.73> (last accessed 25 November 2021).

Batt, Jennifer, 'Poems in Magazines', *The Oxford Handbook of British Poetry, 1660–1800*, ed. Jack Lynch (Oxford: Oxford University Press, 2016), 55–71.

Beachcroft, T. O., *The Modest Art: A Survey of the Short Story in English* (London: Oxford University Press, 1968).

Beetham, Margaret, 'Towards a Theory of the Periodical as a Publishing Genre', *Investigating Victorian Journalism*, eds Laurel Brake, Aled Jones and Lionel Madden (Basingstoke: Macmillan, 1990). 19–32.

Beetham, Margaret, *A Magazine of her Own? Domesticity and Desire in the Woman's Magazine 1800–1914* (London and New York: Routledge, 1994).

Behrendt, Stephen C., *British Women Poets and the Romantic Writing Community* (Baltimore: Johns Hopkins University Press, 2009).
Benedict, Barbara, 'Literary Miscellanies: The Cultural Mediation of Fragmented Feeling', *ELH* 57.2 (1990): 407–30.
Bennett, Shelley M., *The Mechanisms of Art Patronage in England circa 1800* (Columbia: University of Missouri Press, 1988).
Black, Jeremy, *The English Press in the Eighteenth Century* (London: Routledge, 2011).
Bohrer, Martha, 'Thinking locally: novelistic worlds in provincial fiction', in *The Cambridge Companion to Fiction in the Romantic Period*, eds Richard Maxwell and Katie Trumpener (Cambridge: Cambridge University Press, 2009), 89–106.
Bolter, Jay David, and Richard Grusin, *Remediation: Understanding New Media* (Cambridge, MA: MIT Press, 1999).
Boaden, James, *Memoirs of Mrs. Inchbald Including her Familiar Correspondence with the Most Distinguished Persons of Her Time*, 2 vols (Cambridge: Cambridge University Press [1833] 2013).
Boulukos, George, *The Grateful Slave: The Emergence of Race in Eighteenth-Century Britain and America* (Cambridge: Cambridge University Press, 2008).
Brake, Laurel, and Julie F. Codell, 'Introduction: Encountering the Press', in *Encounters in the Victorian Press: Editors, Authors, Readers*, eds Laurel Brake and Julie F. Codell (Basingstoke: Palgrave Macmillan, 2005), 1–7.
Brock, Claire, *The Feminization of Fame, 1750–1830* (Basingstoke: Palgrave Macmillan, 2006).
Brooke, Frances, *The Old Maid. By Mary Singleton, Spinster* (London: A. Millar, 1764).
Bryan, Helen, *Martha Washington: First Lady of Liberty* (New York: John Wiley, 2002).
Carlile, Susan, *Charlotte Lennox: An Independent Mind* (Toronto: University of Toronto Press, 2018).
Carlile, Susan, 'Eyes that Eagerly "Bear the Steady Ray of Reason": Eidolon as Activist in Charlotte Lennox's *Lady's Museum*', in *Women's Periodicals and Print Culture in Britain, 1690–1820s: The Long Eighteenth Century*, eds Jennie Batchelor and Manushag N. Powell (Edinburgh: Edinburgh University Press, 2018), 357–76.
Carnell, Rachel, 'Protesting the Exclusivity of the Public Sphere: Delarivier Manley's *Examiner*', in *Women's Periodicals and Print Culture in Britain, 1690–1820s: The Long Eighteenth Century*, eds Jennie Batchelor and Manushag N. Powell (Edinburgh: Edinburgh University Press, 2018), 153–64.
Charlton, Mary, *Rosella, or Modern Occurrences*, 4 vols (London: William Lane at the Minerva Press, 1799).
Claes, Koenraad, 'Vindications and Reflections: The *Lady's Magazine* during the Revolution Controversy (1789–1795)', in *Women's Periodicals and Print Culture in Britain, 1690–1820s: The Long Eighteenth Century*, eds Jennie Batchelor and Manushag N. Powell (Edinburgh: Edinburgh University Press, 2018), 67–81.
Clark, Anna, *Scandal: The Sexual Politics of the British Constitution* (Princeton and London: Princeton University Press, 2004).
Cohen, Margaret, and Carolyn Dever, eds, *The Literary Channel: The*

Inter-National Invention of the Novel (Princeton: Princeton University Press, 2002).

Cohen, Michèle, '"Familiar Conversation": The Role of the "Familiar Format" in Education in Eighteenth- and Nineteenth-Century England', in *Educating the Child in Enlightenment Britain: Beliefs, Cultures, Practices*, eds Mary Hilton and Jill Shefrin (Farnham: Ashgate, 2009), 99–116.

Coles, William A., 'The Correspondence of Mary Russell Mitford and Thomas Noon Talfourd', Unpublished PhD dissertation (Cambridge, MA: Harvard University, 1956).

Coles, William A., 'Magazine and Other Contributions by Mary Russell Mitford and Thomas Noon Talfourd', *Studies in Bibliography*, 12 (1959): 218–26.

Copeland, Edward, 'Money Talks: Jane Austen and the *Lady's Magazine*', in *Jane Austen's Beginnings: The Juvenilia and Lady Susan* (Ann Arbor: UMI Research Press, 1989), 153–71.

Copeland, Edward, *Women Writing about Money: Women's Fiction in England, 1790–1820* (Cambridge: Cambridge University Press, 1995).

Copeland, Edward, 'Money', *The Cambridge Companion to Jane Austen* (Cambridge: Cambridge University Press, 2010).

Cox, Olivia, 'The *Lady's Poetical Magazine* and the Fashioning of Women's Literary Space', in *Women's Periodicals and Print Culture, 1690–1820s: The Long Eighteenth Century*, eds Jennie Batchelor and Manushag N. Powell (Edinburgh: Edinburgh University Press, 2018), 129–48.

Coxhead, A. C. (RA), *Thomas Stothard: An Illustrated Monograph* (London: A. H. Bullen, 1906).

Crabbe, George, *Poems by George Crabbe*, ed. Adolphus William Ward, 3 vols (Cambridge: Cambridge University Press, 1905–7).

Davidson, Hilary, *Dress in the Age of Jane Austen* (New Haven, CT: Yale University Press, 2019).

Davies, Kate, *Catharine Macaulay and Mercy Ottis Warren: The Revolutionary Atlantic and the Politics of Gender* (Oxford: Oxford University Press, 2005).

Deazley, Ronan, *On the Origin of the Right to Copy: Charting the Movement of Copyright Law in Eighteenth Century Britain (1695–1775)* (Portland, OR: Hart Publishing, 2004).

DeLucia, JoEllen, 'Radcliffe, George Robinson and Eighteenth-Century Print Culture: Beyond the Circulating Library', *Women's Writing* 22.3 (2015): 287–99 (292).

DeLucia, JoEllen, 'Travel Writing and Mediation in the *Lady's Magazine*: Charting "the meridian of female reading"', in *Women's Periodicals and Print Culture in Britain, 1690–1820s: The Long Eighteenth Century*, eds Jennie Batchelor and Manushag N. Powell (Edinburgh: Edinburgh University Press, 2018), 205–16.

De Ritter, Richard, *Imagining Women Readers, 1789–1820: Well-regulated Minds* (Manchester: Manchester University Press, 2014).

DiPlacidi, Jenny, '"Full of Pretty Stories": Fiction in the *Lady's Magazine* (1770–1832)', in *Women's Periodicals and Print Culture in Britain, 1690–1820s: The Long Eighteenth Century*, eds Jennie Batchelor and Manushag N. Powell (Edinburgh: Edinburgh University Press, 2018), 263–77.

Donoghue, Frank, *The Fame Machine: Book Reviewing and Eighteenth-Century Literary Careers* (Stanford [CA]: Stanford University Press, 1996).

Dow, Gillian, 'Criss-Crossing the Channel: the French Novel and English

Translation', in *The Oxford Handbook of the Eighteenth-Century Novel*, ed. J. A. Downie (Oxford: Oxford University Press, 2016).

Drouin, Jeffrey, 'Close- and Distant-Reading Modernism: Network Analysis, Text Mining, and Teaching *The Little Review*', *Visualizing Periodical Networks*, ed. J. Stephen Murphy. Special issue of *Journal of Modern Periodical Studies* 5.1 (2014): 110–35.

Dyer, Serena, and Chloe Wigston Smith, eds, *Material Literacy in Eighteenth-Century Britain: A Nation of Makers* (London: Bloomsbury, 2020).

Eliot, Simon, The Reading Experience Database; or, what are we to do about the history of reading', *The Reading Experience Database* <www.open.ac.uk/Arts/RED/redback.htm> (last accessed 8 October 2020).

Ellis, Markman, *The Politics of Sensibility: Race, Gender and Commerce in the Sentimental Novel* (Cambridge: Cambridge University Press, 1996).

Engel, Laura, *Austen, Actresses and Accessories: Much Ado about Muffs* (Basingstoke: Palgrave Macmillan, 2015).

Ezell, Margaret J. M., 'The *Gentleman's Journal* and the Commercialisation of Restoration Coterie Literary Practices', *Modern Philology* 89.3 (1992): 323–40.

Ezell, Margaret J. M., *Writing Women's Literary History* (Baltimore: Johns Hopkins University Press, 1993).

Ezell, Margaret J. M., 'Reading Pseudonyms in Seventeenth-Century Coterie Literature', *Essays in Literature* 21 (1994): 14–25.

Ezell, Margaret J. M., *Social Authorship and the Advent of Print* (Baltimore and London: Johns Hopkins University Press, 1999).

Ezell, Margaret J. M., '"By a Lady": The Mask of the Feminine in Restoration, Early Eighteenth-Century Print Culture, in *The Faces of Anonymity: Anonymous and Pseudonymous Publication from the Sixteenth to the Twentieth Century*, ed. Robert J. Griffin (New York: Palgrave Macmillan, 2003), 63–79.

Facer, Ruth, 'A Passage of Words: The Transmission of the Novel though Select Hampshire Newspapers, 1772–1800', *Proceedings of the Hampshire Field Club Archaeological Society* 56 (2001): 254–65.

Faulkner, Thomas, *The History and Antiquities of the Parish of Hammersmith* (London: Nichols and Son; J. Weale, E. Page, T. S. Rayner; and Simpkin, Marshall & Co., 1839).

Fergus, Jan, *Provincial Readers in Eighteenth-Century England* (Oxford: Oxford University Press, 2006).

Ferguson, Moira, 'Mary Wollstonecraft and the Problematic of Slavery', *Feminist Review* 42 (1992): 82–102.

Fitzpatrick, Barbara Laning, 'Physical Evidence for John Coote's Eighteenth-Century Periodical Proprietorships: The Example of Coote's *Royal Magazine* (1759–71) and Smollett's *British Magazine* (1760–7).' *Analytical and Enumerative Bibliography*, new ser. 11 (2000): 211–58.

Forster, Antonia, ed., *Index to Book Reviews in England, 1749–1774* (Carbondale and Edwardsville: Southern Illinois University Press, 1990).

Foucault, Michel, 'What is An Author', repr. in *Modern Criticism and Theory: A Readers*, eds David Lodge and Nigel Wood, 3rd edn (London: Longman, 2008), 281–93.

Fox, Claire Gilbride, 'Catherine Macaulay, an Eighteenth-Century Clio', *Winterthur Portfolio* 4 (1968): 129–42.

Gardiner, Reginald, *Admission Registers of St. Paul's School, 1748–1876* (London: G. Bell and Sons, 1884).
Genette, Gérard, *Paratexts: Thresholds of Interpretation* (Cambridge: Cambridge University Press, 1997).
Goring, Paul, 'The Evolution of "A Sentimental Journey. By a Lady" in The Lady's Magazine', *The Shandean*, 39.3 (2020): 67–100.
Grant, James, *The Great Metropolis*, 2 vols (London: Saunders and Otley, 1836).
Green, Katherine Sobba, *The Courtship Novel, 1740–1820: A Feminised Genre* (Lexington: University Press of Kentucky, 1991).
Greenfield, Sayre, 'The Source for the Theatricals of Jane Austen's *Mansfield Park*: A Discovery', *Persuasions*, 18 (2016): 197–204.
Griffin, Robert J., 'Anonymity and Authorship', *New Literary History* 30.4 (1999): 877–95.
Griffin, Robert J., 'Introduction', *The Faces of Anonymity: Anonymous and Pseudonymous Publication from the Sixteenth to the Twentieth Century*, ed. Robert J. Griffin (New York: Palgrave Macmillan, 2003), 1–17.
Grundy, Isobel, 'A moral paper! And how do you expect to get money by it?' Lady Mary Wortley Montagu and Journalism' in *Women's Periodicals and Print Culture in Britain, 1690–1820s: The Long Eighteenth Century*, eds Jennie Batchelor and Manushag N. Powell (Edinburgh: Edinburgh University Press, 2018), 165–77.
Guest, Harriet, *Small Change: Women, Learning, Patriotism, 1750–1810* (Chicago: University of Chicago Press, 2000).
Harris, Michael, 'London Newspapers', in *The Cambridge History of the Book in Britain. Volume V 1695–1830*, eds Michael F. Suarez, S. J., and Michael L. Turner (Cambridge: Cambridge University Press, 2009), 413–33.
Habermas, Jürgen, *The Structural Transformation of the Public Sphere*, trans. Thomas Burger with the assistance of Frederick Lawrence (Cambridge: Polity, 1989).
Halsey, Katie, *Jane Austen and her Readers, 1786–1945* (London: Anthem Press, 2013).
Haywood, Eliza, *The Female Spectator: The Selected Works of Eliza Haywood. Part 2. Vols 1–2*, eds Kathryn R. King and Alexander Pettit (London: Pickering and Chatto, 2001).
Heath, John, *The Heath Family Engravers 1779–1878*, 2 vols (Aldershot: Scolar Press, 1993).
Higgins, David, *Romantic Genius and the Literary Marketplace: Biography, Celebrity Politics* (London: Routledge, 2005).
Hoeveler, Diane Long, 'Prose Fiction: *Zastrozzi*, *St. Irvine*, *The Assassins*, *The Coliseum*', *The Oxford Handbook of Percy Bysshe Shelley*, eds Michael O'Neill and Anthony Howe, with the assistance of Madeleine Callaghan (Oxford: Oxford University Press, 2013), 193–207.
Hudson, Hannah Doherty, '"The Lady is Descended from a Good Family": Women and Biography in British Magazines, 1770–1798', in *Women's Periodicals and Print Culture in Britain, 1690–1820s: The Long Eighteenth Century*, eds Jennie Batchelor and Manushag N. Powell (Edinburgh: Edinburgh University Press, 201), 278–93.
Hughes, Gillian, 'Fiction in the Magazines', in *English and British Fiction,*

1750–1820, eds Peter Garside and Karen O'Brien (Oxford: Oxford University Press, 2015).
Hughes, Linda K., 'What the *Wellesley Index* Left Out: Why Poetry Matters to Periodical Studies', *Victorian Periodicals Review* 20 (Summer 2007): 91–125.
Hunter, Jean E., '*The Lady's Magazine* and the Study of Englishwomen in the Eighteenth Century', in *Newsletters to Newspapers: Eighteenth-Century Journalism*, eds Donavan H. Bond and W. Reynolds McLeod (Morgantown: School of Journalism, West Virginia University, 1977), 103–17.
Ingrassia, Catherine, 'Eliza Haywood's Periodicals in Wartime', *Women's Periodicals and Print Culture in Britain, 1690–1820s: The Long Eighteenth Century*, eds Jennie Batchelor and Manushag N. Powell (Edinburgh: Edinburgh University Press, 2018), 178–89.
Italia, Iona, *The Rise of Literary Journalism in the Eighteenth Century: Anxious Employment*. London and New York: Routledge, 2005).
Italia, Iona, 'Fair-Sexing It', *Media History* 14:3 (2008): 323–35.
Johnson, Samuel, *A Dictionary of the English Language*, 2nd edn (London: J. Knapton; C. Hitch and L. Hawes; A. Millar; R. and J. Dodsley; and M. and T. Longman, 1756).
Kamrath, Mark L. 'An "inconceivable pleasure" and the "Philadelphia Minerva": Erotic Liberalism, Oriental Tales and the Female Subject in Periodicals of the Early Republic', *American Periodicals* 14.1 (2004): 3–34.
Kaplan, Marijn S., *Translations and Continuations: Riccoboni and Brooke, Graffigny and Roberts*, ed. Marijn S. Kaplan (London and New York: Routledge, 2016).
Keen, Paul, *The Crisis of Literature in the 1790s: Print Culture and the Public Sphere* (Cambridge: Cambridge University Press, 1999).
[Kendall, Ann], *Derwent Priory; or, Memoirs of an Orphan* 2 vols (London: H. D. Symonds, 1798).
Kerfoot, Alicia, 'Shoe Conversations; or, What the *Lady's Magazine* Stitch Off Taught me About Eighteenth-century Footwear, Embroidery, and Community' <https://blogs.kent.ac.uk/ladys-magazine/2016/03/24/shoe-conversations-or-what-the-ladys-magazine-stitch-off-taught-me-about-eighteenth-century-footwear-embroidery-and-community/> (last accessed 8 October 2020).
Killick, Tim, *British Short Fiction in the Early Nineteenth Century: The Rise of the Tale* (Aldershot: Ashgate, 2008).
King, Kathryn R., 'Patriot or Opportunist? Eliza Haywood and the Politics of *The Female Spectator*', in *Fair Philosopher, Eliza Haywood and the "Female Spectator"*, eds Lynn Marie Wright and Donald J. Newman (Lewisburg: Bucknell University Press, 2006), 104–21.
King, Kathryn R., 'Scribal and Print Publication', *The History of British Women's Writing, 1690–1750. Volume 4*, ed. Ros Ballaster (Basingstoke: Palgrave Macmillan, 2010), 127–44.
King, Kathryn R., 'Frances Brooke, Editor, and the Making of the *Old Maid* (1755–1756)', *Women's Periodicals and Print Culture in Britain, 1690–1820s: The Long Eighteenth Century*, eds Jennie Batchelor and Manushag N. Powell (Edinburgh: Edinburgh University Press, 2018, 342–56.
King, Rachel Scarborough, *Writing to the World: Letters and the Origins of Modern Print Genres* (Baltimore: Johns Hopkins University Press, 2018).

Klancher, Jon P., *The Making of English Reading Audiences, 1790–1832* (Madison: University of Wisconsin Press, 1987).

Kotzebue, August von, *The Negro Slaves: A Dramatic-Historical Piece, in Three Acts, from the German of the President de Kotzebue* (London: T. Cadell, Jr and W. Davies, 1796).

Kroeber, Karl, *Styles in Fictional Structure: Studies in the Art of Jane Austen, Charlotte Bronte, George Eliot* (Princeton: Princeton University Press, 1971).

Labbe, Jacqueline M., ed., *The History of British Women's Writing, 1750–1830. Volume 5* (Basingstoke: Palgrave Macmillan, 2010).

Lanser, Susan S., 'The Author's Queer Clothes', in *The Faces of Anonymity: Anonymous and Pseudonymous Publication from the Sixteenth to the Twentieth Century*, ed. Robert J. Griffin (New York: Palgrave Macmillan, 2003), 81–102.

Latham, Sean, and Robert Scholes, 'The Rise of Periodical Studies', *PMLA* 121. 2 (2006): 517–31.

Ledbetter, Kathryn, 'The Copper and Steel Manufactory" of Charles Heath', *Victorian Review* 28: 2 (2002): 21–30.

Ledbetter, Kathryn, *British Victorian Women's Periodicals: Beauty, Civilization, and Poetry* (New York: Palgrave Macmillan, 2009).

Levy, Michelle, *Family Authorship and Romantic Print Culture* (Basingstoke: Palgrave Macmillan, 2008).

Lubey, Kathleen, *Excitable Imaginations: Eroticism and Reading* (Lewisburg: Bucknell University Press, 2012).

Lupton, Christina, *Knowing Books: The Consciousness of Mediation in Eighteenth-Century Britain* (Philadelphia: University of Pennsylvania Press, 2011).

Lupton, Christina, *Reading and the Making of Time in the Eighteenth Century* (Baltimore: Johns Hopkins University Press, 2018).

Mackie, Erin, *Market à la Mode: Fashion, Commodity, and Gender in* The Tatler *and* The Spectator (Baltimore and London: Johns Hopkins University Press, 1997).

Mackinnon, F. D., *Grand Larceny, Being the Theft of Jane Leigh Perrot, Aunt of Jane Austen* (Oxford: Oxford University Press, 1937).

Mason, Nicholas, 'Building Brand Byron: Early Nineteenth-Century Advertising and the Marketing of *Childe Harold's Pilgrimage*', *MLQ*, 63 (2002): 411–40.

Mason, Nicholas, *Literary Advertising and the Shaping of British Romanticism* (Baltimore: Johns Hopkins University Press, 2013).

Mason, Nicholas, and Tom Mole, eds, *Romantic Periodicals in the Twenty-First Century: Eleven Case Studies from* Blackwood's Edinburgh Magazine (Edinburgh: Edinburgh University Press, 2020).

Maurer, Shawn Lisa, *Proposing Men: Dialectics of Gender and Class in the Eighteenth-Century English Periodical* (Stanford: Stanford University Press, 1998).

Maurer, Shawn Lisa, 'The Periodical', in *The History of British Women's Writing, vol. 4 1690–1750*, ed. Ros Ballaster (Basingstoke: Palgrave Macmillan, 2010).

Mayo, Robert D., 'Gothic Romance in the Magazines', *PMLA* 65.5 (1950): 762–89.

Mayo, Robert D., *The English Novel in the Magazines, 1740–1815* (London:

Oxford University Press; and Evanston: Northwestern University Press, 1962).

Mazella, David, 'Temporality, Microgenres, Authorship and the *Lady's Magazine*' (unpublished).

Meaney, Geraldine, Mary O'Dowd and Bernadette Whelan (eds), *Reading the Irish Woman: Studies in Cultural Encounter and Exchange, 1714–1960* (Liverpool: Liverpool University Press, 2013).

Mole, Tom, ed., *Romanticism and Celebrity Culture, 1750–1850* (Cambridge: Cambridge University Press, 2009).

Moore, George, *Grasville Abbey*, ed. Robert D. Mayo (New York: Arno Press, 1974).

Morison, Stanley, *A Memoir of John Bell, 1745–1831* (Cambridge: Cambridge University Press, 1930; repr. 2009.

Mullan, John, *Anonymity: A Secret History of English Literature* (London: Faber & Faber, 2007).

Murphy, Olivia, *Jane Austen: The Artist as Critic* (Basingstoke: Palgrave Macmillan, 2013).

Nichols, John, *Literary Anecdotes of the Eighteenth Century*, 6 vols (London: printed for the author, 1812), 3: 719.

O'Brien, Karen, *Women and Enlightenment in Eighteenth-Century Britain* (Cambridge: Cambridge University Press, 2009).

Oldfield, John R., *Transatlantic Abolitionism in the Age of Revolution* (Cambridge: Cambridge University Press, 2013).

Orr, Leah, 'The Basis for Attribution in the Canon of Eliza Haywood', *The Library* 12.4 (2011): 335–75.

Parker, Mark, *Literary Magazines and British Romanticism* (Cambridge: Cambridge University Press, 2004).

Parsons, Nicola, 'The Ladies Mercury (1693)', in *Women's Periodicals and Print Culture in Britain, 1690–1820s: The Long Eighteenth Century*, eds Jennie Batchelor and Manushag N. Powell (Edinburgh: Edinburgh University Press, 2018), 315–26.

Pearson, Jacqueline, *Women's Reading in Britain 1750–1834: a Dangerous Recreation* (Cambridge: Cambridge University Press, 1999).

Penant, Thomas, and John Wallis, *London: Being a Complete Guide to the British Capital*, 4th edn (London: Sherwood, Neely, and Jones, 1814).

Pike, Judith E., and Lucy Morrison, eds, *Charlotte Brontë from the Beginnings: New Essays from the Juvenilia to the Major Works* (London: Routledge, 2017).

Pitcher, E. W., 'The Miscellaneous Periodical Works and Translations of Miss R. Roberts', *Literary Research Newsletter* 5.3 (1980): 125–8.

Pitcher, E. W., 'William Mugleston and "The Matron": Authorship of a *Lady's Magazine* Essay Serial, 1774–91', *ANQ* 12:1 (1999): 28–9.

Pollard, Graham, 'The Early Poems of George Crabbe and *The Lady's Magazine*', *The Bodleian Library Record*, 5: 3 (July 1955): 149–56.

Poovey, Mary, *The Proper Lady and the Woman Writer: Ideology as Style in the Works of Mary Wollstonecraft, Mary Shelley, and Jane Austen* (Chicago and London: University of Chicago Press, 1984).

Porter, Roy, 'Lay Medical Knowledge in the Eighteenth Century: The Evidence of the *Gentleman's Magazine*', *Medical History* 29 (1985): 138–68.

Powell, Manushag N., *Performing Authorship in Eighteenth-Century English Periodicals* (Lewisburg, PA: Bucknell University Press, 2012).

Powell, Manushag N., 'Eliza Haywood, Periodicalist(?)', *Journal for Early Modern Cultural Studies*, 14.4 (2014): 163–86.

Powell, Manushag N., 'Women Readers and the Rise of the Periodical Essay', *A Companion to British Literature, Vol. III: Eighteenth-Century Literature 1660–1837*, eds Robert DeMaria, Jr, Heesok Chang and Samantha Zacher (Chichester: Wiley-Blackwell, 2014), 78–94.

Ratchford, Fannie Elizabeth, *The Brontës' Web of Childhood* (New York: Columbia University Press, 1941).

Raven, James, *London Booksellers and American Customers: Transatlantic Community and the Charleston Library Society, 1748–1811* (Columbia: University of South Carolina Press, 2002).

Raven, James, 'The Anonymous Novel in Britain and Ireland, 1750–1830', in *The Faces of Anonymity: Anonymous and Pseudonymous Publication from the Sixteenth to the Twentieth Century*, ed. Robert J. Griffin (New York: Palgrave Macmillan, 2003), 141–66.

Raven, James, *The Business of Books: Booksellers and the English Book Trade, 1450–1850* (New Haven and London: Yale University Press, 2007).

Reeve, Clara, *The Progress of Romance, through Times, Countries and Manners*, 2 vols (Colchester: W. Keymer, 1785).

Richardson, Charlotte Caroline, *Waterloo, a Poem on the Late Victory ... To Which is Added Truth, A Vision, By the Same* (London: Theodore Page, 1817).

[Richardson, Elizabeth], *Poems. By Mrs Richardson (Formerly "Betty Smales")* (London: Simpkin, Marshall & Co., 1846).

Richardson Megan, and Julian Thomas, 'Rethinking "Romantic" Authorship', in *Fashioning Intellectual Property: Exhibition, Advertising and the Press, 1789–1918* (Cambridge: Cambridge University Press, 2012).

Roberts, R., *The Triumph of Truth; or, Memoirs of Mr. De La Villette, Translated from the French by R. Roberts*, 2 vols (London: [n. pub], 1775).

[Roberts, Radagunda], *Select Moral Tales: Translated from the French, by a Lady* (Gloucester: R. Raikes, 1763).

[Roberts, Radagunda], *Elements of the History of France, translated from the Abbé Millot*, 3 vols (London: James Dodsley and Thomas Cadell, 1771).

Ross, Slaney Chadwick, 'John Dunton's *Ladies Mercury* and the Eighteenth-Century Female Subject', *Women's Periodicals and Print Culture in Britain, 1690–1820s: The Long Eighteenth Century*, eds Jennie Batchelor and Manushag N. Powell (Edinburgh: Edinburgh University Press, 2018), 327–41.

Royds, E., ed., 'Stubton Strong Room – Stray Notes (end Series): Moore and Knowles Families – Two Sisters', *Reports and Papers of the Architectural Societies of the County of Lincoln, York, Archdeaconries of Northampton and Oakham and County of Leicester* 38.2 (1927).

Russell, Gillian, *The Ephemeral Eighteenth Century* (Cambridge: Cambridge University Press, 2020).

Sagal, Anna K., 'Constructing Women's History in *The Lady's Museum*', *Women's Periodicals and Print Culture in Britain, 1690–1820s: The Long Eighteenth Century*, eds Jennie Batchelor and Manushag N. Powell (Edinburgh: Edinburgh University Press, 2018), 53–66.

Schellenberg, Betty A., *Literary Coteries and the Making of Modern Print Culture, 1740–1790* (Cambridge: Cambridge University Press, 2016).
Sher, Richard B., *The Enlightenment and the Book: Scottish Authors and Their Publishers in Eighteenth-Century Britain, Ireland, and America* (Chicago and London: University of Chicago Press, 2006).
Sherbo, Arthur, 'Roberts, R. (c.1728–1788)', *Oxford Dictionary of National Biography*, Oxford University Press, 2004 <www.oxforddnb.com/view/article/69592> (last accessed 8 October 2020).
Shevelow, Kathryn, '"C— L—" to "Mrs. Stanhope": A Preview of Charlotte Lennox's *The Lady's Museum*', *Tulsa Studies in Women's Literature* 1.1 (Spring 1982): 83–6.
Shevelow, Kathryn, *Women and Print Culture: The Construction of Femininity in the Early Periodical* (London: Routledge, 1989).
Shteir, Ann B., *Cultivating Women, Cultivating Science: Flora's Daughters and Botany in England, 1760 to 1860* (Baltimore and London: Johns Hopkins University Press, 1996).
Simpson, Kim, 'Becoming Jane: the Case of a *Lady's Magazine* Emigrant', *The Lady's Magazine* (1770–1818): Understanding the Emergence of a Genre' <https://blogs.kent.ac.uk/ladys-magazine/2016/06/22/becoming-jane-the-case-of-a-ladys-magazine-emigrant/> (last accessed 8 October 2020).
Siskin, Clifford, *The Work of Writing: Literature and Social Change in Britain, 1700–1830* (Baltimore: Johns Hopkins University Press, 1998).
Siskin, Clifford, and William Warner (eds), *This is Enlightenment* (Chicago and London: University of Chicago Press, 2009).
Slauter, Will, 'Upright Piracy: Understanding the Lack of Copyright for Journalism in Eighteenth-Century Britain', *Book History* 16. 1 (2013): 34–61.
Slauter, Will, *Who Owns the News?* (Stanford: Stanford University Press, 2019), p. 74.
Smith, Charlotte, *The Young Philosopher*, ed. Elizabeth Kraft (Lexington: University of Kentucky Press, 1999).
Smith, Chloe Wigston, 'Fast Fashion: Style, Text, and Image in Late Eighteenth-Century Women's Periodicals', in *Women's Periodicals and Print Culture, 1690–1820s: The Long Eighteenth Century*, eds Jennie Batchelor and Manushag N. Powell (Edinburgh: Edinburgh University Press, 2018), 440–57.
Smith, Margaret, ed., *The Letters of Charlotte Brontë with a selection of letters by her family and friends, Vol. 1 1829–47* (Oxford: Clarendon Press, 1995).
Sodeman, Melissa, *Sentimental Memorials: Women and the Novel in Literary History* (Stanford: Stanford University Press, 2015).
Springbourg, Patricia, *Mary Astell: Theorist of Freedom and Domination* (Cambridge: Cambridge University Press, 2005).
Steele, Richard, *The Tatler*, ed. Donald F. Bond, 3 vols (Oxford: Clarendon Press, 1987).
Stewart, David, *Romantic Magazines and Metropolitan Literary Culture* (Basingstoke: Palgrave Macmillan, 2011).
Suarez, Michael, 'Introduction', *The Cambridge History of the book in Britain: Vol. V, 1695–1830*, eds Michael Suarez, S. J. and Michael L. Turner (Cambridge: Cambridge University Press, 2009), 1–35.
Summers, Montague, *A Gothic Bibliography* (London: The Fortune Press [1941]).

Swaminathan, Srividhya, and Adam R. Beach, 'Introduction: Invoking Slavery in Literature and Scholarship', *Invoking Slavery in the Eighteenth-Century British Imagination*, eds Srividhya Swaminathan and Adam R. Beach (London and New York: Routledge, 2016), 1–20.

Swift, Jonathan, *Journal to Stella*, ed. Harold Williams, 2 vols (Oxford: Clarendon Press, 1948).

Taylor, Richard C., *Goldsmith as Journalist* (Rutherford, Madison, Teaneck: Farleigh Dickinson University Press; London and Toronto: Associated University Presses, 1993).

Thomas, Peter D. G., 'John Wilkes and the Freedom of the Press (1771)', *Historical Research* 33 (1960): 86–98.

Timperley, Charles Henry, *A Dictionary of Printers and Printing with the Progress of Literature, Ancient and Modern: Bibliographical Illustrations* (London: H. Johnson, 1839).

Tyner, Judith A., *Stitching the World: Embroidered Maps and Women's Geographical Education* (Oxford: Routledge, 2016).

Waldron, Mary, *Jane Austen and the Fiction of her Time* (Cambridge: Cambridge University Press, 1999).

Warner, William B., *Licensing Entertainment: The Elevation of Novel Reading in Britain, 1684–1750* (Berkeley and Los Angeles: University of California Press, 1998).

Weeton, Ellen, *Journal of a Governess*, ed. Edward Hall, 2 vols (London: Oxford University Press, 1936).

[West, William], *Fifty Years' Recollections of an Old Bookseller* (London: printed by and for the author, 1837), 92–5.

[West, William], 'Notice of the Robinsons', *Aldine Magazine of Biography, Criticism and the Arts* 1.9 (26 January 1839): 132–5.

Wheatley, Kim, ed., *Romantic Periodicals and Print Culture* for *Prose Studies: History, Theory, Criticism* 25:1 (2002).

White, Cynthia, *Women's Magazines, 1693–1968* (London: Michael Joseph, 1970).

Williamson, Gillian, *British Masculinity in the Gentleman's Magazine, 1731–1815* (Basingstoke: Palgrave Macmillan, 2016).

Wolfson, Susan, *Romantic Interactions: Social Being and the Turns of Literary Action* (Baltimore: Johns Hopkins University Press, 2010).

Woolf, Virginia, *A Room of One's Own* (1929), repr. in *A Room of One's Own and Three Guineas*, ed. Anna Snaith (Oxford: Oxford World's Classics, 2015).

Wynne, Charles Edward, 'Account of Mr John Huddlestone Wynne', *Monthly Magazine* 22 (August 1806): 16–20.

Index

Aberdeen Magazine, The, 155
abolition 90, 91–2, 94–8, 99
Adburgham, Alison, 6, 127, 222
Ackermann, Rudolph, 171, 190, 203
Addison, Joseph, 24, 25, 28, 31, 194, 219
Adventures of Telemachus, The, 148, 149
advice columns, 5, 15, 21–2, 58, 73, 80, 85–6, 94–5, 101, 108–9, 111–15, 123, 135, 181, 239; see also medical columns
Albert, Edward and Laura, 146
Algerine Captive, The, 159
Allchin, Richard, 221
amateurism, 4, 7, 75, 127–30, 138–9, 140, 143, 156, 158, 161, 200, 202–3, 226 243
American Revolution, 88, 99, 103
Amulet, The, 174, 175, 203–4
annuals, 15, 152, 174–9, 203–5, 206
anonymity, 3, 6, 126, 137–41, 142, 143, 155, 197, 236; see also pseudonymity
Athenian Mercury, The, 21, 23, 37
Austen, Jane, 4, 10, 11, 75, 92, 138, 215, 228–41, 243
authorship, 6, 9–10, 11, 82, 117, 127–8, 131–9, 160–1, 226, 237–9, 244
  unRomantic, 10, 11, 126–7, 161, 242, 243

Bahktin, Mikhail, 84
Bailey, Joanna, 158

Baldwin, Abigail, 13
Ballard, George, 71
Ballaster, Ros, 6, 30, 48, 54
Bannet, Eve Tavor, 23, 28, 105, 249n26
Barbauld, Anna (Aikin), 118, 216, 215 219
Barchas, Janine, 231
Baretti, Giuseppe Marco Antonio, 51
Batt, Jennifer, 95
Beachcroft, T. O, 115
Beau Monde, Le, 189
Bee, The, 45
Beetham, Margaret, 7, 81, 86
Behn, Aphra, 23, 97
Behrendt, Stephen, 152
Bell, John, 78–9, 165, 189, 190, 258n64
Bell, John Browne, 189, 190
Bell, Mary Anne (Mrs Bell), 190
Belle Assemblée, La (1806–32), 7, 79, 165, 171, 174, 184, 189–90, 196, 220, 245n11, 268n52
Beach, Adam R., 92, 98
Benedict, Barbara, 19
Bennett, Shelley M., 174
biography, 34, 71–2, 73, 99, 100, 101, 117, 146, 175, 188, 194, 210, 212, 218, 241
Blackwood's Magazine, 2, 3, 11, 139, 198–200, 242
boarding schools, 53, 116–17, 120
Boulter, Jay David, 84
Brighty, G. M., 174
Britannia, 100, 169

British Lady's Magazine, The, 7, 275n30
British Magazine, The, 49, 174, 194
Brontë, Charlotte, 1–3, 9, 11, 124, 127, 139, 155, 201, 208, 211, 215, 227, 243, 244
Brontë, Patrick, 2, 11, 200
Brooke, Frances, 13, 27, 32–3, 34, 59–60, 71, 147, 148, 149, 216, 219
Brooke, John Moore, 147
Burke, Edmund, 99
Burney, Frances, 11, 75, 140, 216, 228, 231, 281n55
Burney, Edward Francis, 174
Byron, George Gordon, Lord, 196, 219, 243

Cardonne, Denis Dominique, 53, 92, 143
Cadell, Thomas, 78, 132, 149
Carlile, Susan, 16, 34,
Carter, Elizabeth, 40, 117, 216, 219, 222, 225
'Castle of Le Blanc, The', 159
Castle of the Rock, The, 156, 159
Catley, Ann, 184
Cave, Edward, 13, 16, 35, 37
Chandler, Mary, 220
Charlotte, Princess (death of) 100, 101
Chapone, Hester, 216, 219
Charlton, Mary, 127
Chatterton, Thomas, 141, 142, 171, 242n41
Chudleigh, Elizabeth (Duchess of Kingston), 108, 169, 229
Claes, Koenraad, 87, 242
Clare, John, 203
coffee-house culture, 25, 224
Cohen, Margaret, 53
Coleridge, Hartley, 1, 2, 3, 155, 211, 244
Coleridge, Samuel Taylor, 154, 198, 203
Collier, Jane, 147, 269n67
Collyer, Joseph, 171, *173*, 175
community, 9, 10, 22, 30, 32, 56, 127, 153–5, 195, 211, 214–15, 222–6, 244

conversation 20, 25, 38, 41, 43, 48, 56–63, 84, 108, 119, 120, 123, 211, 225; *see also* miscellaneity
Cook, James (Captain), 148, 169, 175
Cook, John (Dr), 109, 110–11, 169, 175
Coote, John, 2, 8, 42, 43, 45, 46, 48, 49, 63, 65, 68, 76
Copeland, Edward, 4, 6, 56, 179, 193, 231–2, 233, 240
Corbould, Henry, 174
'Correspondents' column, 9, 57–8, 83, 125, 129, 135–8, 144, 171, 202, 205, 224
coterie culture, 23, 225–7
Cowley, Hannah, 215, 216
Coxhead, A. C., 174
Crabbe, George, 4, 9, 76, 78, 141, 142, 202, 258n62
Craven, Elizabeth, 216
Critical Review, The, 47, 87, 157, 194, 195
Cuthbertson, Catherine, 159

Dacier, Anne, 117, 216
Dacre, Charlotte, 157
Davidson, Hilary, 192–3
Davison, Thomas, 137
debating societies, 224–5
'Defence of Women, A', 234–6
Defensa de las Mujeres, 40, 234, 235
Defoe, Daniel, 142
DeLucia, JoEllen, 50, 87
'Derwent Priory' 155–6, 201
  republished in volume form, 155, 157, 197
Dever, Carolyn, 53
DiPlacidi, Jenny, 76, 160, 228, 242
Dodlsey, James, 149
Dodwell, Mary, 100, 155, 202, 261n39
Dow, Gillian, 53
Drouin, Jeffrey, 85, 86
Dunton, John, 21

Edgeworth, Maria, 116, 228
Edinburgh Review, The, 194
Edric the Forester, 196
education, 5, 7, 9, 10, 18–20, 27, 28,

Index   299

32–2, 33–5, 40, 56, 58, 62, 67, 73,
    75, 81, 86, 105, 116–20, 122–3,
    147, 149, 206, 212, 234–6, 244
Elements of the History of France, 144,
    147, 148
Eliot, Simon, 227
Ellis, Markman, 224
embroidery patterns, 5, 13, 16, 18, *82*,
    86, 117, 120, *121*, 125, 166, 167,
    181–14, 189, 193, 205, 247n3,
    275n28, 275n29
Emma, 232–4, 235
Epistles to the Ladies, 27, 220
European Magazine, The, 166, 169,
    261n38, 262n54
Examiner, The, 13
Ezell, Margaret J. M., 23, 139, 226

fashion, 7, 13, 18, 20, 40, 62, 69–71,
    85–6, 179–81, 184–93, 196, 208
Fashionable Magazine, The, 184
fashion plates, 18, 40, 69, 70, 71, 117,
    166, 167, 169, 174, 179, *180*,
    181, 185, *186*, *187*, 188–90, *191*,
    192–3, 196, 205, 206
Feijoo, Benito Jerónimo, 40, 234–5,
    281n56
'Female Rambler, The', 54, 56, 73, 109
Female Spectator, The, 13, 15, 27–32,
    33, 34, 38, 41, 220, 250n31
Female Tatler, The, 13, 30
Fergus, Jan, 6, 48, 124
Ferguson, Moira, 94
Ferrier, Susan, 228
fiction (magazine), 3, 5, 9, 11, 13, 23,
    28, 34, 39, 49–50, 51–4, 75–6,
    101, 103–5, 113–15, 128, 129,
    131, 136, 155–61, 175, 181,
    200–2, 203, 205, 228, 231–7, 238,
    240, 242
    gothic fiction, 11, 52, 155–7, 158,
        159–60, 201, 240
Fielding, Henry, 47
Fielding, Sarah, 218
Finch, Anne, 23, 220
Fitzpatrick, Barbara Laning, 45
Follet, Le, 206–7
Foote, Samuel, 69
Fordyce, James, 108

Foster, James, 158
Foucault, Michel, 139
Forget Me Not, The, 203–4
Foundling of Devonshire, The, 159
Fox, Claire Gilbride, 214
Frances, Henry, 96, 260n29
French Revolution, 88, 99
Friendship's Offering, 174
frontispieces 29, 54, *55*, 76, 77, 100,
    105, *106*, *107*, *165*, 169, 171, *173*,
    174, 214, 257n50, 273n9

Gallery of Fashion, The, 188
Genlis, Stéphanie Félicité de, 83
Gentleman's Journal, The, 23–4, 226
Gentleman's Magazine, The, 5, 6, 13,
    16, 35–6, 38, 39, 86, 87, 149, 153,
    166, 194, 246n17
Gessner, Saloman, 157
Godwin, William, 47, 87
Goldsmith, Oliver, 39
Goodwill, Jasper, 38
Gordon Riots, 88, 100, 118, 240,
    263n64
Goring, Paul, 49
Graffigny, Françoise de, 144, 148
Grant, Beatrice, 141, 268n52, 276n39
Grant, James, 136
'Grasville Abbey', 156–8
    republished in volume form, 156–7,
        197
Gravelot, Hubert-François, *145*
Green, Katherine Sobba, 59
Greenfield, Sayre, 229, 231
Gregory, John, 108
Grey, Mrs *see* 'Matron, The'
Griffin, Robert J., 139
Griffith, Elizabeth, 215, 216, 219,
    278n9
Grusin, Richard, 84
Guest, Harriet, 33
'Guilt Pursued by Conscience', 232–3

Halsey, Katie, 237
Hamilton (senior), Archibald
    (1719–93), 46, 47, 254n20
Hamilton (junior), Archibald (d. 1792),
    47, 273n8
Hamilton, Caroline, 175

Hamilton, Elizabeth, 116
Hamilton, Samuel, 137, 165, 167, 175, 179, 273n8
'Harriot and Sophia' (*Sophia*), 34, 49, 75
Harvest, A Poem, 150
Hastings, Warren, 88, 229
Hawkesworth, John, 148–9, 270n73
Hawkesworth, Mary, 148
Haynes (Golland), Catherine Day, 4, 159–60, 198
Haywood, Eliza, 11, 13, 26, 27–32, 33, 34, 36, 38, 220, 250n41
Heath, Charles, 137, 175–9, 273n8
Heath, James, 175, *177*,
Heath, John, 175
Heideloff, Niklaus Wilhelm von, 188
Hemans, Felicia, 203
Hendry, Sophia *see* Troughton, Sophia
Hibernian Magazine, The, 155, 184, 275n32
History of Emily Montague, The, 59–60, 71, 82, 141, 148
Hofland, Barbara, 9, 198, 204, 267n33
Hofland, Christopher, 267n33
Hogg, Alexander, 162–5, 184, 188
Holcroft, Thomas, 47, 83, 87
Hood, Thomas, 132, 134, 189
Hudson, Hannah Doherty, 71
Hughes, Gillian, 222
Hunter, Jean E., 57
Hutton, Charles, 150

Inchbald, Elizabeth, 47, 87, 195, 276n51, 281n44
illustrations, 5, 13, 16, 34, 39, 49, 69, 100, 114, 144, *145*, *168*, 169–75, *176*, *177*, *178*, 194, 196, 211–12, 214, 229, *230*; *see also* fashion plates; frontispieces
Irwin, Elinor (Charlotte Barrett), 234, 235
Italia, Iona, 15–16, 26, 30

Johnson, John, 65
Johnson, Samuel, 16, 47, 139
Johnston, William, 46
Jones, Mary, 220

Journal des Dames, Le, 188
Journey from London to Genoa, 51–2

Kamrath, Mark L., 52
Kauffman, Angelica, *173*
Kearsley, George, 45
Keen, Paul, 138
Keepsake, The, 174, 175, 203
Kendall, Ann (Mrs Kendall), 9, 156, 158, 159, 241
Kenrick, William, 108
Ker, Anne, 196
King, Kathryn R., 26, 161
Klancher, Jon P., 48, 195, 223
Kotzebue, August von, 97–8

Labbe, Jacqueline M., 140
Lacey, James Murray, 100, 141, 142, 153, 202, 261n38
Ladies Diary, The, 151–2
Ladies Magazine; or, the Universal Entertainer, The, 38–9
Ladies Mercury, The, 12, 21–3, 24
Lady's Magazine; or Entertaining Companion for the Fair Sex, The
    circulation, 3, 42, 47, 125, 137, 157, 163, 206
    concurrent versions of (1771–72), 4, 8, 43, 48, 67–79
    culture of reprinting and, 4, 6, 10, 11, 36, 59, 60, 82–5, 86, 91, 108, 126, 164, 195, 198, 202, 219–20
    launch of, 12–13, 15, 42, 166
    layout and design of, 10, 16, 166–9, 174, 196, 205
    literary history and, 7–8, 10–11, 127, 149, 192, 197, 209–11, 216, 218, 219–22, 228, 240–1, 243–4
    new series, 88, 136, 160, 167, 201, 237, 240
    payment for contributions, 6, 9, 125, 126, 130–1, 131–9, 161
    Romanticism and, 6–7, 10–11, 211, 221, 226, 236, 242–4
    sale to Robinson and Roberts, 8, 43, 46, 63, 76, 78
    trial following sale, 8, 43, 45–6, 63–7, 163, 198
    Wheble's *Lady's Magazine*, 4, 8, 19,

48–52, 54, 56–61, 67, 68, 78, 143, 194
Lady's Magazine; or, Polite Companion for the Fair Sex, The, 39–41, 45, 188, 208, 218
Lady's Magazine; or, the Compleat Library, The, 37
Lady's Magazine; or Universal Repository, The, 37
Lady's Monthly Museum, The, 71, 132–4, 143, 153, 156, 165, 171, 188–9, 190, 192, 194, 208, 245n11
Lady's Museum, The, 7, 13, 26, 27, 33–5, 40, 45, 71, 73, 248n15
Lady's Poetical Magazine, The, 174
Lady's Weekly Magazine, The, 38
Lalla Rookh, 178, 196
Landon, Laetitia Elizabeth, 203, 204
Lasting Impressions, 153
Latham, Sean, 6
learned women, 71, 72, 117, 215–18
Ledbetter, Kathryn, 150
Legg, John, 9, 128–9, 137, 141, 142, 160, 265n12
Lesage, Alain-René, 142
Lennox, Charlotte, 7, 13, 16, 26, 27, 32, 33–5, 40, 45, 49, 71, 73, 216, 218, 219
Leprince de Beaumont, Jeanne-Marie, 144
Lévy, Maurice, 157
Levy, Michelle, 226
Lewis, Matthew, 11
Literary Souvenir, 176
Lives of Cardinal Alberoni, 158
Locke, John, 47, 118, 122, 217
Lockstone, John, 141, 256n41
Loiterer, The, 233
London Magazine, The, 136, 166, 195
Longman, Thomas, 46
Lounger, The, 18–20
'Love and Freindship', 229
Lubey, Kathleen, 217
Ludolph, or the Light of Nature, 151
Lupton, Christina, 83

Macaulay, Catharine, 116, 118, 212–16, 217, 218, 222, 277n5

Macdonald, Miss, 190, 193
Mackenzie, Henry, 18
Magazine à la Mode, The, 188
Magazine of Female Fashions, 188
Maintenon, Françoise d'Aubigne, 59, 60, 71
Malcolm, 144
Manley, Delarivier, 11, 13, 38, 83, 217, 220, 221
Mansfield, William Murray, first Earl of, 63, 91
Mansfield Park, 75, 240
Marmontel, 54, 144, 146, 147
marriage, 21, 25, 32, 36, 37, 51, 58–63, 76, 88, 93–4, 112–15, 135, 146, 231, 242
Mason, Nicholas, 196, 242
'Matron, The' (agony aunt), 21, 85–6, 94–5, 109, 111–13, 115–16, 142, 181, 215, 224, 262n54, 262n55, 262n56
Maurer, Shawn Lisa, 13, 18
Mayo, Robert D., 6, 49, 75, 115, 128, 130, 156, 158, 200, 222
Mazella, David, 81
Meaney, Geraldine, 184
medical columns, 16–8, 109–11, 120, 143
Mélanges de Littérature Orientale, 53, 92, 143
'Memoirs of a Young Lady of Family', 75–6, 159
Middlesex Journal, The, 42, 45
Millot, Claude-François-Xavier, 144
Minerva (goddess), 56, 105, 132, 169, 214
Minerva Press, 132, 135, 155, 157, 159, 160, 198, 199, 265n8, 276n55
miscellaneity, 5, 15, 20, 23–4, 25, 34, 40, 54, 56, 59, 60, 81–2, 84, 101, 105–8, 116, 119, 122, 123, 221, 226, 227, 243
Mitford, Mary Russell, 4, 9, 10, 125, 136–7, 138, 141, 160, 203, 204, 240, 241, 264n4, 267n33, 282n64
'Monks and the Robbers, The', 158–9, 201
republished in volume form 159

Montagu, Elizabeth, 147, 216, 225
Montagu, Lady Mary Wortley, 13, 216, 220
Montbar; or the Bucaneer, 158
Montgomery, James, 96
Monthly Mirror, 157
Moodle, Susanna *see* Strickland, Susanna
Moore, George, 9, 156, 157–8, 160, 271n103
Moore, J. F., 212
Moore, Sarah, 147, 269n67
Moore, Thomas, *178*, 196, 200, 274n18
'Moral Zoologist, The' 119, 171, *172*
More, Hannah, 95, 96, 108, 116, 134, 148, 215, 219, 278n9
Moreland Manor, 156
Motteux, Peter (Pierre) Anthony, 23
Mugliston, William, 109, 215, 262n54
Murry, Ann, 119, 169

Nature and Art, 195
Negro Slaves, The, 97–8
Nelson, Lord, 88, 100–1, 102, 104, 175
Newbery, Ellizabeth, 132
Newbery, John, 45
Newby, Thomas, 141, 202, 274n12
New Annual Register, The, 87, 163, 164, 254n19
New Lady's Magazine, The, 162–5, 184, 188, 194
New Novelist's Magazine, 174
Newman, A. K., 132, 159–60
news, 9, 18, 23, 24, 36, 38, 39, 86, 88–91, 92, 98, 99–105, 108, 116, 119, 120, 169, 174–5, 196, 217
newspapers, 31, 35–6, 37, 90–1, 194, 202, 229
Nichols, John, 45
Nicholson, Margaret, 175
Nonsense of Common-Sense, The, 13
Northanger Abbey, 238, 239, 240

O'Dowd, Mary, 184
Oldfield, John R., 98
Old Maid, The, 13, 15, 27, 32–3, 34
  men and, 32
Opie, Amelia, 9, 95, 99, 198, 204

oriental tales, 11, 50, 51–3, 58, 76, 92–4, 201, 205
'Our Village' (*Our Village*), 136, 137, 201–2, 236–7

Paine, Thomas, 87, 88, 99, 229, 254n21
Parrot, The, 15, 27, 220
Pastor's Fire-Side, The, 158, 197
Paternoster Row, 2, 8, 43, 44, 45, 46, 47, 67, 135, 147, 157, 163, 164, 205, 208, 223, 245n10, 252n2
Pawsey's Ladies' Fashionable Repository, 151
Pearson, Jacqueline, 6, 118
Perceval, Spencer, 169
Perrot, Jane Leigh, 229, *230*
Persuasion, 231, 232, 235, 238
Peruvian Letters, 144, 148, 149, 269n69
Pierpoint, Miss, 192, 193
Pilkington, Mary, 9, 132–5, 137, 138, 143, 160, 188, 198, 241, 265n16
Pitcher, E. W., 145, 146, 262n54, 269n63
Pitt, William, 88, 175
poetry, 5, 9, 12, 23, 32, 36, 37, 40, 47, 53, 57–8, 76–8, 101, 102–3, 136, 140, 149–55, 166, 188, 194, 196, 200, 202–4, 205, 240
politics, 5, 6, 9, 24, 30–1, 32, 47, 62, 71, 86, 87–90, 95, 98, 99
Poovey, Mary, 86, 105
Pope, Alexander, 47, 83, 194
Porter, Jane, 102, 104, 158, 196–7
Porter, Roy, 110
Powell, Manushag N., 12, 33
Pride and Prejudice, 236
Prisoner of Chillon, The, 196
professionalism, 2–3, 7, 9–10, 126, 128, 130, 135, 137–9, 150, 156, 158, 160–1, 174, 192, 204, 208, 210, 223, 226–7
pseudonymity, 6, 23, 57, 126, 127, 128, 140–4, 156, 159, 161, 225; *see also* anonymity

Quarterly Review, The, 194
question and answer sheets, 8, 21–3

Radcliffe, Ann, 11, 47, 156, 157, 159
Raikes, Robert, 147
Raven, James, 44, 139, 169
reading practices, 8, 9, 16, 18–20, 35, 41, 50, 53, 81, 84–6, 105–8, 115–16, 120–3, 243
Reeve, Clara, 129–130, 160, 216, 220, 221, 222, 265n14, 269n69
remediation, 9, 59–60, 82–5, 86, 122–6
Repository of Arts, The, 171, 184, 190, 261n38
reviews, 5, 18, 39, 166, 175, 188, 193–7, 200, 204, 205, 210, 241; *see also* theatrical reviews
Reviews, 6, 15, 139, 197–8, 204, 210, 221–2, 236, 237, 239, 240, 241
Richardson, Charlotte Caroline, 10, 150–5, 160, 202
Richardson, Eleanor, 151
Richardson, Elizabeth (Smales), 151–2
Richardson, Elizabeth, 151
Richardson, Mary (Molly), 46, 253n16
Richardson, Samuel, 2, 142, 164
Ritter, Richard de, 6
Rivington, John, 46
Roberts, John, 8, 42, 43, 46
Roberts, Radagunda, 9, 54, 143–9, 160, 169, 218, 278n14
Roberts, Richard, Rev Dr, 144, 147
Roberts, William, 147, 278n14
Robinson and Roberts, publishing firm, 46–7, 63
 Lady's Magazine (1771–2), 48, 65–7
Robinson (senior), George (1736–1801), 2, 5, 8, 42, 43, 45, 46–7, 87–8, 131, 158, 162, 163–5, 175, 194, 195, 217, 218
Robinson (junior), George, 134, 157, 159, 164, 175, 272n6
Robinson (III), George, 131, 167, 205, 252n2, 273n7
Robinson, Mary, 85
Robinson, Samuel, 131, 167, 205, 252n2, 273n7
Robinson publishing house, 47, 87, 131, 135, 146, 156, 157, 175, 185, 195, 216, 219, 254n19, 254n21
Rousseau, Jean-Jacques, 108, 116
Romance of the Pyrenees, The, 159

Romantic periodicals, 6–7
Rowe, Elizabeth, 194, 216
Royal Female Magazine, The, 49
Royal Literary Fund, The, 134, 138

St Paul's School, 144, 147, 149
Schellenberg, Betty, 226, 227
Scholes, Robert, 6
Scott, Walter, 177, 197, 200, 219
Scudéry, Madeleine de, 217
Select Tales from Marmontel, 54, 144
Sermons Written by a Lady, 144, 147
Sense and Sensibility, 138, 228, 231–2, 233, 235, 240
Sentimental and Masonic Magazine, 156
'Sentimental, Journey, A', 49–51, 54, 56, 58, 65, 66, 76, 141, 144
Sévigné, Francoise-Marguerite de, 216, 222
Shelley, Percy, 204
Shevelow, Kathryn, 7, 20, 24, 25, 117, 181–2
'Shipwreck, The', 231, 233
Sir Eldred of the Bower, 148
Siskin, Clifford, 83, 138, 139, 210, 228, 233
Slauter, Will, 36, 90, 251n66
slavery, 52, 91–8, 115, 218
Smith, Charlotte, 47, 87, 127, 154
Smith, Chloe Wigston, 181, 182
Smith, Mrs W., 190, 193
Smollett, Thomas, 45, 49
Soldier's Child, The, 151
song sheets, 5, 16, 23, 34, 39, 117, 164, 166
Southey, Robert, 1, 3
Spectator, The, 7, 13, 15, 24–6, 27, 61, 216–7
Spencer, Margaret, Lady, 136
Squire, Joanna (Carey), 152–4, 202, 271n90
Statute of Anne, The, 26, 27
Steele, Richard, 24
Stewart, David, 7
Stothard, Thomas, 174–5, 176
Strickland, Susanna, 95, 204
Styart, Charles, 184
Suarez, Michael, 26

Swaminathan, Srividhya, 92, 98
Swift, Jonathan, 13
Symonds, Henry D., 155, 156, 159

Talbot, Catherine, 216, 225
Tales of my Landlord, 197
Tales of the Passions, 158
Talfourd, Thomas Noon, 125, 137, 267n32, 276n39
Tatler, The, 7, 15, 24–6, 27, 31, 37, 41, 217
theatrical reviews, 23, 68–9, 78, 193–4, 196, 257n53
Theodosius de Zulvin, 157
Thicknesse, Ann, 71, 108, 239
Thicknesse, Philip, 171
Tooke, John Horne, 88, 229
Town and Country Magazine, The, 47, 71, 88–90, 166, 174, 194
translation 4, 5, 40, 47, 48, 50, 53–4, 56, 61, 66, 68, 83, 84, 92, 97, 120, 129, 130, 131, 142, 143–6, 147–8, 149, 157, 200, 201, 220, 234–6, 269n69, 270n76, 278n14
Trapp, Joseph, 36, 131
travel writing 9, 13, 47, 50–1, 54, 82, 148, 169, 175, 197
trial proceedings, 39, 88, 108, 169, 229
Trimmer, Sarah, 116
Triumph of Truth, The, 144
Troughton, Sophia (Sophia Hendry), 9, 136, 138, 160, 201, 222, 267n27

Universal Magazine, The, 166, 169
Universal Museum, The, 49, 255n29, 256n41
Universal Spectator and Weekly Journal, The, 37

Vernor, Thomas, 132, 134, 189
Vicissitudes of Life, 159
Vindication of the Rights of Woman, A, 108

war, 99, 101–5
Warner, William, 83
Washington, George, 124
Waterloo, A Poem, 153
Webb, John, 102, 104, 155, 202, 261n41
Weeton, Ellen, 125, 183, 193
Wellesley Index, 150
West, Jane, 159
West, William, 46
Westall, William, 174
Westminster Magazine, The, 169
Wharton, Anne, 23
Wheatley, Phillis, 218
Wheble, John 2, 8, 42, 43, 45–6, 63
Whelan, Bernadette, 184
White, Cynthia, 6, 127
Whyte, Samuel, 119
Wilberforce, William, 96
Wilkie, John, 45, 78
Williams, Anna, 218
Williams, Helen Maria, 87, 95, 99, 216, 261n37
Williams, Renwick (Rynwick), 169, 170, 229
Williamson, Gillian, 6, 37
Wilkes, John, 46
Wilson, John, 2, 45, 198
Wollstonecraft, Mary, 99, 116, 219, 221
women's magazine, the, 6, 7, 8, 12–14, 18–19, 37–41, 48, 80–1
Woolf, Virginia, 140
Wordsworth, William, 203
World of Fashion, The, 190
Wynne, John Huddlestone, 256n45

Yeames, Catharine Bremen, 16, 18, 104, 135, 261n42
Yeames, Elizabeth (Mrs Robert Clabon), 135–6, 137, 138, 160, 222, 243, 266n26, 267n39
Young Lady, The, 27

EU representative:
Easy Access System Europe
Mustamäe tee 50, 10621 Tallinn, Estonia
Gpsr.requests@easproject.com

www.ingramcontent.com/pod-product-compliance
Lightning Source LLC
Chambersburg PA
CBHW051110230426
43667CB00014B/2511